Works by Marc J. Seifer

Framed! Murder, Corruption, and a Death Sentence in Florida

Transcending the Speed of Light: Consciousness and Quantum Physics

The Definitive Book of Handwriting Analysis

Wizard: The Life and Times of Nikola Tesla

The Man Who Harnessed Niagara Falls

Where Does Mind End?

Rasputin's Nephew

Doppelgänger

Crystal Night

MARCSEIFER.com

Framed!

Murder, Corruption,
and a Death Sentence in Florida

Marc J. Seifer
with Stephen Rosati

Tantor
m e d i a

Tantor Media, Inc.
6 Business Park Road
Old Saybrook, CT 06475

tantor.com
tantorpublishing.com

Framed! Murder, Corruption, and a Death Sentence in Florida

ISBN: 9780988349452

TABLE OF CONTENTS

In Memory of Carl H. Rosati and Stephen Rosati

Like a spiral down into a labyrinthine realm of irrationality we entered the depths of hell. The madness of the system, its tentacles, the way they hold you by the jugular, and the way they force the very life out of you. If a person is guilty, he admits it, but if he is not guilty, then he is just swallowed up by the system.

—Esther Rosati

PREFACE

This book is a straightforward, investigative report that will help readers follow the events that resulted in a miscarriage of justice that sent three innocent men to jail, accused of murder. This is a true story that documents Stephen Rosati's experiences from the time he and two other men were wrongly accused and follows him as he is incarcerated and begins a nightmarish journey through the legal system. To write Stephen's story, I relied on over 3,000 pages of police logs, court transcripts and sworn depositions, approximately 200 newspaper articles, television news reports, and hundreds of hours of extensive interviews.

In order to maintain anonymity out of respect for the privacy of some characters and locations, I have in some instances changed the names of individuals and places. As much as is possible I have tried to accurately document events and conversations as they happened. Certain scenes involving tertiary characters have been embellished for aesthetic reasons.

The story of the extradition hearing and incarceration of Stephen Rosati, Peter Dallas, and Peter Roussonicolos is an inside look at an instance of injustice that, on the face of it, seems barely credible. Consider what has to be involved to gain a false confession, get a bevy of eyewitnesses to help support a manufactured case, and also get prosecutors from two different states and a couple of judges to play along. When you read this extraordinary story and see how far some in law enforcement and the legal profession would go to fabricate evidence, you will realize that what happened to Stephen could happen to anyone—even to you.

Marc J. Seifer, PhD
February 17, 2014

ACKNOWLEDGMENTS

I would like to thank Carl, Esther, and Stephen Rosati for allowing me into their lives to reconstruct their story and the chain of events that led to the incarceration of three innocent men. I interviewed the Rosatis over many months and years. Stephen painfully recounted his entire ordeal, and Carl laid out the entire chronology. Esther, who provided me with numerous details, newspaper articles, and other documents, sacrificed everything to fight a corrupt system to save her son. She courageously soldiered on daily for nearly a decade after her husband died with the sole aim of bringing to light, in a court of law, the case of her son's wrongful imprisonment. Her financial sacrifice and mental and spiritual fortitude, along with Stephen's terrible suffering, are worthy of a book in itself.

There are a number of heroes in this tale, among them Stephen's lawyer, the inimitable criminal attorney Jack Cicilline in Rhode Island, who fought the good fight; prosecutors John Aguero and Cindy Imperato in Florida; Stephen's parents, Esther and Carl Rosati, who sacrificed

3

everything to right an injustice and help rehabilitate their son; and the real hero of this story, Detective Michael Breece of the Florida Department of Law Enforcement (FDLE), the one person ultimately responsible for saving the lives of three innocent men.

At Tantor, I would like to thank Kevin Colebank, Ron Formica, Allan Hoving, Jaclyn Wilson, Hilary Rose, and my editor Lily Nesco, for all their work in helping produce this amazing story. I would also like to thank "Prince of the City" Robert Leuci, who himself witnessed police corruption, for his timely advice; reporter Jim Hummel, for his inside look at this case which he covered for the *Providence Journal* as it was unfolding; Nelson DeMille and Uri Geller, for their continuing encouragement; Howard Smukler Elliott Shriftman, Betty Jane Jacobs, and Judge Jonathan Calianos, for their legal advice; Mindy Branstetter, Michael Gold, Jon and Jeanne Cutler, Tommy John Catudo; editors Adam Kay, for his cogent assessment of numerous aspects of the text, and John Paine, who read the manuscript twice and then helped cut its length by two hundred pages; and my agent, John White, for supporting this project for so many years.

Finally, I would like to thank my parents for their encouragement, my sister Meri for helping with the artwork, my brother Bruce for thinking of better ways to produce the book, and my wife, Lois Mary Pazienza, for reading the manuscript and living with this story for nearly a quarter century.

PROLOGUE:
August 1992

Known as "the big guy" to everyone investigating the crime, the accused murderer stared vacantly at the concrete walls of his cell for the thousandth time, as his hands braided the escape rope in mechanical fashion. Denied medication for his clinical depression and sent to maximum security because of disorderly conduct, the big guy swore to himself as he tore another strip from the sheet and glanced over to the clock: 7:47 p.m.

Hounded by guilt and feeling down in the dumps, he was even on the skids with his girlfriend. Out of tears, he was no longer able to cry.

"Come clean and I'll see if I can get you twenty years instead of the electric chair," the cop had said, as if there was a difference. No wonder he'd been jailed once before for beating up a cop. The big guy's fingers worked methodically as he began to calculate it out. Twenty years times twelve months: two hundred and forty months. He glanced once more at the clock: 7:47.

The veins in his neck became taught. He felt that his heart was about to explode. He wanted to smash the clock against the wall, but what good would it do?

My God, I'm innocent! His mind screamed in silent desperation. *I did not kill anyone. It wasn't me.* But what good did the truth do?

Sure, he had busted in on the guy. Yes, his face had been scarred with powder burns from the gunshot. His shirt had been splattered with the dead man's blood, but he didn't pull the trigger. It wasn't him. He never wanted anyone to die. That wasn't the plan. They were just going to rip the guy off.

With the police on a wild goose chase for all those years, he thought for sure that he was home free. That deal had gone down in another lifetime. But now the snare had been closed, new witnesses had surfaced, fall guys were being set free, and he was a dead duck.

The big guy related the whole story to one of his cellmates before he was put in solitary: how it went down, how his partner had whacked the guy in a scuffle, and how they ditched the guns in a lake. But the bottom line was that it wasn't him. He never even fired his weapon.

The words *I'm innocent, I'm innocent* reverberated through his cranium. At the same time they seemed to echo down the cavernous halls of the sleepy prison. Dominating his every thought, he repeated over and over again, *If I didn't kill anybody, why should I pay?*

Unable to bear it for even another second, he kept his mind straight just long enough to climb onto the top bunk, place the noose securely around his neck, and tie the other end to the farthest bedpost. *Don't fuck this up* was his last thought. Finally, he was free.[1]

INTRODUCTION

It was a beautiful fall weekend in 1990, and my wife and I were just about out the door to spend a few days in Maine, to catch some early colors, when the phone rang.

"Dr. Seifer, this is Jack Cicilline," a deep voice clipped. "I've got a murder case for you. A fellow by the name of Rosati got mixed up with a drug deal that went bad in Florida. I want you to meet with his parents and look over some documents at their place. Eventually, you'll probably have to testify in Florida. What would you like for an advance?"

"Four hundred," I said, picking a figure out of the air.

"No, darlin', this is a big case. I'm going to get you an even thousand. Call me tonight for directions."

Did he just call me "darling"?

The following Monday, I was on my way to see the parents of a guy accused of murder named Stephen Rosati. As a handwriting expert, I had difficulty connecting the dots. Most of my cases were signatures on contracts, disputed wills, or anonymous notes. I had been a handwriting expert for nearly twenty years, and I couldn't remember a single case that involved murder.

I envisioned a distraught father in a backwater real estate shack in the pit of Warwick wearing a T-shirt and an old pair of baggy pants, sitting around a makeshift table with a bunch of documents strewn every which way. However, the directions I was given led to an exclusive professional complex with manicured lawns and a long floral-lined driveway. As I drove to the top of the hill, I rattled my head to dispel my preconceived notions. I parked the car, entered the building, and took the elevator to the third floor, where I entered the posh offices of The Rosati Group.

I would soon come to see not only how wrong my speculations had been but also how wrong everything would be.

CHAPTER 1:
A Family United

The reception area of the Rosati Group was elegantly styled in an English Garden motif, with tropical trees made of silk, a waist-high statue of a pert canine by the front desk, and mottled green, copper-webbed chairs in the foyer. Dressed in a well-tailored conservative suit, Carl Rosati greeted me with a warm handshake. A genteel man in his early sixties, he appeared extremely concerned and exceedingly thin.

"I just don't think my son could have done this," he said matter-of-factly, jolting me with his sincerity.

Stephen's mother, Esther, dressed in Bloomingdale attire with a cosmopolitan hairstyle that seemed more Madison Avenue than Warwick, Rhode Island, came in, flanked by two young men. She and her bodyguards eyed me suspiciously as she gave me a firm wiry handshake.

"We want you to look through these documents and verify whether or not they're Stephen's handwriting." I watched as one of the men lugged over a sizeable carton. "These documents are *very valuable* and may free Stephen. They are a daily accounting of my son's life. Naturally, we can't let them out of our sight."

"By all means," I replied, reaching for my magnifying glass. "I simply want to make a cursory examination, and then we can make copies. By all means," I repeated, trying to deflect an intense atmosphere, "you keep the originals. I only need to verify that I've seen them by placing my initials in the corner."

As a handwriting expert, I had learned long ago never to believe anyone about anything. That is the first cardinal rule in handwriting examination. Frankly, as with many others in my field, I have been involved in numerous cases whereby a person proclaims his innocence by swearing that he never signed a document, but after careful analysis and comparison to exemplars (known signatures), more often than one would generally think, the statement turns out to be flat-out untrue.

"We want you to remove any document that Stephen did not write," Carl stated frankly.

"Did he write all of these?" I inquired, looking at the great variations in the writings.

"We believe he did."

"But the handwritings look different."

"He had different styles."

The next day, after a conference call with Cicilline, we decided that I would go to the Adult Correctional Institute (ACI) to obtain samples. It would be my first time inside a major jail. I remember driving past a wall topped with razor wire before reaching the entrance to the building, where I was frisked and asked to empty my pockets before entering a double-locked security area. Then I was led into a holding room, maybe ten feet square, where I sat and waited to meet the alleged killer, Stephen Rosati. A few minutes later, in walked a well-built young man dressed in a blue jumpsuit, which somehow looked fashionable on him. He gave me a tentative handshake, sat down, and at my instruction proceeded to write a series of words that I had typed out for him.

Sometimes he laughed at the task, but he did proceed in a diligent fashion. Because of the great variety in the questioned documents—there were four distinct writing styles: cursive, printing, and two different types of signatures—I had to return to the prison on three separate occasions.

While I was there, I avoided all discussion of the case, and naturally, the prisoner never saw the documents I was studying. Rosati only saw a copy I had typed myself of words and phrases from the checks, receipts, and other pages in question. I gave Rosati assignments for writing in cursive, printing passages, and for signing and printing his name both with his eyes open and closed. I also had him do the same thing with his opposite (left) hand.

About this time, the story was already a front-page burner in the *Providence Journal,* Rhode Island's only major newspaper. They broke the story on Sept. 13, 1990. The article described a murder in Florida where a man and two accomplices entered the home of a major drug dealer on October 12, 1986, shot the dealer to death, and stole a kilogram of cocaine. It went on to say that Stephen Rosati, 30, the alleged killer, had been arrested for shooting and killing a man name Joseph Viscido.[1]

Over the next few months the story would be all over the media, and in January of 1991, the *New York Times* would interview the dead man's father. Reading his words made me aware of just how deep feelings ran when it came to this case.

Mr. Viscido was dissatisfied with the investigation that the Broward Police Department had done. Their probe had uncovered three suspects: a man named Peter Dallas; Stephen Rosati, who they had yet to locate; and a third individual known as Pete the Greek, but the evidence was slim. Mr. Viscido decided to take matters into his own hands. "I felt I had three choices: I was either going to get killed, die of a broken heart or get enough evidence to bring them to justice," Mr. Viscido said. "[His son] was buried the day before his 28th birthday." Hiring his own private investigator and doing a good bit of legwork on his own to try and locate Rosati, Mr. Viscido went on to say, "Tracking down leads was like looking for serpents. Every time I turned over another rock, I'd find another snake."[2]

Mr. Viscido's "story will become a book, perhaps a movie. . . . He set out with a hidden microphone, supplied by police, to talk to his son's friends. Soon he filled four notebooks and [a] 1,300-page file with notes—information the prosecutor used to get an indictment. . . . 'For a while there I didn't think I could make it,' Viscido says. 'I now have peace of mind knowing . . . that they're going to pay.'"[3]

Now the newspapers were billing the dead man's father as a hero who was helping to track down the scum that killed his son, while Rosati, the son of a real estate tycoon, was depicted as a Florida male stripper and one of their prime suspects.

After reading these articles, I sensed that Mr. Viscido would do

13

everything in his power to find his son's killer, I also knew that Carl and Esther Rosati would do everything possible to prove that it was not their son.

CHAPTER 2:
The Early Years

The Rosatis had raised two children: Carlyn, born in 1953, and Stephen, born six years later. Both Carl and Esther descended from prominent Italian families. A number of Rosatis had been priests, and one of them, Father Joseph Rosati—a bishop ordained by the Pope in 1811—was one of the founders of St. Louis Hospital and College in Missouri. In 1906, in Italy, Mt. Vesuvius erupted. Some of the Rosatis were killed, and their housing complex and retail store were wiped out. Consequently, Carl's father, only ten at the time, was sent to America to live with his cousins in Centerville, Rhode Island.

Fluent in French, German, and Yiddish, as well as Italian and English, Carl's father was able to save his money and, when he was old enough, purchase a service station and establish a successful fuel and trucking business. In 1925, he married Jennie Patriarca, who also came from a prosperous family. Where most other Italian immigrants were poor, Carl's uncles on both sides were affluent. They owned several restaurants, a bar, a car dealership, a real estate company, and a Narragansett Beer distributorship. When Carl was just eight years old, his mother passed away. This was a turning point in Carl's life, and he was still pained by the loss even as an older man. Carl attended Rhode Island State College (now called the University of Rhode Island) as World War II was ending, and that is where he met Esther Marino.

Esther's maternal grandfather, Joseph Pannone, left Italy at the turn of the century to avoid military service. Caroline, his wife to be, was the daughter of the mayor in a town just south of Rome. Not wanting to emigrate, but in love with her husband, Caroline followed Joseph to America, where they got married. But Joseph died young. He was only in his early forties. Caroline, Esther's grandmother, never learned to speak English, and so she spent the rest of her life isolated, feeling bitter and remorseful. Unwilling to adjust to America, the aristocratic gentlewoman also dared not return to her home country because of the shame she felt at her husband's decision to leave Italy. She favored her son and transferred her grief to Esther's mother, Rachel. Thus, this daughter grew up with an artificial side and a cold spot to her nature. Esther remembered her mother as someone who was domineering and overbearing. "She used people for a purpose," Esther said, "I never remember any embraces from her."

Unlike Carl, who had a loving and tender mother who disappeared from his life early on, Esther's mother, Rachel—who lived to be ninety—was bitter. Like her mother, Caroline, she favored her first son, Joseph, and took out her anguish on Esther. In one instance, she posted a sign that read *Sick Child*. In this way, she kept young Esther in bed throughout an entire summer as an excuse to slow cars down in the neighborhood. When another daughter died shortly after birth, Rachel went into a depression. She told Esther that it was too bad that Esther lived and her sister died.

"My mother said that this sister was beautiful and that I was ugly," Esther painfully recalled.Ironically, Esther was stunning and had won beauty contests for two consecutive years at Rhode Island State College. Nevertheless, Esther felt hollow inside, a separation from her real self. She likened this feeling to an out-of-body experience. Even after she married Carl, during the Korean War, she felt unsure of herself. Living her life as a dutiful wife throughout the 1950s, she took a back seat to her husband, first when Carl was called overseas to fight in the Korean War and she had to move back home, and then later when Carl returned.

16

"I felt trapped because I was back with my family, and trapped because in some sense I had lost my identity when I became a married women."

Fortunately for Carl, he had been stationed in Okinawa and not Korea. Involved in running a radar station, he used much of the time to study for his real estate license and also studied insurance. Upon his return to Rhode Island, Carl worked seven days a week, going from door-to-door and from business-to-business. "Through the years," Carl recalled, "I landed some major accounts."

But he really got his start by selling insurance to his extensive and prosperous family. A workaholic, Carl not only built up the insurance company, he also began buying large tracts of land to build quality homes. One of them, Knight Farms, in Scituate—located just off the Cranston line where they lived—is almost in sight of the capitol and is still one of the most prestigious housing developments in the state.

That is where the children, Carlyn and Stephen, were raised. Since Carl had owned the entire development, he had the prime house and the nicest property.

In fifth grade, Stephen ran for class president and won. He invited most of the kids back to his house so they could all enjoy his family's fifty-two-foot long swimming pool. Stephen's childhood was in many ways idyllic. The son of one of the most prominent families in the region, Stephen enjoyed the prestige of having parents who gave many parties and were very popular. An excellent hitter, Stephen played center field in Little League and was still able to maintain a B average in school. Childhood friends included Earl Adams, whose father owned a big field where they used to play football; the Finnigan brothers, one of whom became a police officer; David Tasca, whose father owned Tasca Lincoln Mercury, the most successful car dealership in the country; and Billy Wiley, now a defense attorney and the son of Judge Wiley, a prominent African American judge.

Like any typical kid of the day, Stephen built go-carts, raced against his friends, and played touch football. Stephen recalled one game in particular that involved his dog, a boxer named Parfay.

"I remember one day we were playing three on three: me, Tasca, and Maraia against Earl Adams and the Finnigan boys. I hiked it to Tasca, he lateralled it to Maraia, and he hit me with a pass down the field on a dead run. The Finnigan brothers were big, and the older one was about to get me, when out from the sidelines came our boxer, Parfay. He blindsided Finnigan and took him out of the play.

17

Touchdown! They wanted us to do it over, but we said, 'No way'!"

In sixth grade at Providence Country Day School, Stephen remembers one of his best teachers, Mrs. Eaton.

"She was nice because she took us on ecological trips to study plants and local animals. She also motivated us to complete our homework." Stephen remembered a weekend class trip to Alton Jones Campus, "way out in the woods with the lake and peacocks and the hide-away bungalow that President Eisenhower stayed at four million years ago. It was really funny. A kid in the upper bunk, whose father owned an animal hospital in Cranston, peed in his sleeping blanket. That set us off and we tortured him for the rest of the stay. Someone said, 'I don't want to sleep near this guy. He'll pee on my head.'"

In eighth grade, Stephen got into wrestling and won an All–New England tournament in the ninety-eight-pound class. But Stephen wanted to increase his game, and the only way to do that was to transfer to a school that had a better wrestling team. One night at a party, Stephen heard about a crazy coach—a teacher named Gary Gooseberger, from Bishop Hendricken, which was a private Catholic school for boys.

Stephen had heard that Gooseberger was brutal, but all his boys were winners, and he had even coached the state's two top wrestlers, Steven Delaney and Johnny Salvadoro.

"He had me wrestle Salvadoro and even Delaney, who was bigger. Delaney would whip me every day, tie me into a pretzel, and inflict as much pain as possible. One day I bit Salvadoro on the hand, and Gooseberger laughed. 'Rosati, you got balls,' he'd say, and then congratulate me because I tried to hurt back. Then he would throw me into what was known as shark bait, where every two minutes a fresh guy was thrown in at you. It was torture."

Gooseberger was ruthless, and he would do anything to get Stephen to lose the weight necessary to make his weight class. His favorite technique was to turn the heat up to ninety degrees. Stephen was a natural at 119 pounds, but Gooseberger made him wrestle at 112.

"During the tournaments, the Goose would shake me and say, 'you're my man. Go out there and win.' Then he'd slap me in the headgear or the face, and say, 'You go out there and go for a quick pin.' The stands would be packed, and I'd be psyched, enter the mat, and pin my opponents."

That year, ninth grade, Stephen was undefeated, 16–0. Almost all were pins, and his team won the freshman state championship. Stephen was already a skinny kid, but the Goose wanted Stephen not to eat because he had to keep his weight down. "The other coaches didn't like this idea," Stephen said, "but because Gooseberger was producing winners, everyone just shut up.

"I used to look up to the Goose at that time. He was a bodybuilder with a square face, pug nose, red hair, big bushy red eyebrows, and a ruddy complexion, thus his nickname: Red. He was a hefty muscular guy, having been a defensive tackle for Boston College during their heyday. Mister Gooseberger had a great deal of enthusiasm to get the kids riled up, and that's how he produced champions."

"Before some of the big matches, the Goose used to say, 'Any guy who wins a fight gets to screw my wife. And, Rosati, if you win, I'll let you feel her titties.' And then we'd all laugh."

Two or three times during his tenth grade year (1976–77), Stephen went up to his family's condo in Waterville Valley, New Hampshire, with Salvadoro, who was a senior, and Gary Gooseberger (who drove) and his wife.

However, when wrestling season rolled around, everything changed. In one of his classes, Stephen got into a scrap with another student. During the scuffle, he pushed a teacher. Rather than stick up for him, Gooseberger kicked Stephen off the wrestling team. This was a monumental blow to the star athlete. Stephen had little choice. He left Bishop Hendricken and ended up obtaining his high school degree at the Alternative Learning Program. Now that he was able to eat again, he transformed his goals from wrestling to bodybuilding. Soon after, Stephen won a championship in Bermuda and eventually, as a young man, he became Mr. Rhode Island.

In the late 1970s Stephen's father, Carl, purchased an eleven-room mansion complete with swimming pool at Watch Hill, a beach town hamlet reminiscent of Nantucket or Martha's Vineyard, located just inside the border of Rhode Island near Mystic, Connecticut. As a result of investing an additional $175,000 into the property, the Rosatis now had two separate homes, one in the north in Scituate near their real estate agency, and the other— more of a summer residence—in the south, in one of the most exclusive classic villages in New England. But everything changed after Carl suffered his first heart attack in 1980.

At that time, Esther began to take on more responsibility at Carl's office, and they sold, to their chagrin, the magnificent home in Watch

Hill. The following year, Carl suffered his second heart attack. Now, the Rosati Group became truly a husband-and-wife team. Where Carl would be gentle yet determined in business, Esther would manage other aspects of the office. Dressed in the latest fashion, she acted cordial and gracious on the outside, while on the inside, she had a sturdiness that derived from her difficult upbringing.

Unlike her mother, Esther's father, Paul Marino, was a warmhearted man who encouraged her. A highly respected jewelry designer, Paul was also a jewelry manufacturer with a worldwide distribution and showrooms on Fifth Avenue in New York, in Havana, Cuba, and in four other locations throughout the United States. Paul, a teacher at Rhode Island School of Design (RISD), instilled love and kindness in Esther, and she in turn passed that onto her daughter, Carlyn, and her son, Stephen.

Where Carlyn went on to attend the Rhode Island School of Design, the Rosatis schooled Stephen in the manner of Antioch College; that is, by on-the-job training. Just out of his teens and with his father's backing, Stephen opened up East Coast Fitness Center, a health club near the airport. Here, according to Esther, her son could learn marketing, accounting, and management. He hired famous bodybuilders to work out there and began to create one of the most "in" gyms in town. Naturally, Carl was distraught when Stephen left the health club in the hands of his partners in 1984 to become a male dancer in Florida, but Carl hoped that this would be a temporary fling. Stephen was just twenty-four.

Once the real estate market turned around the following year, Carl phoned his son. "Stephen, you're missing the greatest opportunity in Rhode Island you'll ever have. I've got land that I'm just selling to other people and you could be doing this."

Carl still had forty lots at one of his development sites, and he made sure that he kept two for Stephen so that he could begin his life as a builder. At Thanksgiving, 1985, Stephen returned home with his new girlfriend, the striking and exotic Kara Lynx. Quickly, Stephen took back control of his health club, placed Kara in the front as a receptionist, and with Carl's guidance, Stephen began building homes.

Throughout the balance of 1985 and—as would become crucial to the murder investigation—through all of 1986, 1987, and 1988, Stephen continued his work in Rhode Island helping his father build nearly a dozen luxury homes in the some of the most prestigious plats in the state. But by the fall of 1988, the housing market had become depressed, and Stephen had broken up with Kara. No longer tied to Rhode Island, he decided to try his luck in finding potential real estate deals in Florida, where he had lived throughout much of 1984 and 1985. But the real estate market was difficult there as well, and so Stephen stayed in Florida for less than a year, from the tail end of 1988 through May of 1989, and then he returned to Rhode Island.

Upon his homecoming, he moved into one of the large houses he had built with his father in the northwestern part of the state in Scituate. At that time, things had slowed to a crawl, and mortgage money had dried up. During the following year, in early 1990, Stephen got the idea of creating commercial properties that would generate income regardless of market fluctuation. His plan was to build a Quality Inn two exits up from Connecticut in Hope Valley, at the junction of Interstate 95 and Route 138, the main gateway to the University of Rhode Island, Newport, and Cape Cod. The Rosatis also had other properties in the area they were developing, including plans for building an industrial park and the brokering of the sale of a nearby 600-acre parcel to a quarry company in England. That deal alone was in the $20 to $35 million range.

CHAPTER 3:
Like Something out of Kafka

September 12, 1990

The morning Stephen was arrested started as an ordinary day. He awoke in time to flip on *Business Reports* and then began to plot out arrangements for several ventures his company was involved in. Over the weekend he had taken his girlfriend, Suzanne LaPlante, to their site in Hope Valley to see the new venture the Rosati Group was planning. That is when Stephen told Suzanne his idea of expanding the project to build an upscale industrial park to accompany a Quality Inn. Stephen's goal was to create a property that would provide a continual revenue stream.

Simultaneously, the Rosati Group was meeting with an English couple representing a mining concern that was building roads in Great Britain and was interested in part of the property for its quarry value. Beginning negotiations with London showed a potential deal of $35 million, with 10 percent going to the Rosati Group.

In their second parcel, they had invested $180,000 in the creation of roads. Wetlands were tagged and architectural and legal fees were paid. With these three deals, the Rosati Group was beginning to gain control of nearly 1,000 acres in just one section of Rhode Island alone. Stephen was in the middle of a phone conversation going over bore samples they were shipping to England when he was called out of the office. Through the open door, he saw a few police officers.

"I was in my father's office," Stephen remembered, "faxing information to the quarry people in England, when my secretary told me that Fred was on the line. When I picked up the phone, there was no answer. Thinking it was my friend Freddy Palumbo, I figured he would simply call back."

About an hour later, with Rosati on long distance, the secretary interrupted again. "Steve, you have a friend, Brendan Doherty, to see you."

Doherty was, at that time, a state trooper who used to train at Stephen's health club for free along with other policemen he let in as a courtesy. Stephen hadn't seen Doherty* in nearly four years, not since the club was sold in 1986. Four plainclothes cops accompanied the trooper.

"You guys want some money for the softball league?"

"Steve, we want to speak to you privately," said Doherty.

"Sure," Stephen said, wondering what was going on as they took him to one of the side offices, shut the door, and huddled around him.

"Steve, I have some bad news for you. You're under arrest."

"Come on, you guys. How much do you want?"

"This is no joke," Doherty said.

"What are you talking about?"

"You know for what."

"No, I don't know. So why don't you just tell me."

"For a murder in Florida."

"You're crazy," Rosati replied in shock, while subconsciously looking for a way to move past them.

Stephen considered Doherty a friend, and that friend was now accusing him of murder. Five bodies shifted to keep him in place.

---

* A decade later, Doherty would go on to be director of security at Roger Williams University and then get appointed by the governor to head up the Rhode Island State Police. Not too long after that, he would run unsuccessfully for the U.S. House of Representatives, against the incumbent, David Cicilline, the son of Stephen's attorney.

Doherty explained in as kind a tone as he could muster that he was arresting Stephen for first-degree murder.

"These two gentlemen are from the Broward Sheriff County office in Florida. We want to take you to the Hope Valley Sheriff's Office uncuffed to the car, and then we'll have to cuff you when we get downstairs."

"Dad," Stephen spoke plaintively as they left the room and headed toward the front door, "they've just arrested me for murder. Get somebody to help. Get me a lawyer. Do something!"

"Steve, don't worry. I'll call somebody. Your mother and I will meet you at the barracks."

All of a sudden, they ushered Stephen out. "Look," one of the officers said, "he's been charged with murder."

"That's impossible," Carl said.

"We have two policemen from Florida," the cop went on, "and we are taking him to the State Police Barracks in Hope Valley."

Carl recalled, "I'm upset; my wife wasn't there. I can't believe it's happening." Esther was out buying groceries for lunch. "There must be a mistake," Carl tried once more.

"Mr. Rosati, this is no mistake," the officer replied.

"They disappeared with my son," Carl said.

Esther returned a few minutes later and rushed into the kitchen to put out the lunch she had bought.

"Something has happened. The police were here to arrest Stephen."

"For what? A speeding ticket?"

"No. For murder."

"Murder!" Esther exclaimed. "There has to be some mistake."

"Stephen's at the Hope Valley Police Barracks. Two police detectives from Florida said that it has to do with a murder down there."

Stephen recounted that he couldn't stop thinking that they had made a mistake—they had the wrong guy. As they headed out the door, it flashed through his mind that the Rosatis had just hired their receptionist. This was her first day, and he wondered what she would think of him being arrested for murder.

In the elevator, he kept telling himself that if he hadn't done anything wrong, he had nothing to worry about, but at the same time, he remembered repeating to himself, "I can't believe this is happening to me."

Doherty replied, "If you didn't do anything, then you'll be out of there in no time."

Outside, there were two police cruisers. And just as Rosati followed an officer into the back seat of one, they slapped the cuffs on him. Another officer slid in, sandwiching him, and two more sat in front. The other policeman followed them in the second vehicle, and they drove that way to the station.

"I was confused. It was like a nightmare. I couldn't believe what was happening." Stephen recalled sitting in the squad car and repeating, "I don't know what the hell this is all about." But right off the bat, Rosati quickly faced the fact that that nobody believed him and that it was useless to continue to proclaim his innocence. "They just looked at me and said with their expressions, 'Yeah, right, kid. You're a liar.'"

As they continued to the station, Stephen ruminated about his reputation. He kept thinking he would be protected. "You know, 'innocent until proven guilty,' but as he was later to find out, he had no rights."

The first fast move had already taken place because the officers didn't take Stephen to the Hope Valley Police Station, as they had told Carl, but rather to the Scituate barracks. This caused Stephen's parents to go to the wrong end of the state, and that gave the police over an extra hour to interrogate Rosati without any legal counsel.

"Entering the barracks with my head down, I felt ashamed as people stared. It was the worst feeling I have ever had, multiplied a million times," Stephen said. "I saw one of my childhood friends, Greg Long, who is now a state trooper. He shook his head in such a way to show that he understood, as if to say he knew I wasn't guilty."

Greg uttered, "I'm sorry, Steve."

"I'm sorry, too," Rosati replied.

Growing up in Scituate, Greg and his brother Brad had been wild kids, and they had even been on the same Little League team as Stephen. When they got older, they stayed friends. Stephen remembered a time when some guy had humiliated Greg in a fight, and Stephen had gone back with him to arrange a fair return match.

"I stood by his side risking my own ass when he was in trouble, and in that way he got his vindication. Our friendship cut deep, and I could see on his face that he knew they had the wrong guy. But Greg was really the only one who stood up for me."

Rhode Island's a small state, and Stephen knew other troopers, a number of whom had worked out at Stephen's gym. "Vinny Virgilio, for one, who I had traveled to other countries with. Every Christmas I would drive to Vinny's house and deliver a bottle of champagne or red wine, just to keep up the friendship. Vinny told everyone I was guilty."

Stephen doesn't recall being read his Miranda rights. "After you are arrested, you have no rights. They just marched me into a cold room," Rosati said.

CHAPTER 4:
The Tapes

The two policemen from Florida who put the case together were Bobby Coyote and Frank Puccini. They introduced themselves, and Officer Coyote did all the talking.

Dressed in a dungaree outfit, Sheriff Detective Robert R. (Bobby) Coyote took off his jacket and straddled his seat backward like it was a horse. Since he worked undercover, Detective Coyote looked more like a biker than a policeman.

"He had a hot tan, long, curly blond hair, short sleeve T-shirt open to a bare chest so he could show off his gold neck chains, a series of tattoos all over his hands, gold bracelets, and an ominous-looking snake ring on his middle finger, with the serpent sticking prominently out. He flashed the ring in my direction."

Rosati looked squarely at him. "You got the wrong guy. Do I look like a killer? Do I look like I'm lying to you? I'm telling you, I'm innocent. I don't even know who was killed!"

Ignoring these pleas, Detective Coyote began showing his suspect a picture of the dead man, Joe Viscido, lying on the floor in a pool of blood. "You couldn't even see his face. I never heard his name before," Stephen said. The detective then began rattling off a list of names: Peter Dallas, Cory Franco, Jeff Bloom, Michelle Arrieta, Vic Giordano . . .

"I don't know these names! They mean nothing to me," Stephen said, but the detective just kept showing Rosati more pictures. Although he did remember one that was linked to an interrogation he had in Florida the year before, Stephen insisted he didn't recognize any of the pictures or the other names.

"Well, this one knows you. I got tapes." Coyote unfurled a satisfied smirk as he reached over to the recorder and popped in a succession of three or four different tapes.

The first tape blared, "Yeah, that's him. He's the one who busted through the door."

He popped in another tape, and the low, scratchy voice of Peter Dallas, which seemed to quiver, said, "I know Stephen Rosati for months and months. I hung around with him two to three weeks before the incident."

Coyote's voice on the tape asked, "So, at about eleven o'clock, yourself and Steve Rosati get into a car. Can you describe the car for me?"

"It was a car with no doors, just a front windshield," the man identified as Peter Dallas said.

"Now, you get to the house, and I know it's been four years and just try to be, think back exactly as it happened. Who went up to the door? Just go from there."

"It was Steve that knocked. I was standing like behind him, and a little to the left side of him."

"You're both armed?"

As the tape kept going on, Stephen thought, *"It's all fucking nuts."*

"Yeah. Steve had a .45, the kind where you just put a clip on the handle."

I wouldn't know a .45 from a .44. I felt, for an instant, like I was going out of my mind.

"How many people do you remember being in there?" Coyote continued on the tape.

"I can't really remember. Two or three, maybe even four people."

"Was there a female?"

"I can't—I can't . . . If I answer yes, I'll be lying."

"What happened next?"

"Steve took a gun to the guy's head."

"This is crazy," Stephen mumbled, yet in some morbid way, he was curious to hear the rest of the tape.

"Can you remember anybody kicking Joe Viscido?"

"I can't remember that."

"The next thing I remember, he was—he had him back up and told me to go into the room with him and to get whatever was in there."

"Steve Rosati told you to go in the room?"

"Yes, sir. He lifted him off the floor, grabbed Joe, you know, and he told everybody to get on the floor, and he told me to get everything that was in the room, the cocaine, the money."

"You got the wrong guy!" Rosati shouted, interrupting the tape. "That isn't me!"

"Shush, Listen. Your name comes up again," Coyote said.

"So, he's got the other people at gunpoint?"

"Yes, sir. So I take the guy into the back room and closed the door, and . . . um . . . as we were walking, I had the gun out. I didn't even have it pointed at him. I had it down like, and then he swung around and he hit me into the wall."

"He tried grabbing your gun?" Puccini's voice could be heard interrupting.

"I really, I can't—I can't remember, 'cause it was more like a struggle than anything, when I ran into the wall like it was said to me earlier, there was a gun fired, the first gunshot. I don't remember that. Maybe it was at the reaction hitting the wall or maybe it was when he hit me, the trigger got pulled."

"You remember the first gunshot?"

"Sir. No, sir."

"Okay," Coyote's voice continued, "he tries to get the gun and then what?"

"All of a sudden, the door came flying down. Somebody just rammed . . ."

"And who was that person?"

"Steve Rosati. Steve hits the door. It comes flying down, and like we both stopped, and the next thing I remember is that I was told to grab the stuff. The next thing I remember after that was *boom*."

"So, as you're grabbing the cocaine, your back is to Steve Rosati and Joe Viscido, and you hear a shot?"

"Yes, sir."

"And you go running out? Do you remember—did you step or jump over the body?"

"Jumped."

"Where was Steve Rosati at that time?"

"He was at my right."

"Did you see where Viscido had been shot?"

"No, sir. I was in front."[1]

As the tape played, Coyote held a picture of the dead man lying in a pool of blood in front of Rosati who had to sit there and look at it. When he finished playing the tape, Coyote said, "The next tape is a photo lineup," and turned it back on.

"That one, that's the guy," a witness on the tape said.

"You mean Stephen Rosati?"

"Yeah, the big guy. He came in and made us lie down and face the floor."

Stephen listened to the tapes flabbergasted and remembered thinking, *It's like I stepped into the fucking Twilight Zone, only it's my real life. Jeff Bloom had me going into the building and coming out with a bag of cocaine. Giordano had me inside the apartment. Cory Franco said he was working on a truck on the outside. And I never heard of these people. I didn't know who they were, and they were saying my name. I sat there totally dumbfounded, so Coyote backed off a little.*

"Well, maybe you didn't pull the trigger, but we think you know something about it. We don't really care about you. We just want to get Pete the Greek. Do you know Pete the Greek?"

"No," Stephen lied. "After all this bullshit," he didn't want to tell them he knew Pete the Greek, but he suspected that Coyote might have already gotten his previous testimony from the Florida interrogation. Still, he didn't want to tell Coyote that he knew Pete the Greek.

"Look, we're not after you," Coyote said in a friendlier tone. "So if you help us, I can get this all reduced," he stared at the ceiling for a minute calculating, "to only seven years." Coyote paused to let his words sink in, and then his manner and tone became more serious. "But if you don't cooperate, I'll make sure you get twenty to life, or more likely, the electric chair. And if you get the chair, who knows if you'll even make it to death row."

The detective then painted a picture of prison life down in Florida. "You probably won't make it because they'll shank white boys like you down there. It ain't like here, where you're in the majority. Down there, you'll be in the minority. However, if you play along, I'll see that your charge is reduced to second degree. I'll do that today. All we want is for you to help us get Pete the Greek."

"I told you I had nothing to do with this. I just want to talk to a lawyer."

"You can talk to a lawyer till you're blue in the face, but you're going down, Rosati."

"I could see that he was getting pissed because I wasn't playing along. But I had no idea what he was talking about. And, furthermore, there was nothing to consider. 'I'm innocent!' I repeated." Rosati looked Detective Coyote square in the eyes and proclaimed, "I'm not going to take a deal for something I didn't do."

CHAPTER 5:
The Nightmare Begins

Carl and Esther discussed strategy on the car ride to the Hope Valley station, but when they got to the barracks, they found that Stephen was not there. When Carl learned that Stephen was at the opposite side of the state in the Scituate Police Barracks, he became visibly upset.

Angry at the deception, but resigned to it, Carl got back into the car and headed to Scituate. On the way, he used the mobile phone to call Superior Court Judge Tom Calderone. The judge, in turn, called Major Urso at the Scituate Barracks and got clearance for Carl and Esther to immediately see their son when they finally arrived.

The Rosatis learned from the major that seven people had identified Stephen as being involved in the murder in Florida, but it didn't matter to Esther. She never doubted that her son was innocent. First off, they had implied that he was a drug dealer, but Esther not only saw and spoke to Stephen daily, she also knew that for the last five years her son and his father had been building homes in Rhode Island. Later, he was looking for real estate deals in Florida. And even then, Esther and Carl were down in Florida during a good part of those times.

"We were greeted by a police officer that we knew," Esther said. "His expression conveyed sympathy and disbelief. He led us to where Stephen was being held. It was a cubicle. Stephen was standing up, with his hands behind him. The reality of it began to overwhelm him. I looked at my son. My heart welled up in sorrow. I asked if he was handcuffed."

"Yes, Mom, I am handcuffed. Mom, I didn't do this."

"I know, Stephen. I know you didn't do this."

"I don't even know the people that they are talking about, but they say they have witnesses."

"Stephen," Carl said, "if there is anything, anything at all, tell us now because I will do whatever I can to help you. But I have to know the truth so I can help you."

"I don't know," Stephen said in a bewildered state. "I don't even know these names. They're talking about coke. You know I'm not into coke. I can't stand the stuff. They asked me if I knew Pete the Greek. I hedged for a while and then said yes. It must be a case of mistaken identity. I can't even fathom . . ."

"Stephen," his dad said, "whatever is possible to be done, your father and mother will do it. We will get you out of this mess."

When I questioned Carl about this moment, Carl put it all on the line. "I knew that Stephen would be truthful on something like this. One way or another, there was no question in my mind as to his innocence. I also knew that if anything happened to my son, they were going to have to take me with him."

After spending time with their son, the Rosatis met Detective Coyote, the man who had replaced Sergeant McNeil, the original officer who had put this case together against Stephen. From Esther's point of view, since this was obviously a case of mistaken identity, she thought Stephen would be out of jail by the end of the day. But they hadn't reckoned on a detective as dislikeable as this.

"He looked like a cheap cop in a bad movie," Carl said.

Esther had a similar gut reaction. "Dressed in bleached denim pants, with reddish bleached shirt, and long hair, Bobby Coyote struck me as a disgusting individual, sauntering in with all these gold chains around his neck, with an open shirt and a prominent snake ring that sneered out from his little finger.

"In the corner was his partner, Frank Puccini, an overweight glob who looked like a wet rat, sitting with his eyes down, a real nonentity. He seemed weak, and Coyote seemed arrogant. Our immediate reaction to both of these men was one of extreme abhorrence. What I saw was a lot of bravado with no backup. I perceived this immediately, as Coyote started blasting off."

"Your son was heavy, heavy, heavy, heavy into coke. He may seem like a nice kid now, but he was involved in a murder in Florida. In fact, he may not even have had anything to do with it, but he lied to us about knowing Pete the Greek, and we have witnesses that put him there. They prove that he was involved, and if he doesn't speak now, I'll fry him. He'll get the electric chair. If he opens up, I'll probably get him twenty years. But if he really talks, I mean, really unloads, I think I can get him off with seven."

"I can't believe how he says seven like it's nothing," Esther recalled. "He's talking about years! My son will not spend another seven minutes here if I can help it."

"You need to hear some of the evidence we have against him." Detective Coyote pointed to a small tape player. He took out a tape and put it in the machine. The Rosatis listened to a voice say that someone had fingered Stephen as one of the people who killed a person whose name they didn't recognize. Then he turned it off.

"You have not only killed one person with your statements, Mr. Coyote, you have killed the three of us," Esther said. Overcome for the moment, she put her head on her husband's shoulder.

Oddly enough, the other Florida detective, Frank Puccini, told the Rosatis to fight it, and Carl's words assured him that the planned to do just that. "My son is not guilty of anything. We'll take our chance with the electric chair."

"Well, then," Detective Coyote said, "there's nothing I can do for you."

Since there was time, the Rosatis returned to their son. Overcome with great sadness, Esther and Stephen began to sob. Carl cried too.

He said later, "Looking back at the detective, I believe he mistook gentleness for weakness. A man like him wasn't capable of recognizing the difference."

The Rosatis knew that Stephen was not into cocaine because he was so concerned with his body. They also did not believe the audiotapes. They left the police station dumbfounded.

Stephen's next stop was Kent County Courthouse where, by nightfall, he was supposed to be extradited to Florida. However, the Rosatis thought fast. They hired Steven Fortunato, a lawyer who had an office in their business complex, and he came immediately to meet them at the courthouse. It was at that time that the Rosatis found out the date of the murder, which was four years prior, in 1986. They had thought it was a year and a half ago, which was the last time Stephen had been in FloridaKnowing that Stephen had been building houses down near Hope Valley at the time the murder took place in Florida, the Rosatis decided to ask their secretary, Jan Fregolle, to check Stephen's pay stubs and business records and pull checks for the time of the murder. Jan found a number of checks and delivered them to the courthouse. The month Stephen had signed them was the very same month of the murder: October 1986.

On the same afternoon that Stephen was arrested, the Rosatis were able to bring tangible evidence to Stephen's hearing confirming that he was in Rhode Island and not in Florida in October 1986. It was at that time that they first met Randy White, the prosecutor from the Rhode Island State Attorney General's office who would later try the case. When asked about the signed checks, he told the Rosatis that Stephen could have been anywhere, even hiding out in Canada, when the checks were signed and dismissed them as insignificant. Judge Darrigan, however, who was presiding and who at various times had been a candidate for the governorship, saw their importance and delayed the extradition for ten days.

Detective Coyote tried to argue that he had a grand jury indictment, which was not true, and an affidavit giving him the right to arrest Stephen immediately. However, the Rosati's evidence gave them the first round.

"Without those checks, and without a judge like Judge Darrigan, to whom we will forever be grateful, Stephen would have been sent to Florida before sunset," Carl said.

What struck Esther was Randy White's assertion that the checks were probably not signed in a proper manner. "I saw how the prosecution could take the truth and twist it into a lie. Keep in mind these were average everyday checks.

"I looked at Detective Coyote and could see that his expression of arrogance had been replaced by one of insecurity. Quite frankly, he was stunned. He had lost some strength in that courtroom that day. But his next stop was New York, where he went to get Peter Dallas.

And so he returned to Florida as a hero bounty hunter, but he had only one body instead of two."

On his way back to the Adult Correctional Institute (ACI), Stephen remembered how he felt. "I was devastated. I truly thought that once we produced the checks, they would realize they had the wrong man, and I would be released. That's how naïve I was. I thought it was that simple."

"Back at our offices, everyone was traumatized. It was a silent gesture of such sympathy," Esther remembered. "Everything was so overwhelming, with Stephen facing charges of murder, robbery, and also facing a death sentence. In the face of human tragedy, people withdraw rather than come to you. Many of our friends felt it was inappropriate to call because it would seem like a curiosity factor. People also thought that Stephen may not have pulled the trigger, but he must have been involved somehow."

Carl, however, had a positive air about him. He believed that they could establish where Stephen was that day and was convinced that they had documentation to prove it. This proof would be in storage boxes they had at home. He remembered the conversation that took place when they moved their offices the year before. Esther had only wanted to keep records that were two years old because they had files dating back to the 1960s, but Carl was adamant about not getting rid of anything and made her promise not to discard the files.

His main concern was potential tax questions that could come up. In retrospect, if it had not been for Carl's insistence, the Rosatis would have had no physical proof to substantiate Stephen's whereabouts during October 1986.

Naturally, the Rosatis were taken completely by surprise when Red Gooseberger walked into their offices the day after Stephen was arrested. Still stocky and dapper, with those caterpillar eyebrows and full shock of red hair, Red was not quite as athletic as they had remembered him from the days when he was Stephen's high school wrestling coach. The Goose, as Stephen liked to call him, had read of Stephen's arrest in the paper and wanted to help. Having run into Stephen a few times since then—Red had dabbled for a while in building houses—he was convinced that Stephen would not have been capable of murder.

Carl was not particularly fond of Red because of the way he had treated Stephen during those wrestling days at Bishop Hendricken and how he had kicked Stephen off the team, but he was moved by his words.

"Carl, I don't want any money for this. I'm out of work, I'm collecting two disability checks, and here is my chance to finally do something good for someone."

"Certainly you can help," Carl said. "We could always use another hand."

Counting the people in the office, Carlyn's husband, Bruce, and some close friends, such as Angela Smith, there were as many as eight people working the case before the Rosatis settled on an attorney.

"Call Alan Dershowitz, will you, Red? Maybe we can get him."

After speaking with Dershowitz, Red said, "Dershowitz said that we have the best criminal lawyer in the entire northeast, right here in Rhode Island."

"Who's that?"

"Jack Cicilline."

"It was well after midnight when the phone rang," Esther remembered after this first incredibly intense day. "Carl and I jumped from our seats. We were still enmeshed in the documents. It was Mrs. LaPlante, the mother of a girlfriend of Stephen's. She had a job in one of the local courthouses."

"Stephen is in very serious trouble," the girlfriend's mother said. "I doubt he will be able to explain his way out of this."

"I couldn't believe that she could call so late. Lacking any tact, her call was a complete shock," said Esther.

"Don't listen to these people," Carl said. "And let's not get anxious. I'm sure she was well-meaning."

No matter how well intentioned she was, Esther thought her attitude was callous. Nevertheless, she had certainly alerted the Rosatis to the seriousness of the situation. They stayed up until three in the morning going over documentation that seemed insurmountable. They decided that the first task would be to arrange everything chronologically.

"We were exhausted going through it and collapsed in our bed," Esther recalled. "I remember putting my head on the pillow and feeling this primal scream of agony coming from me. The extent of the pain was so great that I cannot put it into words. It was as though they had ripped my heart from my body. Tormented, I was in the depths of pain. I couldn't sleep."

Esther told me that Carl had put his arm around her and told her, with a certainty to his voice, that everything would be all right.

"But, still, I couldn't sleep, because my heart and my whole being was next to Stephen in his prison cell. I felt the abandonment, the pain that he was feeling. That was the beginning of the nightmare. Every day, from then on, was a day of great agony—the insanity of it all. Like a spiral down into a labyrinthine realm of irrationality we entered the depths of hell. The madness of the system, its tentacles, the way they hold you by the jugular, and the way they force the very life out of you. If a person is guilty, he admits it, but if he is not guilty, then he is just swallowed up by the system.

"From that time on," Esther continued, "I lived my life in a vacuum, a realm of darkness, a realm of evil that you can actually experience—the people you are thrown in with, the system itself, which as its own entity, supports the dark side of life. There is no presumption of innocence; you are guilty. You are fighting from a position of guilt. How naïve I was. All of us come from a different level of consciousness, and if you are in another stage, you can only say, 'It's irrational. It's insane.' The only thing that gave me the strength to fight was the thought of saving Stephen's life. No one was going to harm Stephen."

The next morning, at 7:00 a.m., the Rosatis met with their staff to explain the tragedy of what had happened and their plans for organizing the data. A friend from Watch Hill came by to help and spent an entire night copying pertinent documents. Having no experience with criminal lawyers, Carl put together a think tank of his most trusted legal and professional associates. He sat with lawyers, a businessman from a Fortune 500 company, and a judge to discuss who to retain. Jack Cicilline's name kept surfacing as the most noted criminal attorney in the state. However, before the Rosatis would consider him, they wanted to interview three others.

CHAPTER 6:
Adult Correctional Institute

After his parents left, Stephen was taken to the local courthouse and fingerprinted. Trooper Doherty sat him down. "Steve," he began softly, "I know that you were involved in a lot of things in Florida."

"He was clearly trying to get something out of me," Stephen recalled, "but there was nothing to get. I'm feeling like a liar, and he's thinking I had to have something to do with this."

Rosati was taken to a bathroom, and then he was photographed holding a number in front of him.

Stephen reflected on how quickly his parents came up with checks he had signed at the time of the murder and how shocked Detective Coyote was, which was at least some consolation for him.

"Your Honor," their lawyer Stephen Fortunato began, "as you can see from these documents, my client was living and conducting business in Rhode Island at the time of the murder."

After the hearing, Stephen thought back on the lack of confidence on Coyote's face during the courtroom procedure.

"I looked over at Coyote. Here it is, the very first day, and I already have signed, documented proof that I'm in Rhode Island. Suddenly, he's got a very worried look. I was sent downstairs to a cellblock in the basement of the courthouse. I sat with a bunch of other guys I had seen upstairs who were also arrested. We waited together to be transported to the ACI.

"Here I am, dressed in nice pants, a $125 shirt, Gucci shoes, and I'm going to the Adult Correctional Institute. I'm going to jail with a bunch of criminals. I look out the window of the van and see my office off the highway. 'That's my office. I work there,' I said to one of the other guys."

The van turned into a barbed wire gate and continued into a carport. A policeman posted with a machine gun draped across his arms guarded the entranceway. Inside, a policeman sat at a desk and routinely checked off names.

"What are you here for?" he says offhand.

"Murder," Rosati said.

"Mouthing the word sounded like an admission of something," Stephen recalled, "Now he looks up at me in my high-style clothes as if I'm a lowlife. But I don't look like a lowlife. He appears puzzled."

Taken to a room to eat, the prisoners were then called back in one by one, strip-searched, and given a uniform. "Open your mouth. Turn around. Spread your legs. Bend over."

"Take a shower, and put on this uniform," one of the guards tells Rosati.

"I know him from TGI Friday's, a local restaurant. We used to date the same girl. I look around. It seems like I know half the guards from training at my gym, the nightclub scene, or growing up. It was like I said. Kara never understood Rhode Island. I know everyone. They take me to a hospital for a physical, check for TB or AIDS. I see one prisoner there, his face all busted up. I see another kid. I know him. He's in on robbery. Big deal. I'm in for first-degree murder. Another guard comes in and takes me to my modular unit, which in prison lingo is called the mod.

"We pass large plate glass windows. Thirty to forty guys look in and stare at me. Everyone's checking me out. I've got this blue denim uniform on and Gucci shoes."

"Hey, man," one of the kids says, "how much are they?"

"Two fifty."

"You must be rich."

40

"I'm doing okay," I respond.

"I look around at all these faces: so many totally ultimately depressed faces. They look like they're all dead. Soon, I understand."

CHAPTER 7:
The Criminal Attorney

Tough as nails is the only way to describe the most famous lawyer in Rhode Island, John F. "Jack" Cicilline. There was a time in the late 1970s when Jack seemed to be on the six o'clock news almost daily because he was working to keep his main client, aging underworld New England kingpin Raymond Patriarca, out of jail. Patriarca had been used as a model for one of the Mafia dons for Francis Ford Coppola's movie *The Godfather*.

Jack was constantly in the news at that time and throughout the 1980s, when it was alleged that his infamous client and his capos were doing deals at Jack's law firm. With Mob executions taking place in upscale Italian restaurants, telephone booths, delis, and pastry shops just doors from his Federal Hill establishment, and Cicilline defending clients with names like "Baby Shanks," "Cadillac Frank," "Fat Tony," and "Vinnie the Animal"—it was no wonder the FBI decided to wiretap Cicilline's office with permission from a local judge.

Growing up in Providence, Jack first gained the attention of the metropolitan community in the mid-1950s when he was co-captain of the football team from LaSalle Academy, a Catholic high school whose main rival was Cranston. Playing center on offense and middle linebacker on defense, at five foot eleven and about 200 pounds, Jack was legendary in the 1955 and '56 championship finals.[1] A graduate of Providence College, and a lawyer since the mid-1960s, Jack obtained his law degree—as did most every other lawyer in the state—at Suffolk University Law School in Boston, because there was no law school at that time in Rhode Island.

Originally interested in the Foreign Service, Jack was an idealist whose hero at that time was Robert Kennedy, Jr. In the mid-1960s, Jack began his career as policy aid to the Democratic mayor of Providence, Joe Doorley. In 1968, the year that Martin Luther King, Jr., and Bobby Kennedy were assassinated, Jack began his apprenticeship clerking at Joseph Bevilacqua's law firm. Within a decade he was full partner.

As Bevilacqua made much of his living defending the head of the New England crime family, Raymond Patriarca, and his many cohorts, Jack took on much of that work. In the late 1970s, when Bevilacqua was appointed first to a judgeship and then to chief justice of the Rhode Island Supreme Court, Jack rose to become Patriarca's head lawyer. Bevilacqua later left this post in heavily publicized disgrace because of charges of adultery at a local motel and continuing ties to alleged Mob figures.

According to *Providence Journal* writer Mike Stanton, who interviewed Jack for a book on Mayor Cianci, Patriarca "had no love for the Kennedys." Having been a rumrunner himself during prohibition, Patriarca saw Bobby Kennedy's father, Joe, as a former bootlegger, but more importantly, as a "double-crosser" who used the support of the Mob to stuff ballots in Chicago to gain the state of Illinois for his son's presidential bid. Then Bobby Kennedy, the new attorney general, set out to destroy organized crime. Patriarca had a special reason to be angry, particularly because, as it has been alleged, the CIA had hired the Mob king to organize a hit on Fidel Castro, even though the plan was never carried out. It wasn't long before Bobby Kennedy's picture came down from Cicilline's wall, soon to be replaced by a life-sized portrait of New England's godfather, Raymond Patriarca.[2]

Throughout his colorful and high-profile career, Jack has handled every kind of criminal case from Mob hits and racketeering, to drug dealing, rape, embezzlement, and multiple murders. Running his law firm out of an unassuming storefront in the Dante Building in the Little Italy section of Providence on Federal Hill, Jack Cicilline was the head of a dynasty of criminal attorneys that included his brother Stephen, who had an office on Broadway, and his sons David and John Jr. In his prime, at fifty-two, he was a large, husky man with short-cropped hair, whose well-worn suits could benefit from being let out a notch. Like clockwork, Jack would arrive at his office at 7:45 a.m., receive a few phone calls, and then spend the day at the courthouse. Many evenings, Jack could be found back at the office. Twelve-hour days were commonplace for Jack Cicilline.

One of Jack's most distinctive features is his voice, a low, crisp staccato, seasoned by a larynx that has filtered its fair share of cigarette smoke. A dedicated scholar with one of the keenest legal minds in the country, Jack Cicilline considered being a criminal attorney his lifeblood.

In 1978, after Patriarca was imprisoned for conspiracy to commit murder, Cicilline made headlines when he hired Nicholas Bianco, a Patriarca wise guy, as a "paralegal" after Bianco was released from federal prison, having served a four-year term for tax evasion. This was during the "Godfather" days, when in New York, Joseph Colombo was assassinated during an Italian American Civil Rights League rally as revenge for Joe Gallo getting whacked in New York's Little Italy. Unwilling to use "such words as Mafia," as the *Providence Journal* reported, Cicilline denied, "in pretrial hearings for Patriarca . . . that an organization exists like the one being portrayed." Dealing with the media was difficult, even though organized crime cases took up less than ten percent of Cicilline's workload. With stone-faced assurance, Cicilline "likened the group to an Elks club."

Jack's illustrious past always made good press, particularly when the media could disclose that he knew John Gotti, head of the New York Gambino family, and it was alleged that he was the conduit between godfathers from Rhode Island and New York.

"The media has no right to decide what kind of people I should represent," Jack said, admitting that he had met the Teflon Don "one time in my life," a decade earlier. When asked about the circumstances, Jack replied in characteristic bluntness, "I met him someplace, period."

* * *

At ACI, Stephen sat alone in his cell crying quietly, trying not to let anyone see, as he looked out the window. He described how he felt:

"I would look out the window. I can't believe it. It's like a bad dream, a bare toilet in the middle of the room. Forget privacy. I made my bed with some sheets and a blanket. Not even a pillow."

Soon Stephen got a roommate, Dale, and this is how he felt about that:

"He's okay. But like everyone else, he thought I was connected. It was the newspaper articles and the weekly TV coverage that started it. My first full day, there's already an article in the *Providence Journal*. The words 'drug lord' and 'shot a man in the head' jump off the page. I'm big, I'm Italian, I'm wealthy. It all fit."

From that point onward Rosati found that he was getting a feeling of total respect from the other inmates. No matter how many times Stephen would say that they had the wrong man, the other prisoners still believed he was a hit man. After a few weeks, it became clear that everyone around him assumed he was guilty. According to Stephen, there was no point in making a big deal about being innocent. It didn't matter.

Stephen did not do well during the time he was being held. For the first three weeks, he would wake up about 4:00 a.m. and think for a millisecond that maybe he was home. Stephen recalled endless nightmares of electric chairs and chain gangs. In one version he found himself clawing up banks and banks of quicksand.

"There was a fiery pit below, silhouettes of laughing faces above me. I'd wake up terrified, disoriented. I couldn't believe I'm here. I couldn't believe it."

He cried silent tears, knowing that no one must see him cry in this place, a place that thrives on weakness. Rosati considered flipping out. But what good would it do?

"Words cannot express the way I felt. You hate the world. Look what they did to you. You know it's only a small group of people, but it doesn't matter."

Stephen said that it felt worse to him than going to a death camp or facing a firing squad.

"At least there they kill you. All I can say is that I was pushed to the limit. The only thing that kept me going was the thought that this can't happen in America, that it all has to work out in the end. It's so absurd, so ridiculous. I thought I would get out any day—everyday, the same thought for 500 days. Waiting every day, watching my life go by, just disappear on me, every day, day after day, the same thing."

When someone would get out on bail, over the loudspeaker you'd hear, "Pack your things, Joe, Fred, Bill, Frank. You're out of here."

But an extradition hearing for a drug deal and murder is not an offense that qualifies for bail. There would be no bail for Stephen Rosati.

Pack your stuff, Rosati, the prisoner would repeat in his head for the umpteenth time. *You're out of here.* Stephen kept waiting for this, and felt jealous anytime anyone else got out.

"I saw some real losers, mostly heroin addicts, come in and out four, five times for petty crimes, but I had the worst charge. Rhode Island doesn't have an electric chair; Florida does. If they get me down there, I could fry."

One guy whose name was Carlos would get arrested. He'd spend a day or two in jail and then get released. Two weeks later, he'd be back in the slammer, be out in a few days, and a month later, he'd be right back in. He couldn't believe Rosati, supposedly wealthy with connections, was still there. It just blew his mind.

Most of the guys had done their crimes, so they figured everyone else must have done theirs.

"I didn't do this crime," Stephen would tell them.

"Sure, sure, Rosati," came their inevitable reply.

Apparently, some of the guards considered that Stephen might, in fact, be innocent. He had cars and money, and girls came to see him every visiting day. It just didn't make sense. A few of the guards who Stephen knew from the gym seemed to be on his side. David Perry, for instance, was a guard on Rosati's mod who saw him everyday from three to eleven.

"He thought I was innocent. You could tell just looking at him."

"Steve," he would say, "I hope you get out, and when you do, we'll have a drink together."

David helped Rosati a lot, and he considered him a great friend. Through Dave, Stephen obtained a position in facility. This meant that he could escape his cell for a few extra hours every day to sweep and clean.

"I washed the halls and bathrooms. Here I am, one time riding around in a Mercedes Benz, wearing Louis of Boston suits, doing million-dollar land transactions, helicopter skiing in Canada, traveling to the Bahamas, Caribbean, or Mexico, and now I'm scrubbing toilets and urinals in a jail and *wanting* to do this because it's my only purposeful job; because it gets me out of the fucking cell; because it makes me feel like I'm doing *something.*"

CHAPTER 8:
Federal Hill

Carl had reservations about Jack Cicilline because he handled Mafia clients. Concerned that this would cast some shadow over Stephen's case, Carl and Esther explored other options. The Rosatis continued to interview other attorneys, but none seemed to satisfy them.

"Going with Jack would be selling your son's life down the river," warned one of Carl's advisers. Esther thought this advice had more to do with ego than with saving Stephen's life.

The next day they drove to the law office of Jack Cicilline, located at street level, along Atwells Avenue in the heart of the Italian district of Providence known as Federal Hill. The moniker on the building was appropriate—the Dante State Bank Building. Passing by a couple of guys who looked like hoods, the genteel couple walked through the entranceway down a long narrow meandering hallway to Jack's space. They introduced themselves and sat down on a couch nestled among a stack of boxes.

"Picture in your mind a beautiful suite of offices such as the kind you see every week on *L.A. Law.* Now erase that picture from your mind," Carl said later.

"I had to close my eyes to some of the people who were in the reception area as we walked back to Jack's office," Esther recalled. "You can imagine my surprise to see a life-size picture of Raymond Patriarca and his son on the wall. He, of course, was the former head of the Mob in Rhode Island."

As usual, Jack's desk was filled with piles and piles of books and briefs, and the Rosatis had to look around them to see him. He sat there with his glasses atop his head.

Even before they had a chance to exchange greetings, Esther said, "I'm here because I have to be here. I really have heard a great deal about you, and I don't like what you do for a living. I don't admire the people you defend, but I need you to save my son's life." This was a greeting Cicilline would never forget.

The Rosatis got right to the point and handed Cicilline the affidavit. He pushed his glasses down onto his nose and took a full fifteen minutes to read over the entire document. The Rosatis had not had the gumption to actually read the affidavit themselves, so they sat there silently and waited for him to finish.

"There was nothing left to do but stare at the portrait of the Mafia don and his son," Carl recalled. *So this is what it's come down to,* Carl thought to myself as he wondered if Stephen's picture would someday end up on Jack Cicilline's wall as well.

Jack finally looked up. "This is very serious," he said, "but I want you to know that I see some flaws here. There's a possibility that something can be done."

The Rosatis told the lawyer about the checks and the health spa and gasoline receipts Stephen signed, and Jack spoke again.

"Get me a framework to go on. I want October 12 as the focal point. Document everything you can for a four-month period surrounding this date—everything."

Carl looked at his wife and could see she was impressed. This was going to be a long relationship, and there had to be good vibes all around. Even so, the Rosatis had no inclination to leave their son's fate solely in someone else's hands, not even Jack Cicilline's.

Cicilline calculated the cost to the Rosatis if the case went to Florida—the fees for a detective, a handwriting expert, and so on—

and he gave the Rosatis a flat rate for what his services would be. With fighting this thing in both Rhode Island and in Florida, they were looking at the possibility of spending hundreds of thousands of dollars. Beyond that, they did not know what they were getting into.

"But I must say," Carl reflected, "the Broward Sheriff's Office and Detective Coyote didn't know what they were getting into either." They hired Cicilline on the spot.

"What do you think about him?" Carl asked his wife on their way out.

"This is a focused individual," Esther said. "I'm impressed with his strength of purpose. He has the ability that we need, and I think he will fight for Stephen. I feel very comfortable with hiring Jack Cicilline."

After the Rosatis left the office, Cicilline was heard to comment to one of the secretaries, "Now, that lady is some piece of work."

Weeding Stephen's papers out from the massive pile of documents and placing them in chronological sequence had to be done within a ten-day period, so the Rosatis could force another stay. They worked through nights when Carl would fall asleep on the conference room floor. Esther worried about his health. She noticed that his face was losing some of its color, and he often sweated profusely. He assured her, however, that he was fine and was just nervous about Stephen.

After the ten-day stay was up, the Rosatis went to court to appear again before Judge Darrigan. They were sitting there waiting for Stephen's case to come up when a sheriff suddenly whispered in the judge's ear.

"Excuse me," the judge said, "Mr. Cicilline is here to see me. The court will be adjourned for a few minutes."

"It was so evident the respect that Jack Cicilline commanded," Carl explained, "and yet what was also ironic was that he doesn't seek it. Jack is not just a good trial lawyer. He's also a student of the law. He had total concentration when he studied this case and immediately got the stay extended."

Jack hired Fran Martin, a delicately built, gray-haired investigator and retired policeman. The Rosatis met with Fran the following week and gave him a stack of documents, which supported their claim that Stephen was in Rhode Island during the time of the murder. Fran Martin was skeptical, as Jack had originally been at the start, but after three weeks of exploring and talking to witnesses, Fran told the Rosatis, "Your son is innocent, and I have all the proof I need." This, of course, he also told Jack.

Once it was official that Cicilline was on board, there was no getting around the supposition that Rosati was a killer for the Mob.

"The more I tried to dissociate myself from the image, the more they believed it," Stephen recalled.

On one level, Rosati was happy with the new image.

"It protected me from the animals. And believe me, when you get into jail, there are a lot of them. I was also in good shape and soon got a reputation of being big and strong, so nobody bothered me."

Rosati willingly admitted that it was not safe in the ACI and that he had to adjust his personality accordingly so as to get along with all types, especially the guards, because they ultimately decided a prisoner's fate.

Approximately one-third of the ACI was Spanish, one-third black, and one-third white. There were also a few Asians mixed in. The largest group seemed to be Spanish, and Stephen became friends with most of them. He told me that if you were okay with them, they were okay with you. He also said that guys labeled as "child molesters" and "baby rapers" were beaten up the most.

One nerdy guy they called Orville Redenbacher was a target of prison gangs and ended up in the hospital because he had molested a little kid. A bunch of the prisoners huddled around him, hit him over the head with a book, and then punched him in the face. Then the cops broke it up and got Orville into protective custody. If the crime the guy was in for was detestable, like this one, Rosati noticed, the cops took a little extra time to break up the action. When they saw the guy's face all swollen up, many of the prisoners laughed as a way to let off steam. Rosati knew this was a dangerous place and that he had to keep his wits about him at all times.

In Stephen's mod, certain prisoners got clobbered five to seven times a week, and rarely was it done without some tacit allowance by the guards.

"After a pounding, the culprits would be all hyped up for a half an hour. The guys who were into it would say, 'Who else can we get?' Obviously, it wasn't just baby rapers, but that's how it played," Stephen said.

After a while Stephen could predict which guys would get a beating and which ones would not. "If a guy mouthed off, he was a likely target," Stephen said. A person had to be savvy to survive. Yet no one was allowed to go into another's cell, so, fortunately, sexual misconduct was rare.

Two of Stephen's friends, Suki and Mooki, were Asian and quite small. Suki and Mooki always had cookies in their room, and sometimes they gave away some to other inmates. Originally from Laos, these two fellows came from upscale working families, and it was doubtful that they had done what they were accused of. According to Stephen, and to many articles that would later appear in the *Providence Journal,* they were most likely imprisoned for a crime they didn't commit. They were at a party when a woman was robbed. The thieves wore ski masks, but she identified Suki and Mooki as the culprits because of their eyes.[1]

One day, a big black kid demanded their cookies and threatened them with a beating if they didn't comply. Rosati, who had several friends who were black, took the guy aside and told him to forget it.

"They have a lot of friends," Rosati said, "and I'm one of them."

There's no doubt Rosati saved his two best friends that day, but beatings still remained a problem. This was the world Stephen had entered.

"Snitches got pummeled the most," he said. "There was a white guy they called The Worm, who wanted to get a joint from one of the other inmates. Grass was always smuggled in during visits. When the man wouldn't give, The Worm told the guards that the guy was carrying grass. So now, in the middle of the night, we all got strip-searched. It was a total invasion of privacy, all our rooms torn apart. Needless to say, The Worm got his arm broken, and then the word got around, and he got beat up on a regular basis in every mod he was sent to. This was not a good guy, but the guards should have put him into protective custody."

"My friends were all colors," Stephen remembers. "Tut was a big black guy in for robbery. I used to work out with him all the time. Another of my best friends was a Dominican kid named Eddie. You could see that the minorities are at a disadvantage, and now I know how they feel. You could just see the frustration on their faces, because you know they don't have much of a chance. No money for a lawyer. And then, of course, there was Suki and Mooki."

For Rosati, being stuck in a small room with a door that locked him in as it clicked shut each night was the worst. The guards would press buttons to open and close them. Every night he could hear the doors slamming in a row—*click, click, click*—and then he remembered the feeling of being captured. Day after day, seven days a week, he heard the sound of clicking doors opening and closing. If he wanted to get out of his cell, he couldn't. The prisoners had only a small window, which looked out onto a yard and more prison cells. Off in the distance, Rosati could see the high-security building, a soccer field, and barbed wire fences. Fantasizing about being out, Stephen would recollect parties, girls, business deals, driving his Mercedes, the dates he went on—anything to avoid thinking about the possibility of being sent to the electric chair.

CHAPTER 9:
The Alibi

On the home front, it didn't seem possible, but things were potentially worse! Esther noticed that every night when they went to bed, she'd wake to find the sheets soaking wet. The doctor confirmed that Carl was running a temperature of 103°, and Esther reasoned that this had to be more than tension. The doctor thought there could be a problem with Carl's heart valve and also a possible aneurysm.

Carl had developed an infection in his heart valve that was life threatening. It was the same one that killed the puppeteer Jim Henson in less than three days. The Rosatis were in a double crisis. Carl was rushed to the hospital, just as they got another stay for Stephen. Placed on intravenous antibiotics feeding for the next two months, Carl was then transferred to Boston, where they were more prepared for special heart surgery, if it was needed. He would be in and out of the hospital throughout the next year, leaving Esther alone to support their son.

With the real possibility that he could die, Carl felt helpless, especially with IV tubes going in and out of his body twenty-four hours a day. Naturally, Carl's problems were compounded by the worry he had about the uncertainty of his son's situation and the fact that he was far away in Boston. But Stephen and Esther called him every day, so he knew what was going on. He could also see how this double hit was affecting her, so he told Esther not to visit him. It was a long drive, but she continued to do so anyway. He discouraged her by making excuses for why she couldn't visit. One day he told her he would be taking tests all day because he knew his wife needed the rest, and this was the only way he could see to give her a break. She was working night and day on the case, which was at a critical stage.

By this time, their son-in-law, Bruce Benkhart, had computerized Stephen's entire file. He had placed all Stephen's documents in chronological order. These included bank checks, gasoline credit card receipts, receipts he signed for incoming clients at the health club they owned, and payroll checks he signed for his employees every Friday. Now they had a day-by-day account of Stephen's activities surrounding the time of the murder. Cicilline was amazed at how much work the Rosatis had done and grateful that they had provided so much information that would help him.

It was really at this point that the invitation to help from Stephen's high school wrestling coach took a foothold. It was a very vulnerable time for Esther when Red Gooseberger became a part of the office. Their staff went through each box of the 1986 files three and four times to make sure they didn't miss anything, and that's how Red came up with the telephone records, which made him a hero in Esther's eyes.

In reviewing events in Stephen's life, Esther remembered that during the time of the Florida murder, four years earlier, Stephen had had a disagreement with Kara about her not wanting to attend "family functions." In this instance, she refused to attend the Christening of Red's son. Stephen decided to drive over to speak to Red and his wife at the church, pay his respects, and apologize for not attending. They were already outside in the parking lot when he got there. When Esther and Red located the invitation, as one of those unbelievable coincidences, it was discovered that the date was October 12, 1986, the *very day* of the murder! This piece of evidence would be held back by Jack Cicilline at the Rhode Island extradition hearing in case they needed a documented bombshell to save Stephen's life, if the case made it to trial in Florida. It also put Red on an entirely different level of potential power because they had the dated invitation as documentation to support their testimony.

Thus, as time went on, Red's position on the team became much stronger. Initially, this was probably because Carl was bedridden and because Red had found some crucial evidence. It was also because he and Esther actually did the legwork, whereas Carl's role was more linked to keeping the businesses afloat and handling the financing for the case. Because of his weakened condition, Carl was not involved in the day-to-day strategy. Having always envisioned Carl as dynamic and successful, Red now saw him as frail and too frugal. He began to lose respect for Carl, and personality conflicts arose.

"Nevertheless," Esther recalled, "Red was very intelligent, saw situations clearly, and knew the case so well, so we put up with his other side as we continued to work new ways to try and free Stephen."

Right from the start, the Rosatis worked around the clock to find additional documentation to prove that Stephen was living in Rhode Island in October 1986. They likened it to being in a war, and they felt worn out.

As the case progressed, Esther began to see that Stephen's frame-up was not an isolated event. The papers were filled with stories of people wrongly convicted of crimes. "If it could happen to Stephen," Esther realized, "it could happen to anyone." The more Esther looked at the facts, the more she questioned her son's connection to this strange murder case. It made no sense to her.

"Stephen is fun loving and has a zest for life. I don't know if he even knows how to hold a gun," she said. "We had lived in Florida for two winters with him, and I always made it a point to stay in contact."

Thus, when Stephen was arrested for murder in 1990, they naturally thought the homicide had taken place sometime around May 1989 when Stephen was back in Florida for the first few months of that year and when he was first questioned by the police. The Rosatis never considered that it could refer to an earlier date.

Once they found out that that the murder had occurred three years earlier, in 1986, the Rosatis realized that Stephen had not been in Florida that year. It had not been easy to trace Stephen's whereabouts back to a specific week four years before, but without their documentation, it would have been impossible. They began to think back to what was to them one randomly chosen year out of their lives: 1986, and one random weekend from that year in October. So they went through some mental notes.

In May 1986, Carlyn was married. Stephen and Kara were in

the wedding party. That was how the thought process began. After a time, Carlyn remembered, she had gone to Italy with her husband to photograph Secretary of the Treasury Bill Simon's boat to create a brochure. Stephen had picked her up at the airport. The Rosatis checked the date: Saturday, October 11, 1986, just one day before the murder. But they needed documentation of the trip because without physical proof, Jack wouldn't use the incident.

While Carlyn and Bruce were in Europe, Esther was staying in Newport, taking care of Carlyn's dog, while Carl was staying in Scituate. Esther spoke to Stephen that Saturday to confirm the flight times and saw Carlyn and Bruce when they finally arrived home. Stephen had picked them up at T. F. Green Airport in Warwick, where he had filled up the tank and signed a gasoline credit card receipt, and then he had taken them to their parents' house to pick up their car.

The next morning was the christening, which Esther remembered because Stephen called her to say that he was upset with Kara because she did not want to go. That was October 12, the day of the murder. Esther said that Stephen decided to see his old girlfriend Elodie that day because he was mad at Kara.

On Columbus Day, Monday the thirteenth, Esther spoke to both Stephen and Kara on the phone, which she routinely did everyday, sometimes three times a day; so, if Stephen had taken a two-day plane trip, Esther would have definitely known about it. But she couldn't prove that she spoke to Stephen everyday. She just always did.

Kara, Stephen, and Esther had planned a trip to New York to see a cosmetics doctor on Wednesday, October 15, and Stephen had been to the Greenwood Credit Union to co-sign a loan the day before, on Tuesday, October 14. Since Stephen had signed a gasoline credit card receipt in Connecticut on October 15 and had signed another several days earlier on October 11 at the airport, the Rosatis now had signed dated documents that placed Stephen in Rhode Island and Connecticut on the following dates: October 10, when he signed his employees' payroll checks; October 11 at the airport to pick up his sister; October 14 at the credit union; and October 15, when he filled up the tank in Connecticut en route to New York. With all that documentation, Esther thought for sure the police would simply release Stephen as a case of mistaken identity.

CHAPTER 10:
Prayer Group

Esther said that once Stephen went to jail, she entered a different state of consciousness, "like people that have been in airplane crashes." She felt insulated, "closed off to the terror, no longer in a physical world." High on adrenaline, she never got tired. "It was almost like an out-of-body state. That is the only way that I could explain it, because where else did this tireless effort come from, this strength to fight and fight and fight?"

It was coming from what she was going to do to the people who had wronged her son.

"I truly was never afraid of them. This could have been naive on my part, because I was naive, innocent of a system that had become corrupt. However, I was operating from a position of direct knowing." They were accusing an innocent person. That is what Esther knew.

When Stephen was incarcerated in Rhode Island, she and Stephen would fast before they went to court. As warriors, they claimed that this would help in their spiritual awareness and make their senses keener. Sometimes she would go without food for three days and only drink water. Her weight dropped from 118 to 107. She had trouble swallowing food. She couldn't eat and lived mainly on water and juices, explaining that spiritual people such as Moses and Gandhi often fasted. Since her body was not being nourished, she believed that her mind operated on "a higher frequency." Having studied metaphysical techniques for a number of years before this event, Esther believed that these techniques helped in their struggle against sinister forces.

"I have always thought of God as a state of consciousness. Thus, if you could raise your own consciousness, you would be in touch."

As the trial neared, more and more articles started to appear in the *Providence Journal*. One didn't have to be a brain surgeon to see that the tenure of the articles damaged not only Stephen's reputation but also the reputations of the whole Rosati family as well. Carl noted that when you have adverse publicity, "even a retraction doesn't help. Every piece sounded terrible, like you are guilty before you are tried." Carl became deeply saddened and began to despair. Here is just a small sample of what the papers were printing:

Rhode Island Murder Suspect Denies
Being in State Where Crime Occurred

Witness Identifies Cranston Man

Carl Stephen Rosati, 30, has been in the Adult Correctional Institution since his arrest Sept. 12 by state police on a fugitive warrant. He was indicted, along with two other men; by a Florida grand jury in connection with the slaying of Joseph Viscido Jr. of Deerfield Beach on October 12, 1986. . . . Two witnesses identified Carl Stephen Rosati of Cranston as one of the gunmen from photographs presented to them. One of the Florida men, Peter Dallas, last month pleaded guilty to second-degree murder and is expected to testify against Rosati if he is brought to trial in Florida. . . . Viscido was found shot to death on the

floor of his apartment. Rosati has been
held without bail since his arrest.[1]

Similar articles appeared almost daily. The Rosatis had prided themselves, in Carl's words, "on living a decent and honest life in business and in every other way. To see this happening, I felt that this could possibly destroy our family. But I knew that I could not let this happen. Nothing else mattered other than to save Stephen's life and reputation and ours." If it meant using every one of his resources, Carl was prepared to do that.

Where some people they had thought of as friends began to distance themselves, the Rosatis found that others came out of nowhere to offer their services and help in any way that they could. "For those, we are forever grateful. For the others, I reserve my thoughts," Carl said.

Life as Carl and Esther had known it ended the day Stephen went to jail. They stayed at home or at the office working around the clock on the case, and because this was a time before cell phones, they had to make sure they would be home or in the office in case Stephen called. Esther had read about people who just died in prison. She had to be there for her son in every way.

One day Stephen called to tell his mother of a nightmare that he had.

"It was so real, I didn't feel I was in my cell anymore. I was behind a boiler perspiring, curled up in a corner. Everything was so hot; I thought I was on fire. I was hiding because Puccini and Coyote were going to get me."

"I knew he was in pain," Esther said, "so I called our priest, Father Turilli."

"Stephen is just a spoiled rich kid, so now he is doing his penance," the priest said, to Esther's dismay.

Father Turilli, in his mid-sixties and from the old school of thinking, equated having money with sin. However, Esther knew that Stephen would need inner strength to get him through this crisis, so she ignored the remark and made the mistake of asking the priest to go to the jail.

After seeing Stephen, the priest said, "Oh, I'm never going back there again. It got so late that I thought they were going to put me behind bars with Stephen, and I didn't know how I would get out."

As much as Esther wanted spiritual guidance to help them through what was going on around them, she also knew they wouldn't get it from their church. Although Carl was a trustee of the church, they would have to get what they needed elsewhere. So they did.

A deacon from the new church they found took a moment to pray with them and with Stephen over the phone. He also recommended a prayer group that met at the local VFW Hall. Carl and Esther joined this group at Pastor Lottie's house. There, they also met other disgruntled Catholics, and took part in prayers with them. They also invited these people back to their home in Scituate, and this became something they did regularly two nights a week for nearly a year.

With a ritual of singing and praying, the Rosatis embraced this group as family. They cared for each other, and whenever Esther was feeling anxious, she would just call one of the members. Many in the group were poor, most uneducated, and the Rosatis saw an entirely different world than they had ever known. There was never a discussion about innocence or guilt. Rather, it was a place to pray for someone who was ill, for someone who lost a job, or for Stephen.

"It gave me a great deal of comfort and a great deal of peace in a time of turmoil." Esther said. "It was the idea of tuning into God consciousness that I clung to." For Esther, it became her "lifesaver." The experience was now becoming a mission for Esther, "to show that when you have the truth, you have strength and you have power. That's why the negativity did not enter into it. I had to prove that right was right."

The entire prayer group would come to court. They were faithful, considerate, and supportive. It was heartrending for Carl and Esther to realize that when their own church did not know how to react in their time of need. There were other religious people out there that could help give them the spiritual support they would need to fight this shattering injustice.

CHAPTER 11:
Barbells

Stephen was arrested in September when the weather was still warm. He found himself looking out of his cell window at the courtyard below, where he would see other inmates working out with weights. It was natural for him to want to join in.

The equipment at the facility was minimal. There was a bench, two 40-pound dumbbells, and one long 150-pound barbell, all chained to a wall. Stephen thought to himself, *I'm gonna go nuts. I'm gonna drop dead—destroy myself with these weights.* Filled with rage, as a prisoner he was unable to speak out, yell, or even cry. The way to deal with the situation, he believed, was to take his workouts to the maximum, so he could work himself into exhaustion.

He figured out a way to loop the chains from each 40-pound dumbbell to the outside of the long barbell and keep them tight by fastening them with the rawhide laces from his shoes.

"A hundred and fifty pounds was not enough for me to do any

serious squatting, because I was used to working out with as much as 400 pounds. With that kind of weight behind my neck, I could do six squats or knee bends. This procedure would be called six repetitions, or six reps. With this lighter weight of 230 pounds, I would do twenty reps and repeat this procedure fifteen times, or to put it in proper lingo, fifteen sets of twenty reps, a totally insane workout."

The other guys from the other mods had never seen someone work the legs so much. They were used to bench presses, which, of course, Stephen also did. They saw the physique of a state bodybuilding champion and watched how he worked his arms by curling the 150-pound barbell for ten reps, or bench press 230 pounds for seven sets of ten reps.

"Some guys were as strong as me on the bench press, but nobody worked their legs the way I did," he said.

Stephen would stretch his hamstrings using his bunk and then go down to the courtyard. When he started working out, more and more guys would come down, so he began a training program, teaching his fellow prisoners how to squat properly, how to keep their backs straight and their chins up, and how to sit back correctly on their heels.

"Dip your ass and just break parallel. Keep your body in a rigid position. That's it," he would instruct them.

This became a serious ritual for the inmates, and it was what kept Rosati sane. He even got Suki and Mooki to lift weights, but Chanta, another Laotian friend of his, was the one he worked out best with.

"Chanta couldn't do as many squats as I could, but he tried to keep up, and both of us got really destroyed together. When it was his turn, I used to sit on the bench and look at the big tattoo of a tiger he had that ran across his chest. If we're talking tattoos, his was the best."

Most of the other guys had "jailhouse tattoos," insignias made from ashes from a cigarette and a pin. Crosses on the fingers or hearts on the back of their hands seemed to be the most common designs.

The first time Rosati met Jack Cicilline was fourteen long days after he was incarcerated. Jack, attired casually in shorts and sandals, started taking Stephen's statement as soon as he arrived. "There was no bullshit."

"How you doing? I'm Jack," Cicilline said in his distinctive low monotone. "Sit down and tell me anything you can about this case."

"I have nothing to do about this."

"Nothing?" the lawyer grilled.

"Not a thing. I heard you are the best, and I need you to fight for me."

Cicilline sat poker faced, silently reading. Rosati found himself staring at a large gold watch affixed prominently to Cicilline's wrist.

"Do you know Michelle Arrieta?" asked Cicilline.

"No."

"Vic Giordano?"

"No."

"Joe Viscido?"

"No."

"Peter Dallas?"

"No."

"You don't know this guy?"

"No, I don't know this guy. I don't know any of these people. I don't know why this is happening. It's just happening."

"None of them?"

"I know Pete the Greek."

"You don't know anybody else? Anybody?"

"No."

"Not even Dallas! Jesus, I've got to get a statement from Dallas," Jack exclaimed. "Anything . . . You know, no matter what, we are probably going to have to go to Florida."

Stephen put his head down and gasped, suddenly overwhelmed by a sick feeling. His biggest fear was that he would be sent to Florida. If they were unable to win the case in Rhode Island, he'd really be sunk. Coyote had made it abundantly clear that if Stephen got down there, he could spend the rest of his life in jail or get the electric chair.

Cicilline sized up his client. "You're in a serious situation, kid. We'll just have to fight this here. And then in Florida."

Cicilline held nothing back. He let Rosati know they had few options. At that moment, another inmate stuck his head in the door to say hello. Jack knew the kid's father. "Now, there's a guy who *is* guilty," he said in a lighter tone.

After Cicilline left, Rosati went into a depression. "Once he said that I was probably going to have to go to Florida, it just took the wind out of my sails. At least he didn't bullshit me. I stared at the window in my cell and wondered who this was, who I had entrusted my life to."

Stephen thought about his alternatives. "Suicide was a serious option, but I had a number of cards to play before that one. Up until two weeks earlier, I had thought I was indestructible; now I lost all confidence. It never occurred to me that something like this could happen. Now I saw anything can happen. I could be convicted."

Later in a phone conversation, Esther reassured Stephen without a hint of doubt in her voice that they had only begun to fight.

"Stephen, you are not going to Florida. We are going to fight this thing. We have documentation. I told Jack to pull out every stop. Fighting extradition is our only option."

"Mom, that's just you talking. I'm getting fucked."

"Stephen, can't you express yourself in a more dignified manner?"

"You're worried about my language? Okay, I'm getting railroaded. They're going to take me to Florida and give me the fucking electric chair."

"You are not going to Florida."

Stephen was pretty sure that Cicilline believed him right from the start because he had already met with Carl and Esther and had seen a carton of documents, which established concretely that Rosati could not have possibly been living in Florida during the time of the killing. Rosati even had phone records proving he was in Rhode Island on the day of the murder. From the Rosatis' point of view, the documentation they had was incontrovertible.

The proof for them was that Detective Coyote would have certainly snared Stephen on the first day if they didn't have documents. The central problem to the prosecution's case was the contention that Rosati was *living* in Florida. The Broward detective was not just trying to place Stephen in Florida for a single day. He was going to try to portray an entire lifestyle, which was supported by the witnesses he had amassed against Rosati.

"If I had been just a poor dumb schmuck drifting about," Stephen recalled, "I would have been a dead man. But I wasn't. I was a businessman, running East Coast Fitness Center, buying and selling houses, at that very time, living with Kara almost as husband and wife. The fighting of the extradition became our primary task. Simply stated, if I could prove that I was in Rhode Island at the time of the killing, then obviously I could not have killed Viscido in Florida, and thus they could not extradite me. It was as simple as that.

"Jack Cicilline was my kind of man because he didn't appear to be a systems type person. He wasn't a hand holder either, that's for sure, but that helped force me to stand on my own two feet. He didn't give a shit about kowtowing to the prosecution or the cops or anybody, because he knew what he was doing. Whenever he came onto the scene, he got total respect.

64

"A maverick, Jack just had that kind of professional swagger. A seasoned pro, he was totally serious. Nothing fazed him. I was in awe of his abilities. Although I only saw him two times that first month, my parents were working with him on almost a daily basis. Nobody worked as hard as Jack Cicilline. He fought for me in the best possible way. He bellowed for me, day after day, during the longest extradition the state of Rhode Island has ever seen.

"Not the sort to get intimidated by an attorney general's prosecutor, even by Jack just entering the courtroom, I felt we had the edge. When I walked into court, I knew I had a substantial force at my side, a guy who wouldn't bend to the unwritten bullshit rules. He believed that I was innocent, and he knew he had to fight for me. The prosecutor, Randy White, would go around and around, but Jack went at it like an arrow. He would hit the witnesses with just plain facts. I respect him more than anyone, trusted him completely, and owe him my life."

CHAPTER 12:
An End Run

Monday, October 10, 1990, was a holiday. That was the day Florida came to kidnap Stephen Rosati. He was in the yard working out with weights, like he did practically every day, when a policeman from Florida showed up with an authorization ostensibly giving him the right to take Rosati.

Affidavit in Aid of Extradition

Two witnesses have positively identified Carl Stephen Rosati as being one of the suspects who forced their way into Mr. Viscido's apartment on October 12, 1986 and forced him into the bedroom where shots were fired that resulted in the death of Mr. Viscido. . . .

> Another suspect . . . identified as
> Peter Dallas . . . gave a sworn statement
> in which he admitted his involvement in
> this homicide and identified Carl Stephen
> Rosati as the other person who was with
> him . . . [and] as the man who fired the
> shot that killed Joseph Viscido . . . The
> grand jury returned an indictment . . .
> [against] . . . Rosati [who] is now to the
> best of my knowledge a fugitive from the
> state of Florida.
>
> *Robert Coyote, Broward Sheriff's Office*[1]

"All the guys were with me. Richard Ball, one of the guards, approached. He showed me an affidavit written by Detective Coyote, 'sworn to and subscribed' before Florida circuit judge Stanton S. Kaplan." Rosati had been in jail exactly one month.

"Florida's here, Steve. They got a warrant. You have to go upstairs and pack your things," Ball said.

"What?" Rosati said, stunned. The extradition trial hadn't even begun. Ball used to tease Rosati about going to Florida, as they all knew he was fighting extradition. "Are you kidding?" Stephen said.

"No. You have to go. They say you waived your right to an extradition hearing."

"I didn't waive any rights." Stephen spoke to a deaf ear.

When he went up to the mod, he asked to use the phone. Guards weren't supposed to let prisoners use the phone at this particular time. Uncharacteristically, the guard replied, "I usually say no, but since you're facing the electric chair, go ahead."

Stephen called his parents. There was no answer, and Stephen assumed they were not home. In actuality, Carl and Esther were in their basement searching through files and working on the case. They simply never heard the phone ring.

In a panic, Stephen dialed his sister. The time between rings seemed to be an eternity. "Carlyn, you gotta call Jack; Florida's here. Hurry up. I don't have much time—ten, maybe fifteen minutes. Maybe less."

Stalling as much as he could, Stephen took extra time packing his gear. "I pictured myself on a chain gang out in the swamps. I didn't know anybody in Florida. All I could envision was a shank in my back, or being strapped to the electric chair. Aside from everything else, I was innocent, and this increased the terror tenfold, as I could see how helpless I had become, how utterly unable I was to influence my own fate."

Carlyn called Jack at his home. By sheer luck, he was there. He said he would try to call a judge. At the same time, he called the ACI.

"The kid's not supposed to be sent," he barked. "Rosati didn't waive any rights. Give me some time; I have to call a judge. This is illegal, boys."

The guards remained unconvinced as they stared at the official-looking warrant, but that did stall them.

"I was led out to an ominous-looking car with all the windows blackened. I dragged my heels," Stephen said. "The driver was big and mean looking. He just stood by the car with his legs apart, his hands behind his back, waiting.

"My mind was racing, my heart was pounding. All I could think of was Coyote's earlier words: 'You may do fine at the ACI in Rhode Island, but a white boy like you in a Florida prison won't stand a chance.'

"These Florida assholes were robbing me of my rights, and the idiot ACI guards just stood there letting it happen." As if in slow motion, Stephen felt like a drowning man in some surrealistic dream, and those that could save him just looked down blankly and stared.

"Steve, you are going to have to be cuffed to the back seat of his car, so he can drive you down," one of the ACI guards said, jolting him.

Rosati's heart was now pounding as if it would burst through his chest. "Where am I going to sleep?" he said, doing his best to contain a sickening feeling of panic that threatened to overwhelm him.

"Come on, let's get a move on," the Florida man motioned impatiently.

"They got plenty of prisons along the way you can spend the night at," one of the guards cajoled. He started to smile, but he knew Rosati did not think it was funny. The Florida man glared with the kind of tight-lipped sneer that made Rosati think that he might never even make it to Florida.

"They wanted a body to close their case, and obviously they didn't care how they got one. This was kidnapping pure and simple, coming on a holiday with phony papers saying I had given up my rights. They didn't care about rights, about playing by the rules. I was against a ruthless bunch."

The driver turned his wrist over to check his watch. His right foot began to tap. Rosati had the urge to bolt. "Let's go," the ACI man said.

Stephen walked toward the car and thought again how ridiculous this was—how he had gotten into this mess. "Scared shitless, I seemed to see my whole life flash before me."

Stephen sat back and tried to think about anything but prison. He wanted to think about those times when he felt good, like the summer in Scarborough Beach when he first got his license—the summer he was young and *free*.

CHAPTER 13:
Mr. Rhode Island

Nearly a mile long, with flagstone pavilions, white sand and surf, and girls in bikinis, Scarborough Beach had always been *the* place to strut your stuff in the summer if you were a healthy guy, had a car, and lived in Rhode Island. During his sophomore and junior years in high school, Rosati used to hang around with the guys and his girlfriend on the boardwalk. But because he had been kicked off the wrestling team he decided to take time off.

Having come from a successful family, the arrogant and headstrong youth felt he didn't need school to learn how to go into his father's business, which was mainly selling insurance and building homes.

"I knew how to read and write; I had some math skills. That was all I would need, and I knew it."

His parents helped him through this difficult period by first setting him up working in the jewelry business with his maternal grandfather, but then Esther got Stephen back in school by enrolling him in the

Alternative Learning Program.

No longer a wrestler, Rosati did not have to keep his weight down, so he began to eat, lift weights, and build himself up. Bodybuilding became his next goal.

Before he graduated high school, Stephen began his apprenticeship with his father. Carl was busy developing 110 lots in a subdivision of West Warwick known as Juniper Hills. Stephen asked his father how he sold the lots and what his profit margin was, and Carl saw Stephen's curiosity as an opportunity to introduce his son to his world. They were very successful, and Carl's young son was supremely confident.

In 1978, Rosati graduated and received a Jeep as a present, but he soon traded it in for a Corvette. He also went to the Bahamas to enter the Mr. Teenage Bahamas contest, traveling with fellow weight lifter Mark Wilson.

One of the directors, Darwin Baldwin—a handsome black man who spoke with a proper British accent—was a former Mr. Bahamas, and he greeted Rosati when he arrived. He offered to teach Stephen posing routines and weight-lifting techniques.

"He was one of the nicest human beings I have ever known," Stephen recalled.

With Mr. Baldwin's guidance, Stephen beat out thirty other boys to win the competition. Some of the judges felt that Rosati was too advanced for the competition. Others complained that since he wasn't really a citizen of the Bahamas, he had no right to compete. But Mr. Baldwin and the balance of the judges stood on Stephen's side, and the youngster returned to Rhode Island with the Mr. Teenage Bahamas trophy.

Rather than continue in college, Stephen discussed with his father the idea of opening up a gym by the airport, which he wanted to call East Coast Fitness Center. An old homeroom teacher from Bishop Hendricken, Denny O'Donnell, a lawyer and state representative, had become more like a friend than a teacher and was instrumental in getting the gym started. The year was 1979.

Just as this project was getting underway, Denny invited Stephen to Florida to stay on Mayor Doorley's cousin's yacht in Fort Lauderdale. Doorley had been the sonorous mayor of Providence before an even more flamboyant politician deposed him. The inimitable Buddy Cianci, a Napoleonic overlord, would come to rule Rhode Island's capitol and oversee its remarkable renaissance for the next three decades. Still, it was a trip for the young man just to sit out on the boat that the old mayor used to frequent. Stephen had been to Florida as a child with his parents, but this was the first time he was there on his own.

Chicks were easy to come by when you were living on a yacht for two weeks, and it seemed like they had a different girl every other day. At night they would go to discos to meet girls. Stephen recalled one girl whose license plate read Z-Rated.

"We'd invite them out to the boat the next day. All I can say is that two-week period was one weird and fantastic time. It gave me a taste of the high life in Florida, and thereby served to entice me into a world that eventually came to cause me great anguish and pain," Stephen recalled.

On their return home, Denny called with terrific news. He had found a space at the Airport Plaza that had been a Swedish massage parlor and thought it would be a good place for the fitness center. The space had usable whirlpools and saunas, but it also had a lot of little cubicles, which could be torn out. Carl put up $40,000, they hired a builder, and East Coast Fitness Center was born.

Calculating they would need between 500 and 600 active members to keep the gym running, the Rosatis designed an advertising campaign and also sought different ways to attract interest. One way to help was to get Stephen's girlfriend, Mary Ann Delorea, to run the front desk. Mary Ann, a beautiful French girl, had light brown hair, stood five-foot seven, and was Stephen's first real live-in lover. They had dated since high school and had moved into an apartment together that the Rosatis had in Warwick.

No doubt, Stephen's biggest break came because of a car show that was running at the Providence Civic Center. The show was featuring the Incredible Hulk (Lou Ferrigno). Meeting Ferrigno was a rush, and Stephen asked him if he wanted to train at East Coast while he was in town. Ferrigno agreed. They took videos and also got local TV coverage.

Shortly after that Stephen met Tony Pierson, a well-known black professional bodybuilder and Mr. Universe champion. Stephen paid him $150 a week just to come down to the gym to train on a regular basis.

"Here I was twenty years old, living with my girlfriend, paying her $225 a week to run the club, driving my new Corvette, working out every day, running seminars with Tony, and basically becoming the hub of the bodybuilding scene for our state. It was excellent. Everyone came to see Tony Pierson train. We had customers driving in from New York and Boston. We did a quarter of a million that year."

One of the reasons it worked out so well was that it was a perfect fit for Mary Ann. She loved to read and was preparing for college, so when business was slow, she could study, and that was fine with Stephen. Occasionally, they would get away to Boston or Manhattan, and in the summer they zipped over to Scarborough or down to Misquamicut Beach.

"This period was like one long party," Stephen recalled.

By 1982, it became apparent that Rosati would have to renovate East Coast Fitness Center. Carl calculated that it would run between $25,000 and $30,000. On top of that, the gym was getting hurt because a gaggle of other clubs began springing up. To cut expenses, Stephen closed out his deal with Tony and sought to increase capital by taking in two new partners: Lance Arno, who had been working for the gym as a salesman, and Gary Woodrow, a former troubleshooter for American Health, who had a reputation for rejuvenating ailing fitness clubs. For $10,000 apiece, they each got a third of the business, and in that way, Stephen received most of the resources that were required for renovations. One of Stephen's ideas was to make the women's room more attractive, but ultimately the entire club got a facelift. Gary was in charge of promotion, Lance took care of the books and filled in wherever else he was needed, and Stephen continued to recruit new members.

In June 1982, Stephen also entered a number of competitions. In the Mr. Rhode Island competition, he won Most Muscular and came in second overall. These wins naturally added to the prestige of the club. The downside was that with his added bulk, Stephen had become too big for his Corvette, so he traded it in for a big Eldorado. Things were working well, and by 1983, they did $375,000 worth of business.

"The best times," Stephen recalled, "were at night during the Christmas season. East Coast would order a full buffet for the members, lady dancers would be hired, and the more friendly ones would join various members in the whirlpool. People loved it, and a lot of the guys still talk about those times, even to this day, over a decade later.

"Yet, instead of this success encouraging my partners to improve the business even more, it caused them to get complacent. Gary was basically just sitting on his ass, and Lance, with a new girlfriend, began copping an attitude. It started to become clear that the two of them

73

were attempting to maneuver me out of my own business. We began to argue, and I became more introverted when they were around. To get away from it all, I cut down personal training of the members, as I wasn't really getting paid extra for this, and at the same time began increasing my own personal workouts."

In 1983, Stephen won the Tall Class Mr. New England division, won the state championship, and became Mr. Rhode Island. Held under the auspices of the National Physique Committee (NPC), these amateur competitions were judged by nationally known professional bodybuilders. Mike Katz, who had a part in *Pumping Iron*, was there, along with Steve Mahalic, Tony Pierson, and Danny Padilla.

"These guys were the top of the line, and with my connection to them, we were continuing to attract serious bodybuilders. My partners were complaining that I was spending too much time in workouts and not enough time in teaching or gaining new clients, but my wins at these contests were helping promote the club in a more substantial way."

From 1982 through 1984, Stephen was the best in the region, and his club was the "in" place to be. Rosati would still personally train the youngsters who joined and put them on a nutritional program. That was all for one membership fee of $350 per year. But to maintain his personal edge, like every other hard-core weight lifter, he had to tamper with nature.

"Don't let anybody tell you different. Arnold Schwarzenegger didn't just pump iron. That's why, underneath it all, I knew I was never going professional. It would take some serious drugs to get me anywhere near the place I would have to be, and there was no way I was going to do that!," Rosati said.

"One pain-in-the-ass problem in running a place like this was that, like anybody else, the guys in the gym were slobs. Half the time they'd leave their weights all over the place, and you'd have to tell them to pick them up. Lance or Gary couldn't do it, so I had to. Occasionally, that meant getting physical, but in all the time I had the club, I never kicked a single person out, no matter how ornery he was."

Usually at the end of the day, Rosati would grab the microphone and blast them. "Okay, all you skinny wimps, we're closing in ten minutes. I want all of you to put your weights away, now. If you don't do it, I'm not going to take your membership away, and I'm not going to throw you out. I'm just gonna fry your nuts."

That's what Rosati was thinking about as he put his hands out to be cuffed. He braced himself to be taken—against his will—into the nightmare that took the form of a Florida cop, who wore dark glasses and carried a key chain that he swung like a billy club. Stephen and the cop with the holstered gun stood next to the unmarked police car that would drive him 1,500 miles south and deliver him into Detective Coyote's clutches.

Fortunately, Cicilline was able to reach Judge Capanella, who was actually out on the golf course, but the judge was able to get to a phone, call the prison, and overrule the illegal order.

"Another thirty seconds and Coyote would have had me," Rosati recalled. "I stared at the driver and yelled, 'Good!' turned around, and walked back to the mod."

CHAPTER 14:
Jack and John

When working on this chapter of Stephen's life, one of the questions I had concerned the legality of the tactics the Broward Sheriff's Office used to try to take Stephen from the ACI before the extradition hearing really got under way. I sat down with Jack Cicilline and questioned him about the issue of bounty hunters coming into a state to usurp a local court ruling. "Ultimately, would this be legal?" I asked.

Jack replied, "The law is fairly clear in this area. Had the kidnapping been successful, once in Florida, regardless of how Stephen got there, jurisdiction would attach."

"Could the state of Rhode Island make a case against these kidnappers?" I asked.

"Sure," Cicilline replied bluntly, "but I wouldn't want to be in the desert waiting."[1]

Esther told me later that Cicilline had gone to see Stephen at the

ACI for the sole purpose of finding out if Stephen was telling the truth. Once Cicilline believed in Stephen's innocence, he agreed that it was best to fight the battle in Rhode Island by blocking extradition to a faraway state where Rosati could face the executioner.

"Jack, how many people have you defended in all your years who have been completely innocent in this kind of a way?" Esther asked.

"One," Cicilline confessed. "Me, when I was indicted by U.S. attorney Lincoln Almond for misconduct when the FBI wired an informant who came to my office and said I asked him to lie for a client. And, believe me, it cost me a lot of business."*

Six years earlier, in 1984, the *Providence Journal* ran the headline: "Perjury Trial of Cicilline."

The article alleged that "Lawyer John [Jack] F. Cicilline plotted with mobster Frank L. 'BoBo' Marrapese, Jr., and another man to have a witness lie 'to corruptly win an unjust verdict' in a stolen-goods trial last year, a prosecutor told a federal court jury yesterday." The article ended with a cliff hanger, as Marrapese, "who is also charged . . . says that he plans to take the stand and exonerate Cicilline."[2]

Two days later, the *Providence Journal* reported that the informant recanted his testimony and an FBI tape recording "establishes the innocence, not the guilt of Mr. Cicilline."[3]

Even though the vote was 11–1 in Cicilline's favor, the jury was hung; the case had to be tried again.[4] With his image tainted in the eyes of the public, his career and essentially his life were now on hold. Cicilline waited sixteen long months for the retrial. Here he was, in his mid-forties, at the height of an amazing career, but now everything was on the line.

Rather than defend himself, Cicilline hired the tough litigator John F. Sheehan. A man nearly fifteen years his senior, Sheehan was fresh off his victory—with a little help from Alan Dershowitz—defending Claus von Bülow in the attempted murder of his wife, Sunny. (She died decades later in December 2008 after spending twenty-eight years in a coma.) Accused of trying to kill his wife by injecting her with insulin, von Bülow had asked Senator Claiborne Pell for advice in choosing a lawyer. Pell recommended John Sheehan. Later, the trial was reenacted on film in the prominent movie *Reversal of Fortune*, which starred Jeremy Irons in his Academy Award–winning performance as von Bülow.

---

*   Lincoln Almond would go on to become governor of Rhode Island from 1994 to 2002.

John Sheehan, born in 1924, joined the army paratroopers during World War II and lost his left pinky finger during a jump. Having attended Brown University, Sheehan left school in 1949 three courses shy of graduation because of poor grades and later obtained a law degree from Boston University. Sheehan then advanced to the Bar. By 1959, the chronic three-pack-a-day smoker of classic unfiltered Chesterfields found himself well connected. Law partners included Clifford Cawley, who became a judge, and Dennis Roberts II, who became attorney general.

A traditional Irishman of modest height, with a rotund body and thinning gray hair, Sheehan was known for his tweed jackets, acerbic wit, passion for golf, family, and pet dogs. At the time he was defending Jack Cicilline, Sheehan had recently lost a bid to become a superior court judge. "Trial work," he told the *Providence Journal* "is for the young man. Each case takes a little out of you. When you're waiting for that jury to come back [with a verdict] a little bit of you dies."[5]

But trial work was John's forté. As reported in the *Brown University Alumni Magazine* in 2003, "What most people don't know is that John Sheehan, the man wearing reading glasses who sits next to von Bülow in court everyday, was the main architect of the von Bülow defense team."

Jack had known John for many years. Both lawyers had represented accused crime bosses, and both had a droll sense of humor. When just out of law school, Jack prepared briefs for John. Later, they also worked together as co-counsel in two separate high-profile murder cases. Quick-witted, with a lugubrious side, John Sheehan was a good listener. Shortly before he actually became a judge, John took over the serious responsibility of Jack's appeal.

The *Providence Journal* described the scene in the courtroom that day.

"The courtroom was packed with Cicilline's family, friends, and fellow lawyers when the verdict was handed down. Jack's wife, Sabra, five children and two brothers and sister linked hands and many of them began to sob even before the results were known."

As the ruling came in, even the hard-edged Cicilline had to blink back tears. The *Providence Journal* reported the decision in a bold headline: "Jury Clears Cicilline."[6] For the first time in two-and-a-half years, Jack Cicilline did not have an indictment hanging over his head. John Sheehan had come to Jack's rescue.

Jack had learned a hard lesson, and that made him identify with Stephen's plight. He was going to do whatever he could to block Stephen's extradition. Jack met with the Rosatis and began coordinating my testimony—as the case's handwriting expert. Jack also strategized with his detective, Fran Martin, and he coordinated the compilation of the many witnesses that had seen Stephen in Rhode Island at the time of the murder in Florida.

CHAPTER 15:
The Trial

Opening Day: December 10, 1990

The Kent County Courthouse was just minutes from the Rosatis' place of business, although in Rhode Island practically every place is just minutes from every other place. Unlike the regal municipal buildings that anchor Providence and many of the other towns, the Kent County Courthouse appears like a corrugated metal afterthought. There doesn't appear to be a main entrance. One enters a nondescript side door from the end of a lower parking lot that looks like a back entrance for deliveries. There, in this narrow corridor, a policeman and a metal detector greet visitors who can then take the elevator or use the steel staircase to reach the second level, where the courtrooms are situated.

Before the trial started, Randy White, the state representative, came over to the Rosatis and introduced himself as the prosecutor.

"I just want you to know that when I get up there, I'm doing my job. It has nothing to do with feelings, but with my job," he told them.

"We understand that," Carl said.

"We just want you to be fair," Esther added.

"I'll do my best," White replied.

The Rosatis had heard that White had told the Florida prosecutor, Chuck Morton, that in the beginning White thought Stephen was innocent, but as the hearing progressed, he thought he was guilty.

"Once the proceedings began," Esther recalled, "I saw Randy White as an individual who put his head down like a bull charging blindly forward. Once he started, he never looked up."

As the local handwriting expert, I was the first witness. It had been three months since I first worked the case, but I was well prepared. I had all the visuals in a carrying case when I met with Jack Cicilline in a separate chamber. Also present was his private investigator, an aging, rail-thin former Rhode Island cop named Francis Martin.

I looked over at the imposing, barrel-chested professional and had every expectation that we would spend some time reviewing strategy.

"Let's see what you got." Cicilline glanced down at the visuals and nodded. Then he took a deep drag on his cigarette, drawing the smoke into his lungs with such intensity that it looked as if he could consume it in one breath. Crushing out the stub in the ashtray, he made it known with few words that he simply assumed that the document examiner was prepared. Then he turned and walked away.

Martin had been initially skeptical about this case. However, once he began his investigation, he changed his mind. A former policeman with twenty-two years experience, Martin had seen his share of the worst humanity had to offer. He knew a criminal when he saw one, and he knew that the vast majority of people who were arrested were linked to the crimes they were accused of. But this case was in a category all its own, and it sickened him. The Florida detective, in his eyes, was putting a black mark on a noble profession.

Because of Martin's passion for the case, it was Cicilline's plan to have him talk plainly to the judge and the opposition. If they could all talk *mano a mano* without the constraints of legal proceedings and make it clear that they had the wrong person, perhaps the prosecution could cut its losses before going into a long protracted hearing. In either case, Cicilline hoped to make a strong impression on the judge.

Cicilline went off to the judge's chambers along with his frequent opponent, Randy White, the assistant attorney general. At age forty-two, White was ten years Cicilline's junior and had attended the same law school as Cicilline. Tall and trim, White had the air of a thoroughbred, and his premature gray hair flowed to his shoulders. He was one of those few individuals with hair of that length who could pass for a business professional. White was the brother of local celebrity Doug White, a television news anchor on NBC TV. Dressed in his newly pressed pinstriped suit, White stood in marked contrast to the stocky, no-nonsense, gravel-voiced criminal attorney from Federal Hill.

According to Cicilline, Randy White ran the show from the attorney general's office in Kent County. He and Jack had been up against each other many times, but one case had particularly irked the prosecutor. White had won a murder conviction, in part because he was able to establish the angle at which a bullet had shattered the glass when it hit a car window. This tenuous thread was overturned on appeal, and Cicilline came out the victor. "White was very bitter about the loss," Cicilline recalled. Now he had a chance to even the score. [1]

Where Cicilline was accompanied by one frail aging private investigator, White was accompanied by his Florida counterpart, Jeffrey Driscoll—assistant state attorney general for Broward County—a thin, virtually invisible fellow with a short haircut, and Driscoll's associate, the wrangly undercover detective Sheriff Robert R. Coyote, who had replaced Detective Sergeant Chevy McNeil as head of the Viscido homicide case. Like Rosati, Coyote was muscular. Dressed in a gray suit one size too tight, with tattoos bleeding under his cuffs and long dirty blonde hair swept back like a biker, the sheriff exuded a kinetic energy that seemed ready to leap out of his clothing.

The case had been originally assigned to the venerable Judge Americo Campanella, who knew and socialized with the Rosatis, so the case was transferred to a newly appointed judge, the Honorable John F. Sheehan, Cicilline's former co-counsel in 1976 and litigator for Cicilline in 1984 in the FBI wiretap scam. A lawyer for thirty-one years, the balding, sixty-six-year-old judge notified White of his former connection with Cicilline. Sheehan was well respected in the small state of Rhode Island. His law partner was a former attorney general, a friend of Senator Claiborne Pell, and he had earned his judgeship. A quarter century older than Randy White, the assistant attorney general reluctantly agreed that there would be no conflict of interest. Sheriff Coyote wasn't so sure, and the judge sensed this.

"Obviously, you have made a mistake here," Cicilline began with characteristic bluntness. "You've got the wrong man, so let's just drop this case, and let Mr. Rosati go."

Implying that he didn't care if Rosati was innocent or guilty, Detective Coyote said, "I want him."

"Look," Martin fired back testily, "you people have *not* prepared this case well. We have a tremendous amount of evidence to prove that this Rosati kid was living in the state of Rhode Island at that time. I think you guys should go back and reinvestigate."

"We've got seven eyewitnesses," Coyote shot back.

"My eye!" Martin retorted incredulously.

As tempers flared, Sheehan stepped in. "My God, Fran," the judge said, "you've certainly changed your stripes."

"I've good reason, Your Honor. This man is innocent. And we've got tons of proof." According to Martin, the judge believed him, but he was strapped by the warrant. He knew that no matter what the feelings, he would have to proceed with the hearing.[2]

Concerned over the outcome, Cicilline left the chambers, returned to Stephen's parents, and explained what had happened.

"Esther, I think we're going to have to go to Florida."

"Jack, we are *not* going to Florida. We are going to *fight* this."

CHAPTER 16:
Discovery

Only a few days into the extradition hearing, Sheehan announced a three-week break for the Christmas holiday. The Rosatis went home and did nothing for an afternoon, which was enough of a break for Esther. She did not want to waste three weeks being idle, so they talked it over with Jack.

"I know my side of the case backwards and forwards," Jack told Carl, "but I only have bare bones information on the prosecution's case. If you can find something out about their case, we'd be in a much stronger position."

Carl made a call to Tony Natale, an attorney in Florida and a friend of the family. He had assisted Stephen in 1985, when he had gotten into a brawl with an ex-cop who shot his car, and Natale knew Pete the Greek's lawyer, John Howes, a criminal attorney from Fort Lauderdale. He found out that Howes probably had access to vital information, so Natale called back to say that he would like to take the case and asked for a fee of $35,000, with an advance of $10,000. Carl offered him five, and told him to look for anything he could find: files, papers, anything at all.

Natale said that he might be able to get the discovery from Howes because Pete the Greek, like Stephen, had been accused of also being involved in the Viscido murder. Carl was just learning aspects of the law and admitted that he didn't know what 'discovery' was. They quickly found out that it was the *actual police records* of their investigation. Howes, as a Florida lawyer defending a man in Florida, was legally entitled to it, but the Rosatis were not sure of their legal rights, since they were in Rhode Island and this was an extradition hearing, not a trial. Thus, this whole affair was handled in a clandestine manner. Because of Carl's health, the Rosatis decided it would be best for Red Gooseberger to go.

"Red, when you get to Florida, I want you to go through these records, find anything you can about the Greek—who his attorney is, anything at all—because Jack is looking for statements on any of the witnesses. How much money do you need?" Carl asked.

It was known that Gooseberger had a few thousand dollars in his pocket at all times, so he told them not to worry about the money and that he would bill them for the expenses when he returned. So the Rosatis paid for the air fare, the hotel, and incidentals, which totaled about $1,100.

While Gooseberger was in transit, Natale called. "I've got the discovery! The whole nine yards. I'm not sure if you are entitled to it, but I am going to give it to Gooseberger when he gets here."

Pete the Greek's lawyer did not want the sheriff or the prosecutor to know that he had given the discovery to Natale.

"Everything played out like a scene from a spy story," Carl said. "Tony met Red out on a deserted patch of highway and dropped the package in Red's car practically without stopping. Copies of the entire transcripts were made. It ran 1,500 pages. One was shipped through the mail, and the other was hand-carried back by Red on the plane."

"Coming back with the discovery reiterated Red's position as hero," Esther recalled, as he had also located the phone records on an earlier occasion. "This laid the foundation for the Goose to become more deeply enmeshed with us."

Once they read the discovery, the Rosatis realized how faulty the police investigation had been. Gooseberger sought to publicize the inconsistencies of the police investigation through the media, and the Rosatis also contacted the FBI. The Rosatis took the position that Stephen's civil rights had been violated.

On December 24, Christmas Eve, the Rosatis drove directly to Cicilline's office and placed the package on his desk. Cicilline was getting ready for his yearly winter sojourn to his condo in Naples, Florida, and he was leaving the following day.

"How the hell did you get this?" Jack asked incredulously.

"Just forget it, and take it with you," Carl responded with a sly smile.

"Should we go to the FBI with this?" Esther asked. "It's obvious that Stephen's rights have been violated."

"You can go to the FBI, but nothing will happen."

Of course, he was right.

According to Carl, "Jack was absolutely amazed by the contents," for in it was the daily report, starting with the very first day of the entire police investigation, including verbatim transcripts of all the major witnesses: Michelle Arrieta, Vic Giordano, Peter Dallas, Chris Jones—everything. Before this, Cicilline had only known Stephen's case, but now he had Florida's, and thus he even had more information than had been available to the Rhode Island prosecutor. Because of this trip, the time he needed to prepare the case, and the upcoming Christmas holiday, part of the trial would be delayed several months.

As soon as Cicilline arrived in Florida, he hurt his back and was immobile for two weeks. "Your mother put the *Malocchio* (curse) on me," Jack teased Stephen on the phone. "Esther did this so I would have to read the case."

"And read it he did," Carl reminisced.

When he finished, Esther said, "Okay, now I release you."

The Rosatis and Red Gooseberger made extra copies of the case, studied it on their own, and then created a unified typed statement to give to Jack. "He had done his homework, however," Carl said, as Cicilline referred mostly to his own notes. "That's how thorough he was. Fifteen hundred pages is a lot of work to go through. After reading their discovery, we became very confident."[1]

CHAPTER 17:
Columbus Day Weekend: 1986

Just ten months before the explosion of the Space Shuttle Challenger, in which seven astronauts died, and just one month *before* the Iran-Contra arms-for-hostages scandal rocked Ronald Reagan's otherwise acclaimed presidency, 1986 had been a time of relative world peace. Nelson Mandela was still in prison in South Africa after having already spent a quarter century there. People were traveling to everyday places, such as the West Bank in Israel, where Bethlehem, Hebron, and Jericho are, to Baghdad in Iraq, and to the fully intact and peaceful country of Yugoslavia.

In sports, for about a decade, Carl Lewis was the star of track and field and considered the fastest man alive; Greg Louganis was the *crème de la crème* of Olympic diving champions; the Aussies, in the biggest upset story in sailing history, still owned the America's Cup; the Russian Gary Kasparov was beginning his long reign as the greatest chess player since Bobby Fischer, unaware that, a decade later, a computer named Deep Blue would embarrass and beat him; Mike Tyson was king in boxing; and Michael Jordon of the Chicago Bulls won his first of seven-in-a-row seasons as scoring champ in basketball—although the Boston Celtics were still, by far, the team to beat.

VCRs became the hottest craze, and video stores began sprouting up like new tulips in the spring, while mobile phones still stayed rooted in cars, a fad of the rich and tech-savvy. It had been just two years since the advent of the Macintosh home computer, with its confounding pull-down menus and peculiar handheld pointer called the mouse, and just two years since the advent of the CD, a new optical recording disk invented to replace the vinyl record. A little more than a decade after the landing on the moon and the introduction of Visa and MasterCard, the 1980s began with the assassination of Beatle John Lennon, the attempted assassination of President Reagan, and the introduction of a strange new bug called AIDS, a sexually transmitted retrovirusthat slithered its way into a person's immune system, where it could hide, replicate, and devastate. Email, already seven years old, was still restricted to universities, the corporate elite, the Department of Defense, and Al Gore.

This was a time before pump-your-own-gas stations, fifty-six-inch LCD TV screens, tongue piercing, Twittering, smart phones, fantasy football, YouTube, Lady Gaga, Tiger Woods, Barack Obama, and a ubiquitous Internet. The top movies of the day were *Out of Africa, Sophie's Choice, An Officer and a Gentleman, Tootsie,* and the best picture that year, Oliver Stone's *Platoon.* The most popular people in the entertainment world included sixty-year-old actor Paul Newman, who finally won an Academy Award for his updated role as an aging Fast Eddie in *The Color of Money;* two singers: Michael Jackson—a handsome black man—and his raunchy white female counterpart, Madonna; and a hulking, overweight football player with a missing front tooth nicknamed Refrigerator Perry, a defensive lineman who also occasionally ran short yardage for touchdowns and ran his heart out in the Super Bowl that year when his team, the Chicago Bears, trounced the New England Patriots.

This was the era of Reaganomics, a new time for fiscal growth for the country, as it began its subtle preparation for the next century. A pivotal time for women, the 1980s heralded a number of female heads of state, including Corazon Aquino, president of the Philippines; Margaret Thatcher, the prime minister of England; and Geraldine

Ferraro, who ran unsuccessfully for the U.S. vice presidency in 1984 with running mate Walter Mondale.

Land prices were on the rise. The average cost of a house in New England was approximately $85,000, and a good salary was about half that much. But houses, wages, and the cost of living were generally cheaper in the South. People of all ages flocked to Florida for as many reasons: the elderly to retire, couples wanting to start new families, entrepreneurs looking for business opportunities, and the young and carefree, who looked to party along one of the longest stretches of white sandy beaches on the planet. From Palm Beach to Boca Raton, Lighthouse Point to South Beach, the southeast coast of Florida was (and still is) one of the most sought-after places to be in the United States. Running parallel to these beaches, down to Miami, is a long deep-water intercostal channel where the cruise lines dock their mammoth ships and the well-to-do display their mansions and perch on their yachts. Yes, vacationers and the everyday Floridians generally see this opulence and easy style of the beach crowd, but Florida also has a darker side: a cesspool of down-and-outers, dirt bags, smugglers, and drug dealers. It was there, amid this dark side in Deerfield Beach, where the seeds of this strange case began.

CHAPTER 18:
Police Log

"To believe [this story] you will
have to believe that the Broward Sheriff's
Office detectives . . . are the lowest of
the low that the police can be."

Defense Attorney Hilliard Moldolf
The Sun-Sentinel, June 8, 1993, p. 3B[1]

October 12, 1986. Detective Sergeant Chevy McNeil was one of
only two detective sergeants working for the Deerfield Beach Police
Department when the police received a frantic call from a man who
said that his friend had been murdered. A criminal justice major from
Northeastern University, McNeil, just five foot eight, was a ten-year
veteran who had worked eight major murder cases. Preferring to work

three cases per year, this one, which came in at 11:30 Sunday night on Columbus Day weekend, would occupy his attention for a lot more time than that. Eighteen years later, he would make national news for what he did and did not do in working this case.

In apartment No. 10 at 1100 Southeast Avenue, just north of Miami Beach near the posh Intracoastal Waterway, the scene of the homicide was one of those dime-a-dozen condos. When McNeil entered, at 11:49, the victim, Joseph Viscido, Jr., was lying face down at the entrance to his bedroom, blood still oozing from a fatal wound to his head. The room was a mess, his blood splattered all over the walls. In the corner on a desk was a half-empty box of hot chocolate mix, a razor blade, and drug paraphernalia, including rolling papers. The door was ripped off its hinges, furniture was knocked about, and the impression of a torso was embedded into the Sheetrock® on the west wall. All this indicated a fight had taken place, resulting in the death of Viscido.

Stuck in the side of the mirror on the bureau was a slightly blurred color photograph of a young man on the beach standing by his surfboard with a slim, pretty girl in a two-piece nuzzling against him. Detective McNeil was drawn to the girl's eyes. They expressed a youthful shyness yet, at the same time, a defiant boldness. At the bottom of the picture was scrawled "Me & Michelle" in a primitive handwriting.

McNeil leaned over the body and noticed a hole above the ear in the back of the head where the bullet had entered, and a grimace that almost resembled a smile on the face of the dead young man.

"Watch it," he told Detective Hodges, one of the junior officers on the scene. McNeil pointed to three bloodstained footprints that exited the room.

"Looks like the owner of them left in a helluva hurry," Hodges said.

"I wonder why," the senior officer deadpanned.

By 12:45 a.m. three more officers from Deerfield had arrived. Each split off to do their respective assignments. Randy Goldberg of Broward County Sheriff's Crime Unit processed the event for forensics and took photographs. The medical examiner, Dr. Ronald Wright, inspected the body. Other detectives searched the rooms and the area around the apartment. More drug paraphernalia was discovered in the bedroom, along with small amounts of cocaine and marijuana and a sizable amount of cash. Four magazines for an automatic 9mm weapon containing eighty-seven rounds of live ammunition were also discovered.

Reluctantly, Viscido's girlfriend, Michelle Arrieta, reentered the crime scene. Barely five foot one, Arrieta was barefoot and dressed in safari shorts and a loosely fitting nightshirt. Her cheeks were still tearstained from the ordeal. Brushing hair from her face, she looked for a chair and unconsciously twisted around her finger what the sergeant later found was her engagement ring. In shock, she moved her eyes vacantly from the detective's bright gold badge to the pair of handcuffsthat he kept secured behind his back.

McNeil was finishing up an interview with a neighbor who had just told him that he heard pounding on Joe's door. McNeil pointed to Michelle and asked her to wait as he took the man into the hall.

"Yeah, then what?" McNeil asked the neighbor.

"Then I heard a loud male voice bellowing, 'BSO. Let us in!' then a rumpus." The neighbor described hearing something like multiple gunshots and then recounted what happened next.

"I hit the deck, and when I got up, I saw two white males run past our apartment windows and get into a car. One was heavyset, wearing a heavy coat. He had curly or fuzzy hair. The second man was short and stocky. That's when I went over to Detective Hodges's pad, he lives around the corner, and I alerted him."

McNeil gave the man his card. "You think of anything else, you give me a call. You got that?"

"Yes, sir."

McNeil found Michelle wandering into the kitchen. He took her to a quiet corner and asked her to explain what happened.

"It was two white guys." Michelle's eyes looked to the floor in disgust, and then she looked up to face him. "They knocked about an hour ago." She stopped for a moment, her head shaking side to side. "Then they asked Joe about some girl named Carrie. 'What were you doing with my fourteen-year-old sister?' the big guy kept asking. 'Carrie who?' Joe asked back. And that's when they pushed their way in, each toting a handgun."

"Can you describe the perpetrators?"

"Yeah. One of them was tall."

"When you say tall . . . ?"

"Oh, I don't know, easily six feet in height, and he had a heavy build, with one of them white Afros."

"And what about his clothes?"

"Jeans, sneakers, and a flannel jacket, and the second man was short, I'd say," she placed her hand about three inches above her head, "probably five foot five to five foot eight, with dark hair—Italian looking—and he had a stocky build. He was the guy who grabbed the Uzi."

"And where'd he get that?"

"From Joe's back pocket. I told him not to carry that thing . . ." Her words drifted off.

The detective wrote it all down in his notebook as fast as he could. "Go on, please."

"They forced us to lie on the living room floor, and the big guy kept looking at me," the girl said. "Like I was going to get up and beat their asses, you know. The big guy said he was BSO (Broward Sheriff's Office) officer so and so. He chose some Italian name like Coppacola. And then the little guy asked Joe for clips to his gun and for him to get the stuff."

"Stuff?"

"The shit, the cocaine. Joe got up and went into the bedroom and the two guys went in with him, and I took off and ran out of the apartment. A minute or two later, I heard what sounded like gunfire, and I saw the two guys take off in a gray-colored car. It was small, possibly a Datsun or Toyota. Then I went back into the apartment and saw my Joe and all that blood." As she finished, she burst once more into tears.

Dr. Wright interrupted, and McNeil told Michelle to wait, pointing at a chair at the kitchen table. "You sit here. Don't move. I'll be back."

McNeil and the doctor went into the room where the body was.

"He's been shot with a large-caliber gun," Dr. Wright began. "It appears that the bullet entered the victim's head on the right side just to the rear of the ear. You can see here some of the exposed brain matter. Note the high-velocity blood spatter on the molding on the door and the low-velocity pooling of blood on the tile here under his head."

"Any exit wound?" McNeil spoke as he examined the angle of the blood spray.

"No, sir."

"Doc, I want an autopsy report, ASAP. We gotta know what kind of gun did him in."

"Yes, sir."

"And, Goldberg, you better locate this kid's parents on the phone, and see if you can get prints around that indentation on the wall."

Detective McNeil exited the room and approached Michelle again. She agreed to go to the police station to make a statement. She also gave the detective the name and number of Joe's father. As soon as Goldberg called him, Joe's father raced out of his house, got into his car, and drove like a madman to the scene of the crime.

Michelle walked with Sergeant McNeil to his vehicle, one of three squad cars parked helter-skelter that still had their flashers on. Their colorful lights pulsated, bouncing rhythmically, as their colors rolled off shrubbery, cars, and adjacent condos. The detective walked over to the passenger side and opened the door. Michelle got in and they drove away.

"Was it just the two of you in the apartment?"

"No," she said. "Vic and one of his friends, I think his name is Chris, was there with us. They arrived about ten minutes before those guys came."

An eerie quiet pervaded the dark streets as they motored on. Michelle squinted from the harsh fluorescent lighting when they reached the police station and went to Detective McNeil's office.

"Vic?" he asked her, as he sat at his desk to take notes.

"Giordano. He does some deals for Joe."

"Why didn't you tell me this before?"

"I don't know. No reason. What are you asking me all these questions for? He's dead."

"I just want to get it right," the detective said. "Let me see if I have it. There were *four* of you in the apartment: you and Joe Viscido, a Vic Giordano, and some guy named Chris?"

"Yeah, and then two guys busted in on us."

"Was Vic there to buy?"

"No, it was Chris. Vic was the middleman. Chris was going to buy half a key. Vic just wanted a quarter ounce."

"Was there any marijuana there?"

"About a pound, maybe two."

"Okay. What about the other guys, the ones with the guns? Did you know them?"

"No."

"Never saw them before?"

"No. They just made us all lie down."

"All of you?"

"Well, me, Joe, and Chris."

"Where was Vic?"

"I don't know, in the back room or somewheres. Then they asked Joe where he kept his stash, and Joe took the little guy into the bedroom. You could hear a fight going on, and so the big guy ran in, and that's when we took off. I heard the shot just as we left the apartment."

"Where'd you go?" the detective asked, unconsciously resting the heel of his hand on his holster.

Michelle's eyes followed the sergeant's move. "I ran into the parking lot and hid behind a car. When they came running out, the shorter guy had something heavy in his hands that looked like Joe's safe. And then they got into a small hatchback vehicle. It could have been a Honda."

"You said Toyota or Datsun?"

"What's the difference?" she snapped back.

McNeil continued the questions. "Which way did they go?"

"South, and I think there was a third guy driving."

McNeil showed Michelle a Smith & Wesson Identi-Kit, to try to ID the guns involved. Then he made an appointment with a police artist to create a composite drawing of the perpetrators. [2]

Back at the crime scene, the medics had just closed up the dark green body bag, placed it on a cart, and were wheeling it toward the ambulance when a car screeched into the driveway. In a daze, the victim's father pushed aside a medic and tried to unzip the body bag.

"You'll have to do that at the morgue," the other medic said.

Falling to a knee, Mr. Viscido placed his head on the chest of his enshrouded son, put both arms around the body bag, and hugged. He would tell his wife later that he was trying to feel whatever warmth remained.

A hand came down hard on his shoulder signaling him to get up. Rigor was just setting in.

"Please, give me one moment," he cried. "I'm begging you." [3]

When Mr. Viscido saw the inside of the house, it was like walking into hell. His son's room was in shambles, cops were all over the place, the wall was dented, and Joe's blood covered the floor.

Detective McNeil thought about Vic Giordano the following day and realized that his first impression of this guy, who had called in the killing, was that Giordano was a greaser. He also reminded McNeil of a skunk. Vic Giordano's most distinguishing feature was not his Mohawk haircut, but the fact that he had bleached the stripe blond. Well known to the police for a previous arrest on drug charges, Giordano appeared undernourished, although he still had powerful forearms. Giordano's height, which would become important later on, was five foot nine.

"I was only in the apartment maybe five minutes," Giordano said.

"Who was the other guy?"

"Chris Jones. We went there to pick up my car keys. I was arranging to meet with him the following day. These guys busted in and made us lie face down on the tile floor in the kitchen."

"I thought it was the living room."

"No, it was the kitchen. The shorter guy went into the bedroom with Joe and a shot was fired. That's when the taller guy went in after them."

"So the shorter guy was the one who did the shooting?"

"The first shot, anyway. We didn't wait around."

"Can you describe these guys?"

"The tall guy was six feet, about 200 pounds," Giordano said, "twenty to thirty years old. He had a mustache, blue shirt, and blue jeans with dark hair parted in the middle. He was carrying a chrome semi. The shorter guy was maybe twenty-seven or twenty-eight years old, five foot nine, about 150 pounds, wearing a blue jacket, blue jeans, and a dress shirt—blue and white. He had a chrome handgun too." Giordano snarled as he spoke, as if to say he too was a tough guy who knew his weapons.

"Did Joe have any guns?"

"An Uzi. But the short guy got it right away and tucked it into the back of his waistband when they came busting through the door. "They told us to lay face down on the floor. Then the one guy came over to Joe and grabbed him from behind and started yelling at him for having sex with his little sister, Carrie. Joe's shouting, 'I didn't do it, I didn't do it,' and then Michelle yells, 'I'm Joe's wife,' and the guy just says to shut up.

"Then the short guy took Joe into the back bedroom while the other guy watched us three. And next thing you know, I heard a fight start and a gunshot. The guy watching us in the living room ran into the bedroom, so I took off—caught up to Chris out in the parking lot. There, by the wall, that's where we saw a car with its engine on and its lights off, just sitting there."

"Can you describe it?"

"I'm not sure. I think it was a silver-colored Toyota or Honda with a white line running along the bottom. It started to go into reverse, and we kept running. Chris wanted to go for his car, but I told him to fuck the car and just haul ass. He went one way, and I went another, turned into Lime Tree Apartments, and made my way to Denny's, where I called you guys. I don't know where Chris ended up."[4]

After the interview, Sergeant McNeil told one of his subordinates to see if he could locate Chris Jones. He reviewed his notes, and kept returning to the name Carrie. He retraced the letters with his pen. If he found her, maybe he could find the big guy.

Before long, he located a girl by the name of Carey who knew Joe Viscido. It was noted that her boyfriend was tall, but he had blond hair and a few days' growth of beard, so that lead was dropped. The autopsy report came in and McNeil learned that the victim was a circumcised adult male, five foot eight, 143 pounds. He had a mustache and brown eyes, and his heart weighed in at 360 grams. The bullet, described as "a flattened, unjacketed .45 caliber missile," had entered the rear of the cranial vault at the occipital lobe and had torn through the midbrain structures en route to the frontal cortex, where it was located. According to the report, no unusual odors from the body cavity were detected.

Using a computer search for recent arrest records, Sergeant McNeil found out that Joe had been running drugs into the Ohio and or Michigan region under the name John Nina. He called up Mr. Viscido, who rushed over to the station.

"Yeah, I knew that my son had been arrested by DEA," Viscido said.

"Did you know that he ID'd two Detroit pushers in exchange for his release?"

"Of course. I encouraged it. He told me he didn't want to rat them out, but I told him he had no choice. I was hoping the arrest would set him straight."

"It didn't though, did it?" McNeil prompted.

"No. It just made him afraid that maybe they'd get out and come down and get him."

Mr. Viscido revealed that a few months back Joe had been frantic after two men with Michigan license plates showed up looking for him at the car dealership Viscido Sr. used to own. "I think Victor Merriman saw them."

"Who's he?" McNeil asked, writing down the name.

"He's a salesman that used to work for me and is still down at the dealership. Good guy who was also a friend of Joe's. Go see him, because I think he got a pretty good look at those guys."

Sergeant McNeil drove out to the car dealership with Detective Kenny, one of the other officers on the case. Merriman wasn't there that day, but a secretary remembered the two men with the Michigan plates. Since she described them as having long, dirty-blond hair, this lead was dropped, because this description bore no resemblance to the dark-haired men Michelle and Giordano had described.

The next day, a young woman named Carrie Boyle, who knew Joe, was brought into the Deerfield Beach Police Department for questioning. After a polygraph, she was found to be squeaky clean. She told the sergeant that Joe was a surfer and that he should question one of Michelle's friends, Elizabeth (Betts) Olivetti, because she might know more.

All the hospitals in the area were investigated to see if anyone had been reported as shot. The police also checked with the traffic department for any vehicles reported stolen or for ones that had been issued recent speeding tickets. The day after the murder, a 1972 Datsun was towed from the crime scene. Chris Jones, the third witness from the apartment and the one the police had yet to locate, owned the car.

Checking with the Detroit police, Sergeant McNeil found out that Joe Viscido, Jr., had been arrested in August with eighty-two grams of cocaine in his possession. In return for his release, he gave information on one Ricky Bly from Toledo, Ohio, and a Dave Pesto from Cincinnati. Thus, the sergeant reasoned that Viscido might have been killed for revenge because another witness told him that Joe had a reputation for shooting his mouth off.

Two days after the homicide, Vic Giordano and Michelle Arrieta worked with a forensic artist to create composite drawings of the killers. That was a difficult task, since the artist used the same nose for each suspect, which could not be right, but changed the shape of the head, along with the eyes, lips, chin, and hair. For the short man, he sketched a vacant-looking face with an exceedingly long, squared-off chin. He also parted the man's hair down the middle in a wide inverted V. For the tall one, the artist drew a strikingly handsome face with young, sexy eyes, a well-groomed mustache, and chic hairdo fluffed out in the center as if it had been blown dry by a professional stylist. Both witnesses thought that the drawing of the taller subject was a pretty good likeness, but they said the smaller one was off base. Since the artist was out of ideas and Michelle had Joe's funeral to attend, she left as soon as she could, and Giordano followed soon after.

Detective Hodges suspected a local pusher by the name of Peter Dallas, a known associate of "Pete Verakis" [Roussonicolos], aka Pete the Greek. Hodges was able to obtain a photo taken from a video, which the Orange County Sheriff's Office supplied. Of poor quality, the image had come from a camera at a bank where Dallas had gone to cash a check.

Other suspects with drug arrest records from Pompano Beach, Loch Comond, Lighthouse Point, and Hollywood were also considered because of their resemblance to the composite drawings. However, all of them proved to be false leads.

The detectives needed to locate the third eyewitness, who was actually in the apartment—Chris Jones—and they needed him yesterday. A week after the murder, he finally phoned in.

"This is Chris Jones," a nervous voice said meekly. "I'm . . . I'm in Canada. And I'm not coming back."

"Canada," McNeil said in astonishment. "You gotta come back. You're a witness to a homicide."

"I've spoken to a judge," Chris Jones confessed, "and to a lawyer to find out if I can avoid going back down to Florida."

"What's going on?" the detective demanded. "We need your testimony."

"I'm afraid. Those guys were crazy."

"We'll protect you."

"Yeah," Chris whined. "I know just how you guys operate. You'll get me on some other rap and keep me there. I had nothing to do with this."

"We didn't say you did. Just tell us what you know. I want everything, word for word."

After some back and forth negotiations, Chris told his story.

"I went to Joe's house to meet Vic. They all were in the bedroom and they gave me papers to roll some joints. We also had a couple of lines of coke set up. We're hardly there five minutes when we hear a knock at the door. Michelle and me went to answer it, and two men entered wearing light clothing, jeans, and T-shirt tops. One of them had Topsiders and was whipping around a revolver with insignias on the side. At one point, one of them put a gun to my head and said that he could do whatever he wanted because *he was a BSO officer.* After Joe and the short guy went into the room, the shot went off. We didn't wait around. We got the hell out of there, and I made it back to my home here in Canada."

What Jones didn't tell Detective McNeil was that he had observed "Joe getting his head blown off, and had seen brain matter come flying out." Jones was terrified that the perpetrators were cops and that if he was taken as a witness, he'd be next.

"You stay in touch," Sergeant McNeil said. " You disappear, you're a fugitive. Like it or not, you may have to come down here to look at lineups and give us a better description of the subjects." [5]

Sergeant McNeil extracted Chris Jones's Canadian address and phone number, and contacted the phone company to get a complete log on the fugitive's incoming and outgoing calls. The detective then called Vic Giordano's probation officer. "You're Mohican's been highly uncooperative," the detective said. "He's lied to us, and he's already skipped two scheduled meetings at the station. I suggest you put the squeeze on him, or I'll put him back in the slammer."

CHAPTER 19:
The Grieving Father

Mr. Viscido drifted aimlessly through the den, reflecting on his past and his son, a star athlete in high school who had such a bright future ahead of him. Before he moved from New Jersey to Florida, while still a young man, Mr. Viscido had applied for and became a corrections officer. He had always been proud to say that he tested first out of 500 applicants. But he didn't become a cop. Instead, he opened up a car dealership and for a number of years ran it with his son, who unfortunately started drifting into drugs and away from him. The night before the murder, Mr. Viscido had discussed with Joe Jr. the idea of building a duplex, which was something they could do together. "He was not only my son and my only child," Mr. Viscido said, "we were more like brothers. He was my best friend." Mr. Viscido had been just on the verge of bringing Joe Jr. back into the fold, and now he was dead. [1]

Dusting off his son's bronzed baby shoes, he rearranged them next to Joe Jr.'s little league awards, surfing trophies, and a life-sized photo of his son, which spookily overshadowed everything else in the space. Fifty-nine and retired from his car dealership, Joseph sat quietly as he looked through pictures of his son in his baseball uniform from junior high and then photos of him as a high school wrestler four years later. Joe Jr. went on to become a surfing champion, and he made a name for himself with the long board. He had surfed not only beaches in Deerfield and Pompano Beach, but also those in California, Mexico, and the Carolinas. *If only I had let him go to Australia when he had that sponsor, like he had wanted,* Viscido thought to himself, *but I just couldn't see how he would make money at it.*

Joe's wife, Rose, tiptoed into the room. "Honey," she said almost in a whisper, "we have to move on."

"Are you out of your mind? How can you say that?!" Joseph exploded, throwing up a stack of papers, clearing a desk with his arm, and scaring the life out of Rose.

"He was my son too," she cried out desperately, and they both broke down once again. Joseph's sobs were deep and uncontrollable.

"Get out," he motioned, pushing her away angrily, wiping his eyes with his sleeve. She left the house with little thought of returning. Half-crazed with grief, Joseph circled the room again, glaring at this shrine to his son. And then he went to the drawer that held his .357 Magnum. Ripping open a box of ammunition, he removed a single bullet and stared at it for a long time before he opened up the revolver and placed it into the chamber. The gun felt heavy. Swinging the piece wildly about with mad thoughts screaming through his mind, he aimed it at targets in the room and outside the window before turning it on himself. Mr. Viscido stared down the barrel. Mesmerized, he spun the chamber, held the weapon to his head, and vowed, "Either I'm in this thing or I'm out of it." He pulled the trigger. [2]

CHAPTER 20:
A Question of Identification

Within a week, yet another Carrie who knew Joe was located, one Carrie Haven. She came to the station on her own accord. She didn't look like a crack whore to the detective. Wearing a low V-cut halter top, she looked more like she could have been a normal college kid.

McNeil cut to the chase. "What do you know about the murder of Joe Viscido, Miss Haven?"

"This was a Mafia hit from up north," she said. "Joe was set up because he was in deep shit with Pete the Greek, and the Greek wanted payback."

"Are you sure it was Pete the Greek?" he asked.

"I'm not saying he did the setup, but he's a sure bet to know what's been going down."

Despite the information about Pete the Greek, the police still had only hearsay evidence. Michelle Arrieta was called in once again, and she declared that the police sketch of the short perpetrator was inaccurate. They had it redrawn for her, but it was still no good. As for Vic Giordano, he simply skipped the appointment for a polygraph, telling his probation officer that he was too afraid to be questioned. After missing another one, he came to the police station with cocaine stashed in his sock and was immediately arrested. With eyewitnesses like this, it was no wonder the case was stalled.

Two weeks into the investigation, the sergeant received an excited call from the father of the murdered man. Viscido told the detective he was fully committed to finding out who killed his son. He had shifted most of his savings to his checking account and called a private detective. Eventually, he also hired two more—one with FBI connections—and placed an ad in the local papers offering $10,000 for any information leading to the capture of the men who murdered his son.

Acting as an unofficial part of the investigating team, Viscido became a veritable haunt, making himself at home on the other side of the glass partition.

A week after the murder, Sergeant McNeil got a call. "Yes, Mr. Viscido, what can I do for you?"

"I'm at my son's apartment. I think I've cracked the case."

"Be right over." Sergeant McNeil grabbed his car keys and drove back to the scene of the crime. Entering the apartment, McNeil made his way down the hall and headed for Joe Jr.'s room. The color of the dried blood on the wall was now a copper brown. Viscido was kneeling on the tile floor, scrubbing it with a rag. Next to him was a bucket of soapy water.

"I've got your man, Sergeant."

"Yes?"

Pausing in his work, Viscido looked up and eyed the detective before he continued. "I've learned that Pete the Greek is responsible for this."

"How do you know?"

"I have my sources." Viscido stood up to stretch, and then he used his foot to slide the bucket to the wall. With rag in hand, he reached down and lathered it up. "I also know that one of the guys who works for him, Peter Dallas, is probably the person Michelle Arrieta described as the little guy."

"We're not playing games here, Mr. Viscido. You're going to have to tell me where you got this information."

"From Joe's friend," Viscido said hedging, "Kit Finch. Kit told me that my son had announced just a few days before the murder that he was afraid that Pete the Greek was going to kill him. They had an argument on the phone in what Finch called a 'territorial war.' It ended badly. And I've got another name for you. The big guy."

"And who's that?"

"Steve Rosati, a bodybuilder and stripper who lives on Northeast Street in Lighthouse Point. This guy drives a Corvette, license plate 825FD6."

"You got any other surprises?"

"You mean witnesses?" the father asked.

"Yeah,"

"I got a few. It's the Greek's operation, and my son paid the price."

For eight months, the police investigators tried to get Chris Jones to return to Rhode Island from Canada for questioning. Finally, in June, McNeil flew Detective David J. Kenny up to Canada instead. Kenny landed at the airport in Toronto, where Sergeant Mario Manuel met him. They had tracked down Jones through his use of an ATM he frequented.

Jones was waiting at the District Police Station when they arrived. They took him to a small interview room surrounded by safety glass, with a few metal chairs, a big wooden desk, and a large framed picture of Niagara Falls on an otherwise stark wall. Jones began speaking after he was read his rights and the tape recorder was turned on.

"They kept asking Joe where the shit was," Jones said, "and no one was saying anything. 'God, please Joe, just give it to them,' I screamed. Then one of them put the gun to my head and told me to shut up.

"'Yes, sir, whatever you say, sir,' I said. 'I won't remember your face, I promise.'

"'It doesn't matter if you remember my face or not,' he says. I thought, they're professionals, we're all . . . they're gonna kill us all and leave no witnesses."

"Then what happened?" Detective Kenny asked.

"After the gun went off in the back room, Michelle was the first one out of there, and I went after, followed by Vic. I skidded to Naples, told my parents everything. Said 'I gotta get out of here. They're gonna find me, and they're gonna kill me!' So I decided that the best thing for me to do in my life at that point was to come up here, and took the next plane out to Canada. I thought you guys could make do with the two witnesses you already have.

"'You're safer here,' I told myself. 'You've gotten a second chance.

105

This cocaine has ruined your life, and now it's back on track.' I regret ever moving there as a child. I don't want anything to do with the diseases of South Florida."

When he was shown a series of photo lineups, Chris Jones did not identify anybody. Detective Kenny had nothing left to do but to let Jones stay where he was. The policeman returned to Florida empty-handed. [1]

The summer of 1987 wore on in a blistering swelter, and Detective McNeil's leads were running dry. With Detective Burndt, McNeil drove to the local prison to interview the well-known and semi-major pusher Robbie Newman. A popular guy, with a popular girlfriend named Sweetie Sartucci, Newman was tall and handsome and well connected; he knew how to throw a party, and he always had a supply on hand. If one of his mules hadn't snitched, he'd still be out on the street. But his lawyer was working on it, and the cops knew that their hold on him was tenuous.

"Yeah, Pete the Greek ripped me off," Robbie said, his mood turning sour.

"What'd he do?"

"He broke into my apartment on two occasions—that's what he did, he and his crew. And then they robbed me."

"Do you think Pete the Greek had anything to do with Viscido's murder?"

"Pete was the wheel man."

"What about the other guys?"

"The shooters? Those guys were bodybuilder types. One had low-cut black hair. I think his name was Jeff."

"What about Pete the Greek's partner, Peter Dallas?" the detective asked.

"Don't really know the guy," Newman replied.

The next witness was Betts Olivetti, a well-tanned girl who kept herself on the trim side.

"Did you know that Pete the Greek's been ripping off people at Robbie Newman's place?" the detective began.

"Yeah, but Pete's guys don't kill. I know Pete the Greek's got nothing to do with this. Sure, he cheats people and sells them back their drugs, but it's just a game for him, and half the people that know him expect this. Killing's a whole other thing."

CHAPTER 21:
The Short Guy

Dressed like a Madonna clone, in tank top and spray-on hot pants, Ruby Janeau entered the police station. Miss Janeau claimed she was *not* Peter Dallas's girlfriend, but had dated him around the time of the homicide. "He called me from Chicago," she huffed.

She denied driving Dallas around town, but quickly caved. "Yeah," Ruby admitted, "sometimes I'd drive Peter to meet Pete the Greek where he used to live, at the Brigadoon Motel."

"Is this Peter Dallas?" the detective said, reaching suavely into his desk drawer for the bank surveillance ID he had obtained earlier.

Ruby looked at it, scowled, and then looked back at Detective McNeil. "No."

"What do you mean?"

"That's not him. I don't know who that is."

"That's not Dallas?"

"No effing way."

The detective tried to stifle the red that flushed his face. He stuffed the photo back into the drawer and regained composure, but it was obvious that he was clearly disgusted. Here he was, headed into his second year on the case and he couldn't even get a tenable photo of a major suspect.

"So you think Dallas could have killed Joe Viscido?" he said, trying to mask his embarrassment.

"He frightened me. Yes, and I've been afraid ever since that guy got killed. Dallas has a record, you know."

"And that's what frightened you?"

After some prodding, she answered, "He told me he once leveled some Colombians in a motel room and left a girl alive there."

"Can we put you on tape on this? Get a sworn statement?"

"I can't put that on tape. I want to speak to an attorney," she said, suddenly closing down.

Frustrated by his inability to get a decent photo of Peter Dallas, Sergeant McNeil turned to Bob Whiting from the FBI. Whiting cooperated by sending a report, including fingerprints. Born in Canada in 1963, Dallas stood five foot five and weighed a mere 120 pounds. He had brown hair, hazel eyes, and a scar on his right forearm.

Was this the kind of guy who could have wrestled an Uzi from the surfer Joe Viscido, Jr.? He had been arrested in Mineola in 1984 for grand larceny, in New York City in 1986 for selling drugs, and in Chicago in 1987 for the same offense. Sergeant McNeil requested a photograph, and Whiting promised to see what he could do.

Gritting his teeth mightily, Detective McNeil punched in a phone number he didn't want to dial, Pete the Greek's illustrious criminal attorney, Richard Rendina. From McNeil's point of view, Rendina had one aim in life: protect lawbreakers.

"All we want to do is talk to him, Mr. Rendina."

"I will do my best to locate him," the lawyer replied all too laconically. Detective McNeil slammed the phone down in exasperation.

As Detective McNeil waited for a photo to come in on Peter Dallas, he continued his investigation of his list of Carries. He located three more, but all of those leads took him nowhere. But then Joe Viscido, Sr., called with another tip, one that would reboot the investigation. The victim's father had followed every one of Joe's friends and pumped them daily for information. When Viscido finally called McNeil, he had a whole new series of names to rattle off to the detective.

"I got Jeff Bloom, who saw my son just a few days before the murder, and his brother Skip, who I think was also there, and I've got Tyler Cooke. He sold drugs to my son the night he was killed. But I can't get to him."

"Anyone else?"

"Victor Merriman, the guy from the dealership. He said that Cory told him that Peter Dallas was the one who shot Joe."

This was a key lead, and McNeil pounced. "Cory who?"

"I don't know. I'll try and find out."

"You leave Cory to us," the detective said, amazed at how Joe's father could keep churning out so many new leads.

Detective McNeil drove out to the Bloom residence in Boca Raton to see if either Skip or his brother Jeff was there. A glassy-eyed young man about twenty-one years of age answered the door. It was Jeff Bloom.

McNeil asked Bloom when he last saw Joe Viscido.

"Not in a dog's age." When further pressed, Bloom calculated the last time as three or four months before Viscido died.

"If you remember anything that could lead us to the killers, please let me know." The sergeant handed Bloom his card.

"Will do," Bloom replied.

A few days later, Michelle came in and reluctantly agreed to be hooked up to a polygraph machine. "It's one week before Thanksgiving, Sergeant. Can't you give it a rest?" she asked testily.

"Michelle, I told your mother that I would try to be nice to you."

"My boyfriend's dead and you think I'm involved."

"Don't you see that I have to cover all the bases? After this test you'll be off the hook."

Detective McNeil had half a dozen pictures of known associates of Pete the Greek. She was asked a series of questions, passed them all, and was unable to ID anyone.

"Am I free to go?"

"I have just a couple more questions."

"Yes?"

"Do you know Pete the Greek?"

"Now I do, but didn't before. I seen him a few times since the murder."

"Do you think that he was involved?"

"No."

"Do you know Jeff Bloom?"

"Yeah, I know Jeff. In fact I saw him at Joe's apartment the Friday before he was shot. Now, can I go?"

This was a key contradiction, and McNeil jumped all over it. "Are you sure about Bloom?"

"Yeah, I'm sure. I remember it was Friday, because the weekend was coming up."

"Did Jeff know Pete the Greek?"

"Of course. He was a go-between. Jeff was always hounding Joe, saying Pete was going to rip him off."

"And Joe said something like he would be ready for him?"

"Yeah, but I always thought it was just Joe reacting to Jeff talking."

"What do you mean?"

"I figured he was going to come after him sooner or later to rip him off, but I never figured he was going to kill him. Joe didn't even know Pete the Greek, and Jeff was always starting trouble between them."

"How long was this before Joe's death?"

"Very shortly, like a week."

Several days later, the Peter Dallas photo arrived in a priority mail dispatch from New York City. It was November 30, 1987. Upon Sergeant McNeil's request, Dallas's girlfriend, Ruby Janeau, still dressed in her Madonna outfit, stopped by the precinct again. He wondered if she had any other clothes.

"Is that Peter Dallas?" the sergeant said, flashing the photo.

Miss Janeau crossed one exposed thigh over the other. "Yeah, that's him."

"Get Giordano up here." There were certain perks to having one of the key witnesses in a nearby jail cell.

Sergeant McNeil smiled to himself at Giordano's buzz cut as he shuffled six pictures and randomly attached them in rows, three across, and two down. Dallas was placed in position No. 3.

"You know Pete the Greek?" the sergeant asked Giordano.

"The Pete I know is Pete Verakis, who I think could be Pete the Greek."

"Did he have a fight with Joe Viscido?"

"Yes, but he called him just a few days before the killing to say that everything would be all right. I told Joe that this may be just a come-on and that he should keep his guard up."

Unlike the composite drawing of the short guy, the photo of Dallas displayed no part in his hair, and unlike the drawing, Dallas had a very short chin. In fact, his face didn't look anything like the

110

composite. Dallas stared out at the camera with lazy, cold eyes. He was the short guy. Detective McNeil knew it. Neither Michelle Arrieta nor Vic Giordano had liked the police artist's drawing of the short guy, although they both agreed that the big guy's representation was excellent.

"If I cooperate, Sarge, can't you get me sprung?"

"Cocaine is cocaine, son. And you brought it to the police station."

"All right, all right. I'm just trying to be cooperative."

"And that's all we're asking," McNeil said. "Now, look these over carefully and tell me if you see anyone you recognize."

Giordano looked the six pictures over, bit his lip, and concentrated. "That's him, I think. I mean it could be," the prisoner said.

"All right, No. 3," the sergeant was about to say, when Vic Giordano pointed to No. 6, Joseph Bagley.

A week later, Michelle Arrieta was called in. Again Peter Dallas was positioned in the slot No. 3, and Bagley in slot No. 6.

"Recognize anybody?" the sergeant said expectantly, hoping.

Michelle grabbed the page and stared at it concentrating. "No." She spoke definitively and then signed the lineup sheet and boldly wrote in the margin: "I didn't see anybody. Michelle Arrieta."

It had taken Detective McNeil more than a year to get a visual record of Peter Dallas, and he wanted someone other than Ruby Janeau to confirm that photo. *The entire case would turn on his next decision.* He took the photo to the Brigadoon Motel where Pete the Greek had lived.

"Yeah, that's him. That's Peter Dallas," the motel owner corroborated. Finally, confirmation! Now Sergeant McNeil could home in on the kill.

* * *

Cicilline carefully checked the chronology of BSO's investigation as dutifully recorded in their logbook. With a pencil between his teeth, he stopped his momentum to remove every book from his desk so he could clear an area to spread out the interviews, depositions, and photos. The defense attorney worked almost around the clock so that he could untangle the real thread of the story and try and figure out exactly why the police had settled on Dallas when it was clear that both Michelle Arrieta and Vic Giordano had not, at the outset, picked the guy out in the photo lineups.

The most damning evidence against Dallas seemed to come from a deadbeat by the name of Cory Franco, who was a cohort of the

Bloom brothers. Although Franco would cooperate fully with the investigation, what he didn't tell the detective was that he was "scared shitless" because Joe Viscido, Sr., had stalked him while he was out bike riding. Pulling out a .357 Magnum, Viscido had forced Franco to the side of the curb, where he interrogated him. Thinking he was going to be shot, Franco gave Viscido enough information to make him a major player in the case.

Cory Franco was called into the precinct shortly after this encounter. He said that he would cooperate. An admitted crackhead who had difficulty telling even what day of the week it was, Cory confirmed that he was with Peter Dallas and the Bloom brothers the night of the homicide. Although evasive in the extreme, for Detective McNeil, this deposition would be the turning point in the case. Jeff Bloom had lied to him, and Franco was going to tell him why. The detective reached over to the tape recorder and pressed the start button. Franco watched the tape spin round and round as he was sworn in.

"I was at Jeff Bloom's house. Me and Danny Ek, and Skip, Jeff's brother, was with us. Jeff says that's when the Greek, Dallas, and two other of their buddies were there [at Viscido's apartment]. That's when it went down. I was working on Bloom's truck and overheard Dallas say he had 'wasted Viscido.' I'm pretty sure that's what I heard, but I wasn't right close to him."

"You heard the words 'wasted Viscido'?"

"Yeah."

"Why didn't you come forward before this?"

"I was too afraid."

"Can you point him out in this photo lineup?"

Franco stared at the six photos for only an instant. "Yeah, that's him." He pointed to position No. 3, Peter Dallas.

"And what about this one?" Detective McNeil placed another photo lineup before Cory. "Do you know anyone there?"

"Sure, that's the Greek." He pointed out Pete the Greek.

That night, the detective felt like celebrating. He went to a local Denny's, ordered the double cheeseburger special, and sketched out on the back of a place mat what he saw as a solid scenario:

Men at Safe House Major Suspects
    Jeff Bloom
    Pete the Greek (Wheel Man)
    Skip Bloom

Peter Dallas (Short Guy)
Danny Ek
Stephen Rosati (Big Guy)
Cory Franco

Witnesses at Joe Viscido's Apartment

Michelle Arrieta (Joe's fiancée)
Vic Giordano (Joe's friend from high school)
Chris Jones (A friend of Vic's there to do a deal)

To cover all bases, Sergeant McNeil also located Danny Ek who was living with his grandmother out in Pompano. A sorry-looking man who would commit suicide with a shotgun blast to the chest just a few years later for unrelated reasons, Ek flat out contradicted Cory by stating that Peter Dallas did *not* admit to killing Joe Viscido.

"And you never heard Dallas make any statements?"

"I never did, but Geebs told me."

"Geebs?"

"Cory. That's what we call him, Geebs. He told me Dallas was the one who done it and stuff. That's it."

Ek, however, did confirm that Dallas had a friend from New York who was larger than Dallas, "just a dirty type guy, pretty tall, hair kind of curly, kind of thin."

McNeil considered whether or not this second guy could be the infamous big guy.

The following Friday, Mr. Viscido called with what he thought was great news. He had located Stephen Rosati's address! McNeil raced to the location only to find that the only thing the addressee had in common with Stephen Rosati was a last name. Nevertheless, he had Pete the Greek in several ways, and now he also had leads from informants who said that Peter Dallas was back in the Pompano Beach area. The detective felt that it would be only a matter of days before they nabbed him.

CHAPTER 22:
The Hearing: Working out the Details

Day One: December 10, 1990

With his hands cuffed in front of him, Stephen Rosati was led into the courtroom. Having already been in jail for nearly three months, his mood was grim. Dressed in one of his thousand-dollar suits, Rosati managed a meager smile for his family as he took his seat next to Cicilline. Upon Cicilline's request, the prisoner placed limp hands up toward the officer who reached over to remove the cuffs. To their left at the other table sat the prosecution team.

"All rise," said the bailiff, and Judge John F. Sheehan made his entrance. Wearing flowing black robes and half-moon reading glasses, which came on and off at appropriate times when he spoke, his flushed Irish face and his body language displayed a cordial but commanding presence. [1]

"Contesting extradition hearings are rare," Randy White began ambitiously. "The rules of evidence are inapplicable." Citing *Michigan v. Durand*, the state prosecutor explained, "The asylum state, in this case, RI, [did not, as a rule,] intervene between the initial arrest and trial. Once the governor has granted extradition, a court can do no more than decide whether the extradition documents are in order and whether [the accused] is a fugitive."

White then simply offered, "The governor's warrant requesting Stephen Rosati's return to the state of Florida for the crimes of murder and armed robbery."

"Judge, this is moving a little too rapidly for me." Jack Cicilline interrupted. "The state first gets up and tells you that the rules of evidence don't apply, and I expect what they are asking for is some kind of prehearing ruling concerning what is admissible and what is not."

"Let me see if I can cut through some of this," said the judge. He cocked his broad balding head alternately to eyeball both men. "As I understand the extradition proceedings, and I'm willing to be corrected by either side, first the governor's warrant has to be proper. Secondly, the petitioner, Mr. Rosati, had to have been, in fact, in the state of Florida on October 12, 1986 when the crime was committed; and thirdly, he has to be the person so named in the warrant. Did I, in summary, state what the burden is? Mr. Rosati has to prove by clear and convincing evidence that he was not in the state of Florida on the given date."

"Correct," said Cicilline. "However, I submit to the court that it's not simply the date of October 12. The affidavit indicates that something happened a few weeks before that date. We are going to establish by clear and convincing evidence that the petitioner was not in the state of Florida from some time in 1985. There is something very *wrong* about this case," Cicilline proclaimed. "This petitioner was *not* there at the times other people are saying he was there. And I *object* to any attempt by the state at this time to place limitations on that presentation."

White, about to counter, was checked by the judge. "I'm not limiting anything yet. However, you would agree with me, Mr. Cicilline, if the state of Florida contends and proves that Mr. Rosati was in the state and did commit the crime, now it shifts [to the defense] to prove that he was not there on October 12, 1986."

"By clear and convincing evidence, Your Honor."

"May I respond, Judge?" asked the prosecutor.

"Sure."

"The issue raised in *Michigan v. Durand* overrules and decides that no longer is it a requirement that the person be in the demanding state at the time the crime was committed," White postulated.

"How could he commit the crime you are saying if he was not present at the time it was committed?" the judge asked incredulously.

"Well, as the court is aware, there are crimes which can be committed."

"This is murder and robbery, is it not?"

"Yes, it is, Your Honor."

"He would have to be present, would he not?"

Feigning nonchalance, White replied, "If that's the court's ruling, fine, Your Honor. I'm simply bringing—"

"No, just answer the question." Sheehan pivoted to face White squarely. "Wouldn't he have to be present if he's charged with murder and robbery?"

"I can't pretend precise familiarity with Florida law," White said nimbly, avoiding a direct answer. "Under Rhode Island law there are situations in which persons are not at the scene of the crime. They could be anywhere, could be indicted, charged, tried, and convicted as principals for murder."

"Aider and abettor," the judge said begrudgingly. "Let's proceed and see how far we go."

"I would like to respond." Cicilline was appalled at the prospect of his client being charged irrespective of whether or not he was present when the murder was committed.

"I've yet to finish," White sliced, trying to cut Cicilline off.

"*I* want to respond to what he's already said," defense barked back.

"Slow down!" cautioned the judge, cracking the gavel. "Just relax everyone!"

White deftly changed the subject. "I would ask, respectfully, that those persons who expect to be witnesses be sequestered so that they are not in a position to hear the testimony of each other."

The judge complied.

"I ask that the state's witnesses be sequestered as well," said Cicilline.

"Certainly. It's a two-way street."

Having anticipated this move, White countered by bartering to allow Francis Martin, a recognized investigator, to stay at Cicilline's side, in exchange for keeping Mr. Driscoll of the Florida State's Attorney's Office and Detective Coyote from being sequestered.

Cicilline had no problem with letting Driscoll stay but moved to block Coyote, saying, "He's a critical witness to their case. I ask that he be excluded."

Following the normal procedure of allowing police officers to stay in the courtroom, while noting that no jury would be present, so that no undue influence could occur, the judge naïvely allowed *the* detective who would be testifying to stay.

"Please note my objection," Cicilline said portentously.

"So noted."

At this point, as I was an expert witness, I got up and exited the courtroom.

Fran Martin, Rosati's gumshoe, was the first to take the stand. The investigator said that he had interviewed the Rosati family and had studied the Rosatis' business books and telephone logs.

"On the day of the alleged offense, which was a Sunday, two telephone conversations were made from the offices of the Rosati Group. One, for two minutes, was to a dating service, and the other, for twenty-one minutes, was made from the Rhode Island office to a party in Woonsocket. Also, a phone call the following day was made by the defendant to a party in Woonsocket."

Martin also verified that various records and payroll checks made out to Rosati's employees at East Coast Fitness Center were signed by him on October 9, 10, and 11 of 1986 as well.

Martin confirmed that Rosati had moved into a West Warwick condominium with Kara Lynx in the fall of 1985. He had interviewed the landlord, next door neighbors, business associates, friends who were with Stephen on a fishing trip in New York in early September, and other people who saw Rosati on a regular basis throughout the 1986 period in question.

"At my request, did you make inquiry of airlines?" Cicilline asked.

"Yes, I did. I tried to track down if Mr. Rosati had made any airline reservations between Rhode Island and any place in Florida for that October 12 day or the day before or after." As the airlines only keep records for a few years, they had no substantive information to offer.

On cross-examination, Randall White requested the names of the witnesses, and Martin supplied them. "You didn't find any airline documentation that would assist the court, is that correct?"

"No, I didn't."

"Did your investigations attempt to determine whether there was simultaneously a residence for Stephen Rosati in Florida during this 1986 period?"

"No," Martin said. "From the evidence I had uncovered, I had no reason to believe he lived other than in Rhode Island."

"But you do accept the proposition that somebody can have two residences, don't you?"

"Oh, yes, I do."

"I have nothing further," the prosecutor said.

As the handwriting expert and the next witness, I was summoned back to the courtroom and walked to the stand to be sworn in. Cicilline prompted me to list my credentials, and I braced myself for the counterattack. The prosecutor wanted to know who I worked for at the attorney general's office. I told him. White tried to imply that as a graphologist, I obtained the bulk of my work from analyzing handwriting for personality factors.

"That is not correct." I replied. "Well over 90 percent of my income comes from questioned documents work."

Since I had worked for his department—a point reinforced by an interjection from the judge—White, in a bind, pronounced, "I don't have any problem with this witness being an expert."

Because attacks against expert witnesses can be truly brutal, this came as a welcomed relief. I could also see that Judge Sheehan was very interested in what I had to say because there was a real question in his mind as to where Stephen Rosati had been living at the time of the murder. I brought out twenty large placards and placed them on an easel.

In direct examination, Cicilline had me establish that I had gone to the ACI on three occasions to obtain exemplars, or known samples, of Rosati's handwriting. Further, I had examined numerous questioned documents, such as credit card receipts and canceled checks, which the Rosatis had given me.

"Now, Dr. Seifer, did you undertake to group the forty-eight or so questioned documents?"

"Yes, I did. I put them together chronologically and also by style and compared them to the exemplars of Rosati that I had obtained."

After some bantering between prosecution and defense, document examination moved to the next stage, which was to read into the record each of the forty-eight documents that had signatures:

October 6: Shell credit card receipt from a Rhode Island gas station

October 9: A check from Pine Hill Home Builders

October 10: Paychecks and receipts from East Coast Fitness Center

October 11: Shell credit card receipt from another Rhode Island gas station

October 11: East Coast Fitness Center receipt

October 14: Endorsed check, bank stamp dated

October 14: Notarized board meeting document

October 15: Credit card slip signed in Connecticut at a Texaco gas station

The prosecutor had sat silently until this point. "Your Honor, I object to the continuation of this testimony and its relevance and probative value for the hearing. What difference does it make what Stephen Rosati was doing, assuming he was signing checks or credit cards or the like on October 17, October 20, or thereafter?"

"It goes to weight, Your Honor," Cicilline explained, "the argument being made, and I think I am clearly entitled to show, that he was a permanent resident in the state of Rhode Island throughout this entire period."

"All right," said the judge. "They are only for identification, Mr. White. I know you want to get this moving and I appreciate it, but I will listen. But I understand that the date in question is October 12."

By matching up the various exemplars obtained directly from Rosati with the numerous questioned documents, I established that Stephen Rosati did in fact sign all forty-eight documents. It was also established that Rosati happened to have a variety of styles and signatures, such as when he signed important documents and when he scribbled his name on gasoline credit card receipts. One key discovery that clinched the identification for me was an idiosyncratic propensity that Rosati had for making the letter S with the top part detached as if it were the number 5. This was shown to have occurred in both the questioned documents and in the exemplars.

After an entire day of testimony, Judge Sheehan asked me to summarize. "Do you have an opinion based on scientific certainty?"

"Yes," I said, "I went through all forty-eight documents and found comparisons in all of them. It is my contention that all forty-eight documents were signed by Carl Stephen Rosati, the person who wrote the exemplars."

"Court will recess until tomorrow," the bailiff decreed.

CHAPTER 23:
Bang, Bang

Richard Haffner and Stephen Rosati were the biggest bodybuilders in Rhode Island before Rosati moved to Florida and began trimming down. A friend of Johnny Salvadoro, one of Rosati's old wrestling buddies, Haffner had been Mr. Rhode Island in 1982, the year before Rosati deposed him. Not only did Rosati gain the state championship, he also came in second overall in a regional meet that included bodybuilders from Massachusetts, Connecticut, and New York.

However, as the year wore on, Stephen began to get tired of competing with guys like Haffner. Further, he knew that his physical regimen was getting to be excessive—twelve egg whites and two egg yolks for breakfast, a half loaf of whole wheat bread at lunch, a giant steak at dinner: the whole routine. He got it into his mind that he wanted to change. Having decided not to go professional, Stephen noticed by the end of 1983 that he was also losing his edge.

"When I thought about what I was doing just to maintain, and what I would have to do to compete with the big boys, there just was no way."

Realizing that professional bodybuilders were in a different league, Rosati knew he had to stop.

Sometime in 1982, Stephen broke up with Mary Ann. With his partners, Lance and Gary, Rosati hired a few girls and guys to replace her and to help build up memberships. Good salesmen, Stephen remembered, were averaging over $300 a week. As an incentive to boosting membership numbers, he ran a promotion to extend existing contracts for members who signed up friends. As a state champion, Rosati was persuasive, and his fitness center continued to grow.

The real estate business was booming, so Carl and Esther purchased a large home by the water in Watch Hill. With its own cabana, heated pool, and view of the harbor, it was a magnificent place, which the Rosatis thoroughly enjoyed for a number of amazing years.

"This was an extraordinary move for an Italian family, as this part of the state was strictly WASP territory. Nevertheless," Stephen said, "my parents became well-respected members of that community. I stayed at the house in Scituate, which is in the northern part of the state, and drove down to visit them on weekends and during the summer months."

While at the ocean one day, Rosati met his next girlfriend, Elodie (Ellie) Vanderpyl, and invited her to a pool party he was having at Watch Hill. A hairdresser from Woonsocket, Ellie moved in with Stephen at Scituate shortly thereafter.

Because he was Mr. Rhode Island, Rosati qualified to compete in the 1983 national competition, which was held in San Jose, California. All of the top amateurs in the country were going to be there, so Rosati worked out a little to tone up. However, his head wasn't into it by then, and he wasn't in top shape. Most if not all of those guys were heavy into the steroid scene, and Rosati realized that eventually that kind of lifestyle would have to take its toll. Today steroids are outlawed, but in those days a lot of guys still shot up.

"Bodybuilding is a narcissistic sport, with everyone in love with only themselves. I may have been—and may still be—vain, but not that vain," admitted Stephen.

Gary and Lance began making it obvious that they wanted to phase out the emphasis on bodybuilding to make East Coast more of a health spa. They both had their girlfriends there, and Stephen just didn't feel at home anymore.

"They wanted the business so badly that finally I told them, 'Go ahead; do your thing. I'm going down to Florida.' I knew that the place wouldn't have the right energy without me there, but by this time I just didn't care. I left in June of '84."

Rosati got the idea to go to Florida because he had a friend who had a father who was an attorney there with connections in the construction business. But that deal fell through, and Stephen decided to look for work in the profession that he knew: health clubs. He chose one of the more elite gyms, the Olympiad, a fashionable health spa located in Boca Raton. Rosati told the owner about his own health club in Rhode Island and that he knew how to increase membership.

"The key for success, I told him, was just five words: time, money, need, think, and spouse; and with this key I could combat any resistance offered by a prospective client. For instance, Spouse: Your wife must be glad that you are getting in shape. Think: What's there to think about? You want to get in shape, don't you? Money: You can afford $10 a week to keep yourself in shape, can't you? Let's get started today."

So in this way, no matter what they would say, Rosati would still sign them up. "Sometimes a guy would say no to me seven or eight times, and still, at the end of my rap, he'd whip out his Visa card."

Unable to find a job in her own profession, cutting hair, Ellie became a waitress at LaVoguenique. She wasn't thrilled with the job, but she was with her boyfriend and paying her share. They had a few idyllic weeks together.

Rosati was so successful at the club that, within a month, he became the second highest recruiter. By jogging and working out, he also set the goal of dropping below 200 pounds so he could look like a regular guy on the beach, fit into a Corvette, and pick Ellie up after work in his new wheels. However, about a month into this routine, everything changed. An older fellow, slightly past prime, but with a certain air of confidence, approached Rosati by the shoreline. Tall, lanky, with long brown hair and a chiseled black beard, he asked for Stephen's name.

"Steve Rosati."

"Marc Love," the man replied as he reached out to shake Stephen's hand. "Steve," he nodded, motioning to two pretty girls who were giggling to themselves, checking out Stephen's physique, "what would you think about taking off your clothes in front of women like that and getting paid for it?"

"You gotta be kidding."

"I'm the head of an all-male dance group, and I can see, believe me, you'd make a ton of money. You'd be perfect."

Much to Stephen's surprise, he found himself replying, "Sure, I'll try anything once."

"Come down to the club tomorrow night and meet the other guys." He handed Rosati a business card, which read "2001 Odyssey."

The following night, Rosati was backstage at 2001 being introduced to the other strippers. Most of them were from New York. There was Chris Shea, the Hollywood Swinger, Richie 11 (he wasn't called 11 for nothing!), and Little Rocky, a short guy who somewhat resembled Sylvester Stallone. They were all in good shape, but none of them were bodybuilders like Rosati, and so Stephen saw a way he could be different.

With an all-woman crowd hovering at the front of the stage, and a few guys lingering in the back waiting to score after the show, Marc Love took the microphone to announce the first performer. The Hollywood Swinger opened to a throng of shrieking women— all of them ready to pounce or stuff one- or five-dollar bills into the guy's briefs. Dressed in a sequined outfit designed to rip away, Shea strutted out like a rock star to gasps, blushes, and screams. Little Rocky followed, stripping to Rocky Balboa music, and then Richie 11 emerged. Dressed in a full uniform, he did his routine to a song from the movie *An Officer and a Gentleman.*

"After two or three shots of whisky," Stephen recounted, "I was introduced as a guest dancer. Striking bodybuilding poses, I took off my clothes to Michael Jackson music chosen by the DJ, and strutted into the crowd in a skimpy bathing suit, which is usually called a thong or T-back. The finale was Marc Love taking off his clothes. As he was just about over the hill, it was pretty funny. But he was a bit of a psycho, and this routine enabled him to drag a bunch of women back to his den after the show."

At the end of the evening, after getting satisfied from one of the babes from the crowd, Rosati returned to his apartment with $50 he had earned in tips. It didn't take Ellie too long to see what was happening, and she moved to another apartment at the other end of town. In rapid order, Stephen took in Chris Shea as a roommate to keep expenses down and began taking Little Rocky's advice to create a single theme. Settling on Conan the Barbarian, he quit his job at the Olympiad, and Love booked him and the rest of the dance group around the state.

Although he really didn't know how to perform and was still over 200 pounds, he decided that the perks made learning the trade and dropping the weight worth it. By running, dieting, continuing to work out with weights, and dancing five or six nights a week, his weight continued to drop, and he soon got down to 180.

In the beginning, Rosati was earning around $200 a week, but by the fall of 1984, he started investing in costumes and eventually increased his pay considerably. He bought fur pelts, which wrapped around his wrists; chamois and deerskin loincloths, which he placed around his waist; and a large raccoon coat, which cost more than a few thousand dollars. Settling on dramatic jungle songs, Rosati continued to choreograph the numbers basically on his own until he met a dancer named Hunter, who was from Texas.

Hunter wanted Stephen to go back to Houston with him to dance at LaBarre, a large nightclub, because the club didn't have men Rosati's size. Rosati flew out the next day. The DJ at LaBarre was Big Rocky. "Steve," he said, "you got the body. You got the looks. You got the costumes. All you need is a number." He chose "The Warrior" by Scandal, featuring Patty Smyth, and helped choreograph a routine.

"Bang, Bang, I am the Warrior," the lyrics rang out, as gunpowder sounded on stage with accompanying puffs of smoke. Stephen would have flash pods behind him, which he used in conjunction with each pose timed for each "Bang, Bang." According to Stephen, the crowd went wild. There was a lot of glitter and muscle, and at that time there weren't too many bodybuilders on the circuit. "Many of the guys were skinny: good dancers without much physique."

Big Rocky was generous, and he also helped the newcomer with his overall look. "It was in Houston," Stephen said, "that I really learned how to perform, and worked from 5:00 p.m. to 2:00 a.m. four to five nights per week. As the time went on, I increased my outfits to four."

Besides Conan, Rosati had a motorcycle look, a pirate, and a Roman gladiator. With the increase of his professionalism came a dramatic increase in revenues. Some nights, especially in Texas, Rosati was earning as much as $600 in tips and averaging about $1,200 a week. He expanded his territory in Florida to include guest appearances with other dance groups and performed at clubs as far north as Orlando, traveling back to his base at 2001 or over to Bogie's at Palm Beach or Rosebuds, which was a low-key place on the strip. He also flew out to Houston on a regular basis.

In Florida, Stephen generally worked one show a night: twenty minutes work for four or five nights a week. He spent all his days on the beach.

"I was twenty-five years old and in great shape. Houston was more intense, five or six shows a night, but the income there made it worth the extra effort."

The top guys were doing unbelievably well. One lady, whose husband owned a satellite dish franchise, used to tip Rosati $200–$300 a night,because she just liked his act and never made a pass. With plenty of oil and corporate money in the hands of lonely wealthy women or hot wives or ex-wives on the fast track, many of the dancers made out like bandits. Stephen, however, was in it for a different reason—really for the kick. He saw some of these guys earn as much as $1,700 a night.

"For that kind of money, they tended to spend entire weeks with their babes. They had to talk to them on the phone and generally keep the party going so that they could soak them for even more. Some received jewelry or rings, some even got apartments or cars; and if they worked it right, they were able to change over to respectable day jobs or even marry their benefactress.

"Off nights some of the guys would go to the female strip clubs and tip the girl dancers. They generally tipped the girls $100, and the girls usually reciprocated by coming to the men's clubs and repaying the compliment. It was just one of those things that we did."

The after-hours scene became crazy. "Every night," Stephen reminisced, "hot chicks simply waited at the bar or outside the dressing rooms, panting. The ones with the tape measures sought out Richie 11. Orgies at Marc Love's place or ours, a different babe every night, hundreds if you wanted, and every which way you wanted it, and the girls were more insane than the guys. When men were performing, the girls thought that they had a right to put their hands anywhere they wanted, especially towards the climax of your act when you went into the crowd. Dressed in mini-skirts, low-cut tops, and high heels, it became primeval, intense. Sweating babes would reach over, try to French kiss you, throw napkins or straws, and generally just work themselves into a frenzy. With their hormones gushing, most were just clean college kids down for a week's vacation from New York or Michigan, all just looking for a good time. Others, however, became animals. Bouncers had to carry them out."

CHAPTER 24:
Just Getting Through

Rosati found that he was being moved into the new mod, and Chanta would be his roommate. Chanta had made the mistake of going to a party armed with a pistol and then getting into an argument with another man. Later, when he went upstairs, with his gun put away, a friend of his went downstairs and shot and killed the guy Chanta had argued with. "Chanta may have been guilty of something," Stephen commiserated, "like waving an unregistered gun at a party, but he didn't kill anybody." All the same, they had him for aiding and abetting, and he was facing life.

"Steve, I don't want to be in this jail," Chanta would cry. "Not good people here. They talk the bad talk. You talk the good talk. I no kill this guy." And then he would just cry. After a time, he would cheer up and say, "When I get out, Steve, I'm going to get you Oriental girl," and then they would both laugh.

"Everybody cries in jail because it's so sad," Stephen said. "Eddie

Martinez would come back from court and burst into tears. He'd say, 'Steve, it doesn't look good. They're going to find me guilty.'"

"Of course," Stephen admitted, "the same thing would happen to me. I'd come back from court, and the tears would just start to flow. My old girlfriend would be coming to testify. Sure, I knew she would look amazing, but I could barely look at her, and I definitely couldn't talk about it. No one could imagine what it was like. I never let anyone see, because they prey on weakness in prison. You have to toughen up or you won't make it. So when someone comes to the room, you wipe your eyes and say you're tired.

"I'd go to the church services and pray to God. I asked him why he did this to me. I was so ultimately depressed, and many times, I felt I was going crazy."

What saved Stephen were the workouts. Ironically, though, when he got to the new mod, with all the modern equipment in the weight room—pulleys and pins, and barbells on springs— it just didn't feel the same. The funny thing was that he longed for the old mod and the old courtyard, with the two simple dumbbells, the barbell, and the bench. "I could do so much more with so much less," he said.

Two books also saved Rosati: *Unlimited Power* by Tony Robbins and the Bible. Robbins got Stephen to return to his strength: bodybuilding. But he also talked about how the body sends signals to the mind. "If you walk like you're on top of things and you own the joint, your brain believes it, and you feel that way." Rosati practiced this, and sometimes it helped.

Stephen had a new language student edition Bible, which he read every day cover to cover three or four times over the course of his incarceration. He would read Psalms such as 35:

> *Let their way be dark and slippery, the angel of the Lord pursuing them.*
> *For without cause have they hid for me the pit, even their net,*
> *Without cause have they digged for my soul.*
> *Let destruction come upon him unawares,*
> *And let his net that he hath hid catch himself.*

CHAPTER 25:
The Hearing: Kara

Day Two: December 11, 1990

Preparing to face the prosecutor, I was sitting in the hallway collecting my thoughts when one of the most stunning blondes I had ever seen appeared. She was strikingly beautiful with mesmerizing green eyes. Clutching a white mink jacket, the lady was dressed to the hilt. She wore lavender stockings with scroll designs on the calves, lavender spiked heels, and a knit body-clinging lavender two-piece suit. Keep in mind, this was a Tuesday morning, not Saturday night at the Biltmore. I remember thinking that this young lady, who turned out to be Kara Lynx, looked like the type of gal who could only drive in a Mercedes and only live behind an iron gate.

As I sat and waited, I realized that I really had no opinion about the innocence or guilt of the suspect, but I was inclined to think that Rosati must be involved in some way. The bailiff leaned his head into the hallway and nodded. "Dr. Seifer, you're on." I got up and entered the courtroom.

"I will remind you, sir, that you are still under oath," the judge said.

The prosecutor began, "Now, you testified yesterday that with respect to at least some of the exemplars you took from Mr. Rosati that you provided him with a writing that he was to mimic, correct?"

"No, no."

"No, not to mimic, I mean to repeat?"

"Right."

"And you were paid a fee, correct?"

"Yes."

"And you knew in advance of even taking the first exemplars that Mr. Rosati's position in this was that his son had signed the questioned documents, correct?"

"No."

"Wasn't that what you testified to?"

"No. Mr. Rosati also said that there may be some of *his* signatures in the pile, and he wanted those removed. He only wanted his son's to be used."

White then proceeded to ask a long list of nitpicky questions that began to tax the patience of the judge. Finally, it appeared as if the prosecutor had moved to his climax.

"Now, I would like you to take your time, Mr. Seifer, because this is very important, at least to me."

"I wish you would let *me* know what's so important, quite frankly," said the judge in an exasperated tone, as it was evident to him and most everyone else in the room that as a handwriting expert, I had indeed established that Rosati had signed numerous documents in Rhode Island during the days, weeks, and months surrounding the time of the murder. The judge was also aware that if there had been a real contention about the genuineness of the signatures, then White would have put on his own expert to refute the findings.

"Your Honor," White said, "I would suggest to the court after a few more questions it will become quite evident why it is very important."

His exasperated tone unchanged, the judge replied, "All right, proceed."

After another exhaustive review, White proceeded to reveal that he had uncovered an endorsement on the back of an October 10 check that I had overlooked. The check was endorsed with the name Steven Rosati instead of Stephen Rosati. The handwriting, however, was, without a doubt, the same. Every key feature matched. It was an astute discovery by the prosecutor, but in my opinion it was Stephen's signature, and that point was certainly clear to the judge, who poked fun at White when he said, "I don't want to spend eight years on this case."

Ignoring the editorial comment, White continued, noting that I had grouped the gasoline credit card signatures as a different style than the check endorsements.

"So you entered your scientific analysis with an assumption and a presumption that the credit card slips and the others were written by Stephen Rosati?"

"No."

"Isn't that what you said?"

"No, that was my conclusion, not my premise," I countered. "My premise was that because of the different styles, I didn't think Stephen Rosati had signed both groups, so I set out to try and find out whether he did or didn't do it."

"I have just one more question. As to any of the handwritings, is it fair to say that you do not know nor could you offer an opinion about when any of those questioned documents were written?"

"Well, that's a complex question," I said. "I mean the checks are within a series and they are stamped by the bank, but as to exactly when they were signed, I can't tell you exactly when they were signed, no."

The next witness would testify after lunch break.

* * *

Heads turned when Kara Lynx, in toe-arching spiked heels, entered the courtroom. In her quiet slow Southern drawl, she said she was now living in Highland Beach, Florida. She had known Stephen since 1984 and had met him while working as a model.

"We moved in together in June of 1985 down at Lighthouse Point—that's in between Pompano and Deerfield—and then in late December we moved to Quaker Valley Condos in West Warwick, Rhode Island. That was two days before Christmas 1985." She sighed. "I left December 26, 1987."

Cicilline asked Kara if she had been employed when she was in Rhode Island. Kara said she worked at Stephen's gym five days a week and saw Stephen every day, including, of course, weekends.

"Was there ever a time when Stephen was away from you or away from Quaker Valley Condos for any extended period of time?"

"He went fishing one time, and that was it. No."

"Do you remember when that was?"

"Maybe September of '86."

"In the course of the day, apart from seeing him at the East Coast Fitness Center and seeing him at home at night, would you have any other means of communication?"

"Well, phone calls. Sometimes I would call maybe once or twice a day. Sometimes he would call me to check on business."

Cicilline established that on October 7, 1986, with Stephen's help, Kara was able to get her jewelry insured. "And that was while you were living with Stephen?"

"Yes."

"Do you recognize this," Cicilline asked.

"That's my paycheck. Stephen would come back from the office to the gym and hand me my check and it would have his signature."

"Is that your endorsement on the back?"

"Yes."

"Can you tell us the date of the endorsement?"

"October 17, 1986."

Kara testified that she was with Stephen that Sunday, October 12, the day of the murder. She knew this because she was with Stephen every day she was in Rhode Island.

"Do you know where you were on October 15, 1986?"

"Yes. I drove down with Stephen and his mother to New York. We used to go every three or four months to a beauty clinic."

"Do you have any reason to believe that on any occasions when you went to New York that Stephen had just returned from Florida?"

"No."

"Thank you. That is all."

Randy White approached for his cross. "Why did you move out when you moved out?"

"Because," Kara began with a sigh, "we had been engaged for two and a half years, and I decided it was time to move out. I waited until after Christmas. We spent the holidays together and than I moved out."

"Were you getting along in the days, weeks, and months prior to December 26 of '87?" inquired White.

"We had good days. We had bad days. It just wasn't going anywhere."

"Did you ever talk about setting a date for marriage?"

"Yes. We set a date, but we just didn't get married. We put it off."

"Was it in 1986?"

"Yes. It was a very hasty thing. I wanted to get married. He finally said yes. I called his mother and said let's get the invitations today, as I think it was like three months from when we said we were going to. It lasted about a month and a half that we were actually going to be and then we cancelled." Kara glanced wistfully over at her former beau.

"When did the bad days begin?" White snapped.

"Well, there's bad days with every relationship. I don't know when they began."

"Did they go all the way back to the first day you knew him even back in Florida?"

"Yes."

"Do you remember any particular events of significance in the month before you and he left Florida?"

"I don't believe so."

"Do you know whether or not he went to court anywhere in Florida in November of '85."

"I don't recall whether he did or didn't."

"And is it fair to say that in Florida, as in Rhode Island, for the period you lived with him you saw him every day?"

"Yes, I did."

"And you knew his comings and goings every day in Florida?"

"Yes."

"And is it your testimony that he didn't go to court somewhere in Florida in November of '85 or that you don't know."

"Objection," said Cicilline.

"I will let her answer," replied the judge.

"I'm not positive whether he did or didn't."

This was an essential series of questions for the prosecutor, as Randy White himself had some doubts about the case. Kara's sidestepping at this juncture established her in his mind as an unreliable witness. If she could cover up a court appearance, she could cover up a weekend flight to Florida. He changed the subject and went on.

"Did you know whether or not he had any other girlfriends?"

"I had heard rumors. I had no proof. I had no names."

"Ever heard of Ellie?"

"Yes, that was his girlfriend before me."

"Was he ever married to Ellie?"

"Not to my knowledge."

"Did he have contact with Ellie during '85 to '87?"

"Not that I knew of. Now I know he did, but I didn't know at that time."

"Right under your nose and you didn't know it?"

"Yes."

"And after you broke up?"

"I moved to Providence for a short period of time and then moved to Florida, and then I met somebody and got engaged and got married almost right away, so then I stopped all contact."

"When you were living with Stephen in Florida [in 1985] where did he dance?"

"Rosebud's, Bogies. They were discos."

"During that time, I assume that you knew some of his friends?"

"Yes."

"Do you know Cory Franco?" Randy White hammered.

"It doesn't sound familiar."

"Jeffrey Bloom?"

"No."

"Peter Roussonicolos?"

"No."

"Joe Viscido?"

"I don't know if Viscido is just—I'm not sure. I don't know. The name sounds common. I don't know. I'm just trying to be honest. I don't know."

"The name of Viscido sounds common to you?" White's ears perked up three notches. He was unprepared, however, for Kara's response.

"In Rhode Island, they all sound that way," she said. Both Judge Sheehan and Jack Cicilline stifled their smiles, as did half the crowd.

"Are you originally from Rhode Island," White asked.

"No, I'm originally from No' Carolina."

"They do have different names down there," interjected the judge with a friendly grin.

"What was familiar with the name Viscido?" White wanted to know.

"It's just what I said, Viscido. I don't know if it was Resito, or . . ."

"It ends in a vowel?" Judge Sheehan asked innocently, trying to be helpful.

"Right," Kara thanked the judge, batting her eyelashes.

"How about Peter Dallas?" White tried.

"No."

"Michelle Arrieta?"

"No."

Kara recalled that she had seen Stephen again in Florida in December of 1987 at HoJo's beach or she had heard that he had been in Florida. She wasn't quite sure of the date. It might have been 1988.

"Ever heard of the name Pete the Greek?"

"I'm not sure. Oh, I'm not sure."

"Would you acknowledge that Pete the Greek is a rather unusual name?"

"Objection, Your Honor," said Cicilline. "I don't know how long Mr. White has been around, but I know five or six Pete the Greeks. I mean it's a very common name in Rhode Island. Billy the Greek, Pete the Greek."

"I've met a few myself," said the judge.

"Your Honor," White said unhappily, "for the record, my own preference would be to have the witness answer the question. I don't care how many Greeks my brother knows."

"All right. Please, Mr. Cicilline," said the judge, "Don't make any more comments."

"To you, not to Mr. Cicilline, but to you, Kara Lynx, is Pete the Greek an unusual name?"

"I don't know. If I say no, am I wrong? If I say yes, am I—I don't know."

White wanted to know why Kara had given an ambiguous response to the name Pete the Greek when she was so definitive about Cory Franco and Jeff Bloom.

"The only reason is," Kara began, "because of a couple of the newspaper articles, and I heard the name when a girlfriend called me about the articles. I knew that I have heard the name, but only in relationship to this case, not before. I never actually read the article myself. I said, save it for me, I do want to read it, and I never ever got to see the newspaper article."

"I have no more questions," said the prosecutor.

On redirect, Cicilline sought to correct the weakest link in her testimony. "Now, you have indicated [in depositions] that you did know that Stephen was arrested in Florida sometime."

"Right."

"And it was for what charge did you think?"

"Battery or whatever."

"You never went to court with him?"

"No."

"But I take it you were living with him at the time?"

"Yes."

"Was he ever out at any time during the time he was with you?"

"Only when he went salmon fish'n in September of 1986."

"Did he call you when he went fishing?"

"I assume so, because we called each other every day."

"Where would he call you?"

"At home or at work or wherever I was."

Although the prosecutor objected, Cicilline was able to get Kara to look over a Florida newspaper article about Stephen's arrest. "Do you now know why the name Viscido is familiar?" he asked her.

"Yes," she said. "It's throughout the entire article."

On recross, White asked Kara if she knew where she was four years ago on October 12, 1986. She said, "Not the exact day, no."

"And, therefore, you don't know where Carl Stephen Rosati was on October 12, 1986, do you?"

"I know that evening he was home. He was home every evening."

"Why do you remember that evening as opposed to any other evening?"

"Because he never spent a night without me, so, therefore, I have to assume he was home."

"What about when you put the pieces together [about his affair], when he would have seen Ellie?"

"I would assume midday, morning, or early evening. Occasionally he might go out to dinner without me with a friend, but he was home at night."

"Every single night?"

"Every single night."

"During that two-year period?"

"Except for the fishing trip, yes."

"I have no more questions."

The judge turned to Kara to ask one final question. "I take it that while you don't know exactly where you were on October 12, 1986, you know, or do you know, were you in the state of Rhode Island?"

"Yes," Kara said confidently, "I was in Rhode Island."

"All right, thank you. You may step down."

During recess, Randy White took Jack off to the side and said, cordially, "Jack, do you mind if we speak to Kara Lynx alone for a few minutes?"

"You mean without me present?" Jack said matter-of-factly.

"Yes."

"Sure, go ahead." From Cicilline's point of view, since Kara had nothing to hide, why not let them speak to her. "I never had any doubts about Kara's veracity or her ability to stand up to scrutiny." Jack said later on reflection. "I also felt that Randy White might eventually come to believe her and the entire Rosati defense if we willingly exposed them to questioning. Randy White had blinders on. I was just trying to remove them." Jack, thus, could not have foreseen the mean-spirited attack that Kara was subjected to.

Detective Coyote and the two prosecutors, one from Florida and one from Rhode Island, led Miss Lynx downstairs into a small room. There the detective accused Kara of testifying for money and she denied it. He threatened to impugn her reputation if she didn't admit that she was covering for Stephen.

Kara had come a long way to find herself now married to a multimillionaire, and she didn't get there by retreating or by cowering to bullies. Underneath it all, these were just men.

"You can tell my husband anything you want about me," she said, "if it makes you feel better. But that can't change the truth. Stephen is innocent. I slept with him every night. Every night. And I will repeat this at any time in any courtroom, no matter what you say."

"I hope you can sleep well tonight, Miss Lynx," Randy White said.

"I will sleep very well, thank you. Will you, Mr. White?"

CHAPTER 26:
The Hearing: Character Witnesses

Day Three: January 23, 1991

Jack Cicilline brought in the next witness, the real estate agent who sold the condominium to the Rosatis in November 1985, shortly before Stephen and Kara moved in. She testified that she had seen Stephen and Kara at the premises on numerous occasions. Stephen's next-door neighbor supported this contention. On cross-examination, White asked the witnesses if they knew where Stephen was in October 1986. Neither of them could be sure.

The Rosatis' former bookkeeper, Mrs. Salvadoro, came next. She had a soft spot for Stephen in part because her son, Johnny, had been one of Stephen's old high school wrestling buddies.

"I have known Stephen since he was about fifteen," Mrs. Salvadoro said, a touch of pride to her voice. "He had his own little business, the East Coast Gym, and he also was in the Rosati Insurance Business and worked as a vice president of Pine Hill Estates, which was one of their home building companies. I would make out the checks for Pine Hill, or the gym, and Stephen would come in and sign them. Then I would put them in an envelope, and he would deliver them."

"You personally gave him the checks?" the judge asked.

"Yes," Mrs. Salvadoro said.

"If the check was made out on September 2, I usually would give it to him on that date. Here, for instance, is a check made out to Stephen on October 10 and that was also signed by Stephen and endorsed on the back by Stephen. This was made out to Stephen on the fourteenth and was cashed on the fourteenth. This check was made out on October 17 and cashed by Stephen on October 17."

"Was there ever a time that you mailed a completed check co-signed by Carl the father, or signed by Carl for Stephen, and sent it to Stephen at some other location?"

"No."

White on cross-examination wanted to know if Mrs. Salvadoro was present when the checks were cashed at the bank, and she said she was not.

The next witness was Chris Ianiero. He worked at East Coast Fitness Center from July 1986 until April 1988. Ianiero described his responsibilities as taking care of memberships, sales, and locking up at night. He testified that he saw his boss, Stephen Rosati, "almost every night that I worked—six, seven days a week, depending."

"And how were you paid?" asked Cicilline.

"By check on Fridays. Stephen would come in usually for his workout, and while he was there, he would make out all the checks for everyone."

"You personally would receive your check from him?"

"Yes."

"Was there ever a time that you received a check from anyone else?"

"No."

"Concerning enrollments, this receipt made out to Ed Flanagan [in Rosati's handwriting] has the date [of Saturday] October 11. Were receipts dated the same date that the person made the payment?"

"Yes."

"Here's your paycheck for Friday, October 10. Who was it given to you by?"

"Stephen Rosati."

"Any question in your mind?"

"No."

"That's all," said Cicilline.

Jacqueline Pallazzo was called to testify. In 1986, Jackie was a hairdresser in training at Costins in the Airport Plaza, where the fitness center was located. Because she had signed up for a special $99 yearly membership, she remembered the date of this payment, which turned out to be October 12, 1986, the day of the murder. To her recollection, Stephen and Kara were present when the payment was made.

On cross-examination, White asked why she believed she saw Stephen and Kara there that Sunday.

"Because every time I worked out I would see them there."

"Okay," said White. "You don't have any specific recollection of seeing Stephen Rosati there on the day you got that receipt then, do you?"

"No," Jackie conceded, but she still thought Stephen and Kara were there that day.

George Hanrahan took the stand. A jocular fellow, Hanrahan was the financial controller and general office manager for the Rosati Group. He was responsible for the day-to-day financial aspects of the company. Hanrahan verified that Stephen signed numerous checks as a matter of business, specifically on October 8, 9, 14, and 17 of 1986 for Pine Hill Estates. On cross-examination, White asked Hanrahan who had keys to the office. Hanrahan said that he and two girls who worked at the office held keys, along with Carl, Stephen, and Esther Rosati.

"Did Kara Lynx have a key to the office?"

"I have no knowledge of whether she did or did not have a key to the office."

"On October 16, 1986, at 9:04 p.m., there was a twenty-two-minute-long telephone call made to Fort Lauderdale, Florida, billed at $5.39. Did you make that call?" White jabbed.

"No."

"Do you know who did?"

"No."

"On Saturday, October 18, 1986, at 4:04 p.m., there was another four-minute call to Fort Lauderdale. Did you make that call?"

"No."

With that series of questions, White succinctly established that numerous people had access to the telephone in the off hours. He further was able to confirm that Hanrahan did not see Stephen during the weekends or on holidays.

Nevertheless, Hanrahan concluded by saying, "I can say on the stand, under oath, that there was no block of time during that part of my employment when Stephen was unavailable to me."

CHAPTER 27:
The Hearing: Stephen's Evidence

Day Four: January 24, 1991

Frank Joseph Carbone, owner of a plumbing supply corporation, had known Stephen since they were teenagers. Carbone took care of East Coast Fitness Center and also supplied the plumbing for houses Stephen was building. For 1986, his billing records indicated he worked for Stephen on October 2, 7, and 28. He also said he would run into Rosati whenever he picked up his checks.

On cross-examination, White wanted to know how Carbone knew, for instance, that he had seen Stephen on October 2, 1986.

"Because it put me in a bind that day. There was an emergency. The hot water heater let go at East Coast, and I was up in Cumberland. Carl paged me, and I had to get to the gym to replace the heater, and Stephen was there. The invoice tells me it was October 2."

On redirect, Cicilline asked if Carbone was certain that Stephen was in Rhode Island on October 2, 7, and 28, 1986, and Carbone said that he was certain.

Stephen's brother-in-law, Bruce Benkhart, was sworn in. As a person with computer experience, he testified that it was he who had created a file of Stephen's activities for the days, weeks, and months surrounding the time of the murder. It was literally a daily log with almost no days missing. Days that Stephen signed checks and gasoline credit card receipts were listed accordingly, and for the two days surrounding the murder—Sunday, October 12, and Columbus Day, October 13—phone calls were logged in from the office to Woonsocket and to a dating service. Benkhart testified that he had created the file from original documents he had found in folders containing the business records.

On cross-examination, Benkhart said, "Certainly what we were trying to demonstrate by Mr. Cicilline's instructions—and it only made sense—was not to just focus on October 12 but to collect information surrounding that date to prove his whereabouts. He was living here. We all knew that."

By the judge's inference and the tenor of the testimony, the defense had clearly established that Rosati had been a full-time resident of Rhode Island throughout 1986, including the month of October. This contradicted the thrust of the prosecution's initial case that Stephen was *living* in Florida for that period. The prosecutor, however, was unfazed. In today's jet age, a person could be in three cities in one day. The defense had established nothing ironclad for Sunday night, October 12, and that was the bottom line.

Esther Rosati began to collect a growing file of the many newspaper articles on the case. Combining that information with the discovery, she sensed a danger and informed Jack that the father of the dead man was someone to look out for. Articles with titles like "Dad Helps Indict 3 in Son's Murder," "Devoted Dad Hunts Down Son's Slayers," and "Father's Inquiry Leads to Arrests" ran in such papers as the *Miami Herald*, the *Boston Globe* and the *New York Times*. Mr. Viscido, Sr., was making it perfectly clear that he wanted the three men he believed to be responsible for his son's death—Peter Dallas, Peter Roussonicolos, and Stephen Rosati—to pay for the crime with their own lives as well.

CHAPTER 28:
Winter of Discontent

In the autumn when he was first arrested, Stephen was able to work out in the yard with his precious weights, but in the new mod in the winter, it was a very different story. I asked Stephen to describe the experience.

"It's as tough as it appears in the movies," Stephen said. "Picture a group of totally dejected men rammed together in close quarters, behind bars for a lifetime. It's a primitive world of domination. Everything depends on pull with the guards. They are the ones with the real power, and your link to them creates your power base.

"Late at night, guys used to whisper under Johnny Vay's door."

"Why'd you do it, Johnny?" someone would yell.

"What do you mean?" he'd reply. He was incarcerated for patricide.

"What'd you kill your old man for and stuff him in a pipe at the airport?"

"Other guys would think nothing of bashing your head in before breakfast. There were a lot of nuts in there. I saw this shit everyday, and some of the guards you also had to stay clear of." Rosati revealed that the quickest way to get in trouble was to curse and talk back.

"That would be the first step to get a guard to start busting your balls," and it was worth a two-nighter in segregation; that is, solitary confinement. If a prisoner was too slow getting back to his cell, another two-nighter. "You're going to seg," was all he had to say, and then the prisoner would be placed before a board, which consisted of three or four guards. They were the judges. "It was a big joke."

"If some guy upped the ante, a bunch of the jail keepers would come into a cell like storm troopers and beat the shit out of him and then throw him into seg." If a guard pressed the red button on his belt and yelled "X-rays," ten or more other guards would come flying in and break a few bones, and the prisoners had to go up to the infirmary for X-rays. "After that, they'd all laugh. This was common. You had no rights in there. If some guy was stupid enough to ask for a beating, he'd get one."

In general, Rosati did not think the guards really wanted to do this, but he saw it as a way for some of them to blow off steam, to maintain control, to exercise their power.

"I'm telling you this for the record. But personally, I can't say anything bad about the guards, because they treated me fine."

"Steve," they'd say, "you're one of the few guys in here that's not a scumbag. You're okay. If there's anything we can do . . ."

Rosati's case was on TV almost every day, and the other inmates would call him a movie star. It was a front-page murder mystery that ran for months, and at the end of the line, the prisoner was facing the electric chair. Since there was no death penalty in Rhode Island, this extradition hearing put Stephen Rosati in an entirely different category. On top of that, he had a high-profile family, money, and muscles, and he also had beautiful girls coming to visit him. He was Italian, he had private investigators working for him, and he had Jack Cicilline. All of that gave him a level of respect not only from the inmates but also from the guards. Because he was somebody, Rosati became one of the most powerful guys in the Intake Center. He would deny at every opportunity any involvement with the Mob, but that only seemed to verify to the people in the prison that he was connected.

Stephen likened prison food to something you would find at a sleazy bus terminal. A simple breakfast like bacon and eggs came only one or two times a month. Once in a while, if the prisoners were lucky, they might catch a meal with macaroni and cheese and a salad, but most nights the food was "just tasteless." According to Stephen, Friday dinners were the worst: "fried fish patties, sliced cardboard potatoes out of a bag, and flavorless carrots and peas," but they all ate the food because it "filled the hole." About the meager portions, the guards would say, "If the prisoners give you trouble, they're not going to be so strong."

For some of the inmates, these meals were seen as three squares a day, but this diet was a drastic change for Rosati, and his stomach was having trouble taking it. He began to get sick, and he felt himself getting weaker. He told one of the guards who he had known from East Coast Fitness Center that he was always hungry, and the guard asked if he wanted work in the kitchen. Rosati jumped at the chance.

For the first three weeks, he washed dishes but then graduated to working the line, putting food on trays, and then counting trays and silverware.

"Since I could count, I was considered a genius."

Now he had time in the kitchen. Thus, he was able to prepare omelets with green peppers and onions, and he also had cereal. The guards would let him eat as much as he wanted. Very aware of nutrition, Rosati stayed away from fatty foods. He drained the hamburger patties on paper towels and ate fruit and vegetables whenever he had the chance. In this way, he was able to maintain his size, but a lot of the guys lost weight. Without real food, it played on their heads, and this kept some of them more depressed than they would have normally been, even in prison.

Stephen recalled that he always addressed the guards as "officer" and always treated everyone, guard or prisoner, with respect.

"If you treat others with respect, then they will treat you with respect. In numerous little ways, I did what I could to make the guards look good, then they would do what they could for me. In this way, I never had a problem and essentially operated the same way with the inmates. As I had never taken orders from anyone before in my life, this was a radical change. When I was in our office, I had secretaries, and when I was out in the field building houses, I had entire crews working under me. Now I had to do whatever I was told, such as bend over and lift my balls for a strip search after every visit."

After a month, if you had the money, you were able to order a TV, so Rosati had one in his cell, and that's how he learned a lot about his case.

"I would see it on TV even before my parents or Cicilline told me anything. We also got paid every week with a pack of cigarettes. At first, I used them just to barter with, but after a short time, I began to smoke, even though I was not a smoker. Unfortunately, this habit has stayed with me, and I still smoke three or four cigarettes everyday."

Prisoners at the ACI were allowed up to five visits between 12:30 and 2:00 p.m., two or three times per week, with the days fluctuating seemingly on a random basis. Within a day after Rosati was arrested, his girlfriend, Suzanne, had already seen his arrest papers because her mother worked in one of the courthouses.

"It was illegal, but that's Rhode Island for you. She came on a regular basis for the first two months, but I he could see that doubt had entered her mind. Studying law, she was in a difficult position, but she was also jealous, as she was far from the only girl who visited me. Laurie Peroti, my neighbor from the apartment complex, came almost every day. From time to time, Mary Ann, my first girlfriend from high school, also stopped by. This meant that sometimes Suzanne had to sit around a table with two other girls I still maintained relationships with. She got pissed, and by Thanksgiving she disappeared, never to return. I think she went back to her old boyfriend. I have to admit, I looked forward mostly to Laurie's visits, as she was a real friend. Suzanne, no doubt, sensed this.

"Every visiting day Laurie came, and we would be able to hug once at the beginning, hold hands during her stay, and kiss and hug once at the end. I was not really one for smuggling in contraband, but this kiss at the end usually was the best way for the guys who wanted to snort or do some grass to get some into their cell. Wrapped in a plastic balloon, transferred from one mouth to another, and then swallowed, the shit would be thrown up shortly after going back to the cell. Getting stoned was never really a problem for those who wanted or needed to escape into fantasy, at least for a few hours here and there during the week."

Other visitors, aside from Stephen's parents and sister, included Frank Carbone, a plumber who worked for the Rosati Group; George Hanrahan, the controller for their company; Carlyn's husband, Bruce, a number of Stephen's friends and cousins; and his mother's brother, Uncle Al. For the first four months, Rosati's grandmother didn't even know he was in jail until Stephen called her.

Stephen remembered some of the others who visited him at ACI. "My old wrestling buddy, Johnny Salvadoro, stopped by, in part because his mother worked for us as a secretary. She also testified on my behalf, as she co-signed my payroll checks. And then there was Red Gooseberger, my old wrestling coach from Bishop Hendricken. The Goose was the biggest shock, considering how he let me down in such a drastic way when he kicked me off the wrestling team when I was a kid almost ten years earlier."

Red was helping so much with the legwork and would go back and forth to Cicilline's office with all sorts of information to help prepare Stephen's case. He told Rosati's parents that he knew Stephen could never do what he was accused of and that he believed in his innocence. Red was unemployed due to a disability, so he had unlimited time to devote to helping with the case. Consequently, he was in the picture more and more.

Red showing up really wasn't totally out of the blue. Through the years, Stephen had seen him around because he had become involved in real estate. Red had purchased a number of quality lots and had constructed two or three $600,000 homes, which he had sold. Once the market slowed, he didn't have anything to do, so in 1987 or '88, he came to the Rosatis with an offer to buy one of their lots. He had lunch with Esther and Stephen, and he and Rosati talked about old times, about wrestling, and how Red had kicked Rosati off the team. However, Rosati assured him that he would not hold it against him and would not screw him "too bad" if he wanted to buy a lot.

They all laughed about that until Red became serious and said, "You're getting screwed, Stephen. You're father is not feeling well, but don't worry. I'm going to do what your father can't do." Pressing flesh, schmoozing with the local media, and playing the press agent was how Red Gooseberger ultimately helped the Rosatis put the best possible spin on media coverage, given the seriousness of the indictment.

As winter commenced, the walls of the prison began to absorb the cold. Stephen was freezing. Prisoners were getting sick all the time, so Stephen's parents dropped off a lot of clothes, especially socks and long johns, along with a number of books and magazines. Regulations only allowed a certain amount of underwear, sneakers, books and so on, but the guards pretty much overlooked these restrictions, and Stephen was able to get in three different kinds of sneakers, including Reeboks and pump sneakers, as well as bags full of clothes. The question that came up immediately was how much the sneakers cost.

At night, as if it wasn't cold enough, chilly air blew in through a vent in the room. The prisoners were not allowed to block it. Blocking it could get them at least two days in solitary for disobeying orders, but because of the cold, Rosati had no choice. Like some of the other prisoners, he used to soap up the waxy cover of a slick magazine and paste it against the vent. This helped somewhat, but it was still too cold. At night, he would put on three sets of long johns, two pairs of socks, and a cap, and cover himself with a couple of thin blankets that had been provided.

CHAPTER 29:
The Hearing: Stephen Takes the Stand

Day Five: January 25, 1991

Sitting in the front row of the courtroom, surrounded by a dozen cousins and friends, a Bible wedged between them, Carl and Esther looked up at their son with mixed feelings of concern and admiration. As his handcuffs were removed, Rosati readied himself for the stand. Local TV stations and Jim Hummel, the well-known reporter for the *Providence Journal*, were there to cover the action.

Cicilline asked Stephen what his most recent employment was at the time of his arrest and then had Stephen review his work experience. Stephen said that from 1979 until the spring of 1984 he had lived in Rhode Island. He owned and operated East Coast Fitness Center from 1979 until he sold the company in 1986, but was absent from that company for the period of time he was in Florida, which was June of 1984 until Thanksgiving of 1985. Upon his return to Rhode Island, from 1985 until his arrest in September of 1990, he also worked for his father's company, the Carl H. Rosati Jr. Insurance Company, eventually renamed the Rosati Group.

For the year and a half he was in Florida, he lived first with his girlfriend Ellie Vanderpyl while he worked at the Olympiad Health Club. Then he became a dancer for Marc Love's troupe. He said that he danced at Rosebuds in Fort Lauderdale, La Magique, Gee Willikers, Bogie's, and a few other places in the area around Fort Lauderdale and Pompano. He either lived alone or with one of the other dancers. In July of 1985, he moved in with Kara Lynx at Lighthouse Point.

"And how was she employed?" asked Cicilline.

"She used to do many modeling jobs. She made some TV commercials for hot tubs, did fashion shows, and hair shows. She was a leg model for one of the stores in the mall, a lot of little jobs here and there. She was very successful."

"When you were in Florida, did you come to know a person whose name was Peter Roussonicolos?"

"That name is not familiar."

"Pete the Greek?"

"Yes, I knew him from Rosebuds, the nightclub that I worked at. Like other guys, he would buy me drinks because maybe I would introduce him to girls."

"Did you ever go anywhere with Pete the Greek on any occasion?"

"Possibly once, and I saw him pass in the car from time to time."

Cicilline then asked Stephen what type of car he drove in Florida, and he said an Eldorado in 1984 and a black Corvette in 1985. For the crucial year 1986 when Joe Viscido, Jr., was murdered, Stephen described his work as a builder of nearly a dozen homes at Juniper Hills for Pine Hill Estates, one of his father's companies in Rhode Island. He verified that he worked his jobs on a daily basis and was responsible for contacting subcontractors—framers, plumbers, and electricians. He also obtained bids for lumber costs.

"I would compare quotes and get the cheapest price. I would take slips to the office and sign all of the checks, and I also authorized other checks."

"Was the name Joseph Viscido a name that you knew at that time when you were in Florida?"

"No."

Cicilline asked if Stephen knew Peter Dallas, Danny Ek, Jeffrey

Bloom, Cory Franco, or Victor Merriman.

"No, I didn't know those names."

Time that day was short. Stephen would spend five more days in jail before he would finish his testimony and be cross-examined.

CHAPTER 30:
The Hearing: The Corvette

Day Six: January 30, 1991

Reminiscent of an Irish priest from the old days, the judge flowed into the courtroom with his billowing robes and glanced seriously yet somehow benevolently at Carl and Esther Rosati.

"Good morning ladies and gentlemen," the judge said, and then turned to Detective Coyote to ask if the detective's trip back from Florida had been pleasant.

"It was nice and warm down there, sir," said Coyote.

"It's a little warmer up here too."

"Not as warm as down there."

"Wait until Friday, Mr. Coyote," said the judge portentously.

When the small talk was over, Cicilline resumed his questioning of Rosati, who verified that he cashed his various paychecks, such as one on Friday, October 10, 1986, at his bank in Rhode Island.

"And this is my signature on the gasoline credit card where I gassed up at Cowesett Avenue, Route 3, West Warwick, on October 11."

Jack Cicilline then showed Stephen a receipt from Jackie Pallazzo, which was signed by Chris Ianiero, one of the employees at East Coast, on October 12, 1986, the day of the murder.

"Do you recall where you were?"

"As usual, I was in my office. I recall that I was with Kara that day, and Chris Ianiero was present."

"How were you able to remember that?"

"Because that weekend was a special weekend. I was getting ready to purchase an automobile, and I remember going to my friend's body shop to look at the car later that afternoon. I also remember working out at my gym in the morning. I used to work out every Sunday morning."

Stephen then proceeded to verify his signature on forty more checks all during that time period, and Jack Cicilline inquired what the checks were for. He established that they were all linked to business.

"When you lived in Florida, what type of car did you drive?"

"I owned a Corvette."

"Did you ever own a Datsun 280Z?" Cicilline asked.

"Never."

"Can you describe an incident involving the Corvette that occurred in Florida in 1985?"

"I was coming out of one of the nightclubs where I worked, and I turned on to Okeechobee Boulevard heading east. A car was blocking my way, and I could not go around because the traffic was behind me. A man jumped out of his car and reached into mine and tried to pull me out by my collar. I got out and he took a swing at me. I swung back and hit him. He fell to the ground. At that point I got back into my car. The traffic had cleared. I put it in reverse, went around his car, and as I drove away, he fired a shot into the back windshield of my car. The next day I took it to Corvette Associates in Fort Lauderdale to get the car fixed. I dropped it off."

"Were the traces of the gunshot removed?"

"Yes, they were, and I filed an insurance claim to cover the costs. That was in May of 1985."

"There's no question that the car was repaired in May?"

"No question. The car was impeccable. I wouldn't drive it any other way."

"Any bullet hole in the car after that?"

"Never."

"And do you remember who you sold the car to?"

"Josh Essex," Stephen replied.

Cicilline moved to establish Stephen's residence in Rhode Island. "During the time that you lived with Kara Lynx was there ever a night that she wasn't home?"

Rosati said that except for one or two nights when Kara visited her sister in New Jersey, she was home every night.

"Why did you move to Florida in 1988?" Jack was referring to a time two years after the murder.

"Because building had slowed down here. All my houses were completed. I had gone down to Florida on vacation and met a friend who was a land developer, and he asked if I was interested in working with him down there. So I moved to Florida in November of 1988 until May of 1989."

Cicilline had Rosati verify photos of a fishing trip Stephen had taken with some friends in September of '86. Then he showed Rosati a gasoline credit card receipt for October 15, 1986. Stephen verified that he had driven to New York that October day to bring Kara and Esther down for beauty treatments.

"So you know where you were on October 15, 1986. Do you know where you were on October 11, that Saturday?"

"Yes. I know I bought gas that day at Green Airport, when I picked up my sister and her husband. They were coming in from Europe. I took them to my parents' house."

"So you are certain that you were in Rhode Island on October 11?"

"Yes."

"How about October 12, 1986. Do you recall where you were on that date?"

"Yes, I was here in Rhode Island."

"Is there any question in your mind?"

"There's no question in my mind. I remember because I made a call to my ex-girlfriend Ellie Vanderpyl from our offices. She lives in Woonsocket."

"Why did you call from the office?"

"Because Kara was at my home."

"And do you have a specific recollection of speaking to her on that date?"

"Yes, I do. And I called her the following day, October 13, also from the office, in the morning."

The phone records showed the calls to Woonsocket—one at 2:20 p.m., Sunday, October 12, 1986, for twenty minutes, and another at 10:19 a.m., Monday, October 13, 1986, for twenty minutes. Phone records also established that Stephen called Ellie from his office on August 8 and October 27 of the same year, thereby establishing a pattern.

"Do you recognize this October 16 call to Fort Lauderdale?"

"Yes, that was Bob LeVine's phone number at his Oceanside Gym, Kara's ex-boyfriend. She used to call Bob because she had owned a dog before we came up to Rhode Island, and when we left, she gave the dog to Bob. Kara liked to call now and then to check up on the dog and also to say hello."

"Is there any question in your mind that you were in the state of Rhode Island on October 11, 12, and 13 of 1986?"

"I was definitely here. I picked up my sister at the airport on the eleventh and called Ellie on the twelfth and the thirteenth. There is no question in my mind at all. I was here."

"Mr. White, I assume you would appreciate a recess for lunch before you prepare your cross?" asked the judge.

White said he would, and court recessed until 2:00 p.m.

CHAPTER 31:
The Lynx

Seeing Kara up on the stand, holding her own and fighting to protect Stephen, made him think how sad it all was and what he almost had. What he did have. It had been just three months after he began dancing with the Men in Motion that he met her. In one of his vain moods, he was stalking the beach at HoJo's Lauderdale by the Sea. Feeling great, he found himself singing "I'm Huge (And the Babes Go Wild)," by Stevie Smith and the Nakeds, as he dug the scene. Well aware of his physique, he could feel the gals looking him over. Unlike today, in those days it was unusual to see bodybuilders.

Rosati ogled a blonde perched at a bar stool and wearing a tiny bikini before he walked over and introduced himself.

"Hi, I'm Kara Lynx," she responded in a Southern accent.

"Is that your real name?"

"All the guys ask me that. That's my real name. Jeanette Kara Lynx."

"Where you from?"

"No' Carolina. Morehead City, Atlantic Beach. Now I live here in Fort Lauderdale, off Commercial. You're Italian, aren't you? She said in the same Southern drawl.

"Sure am—I'm from Rhode Island."

"My mom always told me to watch out for Italians, especially if they're from the North."

Kara was gorgeous, with an exquisite body and green eyes, and she drove her own Corvette. Poised and sexy, she radiated a vibrancy that stunned any male who looked her way. Underneath the glitz, however, there was a vulnerability that touched Stephen. Kara worked as a model and did all kinds of shows, which provided her with a good living. Having just broken up with her boyfriend, Kara was unattached, and she and Stephen immediately took to each other. Within a month, Stephen told Kara that he was in love with her, and she told him the same.

Rapidly, Rosati curtailed his extracurricular activities and just went back to her place after his night performances. Eventually, he even eliminated the highly lucrative trips to Houston and instead spent all his time with Kara. For months they lived an idyllic existence (mostly!).

"I was her muscle man, and she was my lov'n puppy," said Rosati.

Kara used to time Stephen's trips to and from the club to make sure he was true, and generally he was. But she was bothered about the way he drove her pink Corvette. Stephen claims that he may have been rough, but he was not reckless. However, after a time she wouldn't let him drive it at all. So he decided to get his own. He traded in the Eldorado as a down payment on a new 1985 black Corvette with darkened windows. It cost him $600 a month for two years. He also allowed his Rhode Island license to lapse and ended up getting one in Florida, instead. This would become important to the case when he was eventually arrested.

After four months, Stephen recalled, "I was really cooking. People don't realize, but I had actually become a star in a sense. It was wild. After the New Year, I entered the 1985 Great American Strip Off. My parents came down from Rhode Island, and my mother saw me perform. Since I won the competition in Florida, this allowed me to fly out to California to compete nationally. Arsenio Hall and the actress Edie Adams saw me perform and congratulated me after the show."

Back in Florida, friends from Rhode Island also came down to see him perform at the club. What they saw totally freaked them out. When three of his friends—Paul, Greg, and a guy named Vaccola—came down Vaccola said, "Steve, I can't believe this. You got three hundred women chanting your name. You're the man, Rosati. Get me some girls!"

However, by June 1985, Stephen was ready to think about going home.

"I knew I was just delaying the inevitable. Being a male dancer was not what I wanted to do with my life. It was just a kick that I had just kind of fallen into. I wanted to be a respected businessman, not a stripper."

Stephen realized that most of the guys that performed had nothing else, not even family. This was the best that they could do, although a few were going to college. Some of the guys, like Robin Roth and Slick Nick, were still stripping eight years later.

At that time, Stephen saw some of these guys on *The Phil Donahue Show*. When he saw them interviewed, he smiled because the guys on that show were from his dance team.

"When I was at my peak," Rosati recalled, "which was after my autumn trips to Houston, guys would ask me to go last because there would be no money left after I went out on stage." Using the name Conan, Stephen Rosati was the hottest male dancer in Southern Florida through much of 1985.

In midsummer 1985, Rosati met Pete the Greek at Rosebuds, a quiet club in Fort Lauderdale out on the strip, by the beach. Steve was working the club Thursday nights. Pete was dating one of the waitresses, but he also had his eyes open. He would call Steve over to sit with him, in part because there were always a lot of girls around Rosati that he wanted to meet. He and Rosati also just clicked.

"We got along. Pete told me that he owned a gas station, and as it later turned out, purely by coincidence, I ended up renting a house with Kara out at Lighthouse Point, just a few blocks away from where the station was situated."

Kara kept saying, "Steve, I'm tired of Florida. You have to start making something of yourself. Your father has a good business to go to. We could go up there and maybe get married."

Stephen's father was also telling him on the phone that the real estate market was turning around again and that this would be a good time to return home to earn some "serious money." As the summer wore on, Rosati knew it was just a matter of time before this crazy period would end, but he wasn't quite ready to let it all go. Rosati had heard from some of the fellows that Pete the Greek was a drug dealer, which didn't mean anything to him, because he didn't do drugs. Rosati used to see the Pete the Greek occasionally when he gassed up the car at Pete's station, and they would talk. Once, they had lunch together.

One bizarre incident that stuck out in Rosati's mind occurred when Rosati was getting gas one day at Pete's station and a cop pulled up in his squad car and began to cruise the lot. Pete came out and started screaming at the guy.

"Get the fuck out of here. Get the fuck off my property!"

Rosati was amazed that anyone would speak to a cop that way and get away with it. The cop didn't do a thing and just drove on out.

It was not uncommon for Rosati to be at parties where there would be coke or grass. For people in their mid-twenties or early thirties, drugs were the rule more than the exception. Stephen was a dancer, essentially taking time off before returning to the fold to reclaim his health club and begin his apprenticeship with his father, selling insurance and building homes.

His relationship to the world of drugs in Florida in his own words was "extremely marginal," but even that cursory link would come back to haunt him. One day, by chance, he was having lunch at Bobby Rubino's Chicken Restaurant, and Pete the Greek came in. Since Rosati was alone, Pete came over and joined him. After lunch, he asked for a ride.

"Come on, give me a ride in your car. I have to see this kid [Kit Finch]. It's just up the road. You'll be back in a flash."

"And then I can drive your Porsche?" Stephen kidded.

"Yeah."

So Rosati let him drive the Corvette to the guy's place, and they both went inside where most likely, Pete sold Finch some weed. Rosati knew Finch from the gym where he used to work out, but not by name. This run-of-the-mill, seemingly incidental event would turn out to be pivotal. In fact, it would be the very reason Stephen Rosati would eventually be arrested and have his entire world, and that of his family, be forever turned upside down.

"Finch," Stephen said, "was one of those Florida local-yokel dirt bags, with long grubby hair and what I would call a semi-build. I was in prime shape at that time, just out of competition, and I could see him staring at me at the gym with one of those 'deliverance' looks that said 'get out of my territory.'"

Rosati knew Finch's girlfriend, a stripper who went by the name Tiffany, who was also there and who eyed Rosati, which Finch picked up on.

"I reacted and told him to get out of my face. Well, as it turned out, that was the guy Pete the Greek was going to see. It was just a coincidence. It's hot as hell that day, and I've got my shirt off when we went into the trailer."

As Rosati later found out, Kit Finch not only knew Pete the Greek but he was also the best friend of Joe Viscido, the dead kid. So he told Viscido's father that Stephen Rosati used to hang around with Pete the Greek.

"He was such an incidental character in my life down there that I barely remembered him, but that's essentially how I was linked not only to Pete the Greek but also to a guy I never met who was murdered a year later, 1,500 miles from where I was living," Rosati said.

One night, shortly before Stephen and Kara left Florida for good, a strange incident occurred where Stephen almost lost his life. He had just come out of Bogie's and was driving his Corvette along the boulevard, when two cars pull up rapidly in front of him causing him to almost hit another vehicle.

At the light, Rosati yelled out, "You asshole! What the hell's wrong with you?"

Suddenly, the guys jumped out and one of them pulled Rosati from his car.

"Needless to say, I beat the shit out of him, while the other guy just looked on." Then Stephen got back into his car as this guy's wife yelled, "You're hitting an off-duty policeman."

"He started it," Rosati yelled back as he pulled away.

The ex-cop then reached into his sock, pulled out a revolver, and got off two shots. Going for blood, he knocked out one of Rosati's taillights and also hit the back windshield, completely shattering it. Naturally, Rosati had no choice but to bring the Corvette to an auto body shop, which he did the following morning, and left it there until it was fixed. The shot in the taillight was barely noticeable, but he had that fixed as well.

The cop, who was on probation for allegedly raping a girl during a police call, reported Rosati. He was arrested and placed on six months' probation for assault and given twenty hours of community service.

"The mistake I made was not beating him up enough. I should have knocked him out. He calls the police first, even though he assaults me with a deadly weapon—I think you could call it attempted murder—and I'm the one who gets in trouble! It just goes to show you how unfair the police in Southern Florida can be.

"It was getting to be a pretty rotten scene down there, and my father's phone calls were really coming through. He kept talking about the building business, how I would fit in, and further, I realized that I wanted to get Kara out of there. Once I began to get back on track, in terms of realizing where I knew I was really headed, I started not to enjoy the dancing anymore. It got stale real fast, and all I could see was myself in the same old routines."

About a month before Stephen left the state, he stopped dancing altogether.

"I left Kara in charge of dealing with her business and closing up the house, while I somehow managed to jam everything of mine into the 'vette and drove it to Rhode Island two weeks before Thanksgiving of 1985. Who knew this date would become so important? I bought a condo in Quaker Valley, West Warwick, and moved in to get the place ready for her. Kara followed about two weeks after that, driving up with the furniture. Christmas 1985 we celebrated in Rhode Island."

Upon his return to East Coast Fitness Center, after a lapse of a year and a half, Stephen found Lance driving a new BMW and East Coast generally run to the ground. Stephen asked to see the books and found glaring discrepancies: too much money had been drawn out of the company.

"I could see Lance's plan was to make the place so unappealing that I would want out of my share. But with me holding the mortgage, I clearly had the upper hand."

Once Rosati threatened to have the books looked at by lawyers and a professional accountant, his partners realized they were the ones who would have to leave. Thus, in this manner, Rosati reclaimed East Coast Fitness Center by buying Lance and Gary out for $3,000 each.

Soon after Rosati took back the gym, he cleaned it up and added some new equipment. He then ran a special promotion for yearly memberships for only $99.

"Certainly, Kara facilitated the membership drive. With her looks, she began to sign up new members at a record-setting pace. Trim, tanned, and with one of her colorful tight-fitting workout suits, what can I say? A lot of the guys would sign on just to come down to look at her."

The promotion paid off, and Rosati was able to pay three months' back rent.

CHAPTER 32:
The Hearing: White on Cross

Day Six, Continued: January 30, 1991

"Good afternoon, Mr. Rosati."

"Mr. White, how are you?"

"Fine. Mr. Rosati, you had testified about your activities and travels over the past several years. When did you first go to Florida?"

"I would say in the early summer of 1984."

"How long had you known Ellie Vanderpyl [before you went down to Florida with her]?"

"About ten months."

"Are you older or is she older?"

"I believe that I am older."

"Okay, you're dating for ten months and that didn't come up? You don't know or you can't remember who is older . . . which is it?"

"I believe I am," he repeated.

Already, a perceptible antagonism had developed. Facing the electric chair in Florida, Rosati perceived White as a threat, but he did not display overt signs of hostility. His answers would be on the mark and to the point. From his point of view, he had nothing to hide, but it had already become apparent to him that this prosecutor was trying to load the dice. The goal, he felt, should have been the unveiling of the truth, but that didn't seem to be what was going on. White was even making an issue out of his date of birth and that of his girlfriend.

Rosati reviewed his life once again for the prosecution: his work at East Coast Fitness Center, interest in weight lifting, previous trips to Florida, the possible job he had lined up down there as a carpenter with the Laborer's Union—which fell through—and his decision to move down there with Ellie. He remembered driving his Eldorado to Florida and trading it in sometime in the spring of '85 for a black Corvette and Ellie joining him after about a month to start a job at LaVoguenique. Finally, he reflected on how he had left his job at the Olympiad Health Spa to become a male dancer at various nightclubs.

"Were you employed alone or as part of a dance troupe?"

"We would travel as a group. The main group I was with was called Men in Motion."

"Did you have a stage name other than Carl Stephen Rosati?"

"Conan."

"And was that the only name you . . ."

"I also went by Steve." Stephen then listed the various nightspots he worked at: Rosebuds, La Magique, Gee Willikers, and Bogie's. "If I danced at LaVoguenique, I would see Ellie, because she was a waitress there. We parted on friendly terms, but I haven't spoken to her in years."

Returning to 1985, White had Rosati describe his life with Kara, their move from Lighthouse Point in Florida to Warwick, Rhode Island, in late 1985, so that he could begin building houses with his father, and their breakup in December 1987.

"Then Kara moved to North Providence, and at first we didn't keep in touch, but we did shortly after that because we broke up on very good terms."

"Is it your testimony that between November of 1985 when you came to Rhode Island until November of 1988, that you never left the state of Rhode Island?" asked White. "Excuse me," he corrected himself. "Except for the fishing trip to New York in September of 1986?"

"And the trip to the doctor," the judge corrected.

"There was a gas station in Stonington, Connecticut," Cicilline interjected.

"That's on the way back from New York," Judge Sheehan added. "I realize you have to go through Connecticut to get to Rhode Island from New York."

"I didn't go to Brown, Your Honor," quipped Cicilline.

"I realize that. It's quite obvious," the judge poked back.

The ease of tension was a respite, so the judge let the moment linger. Then he motioned for Stephen to continue.

"After I broke up with Kara," Stephen said, "I used to go skiing in Vermont, and then I spent New Year's Eve of 1987 and 1988 in Florida, and stayed there approximately two weeks."

"Where did you stay in Florida?" White asked.

"Wright by the Sea Motel."

This was the opening that the prosecutor was looking for. His manner changed, and he hit Rosati with a counterstrike. "When you testified at length earlier today, and when Mr. Cicilline was asking questions Friday, you never mentioned the trip to Florida at the beginning of 1988, did you?"

"Objection!" Cicilline shot in. "I didn't ask him."

"I'll allow the question," said the judge.

"As a matter of fact," White said, playing fast and loose, "at one point you said you never left Rhode Island between November '85 and November '88, isn't that right?"

Not expecting double-talk from a member of the attorney general's office, Rosati was stung, "I don't recall," he answered cautiously.

"When did you remember the trip to Florida at the beginning of 1988? When did it dawn on you? Was it last night? Was it over the weekend? Was it today?"

White kept on him. Starting with a false premise, the prosecutor was trying to rattle the witness, to keep him off guard so that the truth might surface. In fact, Stephen Rosati had mentioned the trip to Florida in his testimony to Jack Cicilline, but he had not dated it. He had simply said that he met a land developer while on vacation in Florida, and then he moved down there later in 1988.

"It dawned on me when you asked the question, is that what you are saying?" Stephen asked warily.

"Yes," said White, and then he jumped to May of 1985, when Stephen's car was shot at while he was in Florida. "And am I to understand that your testimony is you don't know who cut you off?"

"Objection," barked Cicilline.

"Ground?" asked the judge.

Cicilline said testily, "No one asked him that either."

"Well, now he's asking."

"Well that's not the issue. The question is argumentative in the way it was asked."

"Your objection is sustained as to form only. Mr. White, ask Mr. Rosati, 'Do you know . . .'"

Rather than acquiesce, White went on the offensive.

"Judge," he retorted, "if I may be heard. We have proceeded endlessly, interminably through countless witnesses. In accordance with my understanding of the proceedings and the inapplicabilities of the rules of evidence, I have simply allowed things [to go] that ordinarily would put one through the roof and now suddenly we're back into a fine toothcomb. I just . . ."

"I only object to questions which suggest something else to the court," Cicilline growled.

The gavel cracked, "Calm down! Everybody, just calm down," spoke the judge.

Carl watched the proceedings with dismay. As the crowd settled back down, he used the moment to whisper to his wife.

"Esther, Randy White has no discernment. He doesn't want the truth. He's just out to hang us."

"I know, Carl," Esther whispered back.

"I will rephrase the question," said White. "Do you know who cut you off in May of 1985?"

"Do I know his name?" asked Rosati, a touch of anger and disgust to his voice.

"Yes," interrupted the judge, trying to put the witness back onto a calmer track.

"No," said Rosati. But in further answers to White's probing, he recounted the incident again to the best of his ability.

"[One guy, an off-duty policeman] was trying to hit me, so I defended myself, and I hit him back. My car was blocked by the other car. I put it in reverse to go back and then go forward, and *boom* my window went out."

White asked if Rosati had ever reported the event to the police, and he hammered him on other details. The judge interrupted, wanting to know why May 1985 was important for understanding what occurred in October 1986. White argued that it was germane to understanding Stephen's whereabouts with respect to the testimony of other witnesses.

"Let's get on with it," said the judge, wondering just which of the two counsels was proceeding endlessly and interminably. "We are spending too much time on side issues." He gave White a stare. "The horse is almost dead now."

White then asked Stephen how he came to have a Florida license in January of 1988 when he was a resident in Rhode Island and just down for a vacation. Stephen said that when he tried to rent a car in Florida, he found out that his license had expired, so he went to the Florida Registration of Motor Vehicles to reactivate his old Florida license.

"I guess it stays on the computer and you can renew it after a certain amount of time, so I renewed it."

"Why did you tell the Florida Registry that you lived in Boynton Beach, Florida?"

"They required a residence in order to get a license, so I gave the address of a friend of mine."

CHAPTER 33:
The Hearing: White on Cross, Continued

Day Seven: January 31, 1991

"Good morning, Mr. Rosati."

"Good morning Mr. White, how are you?"

"When we talked yesterday, you weren't truthful to the Registry of Motor Vehicles in Florida when you told them you lived in Boynton Beach, correct?"

"Objection."

"Overruled."

"No, I had to give [a Florida] address to receive another license."

White hammered away for fifteen minutes more on the license story. Stephen said that he was living in Rhode Island, that he had no Florida permanent residence, and that he just needed a license to drive and to get into nightclubs.

"They check your ID because that's the law. I guess young people drinking and everything, and that's the reason behind it," said Stephen.

"So you were concerned about abiding by the law, right?"

"I was concerned about getting into nightclubs and being able to have my freedom."

Rosati realized that this prosecutor was simply playing games with his head, and he wondered when the prosecutor was going to get around to asking him about October of 1986. It actually took Randy White two days to ask this question.

"Were you ever in Florida in 1986?"

"Never."

"Never, never in Florida in the entire year 1986?"

"Never, Mr. White."

"Now, you heard Miss Lynx testify that for the year 1986 you and she spent every night together. Do you remember her saying that?"

"Correct."

"That's not true, is it?"

"Nor is that statement," corrected the judge. "Miss Lynx mentioned the fishing trip."

"Except for the fishing trip, I don't recall any other times that she spent the night away from me," Stephen replied. "I was so busy that year that I really didn't have time to breathe and went on a fishing trip with Josh. But other than that, I was so busy with the health spa and the building of companies, the only trips I took were to New York. But now that I think of it, I did take a trip with Kara to Mexico, but I don't remember if that was '87 or '86, just so you know."

"And that was during that period when you testified that you didn't have room to breathe, you were working so hard?" White asked.

"Well, let's see, it could have been '87 when I had a little more time on my hands—maybe '87. And now that you reminded me about Kara's sister, I think we drove down to New Jersey sometime to visit her."

White passed right by the crucial days of October 1986 once again to ask Stephen about his moving to Florida two years later between 1988 and '89 when he saw potential opportunities in real estate at that time.

"Did something happen to you just prior to your leaving Florida in the end of May 1989?"

"Yes."

Stephen described in detail the initial incident when Officer Chevy McNeil of the Broward Sheriff's Department came to interrogate him and McNeil told him that he had almost indicted him for murder. He explained how he had told McNeil that he didn't know what he was talking about.

"Was the trip and the visit by the police officers the first time you had ever heard about the murder that they were talking about?" White asked.

"I didn't know what murder they were talking about."

"They didn't tell you when?"

"Nope."

"They didn't tell you where?"

"Nope."

"They didn't tell you how? They didn't say anything except you're lucky—you were almost indicted?"

"Correct."

"And well, you knew, I assume that you had never committed any murder, right?"

"I never committed—of course not."

"Did you ask them what are you talking about?"

"I didn't want to ask them because I knew that I was innocent. Why should I ask about something I don't even—I have nothing to do with? I don't want to know who it is. It's crazy. I thought it was absolutely insane. To this day I know it's insane."

"You know now what murder they are talking about, don't you?"

"Yes."

"When did you first learn the facts of what murder they were alleging?"

"When that fellow right there," Stephen pointed at Detective Coyote, "brought me into the Scituate police barracks."

"Did Detective Coyote ask you anything about the names of people Mr. Cicilline asked you about when you testified here?"

"He asked me names. I don't remember the names. I was completely bowled over by what happened to me. I was overwhelmed with what had been done—that I could ever be brought into a situation like this. That day was confusing and totally overwhelming to say the least. That day my life was taken away from me."

The crowd was moved. White paused before continuing more quietly.

"The names that were mentioned weren't familiar to you?"

"They mentioned some names that I have heard, and they had mentioned other names that I have never heard."

"Does it refresh your memory if I suggest to you that Bobby Coyote asked you first do you know Pete the Greek and you claim that you didn't know Pete the Greek, and then at a later point he asked you whether you knew Pete the Greek, and you said you did know Pete the Greek?"

"I don't recall. That day was very upsetting to me."

After nailing Rosati on this point for several more minutes, White moved on.

"Directing your attention back to October 11, 12, and 13, 1986. Anything striking about those days in your memory?"

"No."

"Nothing? But your testimony was that you remembered who you called, when you called them, when you picked them up, what you did on October 11, 12, and 13, on days that weren't memorable to you?"

"Well, they are memorable to me now because now that this thing has been brought up against me, these false accusations, I can recall back to what has happened because I looked back in my memory to see exactly what was going on in my life. Then I knew I was buying a car. I was in the process of selling my gym. I had been—I trained every day. I knew I was at the health spa everyday. I remember calling Ellie and I remember talking to her, and those things I do remember because I had been accused falsely of such a thing. I have looked back and searched my memory to that day."

After a short recess, White went on.

"Mr. Rosati, do you know that the Broward Sheriff's Office has accused you of murder?"

"From what I understand, yes."

"Okay, and do you know who they claim you killed?"

"Now I do."

"And who is it they claim you killed?"

"A Viscidio [sic]. I found out after I was arrested and put into the ACI." [It should be noted that Stephen always mispronounced Viscido's name with an 'io' ending, suggesting that he had never heard that name before.]

"How did you first meet Pete the Greek?"

Stephen described again their relationship and how they had met by chance one day at a restaurant when Stephen noticed Pete's Porsche.

"He said, 'You want to take a ride with me? I'm going over a friend's or something.' I said, 'Yes, I'm not doing anything.'"

"And when was that?"

"This must have been in September of 1985, but I'm not sure. So we took a ride to some kid's, either a house, or a house trailer type thing."

"You either went in the black Corvette or the Porsche?"

"Correct. There were one or two people there. I don't recall much more than that."

"Do you know Kit Finch?" White asked after conferring with Coyote.

"The name is not familiar."

"Do you know Sweetie Sartucci?"

"The name is not familiar."

"In 1987, do you remember being at Gee Willikers with your dark Mercedes when Pete the Greek was there?"

"It never happened. I didn't have the car down there until 1988, and I never saw Pete the Greek at that time."

"Now, Mr. Rosati, you have testified that the first time you knew any of the details of the accusations against you were when you were arrested in September of 1990, correct?" White asked.

"Right, when I was in prison."

"And you have been in prison ever since, correct?"

"I have been in prison over five months. That's correct."

"And during that time you have had a lot of time to reflect about the date of the murder. How did you go about jogging your memory to testify to the things you did."

After an objection by Cicilline and a discussion about attorney-client privilege, Stephen resumed. He said that he used a combination of his memory and documents to reconstruct his life for October 1986. White wanted to know when Stephen was first living in Florida and how many nights he had spent with Ellie Vanderpyl after they broke up. Stephen said that after they broke up in Florida, he had a fight with Kara. That was early in their relationship. Kara had met Ellie at LaVoguenique and had stormed out.

"Ellie had a little apartment off of Sample Highway going east, near the water. When I used to get into a fight with Kara, I used to see Ellie. Shortly after that, she moved back to Rhode Island."

"Did you ever see Ellie in person in 1986 while you were living with Kara?"

"Yes, and I contacted her when I first returned to Rhode Island from Florida in November of 1985, in the month before Kara came back."

"You talked to her on the phone?"

"Yes."

"How many times?"

"I don't remember."

"Is this a woman that you were talking to with regularity because the fire is still burning, or is this someone you talked to once in a very blue moon?"

"When I had problems with Kara, I would sometimes call Ellie. I picked up the same process that I was using in Florida."

"How do you know with such precision that you called Elodie on October 12, 1986?"

"Because this is the point of my life that I am being accused of falsely, and I have searched and recollected and looked and now I recall, that's how."

"On your own, you recall this?"

"I recall from memory and from documents."

"And what is in your memory that tells you that you called her on October 12, 1986?"

"Because I remember going to the office to make phone calls or to the gym to call Ellie, because Kara would look at the phone bills."

"What was it about this particular phone call that you remember?"

"Well, I remember the call preceding was to a dating service [verified by phone records] and I said, I don't want to do this. I will call Ellie, and I called her. So that's how I remember the call."

"My question," said White, "isn't what answers are provided by documents. You, Stephen Rosati, how do you know you called on October 12, 1986. Something special about October 12?"

"This is the day I have been accused of falsely. I have searched my mind and my soul, and I remember dealing with Ellie during that time and talking with her."

"What did you talk about?"

"I don't remember exactly. Plans to meet or plans to get together, or I miss you. *We got together,* something to that effect. That's what I always talked about with her."

"In a general sense, what makes October 12, 1986, different? What is it that she said or you said in a specific way that draws that conversation in your memory?"

"We were planning to meet."

"This looks like a good time to break," the judge said, checking the clock, thereby interrupting the most important testimony Stephen

Rosati would ever make.

* * *

After lunch, the testimony continued. Rather than continue to dissect Stephen's activities for the day of the murder, curiously, White changed the subject.

"Mr. Rosati, do you know Calvin Fredrick?"

"Yes."

"Friend of yours?"

"Not a friend of mine. He's somebody I met on two occasions in Florida."

Stephen described in a guarded way an incident whereby Fredrick's people took his Corvette in August 1985.

"Isn't it true that you were a middleman in a deal between Fredrick and somebody else?"

"I was not a middleman, no. I introduced Fredrick to a guy at Gee Willikers. The two had set up whatever was going to happen, an exchange of money for drugs, I believe. They liked each other. They thought they could trust each other from what I understand. At that point I was out of it."

"And you would collect a kickback for being involved, right?"

"Gentlemen," the judge interrupted to the defendant's relief, "correct me if I am wrong, but isn't the only issue before the court whether or not the petitioner was in Florida at the time of the alleged offense?" The judge intimated that any other offense, if there was one, should be tried in the state of Florida, "so whether he was in a drug deal or whether he was ripped off is really of no concern to me."

HABEAS CORPUS:
The Great Writ

Latin for "You have the body." Prisoners often seek release by filing a petition for a writ of habeas corpus . . . [a] judicial mandate to a prison official ordering that an inmate be brought to the court so it can be determined whether or not that person is imprisoned lawfully and whether or not he should be released from custody.

In Brown v. Vasquez . . . (9th Cir. 1991) . . . the court observed that the Supreme Court has "recognized the fact that "the writ of habeas corpus is the fundamental instrument for safeguarding individual freedom against arbitrary and lawless state action."

Judge Sheehan called a sidebar. Randy White, the Florida prosecutor Jeffrey Driscoll, and Jack Cicilline approached the bench. White argued that he wanted to continue this line of investigation because it established a lifestyle down in Florida that was consistent with the crime. The judge said that his only concern was the weekend of October 11, 12, and 13 of 1986.

"Well, let's say, and this is just thinking aloud," said the judge. "I want all your responses. Let's say that the phone call on October 12 was made by this petitioner in Rhode Island, and then I'm confronted with the affidavit saying three eyewitnesses and also an alleged accomplice say that he was in Florida on October 12 and then participated in the shooting of the deceased. Is that not a question of fact for Florida and not this court?"

"No," said Jack Cicilline, already prepared for that dilemma. "You have to determine whether or not the evidence that you hear about his presence in Rhode Island is so compelling that you can't say that he was in Florida at that time. If you find that he was in Rhode Island notwithstanding the fact that there may be contradictory evidence of affidavit, if you find notwithstanding that he was in Rhode Island you must grant the writ."

In two sentences, Cicilline had summed up the entire case for the judge. If the evidence was overwhelmingly in favor of Rosati, the judge had every right to rule to block extradition.

"You are going to have to educate me on the law on that. I think that the law is if there's contrary evidence and by way of alibi or whatever presented by the petitioner contrary to what's in the affidavit, I must send him down to Florida."

"No, alibi by itself is insufficient," said Cicilline.

"I know that," said the judge.

"But if that alibi builds up to clear and convincing evidence that he was here, no matter by what name that evidence is called, whether it be alibi or something else, then you have to grant the writ."

"But if the evidence . . ." Randy White began.

"Is merely contradictory, I know," said the judge, "I don't have to. Do you agree with that, Mr. Driscoll?" he asked the Florida prosecutor.

"Yes, Your Honor. That's fine," the quiet man replied.

Cicilline continued his argument. "If that were simply the

standard," he said, "there would be no office of habeas corpus. Habeas corpus [the writ which entitled Rosati to a trial because of unlawful detention] puts you in a situation where you have to make a judgment as to whether or not the affidavit by itself is sufficient to overcome what he has presented as evidence [that his body was present in Rhode Island]." Cicilline made the point that this was the legal issue that needed to be resolved.

"I don't want either side to think that I have made up my mind," said the judge. He thanked the principals and ended the sidebar conference.

White continued obdurately to hammer away about the Fredrick drug rip-off and then asked if Stephen knew Michelle Arrieta, Vic Giordano, Chris Jones, Jeffrey and Skip Bloom, Danny Ek, or Cory Franco.

"No," the witness said after each name.

"Are you sure?"

"I'm so positive that I don't know them," said Rosati.

Shifting gears, White returned to the time surrounding the week of the murder and asked why Kara had cashed her October 10 and October 17 checks on October 20.

"Because she used to save up her checks and have me pay for everything in between."

"It wouldn't have been that she was out of town and couldn't cash the October 10 check?"

"If she was going to go out of town," Rosati responded confidently, "she would have cashed the check because she would have needed the money."

"Do you remember seeing Pete the Greek with Sweetie Sartucci in April of 1987 in your Mercedes at the Brigadoon Apartments in Florida?"

"No, and never heard of her."

"You're saying that you don't remember that, or it didn't happen?" White asked, ending on this tangent.

"I was never in Florida then. That's absurd."

During the break, Cicilline continued to reflect on the police logbook. It was the name Carrie that kept bugging him.

CHAPTER 34:
Slickville

In April 1988, a warrant for the arrest of Peter Dallas was issued. Sergeant McNeil was able to ascertain that Dallas was out on bail in New York and had to return to their court by May 17. The sergeant was thus able to obtain a set of prints and more photographs of his key subject.

During that same month, an unrelated lead came in that linked up to certain key facts and also to the name Carrie, even though this time the name referred to a male instead of a female. Agent Ken Brennan of the Fort Lauderdale office of the Drug Enforcement Agency was a tall, thin man, known in his department as a straight shooter, a cop with "the eagle eye." So impressed was Brennan with this new lead that he called Detectives Chevy McNeil and Jeff Burndt to say he had an informant who told DEA that a Carey or Kerry, along with someone named Jim, committed a drug rip-off that turned into a homicide in a house in the Deerfield Beach area where there were four people.

"This guy see the composites in the papers?" asked Detective McNeil.

"Yeah," Brennan conceded. "But I'm telling you, he's got one helluva story. Fingered the big perp as one Kerry Carbonell, a drug trafficker with numerous arrests since 1980, including armed robbery. And he's big, mid-thirties, 235 pounds, with dark-colored hair, shoulder length, parted in the middle, just like the composite. Sounds on the money."

"So does $10,000 for the reward. Send the pidge over, and if you got a picture of this Carbonell guy, can you shoot me a copy?"

"Will do," Brennan said.

When the informant came to the police station, the detective was skeptical. The gangly man's name was Jay Prince. "Where you from, son?"

"Slickville," the informant said.

"Slickville? You pulling my chain?" the detective asked. "Where the hell's that?"

"Pennsylvania."

"So let's hear your scoop."

"I was in J. W.'s couple of years ago when Kerry Carbonell comes in, sobbing and shit. 'Bad memories,' he keeps crying, as he's brushing his face, like he's got flies or something. Then he told me. He and his buddy whacked some dude in Deerfield in a drug rip. Said that he accused the dead guy of screwing his friend's sister. Told him he was a cop, 'to make it personal.'"

"Okay, and what about this friend?"

"A mean dude, guy's a bodyguard, killed thirty people or more— stone-cold killer type. These guys are part of what we call the zoo crew. They'll steal, rob, shoot, whatever, to get the job done."

"Anybody else know about this?"

"Lunchmeat."

"Who's Lunchmeat?"

"My friend, man, Terry Malone. We go way back, all the way to grade school."

"And where's that?"

"Slickville," Prince said.

"Shoulda known," McNeil said.

Although this lead was contrary to all the evidence Sergeant McNeil was building, he had to pursue it. After Prince picked Kerry Carbonell out of a police photo lineup, it was decided to put a wire on

Prince and have him talk to Lunchmeat to see if he could substantiate the story. Detective Jeff Burndt was put in charge.

Prince called up Malone, and they met at a local restaurant in Lantana. Malone was waiting outside, pacing back and forth like a caged wolf. He gave his buddy a high five when Prince crossed the street.

"What's shaking, dude?" said Prince, his mike relaying the entire conversation to a tape recorder located in a police van just a block away.

"Nothing, man," Malone hedged. "We could turn into liabilities if we know too much about anything."

"Look, Terry, this is a solid contact [with the police], so let's not mess it up because of some bullshit that we didn't even have no part in. Now, I know these motherfuckers did something wrong from the get-go."

"I want this in strict confidence 'cause I got kids."

"I got kids, too. So tell me, who is he?"

"The dude was Kerry's friend that actually pulled the trigger. There's a motherfucker that I don't like."

"Now, let me get this right. This dude that was with Kerry that night is the same guy that offed the nigger in Lauderdale?" Prince asked.

"I think so."

"Fucking little short dude."

"Talks big, but he ain't, you know. He's the kind that liked to hide behind a baseball bat. You know what I mean? He's got backing to do that."

"Oh . . ."

". . . backed by the cops, okay?"

"The plot gets thicker all the time," Prince replied.

"Correct. So, these guys here were doing cops' dirty work because they were eliminating dope scum off the streets. So, now . . . you got a bunch of people drinking out of the same cup. Okay?" Lunchmeat said bobbing his head.

"Right," Prince bobbed back.

They talked for several more minutes until Malone finally revealed Kerry's last name as Carbonell.

"The dude that was with him that actually shot the fucker is James something; they call him Poppa Jim. That's what Kerry calls him, all right? Now, Poppa Jim is about my height, clean shaven, nearly fifty years old, I'd say forty-six, 165–170 pounds, all right?"

Detective Burndt turned off the tape and turned to Sergeant McNeil expectantly.

"Poppa Jim, 170 pounds?" Detective McNeil said. "I listened to this tape to hear about a guy who's 170 pounds and fifty years old, and you want to link him to the little guy?"

"I know, I know, but some of this fits. This guy Kerry, he's big, got this name that came up, Kerry, and he uses this BSO officer stuff when he pulls the rips."

"All right. We should stick this Kerry Carbonell guy in a lineup and get Giordano up here, and call Michelle."

McNeil wrote in his report, "The subject Carbonell was also placed in photographic lineups and shown to the witnesses Arrieta and Giordano, but they failed to identify him as one of the individuals involved."

Here was a new twist that was quickly sidestepped because of new revelations from a previous witness, Cory Franco. These statements, returned Detective McNeil to his original premise. Cory, we remember, was a fifth wheel at the supposed safe house, a friend just outside of the immediate circle surrounding the Bloom brothers that included Jeff and Skip Bloom, Danny Ek, and Peter Dallas. Sidetracked by these new revelations, McNeil never arranged to have Michelle Arrieta or Vic Giordano see the Carbonell photo lineup even though he wrote in the police log that they did. Thus, McNeil's report did not correlate with what actually occurred.[1]

CHAPTER 35:
Back to Geebs

Sweating profusely as he was being interrogated, Cory, also known as Geebs, was terrified of being implicated. He had blabbed his story to just about everyone and he had also had a run-in with Viscido's father, who threatened him with a gun. Now he had to make good, but his rendition could send his buddies on a fast track to the electric chair. The detective made it abundantly clear that if Franco didn't own up, he too would be on that fast track. Geebs grabbed the bottom of his shirt and pulled it up to wipe his face. Sergeant McNeil offered him a glass of water and tried to calm him down.

"I used to work for Joe as a body man on cars," Franco said, "and I hung out at Jeff and Skip Bloom's all the time."

"We know," Sergeant McNeil said. He called in a prosecutor as another witness and swore Geebs in.

"Now, look at this photo lineup. Is there anybody here that you know?"

"Number three, that's Peter Dallas," Franco responded.

"There's no doubt in your mind?"

"That's him."

"And what statement did you hear him make?"

"He said, 'I killed Joe Viscido.'"

Sergeant McNeil was hoping Franco would say, "I wasted Viscido," because that was the term that he had initially used when he was first interviewed.

"But you can't recall the exact words?"

"Um, it's, 'I killed Joe Viscido.' It's 'killed' or 'murdered' him or . . ." Cory stumbled, aiming to please. "He said it to Jeff Bloom."

"Okay. You seem to be having trouble with the words *killed* and *murdered*. Is it another word he used?" The detective stayed with it, hoping.

Franco searched the reaches of his mind and then gave an expression indicating that he thought he now knew what it was. The sergeant's face lit up in anticipation. "It's . . . 'I slaughter' or 'I slaughtered' Joe, or . . ."

The policeman threw a scowl that caused Franco to shift in his seat. "If you remember the exact word, we'll get back to it," the sergeant said in exasperation. "All right. Did you know Peter Dallas was doing things like this?"

"Yeah."

"How did you know that?"

"Because Jeff Bloom told me and said they done it to a bunch of people."

"Done what?"

"Set them up, ripped them off—drugs, cocaine."

"Who's they?"

"Dallas, Pete the Greek, and two of their buddies." Franco related that when these men went out on their heists, they often wore swat-team uniforms. "Dallas drove a station wagon with no doors."

"No doors?"

"No doors, and no trunk or nothing. Pete the Greek drove a white Porsche."

Detective McNeil pushed further, "Did you know anything about a reward?"

"No."

"You never knew that Viscido's father had issued a reward for information on his son's death?"

"No," Franco began, and then corrected himself. "Well, I kinda heard that there might've been a little bit of an award here or there, but I'm not even interested in the money. Just wanna see these guys get, you know, just like to see 'em behind bars."

"Why didn't you tell us about all of this earlier?"

"Cause I'm scared of them. They're maniacs."[1]

It is unlikely that Geebs had any idea how enraged Joe's father was getting because of his statements about the murder. Here was the verbal corroboration Mr. Viscido needed to confirm his now ironclad supposition—namely that Pete the Greek, Stephen Rosati, and Peter Dallas were in on the hit.

Mr. Viscido checked over his weapons and began making his plans for his admitted second attempt on Pete the Greek's life. Due to other outstanding charges, Pete the Greek was often in and out of the courthouse. Viscido fantasized shooting "the snake" right in front of a judge. That would show them. With all this evidence, he just couldn't believe that arrests were not being made. Sure, it was self-destructive, but what was the point of living when his one and only son was six feet under? Abandoned by his wife and completely committed, Mr. Viscido put on another disguise, packed a hidden shoulder holster, and headed to Coconut Creek. Knowing it would be impossible to get past the metal detector, Viscido lay in wait behind a pillar on the steps of the courthouse.

Ever chipper, Pete the Greek strutted up the stairs like a mini don, chumming with his well-known lawyer, Richard Rendina, enemy of the police, friend of the foes.

Containing his rage, Mr. Viscido checked his position as he eyed the policemen waiting to escort the Greek, who appeared confident as he waltzed with his guard toward the entranceway. With heart pounding, Viscido patted his weapon and slid forward, as Pete the Greek disappeared into the foyer. Frustrated at this missed opportunity, Mr. Viscido shoved the gun under the car seat and hightailed it for Detective McNeil's office.[2]

With such raw emotion in his voice, it seemed as if he could explode when he spoke to McNeil. The detective did his best to calm him down.

"We rush this, Joe, and they'll walk. You get what I'm saying?" Detective McNeil reiterated. "We simply need more evidence."

"How much longer are you going to play that tune?" Viscido said in a contained rage. "Bloom may have clammed up, but now I think

I know why; because he was also in on it. I got information that says that Franco will spill the whole beans, confirm what I'm saying. Give me another wire, and I'll pull it out of that son of a bitch. He's already blabbed it all over town."

"Joe, you've got to cool it," the detective cautioned. "You're too upset."

"Then get Franco in here again and nail this thing shut!" Mr. Viscido retorted.

The cops complied and brought Cory in for further questioning.

"So you didn't tell us the whole truth?" Detective McNeil demanded, with tape rolling.

"No, sir. I was scared," Cory Franco began during this third interrogation.

"What is the truth now?" the detective hammered.

"I was outside of Jeff Bloom's house, working on the truck, and Peter Dallas, Pete the Greek, and that big tall guy come in there, and they wanted some cocaine."

"You've identified Pete the Greek and Peter Dallas," McNeil said. "Can you describe the big tall fellow?"

"He was tall, kinda heavy, like the picture," Franco said, establishing that Franco had seen either the composite or other photos of the suspected big guy, thus potentially tainting any future ID of his.

"Can you point him out in the lineup?"

"That's him, No. 4." Cory Franco pointed to Stephen Rosati.

"So, how did it go down?"

"Jeff says he knew where to get coke, so they all pile into Dallas's car with Dallas driving, with Pete the Greek in the front, and Jeff and the big guy in the back. They left around eleven and were back about eleven thirty. But I'm not too sure. It could have been longer."

"Okay. Who stayed behind in the house?"

"Me, Skip Bloom, two girls, and Danny Ek."

"Okay, and then all of these guys came back?"

"Yeah, and they had a bunch of coke, like a pound baggie. The Greek said that he went in—they went in—he, Dallas, and the big guy to get the coke, and I guess Joe went for a gun or something, and Dallas shot him, killed him."

"Dallas said this to you as well?"

"Yes."

"Did Jeff tell you that he was watching through the window and saw this happen?"

"Yes, sir."

"Has anyone prior to the first statement threatened you or told you how to talk to the police about this?"

Thinking quickly, Cory chose not to tell Detective McNeil that Joe's father had threatened him with a gun and had probably also laid out this entire scenario for him. Instead, he said, "Jeff Bloom told me to lie."

"What did Jeff Bloom tell you exactly?"

"He said just go ahead and lie to cover up, to keep him out of it."

"Cory, I'm going to ask you one more time. What are you not telling us?"

"That's all I know."

"There's something else, isn't there? Now's your chance to get it out and it's all over with. Did you have anything to do with ripping him off or killing him?"

"No," Franco said, scared out of his wits.

"Who did?"

Franco stumbled. "Joe Visci . . . Jeff Bloom."

The detective barked, "Who else?"

"Joe Viscido, Pete the Greek, and Dallas and that big fat guy."

"Big fat guy?"

"The big guy."

"Just the big guy?"

"Yeah, the big guy. No. 4," Franco said, referring once again to Stephen Rosati.

"Did Jeff Bloom say that there was anybody else in the apartment?"

"I just heard from Michelle Arrieta that she was in there, and some other . . . another guy and his girlfriend were in there."

"You talked to Michelle yourself?"

"Yes, sir, I did. All she told me was what was going on there that night."

"Tell us what was going on there," Sergeant McNeil hammered. "We need to hear all about this. Don't cover for Michelle. Start from the beginning and tell us the truth."

"She told me that when Pete the Greek and all them came in, Joe went for a gun and they, Dallas, shot—killed Joe."

"Okay, and everything you are telling us is the truth?" Sergeant McNeil asked again.

"Yes."

"You gonna testify?"

"Yes."[3]

CHAPTER 36:
Heartbreak

It was the fall of '85 when Stephen returned to Rhode Island with Kara. Things couldn't have been better. He built four houses in 1986—mainly colonials and raised ranches—while he worked out at East Coast Fitness Center at night. Kara ran the place full time during the day. Rosati's goal was to rebuild the gym, look for potential buyers, and eventually turn a profit on his investment.

At first, Rosati was earning between $35,000 and $40,000 per house. However, by midyear, housing was booming, and their profit margin increased to over $50,000 per home site. Also doing land deals, Stephen lucked out when he purchased a three-acre parcel for $50,000 and peddled it two months later for $170,000.

In October 1986, Rosati sold his Corvette to Josh Essex, the builder who framed his houses, and he bought a diamond blue Mercedes for $42,000, instead. In December, he unloaded the fitness center to Richard Haffner, another bodybuilder, and used the money from that transaction to pay back the note.

"From one Mr. Rhode Island to another, all and all, it was a neat deal," Stephen said.

Once Kara was no longer at the fitness center, she got a job at Filene's makeup counter and also helped Stephen design the interiors of his houses.

Rosati spoke with pride about his time building houses.

"Of course, I was not physically involved in their actual construction and do not even own a hammer. All of this work was subcontracted out. I was the man on top."

Aside from land development, and the newly spun-off fitness center, the Rosatis also had an insurance business tied into the company, so they had income from about four different venues.

"I was a money machine back then," he said, "and earned nearly a quarter of a million in 1986. We were making so much money, I didn't know what to do with it. Kara and I joined Quidnessett Country Club as its youngest members. I don't play golf. We went there just as a social thing, mainly on Saturday nights. I had been up to Louis Boston, an exclusive men's clothing store, and spent about $15,000 on a dozen suits and silk shirts, ties, and pants, and Kara was purchasing $2,000 evening gowns. It seems so shallow now looking back, but that's what I was into back then."

Dressed to the nines and looking like Mr. and Mrs. Adonis, Steve and Kara would glide into Quidnessett and order dinner.

In 1987, the Rosati Group started a large land project right off the interstate highway in Richmond, Rhode Island, and they also built about ten houses in Hopkinton. At that time, these homes were selling in the $175,000 range. Kara would choose the color of the paint, the type of roof, and the interior tile. She also increased the pressure on Stephen to get hitched.

"I didn't come all the way up here not to get married," she'd drawl. Rosati would balk, and then she'd continue. "Steve, I'm gonna set a date, whether you like it or not."

"She was beautiful and everything, but I was the one who had to cook the dinners at night. She was a showgirl, not the type to become a mother or a wife. She was just too vain to want to have children, and that bothered me. On top of that, as pretty as she was, she was too damn insecure and went to a plastic surgeon a number of times to subtract and mainly add a few inches here and there. She even spent $18,000 to have her jaw broken and rewired just to alter it slightly."

A knockout before any of this surgery, according to Stephen, Kara was absolutely paranoid about getting older and not finding some rich guy to take care of her.

"When I get older, you're gonna drop me for some younger dish, so I'm just gonna have to keep myself up," she would say.

"I had to admit, the doctor did a fantastic job," Steve recalled with a smile. "She was still soft and shapely. Nevertheless, you would think that since she was so beautiful before all of this, she wouldn't be so insecure."

Rosati thought it stemmed from her mother, who had become jealous of her when she was a kid growing up and basically kicked her out of the house in her teens for fear that she would seduce her mother's latest flame.

"I give Kara a lot of credit for pushing me in business and helping me stylize the homes," Stephen said, "but her problems were too much for me to deal with. If I was going to get married, I knew that I would want to have kids."

"I'm gonna marry somebody very rich, even if it's not you, Steve," she told him on more than one occasion.

Kara was also exceedingly jealous and would constantly want to know where Rosati was and what he was doing when he wasn't at the building sites.

"She was constantly on my back," Rosati recalled, while at the same time admitting to "having had a fling every now and then. For instance, I saw Elodie a couple of times, but Kara was cheating on me as well, and I knew she was. Friends would tell me, 'Steve, I saw your girl with another guy.' By this means, I found out that she was seeing Derick Bogard and one of the owners of Barry's Disco.

"A stiff dick has no conscience; I couldn't blame the guys. She was the problem. She always wanted money. I was buying her fur coats and rings. I bought her a Samurai Suzuki; she wanted a Porsche. After that request, it wasn't a Porsche I wanted to give her. She was tough, and we would get into some awful fights. For instance, she wasn't a skier, so she wouldn't let me ski. I was being smothered.

"On top of that, she just never figured out Rhode Island. In Florida, nobody knows anybody. The place is too big. There are too many transients. She thought that she could sneak around in Rhode Island like she did before, not realizing that I knew everybody in the whole state. She never understood this.

"She'd come home at five in the morning and then have the nerve to quiz me! To top it off, she'd say, 'You have no right to ask me where I've been.' And she was doing this up until a month before our marriage date."

Stephen finally told her it was over and asked her to move out. "I really loved her, but she was self-destructive," Stephen said. In the beginning, Stephen would go and sleep down at the gym, and then they jointly decided that they would break up after Christmas 1987.

"We bought each other gifts as if we were going to continue forever. I also continued to see her now and again, and she would call me up in the middle of the night. Then she moved up north and became a show gal at the Fuzzy Grape in Webster, Massachusetts. I couldn't go see her and never saw her perform. She had told me that she would never dance for a living, but within a few weeks of our breakup that's where she was, dating guys at the club, making $1,500-plus every week on the tips alone. That's when I decided to go to Florida again, just to get away for a couple of weeks, and traveled back there in January of 1988. In the back of my mind, I also was thinking about doing real estate deals down there, but this trip was mainly to deal with the emotional pain I was in."

Rosati stayed at Wright by the Sea in Highland Beach, which was the hotel that his parents stayed at when they visited him back in '85. He looked up some old friends and went down to Bogie's, where he also performed as Conan for a few nights for a kick, but it had become passé. He had been out of that scene for over two years.

"I was now a successful businessman," he recalled, "nearly a half-million dollars richer than the green kid I was when I left."

To try to forget Kara, Steve went out every night, hitting all the clubs on the strip dressed in his high-class clothes: Joseph's in Fort Lauderdale, Club Boca in Boca Raton, every night a different place. During the day, he went to the beach, worked out lifting weights, and traveled to different properties to check out the possibilities.

At the Holiday Inn in Boca Raton, he met a girl at four in the morning. His cash was in his pocket, but his wallet with his return plane ticket, credit cards, and license were in a man's club bag, which he naively had laid out on the bar.

"Because of the hour, there were only about a dozen people milling about. I thought it would be okay. There was one kid I knew from the old days, Billy Toronado, and I asked him to watch my things as we danced."

When Rosati returned to the bar, Toronado and the guy he was with were gone along with his bag.

"It was stupid, but it was so late. I was drunk, and I knew the fucking guy. That's Florida for you. I found out at the bar that Toronado's friend was named Steven DelBono."

The next day, Rosati drove down to the Delray Police Department with his date and reported the bag stolen. He gave a description of the guys who had taken it and even supplied their names.

When he went to rent a car, he found out that he couldn't because he didn't have a license. But one of Rosati's friends, Jeff Calese, happened to be a Delray cop, so Rosati called him. He said that he would pick Rosati up and take him to the local registry. At the counter, he discovered through the computer that his old Florida license was still good. By that time he had regained his Rhode Island license, but now it was gone, and the lady behind the counter said that all he needed was a Florida residence. He asked Jeff if it would be okay to use his address, and Jeff agreed.

Steve went back to the car agency, rented a black Lincoln Town Car, and returned to the police station to fill out another report. Unable to remember Jeff's address, Rosati used the address of the girl he was with, which was in Boynton Beach. Somehow this got onto the registry computer, so now Stephen Rosati was listed as having two Florida residences. At the same time, he called up the various credit card companies and had his cards canceled.

"I should have done that first," he said, "as there was already $225 charged on my American Express card for Sharper Image."

He also got a replacement for his return plane ticket and returned home soon after.

Throughout 1988, Rosati was still making a lot of money. He had a condo, cars, and another condo in the works. Kara was gone, he was back in Rhode Island, and he felt a new sense of freedom. After dating a lot of other women, he settled on a beautiful girl who lived in Coventry. A girl-next-door type, she would mainly go to nightclubs with him to dance.

In Scituate, with his father's backing, Stephen began building a $450,000 home in Knight Farms, which was in the exclusive development that the Rosatis owned.

"I wanted to change the look of the development," Stephen said, "so I constructed an executive colonial, like ones I had seen in East Greenwich. A mini-mansion, it took awhile before it was sold, so I moved in. I was able to live like a king in a house that overlooked the

Scituate reservoir for much of the rest of the year, as we continued to look for a buyer."

Before the spring, Rosati flew up to Calgary, Canada, with René Legault, a friend who owned Superior Auto Body in Rhode Island. René had bought a place up in Vermont, and he and Steve used to go skiing there. René told Steve about helicopter skiing, so he decided to try it. From Boston they took a plane to Toronto, changed planes to cross the country to Calgary, and went on to Calgary, where they took a car through the breathtaking snow-peaked mountains to Banff National Park. Picked up by a helicopter, they skied at two sites in the Purcells and the Bugaboo Mountain Range.

The guide, a Canadian who spoke with a broken accent, took eight skiers, some who were from Sweden. Fitted with beepers around their necks in case of an avalanche, they all stepped aboard the craft. The helicopter cut through a pass, banked, and then landed on virgin powder. This would be the first time Rosati had ever skied deep powder. It was a warm sunny day, 50–55 degrees. The guide went down first and then signaled each of the skiers to follow one at a time.

"We each plowed through two to three feet of powder up to the knees. The experience of going through it was really indescribable, probably the best experience of my life. Twelve thousand feet up, two or three thousand feet above the tree line, I felt like I could see across the world. Maybe for the first time, I finally realized how small I really was. It was just beautiful. The vastness. It gave me an open feeling, like a dream. I had always dreamed of having a cabin made of all glass overlooking the whole world, and here I was—free."

The following autumn, the market became depressed. Feeling like he was just marking time, Stephen decided once again to return to Florida. But this time he intended to stay until he found a real estate deal. He had spoken it over with his parents, and they kept him on salary. It was their intention for Stephen to keep his eyes open with the hopes of expanding their base. He closed up the Scituate house, put out a spiffy for sale sign, packed his Mercedes, and headed south.

CHAPTER 37:
Vigilante Justice

Kara was working as a dancer for Solid Gold, and she let Stephen stay at her place. It was 1989, and he was back in Florida. The couple had already been apart for four years, and she was now in love with Gary Crane, a scrawny guy whose father was a multimillionaire. Gary owned eight Crane Motor dealerships in New York and Florida, a million-dollar home, a $300,000 condo on the beach, an apartment in Manhattan, and an offshore racing boat, which he renamed *The Kara*. Although he had memberships in two exclusive clubs and had bought a large BMW for his new girlfriend and a Testarossa Ferrari for himself, Crane was already losing his hair at the age of twenty-eight.

"I never went to his house or out on their boat," Stephen said, "but sometimes I would see them at the beach. But she couldn't come over to speak to me, because he would get mad. That was the one edge he had. They got married soon after."

After a week, Rosati moved out of Kara's condo and found an efficiency apartment at the Quality Inn Oceanside in Pompano Beach. During the day the budding tycoon would travel to different potential building sites, and at night he frequented the clubs. One evening, an exotic dancer whose stage name was Taylor came to his table. According to Rosati, the small, green-eyed beauty had a scrumptious body and earnings in the six-figure range. Stephen believed she was attracted to his expensive suits and overall look and was unaware that he had worked in the business himself. They dated for a few weeks before they moved in together in the Lincoln Harbor Apartments in Fort Lauderdale.

The real estate market in southern Florida was difficult because much of it was overbuilt, and there were many condos still available. Thus, there didn't seem to be much point in erecting new properties, and many of the old sites were being revamped. However, after a few weeks of knocking around, things began to click for Rosati.when he met up with Isaac, a wealthy Israeli who was living at an exclusive resort on Turner Island, and Bob McNeil, a point man for a multimillionaire from Texas staying at the Quality Inn Oceanside. McNeil said that if the two of them could tie up a deal, they could flip it to the Israeli and the Texan, who between them had $35 million to invest.

McNeil started to train with Rosati at one of the gyms, and during prime time, they scoured hundred-acre parcels zoned residential, while they kept in touch with their potential backers. With these large areas going for a million or a million five, a reasonable price at that time, the duo came close to finalizing deals on several occasions. Over the next few months, Rosati spent about $7,000 on lawyer's fees and intent-to-buy deals, and he called his father on a regular basis to discuss the potentialities. However, nothing worked out. The real estate business was in a holding pattern. There simply were too many options available in sites that already existed. McNeil decided to close up shop and return to Texas.

It was midmorning, the last week of May 1989, and Stephen had gone seven months without a deal. The summer was coming up, so he decided to pack his gear and head north. Taylor had been dancing in Hawaii and was on her way back, so Stephen decided to wait to say good-bye. However, before she arrived, he heard a pounding at his door.

Two policemen from Broward City Sheriff's Office appeared: a small detective by the name of Chevy McNeil [no relation to Stephen's

192

real estate colleague] and his very large partner, whose name was Hernandez.

"Can we speak to you?" McNeil said.

"Sure."

"We almost had you indicted for murder," the detective announced to the utter amazement of Rosati as they took a seat. "We were going to come to Rhode Island to get you. A buddy of yours was just killed, and we think it was a vigilante who did it."

Thunderstruck, Rosati muttered, "Who?"

"Skip Bloom."

"Who?" Rosati's heart began pounding so loudly he could hardly think.

"A vigilante. Out there," the detective reiterated, "and we think you could be next."

"What?" The young man was overwhelmed. He simply had no idea what they were talking about.

"They said that you were spotted at the scene of a crime. We want you to look at some pictures." They showed Rosati a picture of a crime scene and some other pictures of faces.

Stephen recalled, "My mind was racing so fast, my eyes couldn't focus. Then they started asking me if I knew a bunch of people. 'Do you know such and such?' they would say as they rattled off a list of names I never heard of. Today, years later, I recognize the names because of the litigation, but at the time I had never heard these names. I'll list some of them here for the record, but you have to understand, back then I didn't know who they were: Joe Viscido, Vic Giordano, Michelle Arrieta, Skip Bloom, Jeff Bloom."

They wanted Rosati to go to the police station with them. But if he didn't do anything and didn't know what they were talking about, he saw no reason to go anywhere to give a statement.

"There was no statement to give," Stephen remembered.

"Do you know Pete the Greek?"

"Yeah, I know Pete the Greek. Everybody in Fort Lauderdale knows Pete the Greek. So what?" Rosati replied.

"Steven DelBono and Billy Toronado?"

"Yeah, I know those two assholes," Rosati said, referring to the two men who had stolen his handbag at a nightclub in Florida the last time he had been there.

"Well, we think you could know more. We want you to come to the station and make a statement." To Stephen Rosati, Detective

McNeil sounded like a spider, and he felt like the fly.

"Okay," Rosati replied, agreeing to anything to get them out of his apartment to give him time to think.

Immediately, he called his father. Carl called an attorney, Martin Temkin, an affable man, but not a criminal attorney, and Temkin called Jerome Rosenbloom, a criminal attorney in Florida. Rosenbloom called Detective McNeil and told him that Rosati would not be coming down. If they had any further information, Rosenbloom said to contact him.

"The way I saw it," Rosati recalled, "I wasn't about to go down to a police station in the state of Florida to give a statement when they told me that they almost had me indicted for murder. I was in a panic. I didn't know what the hell was going on. I only knew I wanted to get out of Florida, to my safe haven in Rhode Island."

Stephen's parents flew down, helped him pack his things, and within two days he was back in Rhode Island. Rosenbloom covered a speeding ticket Rosati had outstanding and said, "If they had anything, you would have known about it. They were just on a fishing expedition. Don't worry, I'll tell them that you have moved back to Rhode Island. If they want to reach you, they'll have to go through me."

Before he left, Rosati called the police and told them he wasn't going to the station.

"We're trying to help you," McNeil told him, "so you should try to help us."

There's a vigilante out there, and we think you could be next, kept rattling in Rosati's head like broken glass in a drink mixer.

"I could tell by his voice that he thought I was guilty of something," Stephen recalled. "I reiterated that since I didn't know anything, there was no point in coming to the station. A father of a dead man was on a crusade."

Skip Bloom—who Stephen had never heard of—and his dog were found dead.

"I just wasn't prepared to deal with it. Here I am being charged and almost indicted. At the time, I didn't even know what the word *indicted* meant. I thought that if I went to the police station that they would have arrested me for something totally ridiculous. It was too crazy to give a statement. I thought it best not to say anything."

Rosati took the next flight out and never saw Taylor again.

CHAPTER 38:
The Hearing: Elodie

Day Eight: February 13, 1991

A trim young woman with a frizzy blue-collar perm, wearing a brightly colored short dress, entered the courtroom. It was Stephen's other girlfriend Elodie (Ellie) Vanderpyl, a hairdresser who was now living in Massachusetts. Elodie was an enticing, dark-haired counterbalance to the ravishing blonde Kara.

"I met Stephen in '83 and moved into his parents' house with him for a short while not too long after that. I also lived at my parents' house in Woonsocket," Elodie began after being sworn in.

Cicilline asked if her phone number was the one that was called on October 12 and 13, and she said that it was.

"Tell us about your trip to Florida."

"Sometime in '84, me and Stephen drove down to Florida, and I lived with him there for about five weeks. It was down in the Pompano area. Then I moved out on my own and became a cocktail waitress at LaVoguenique. I stayed in Florida another four months and then moved back to Rhode Island. That's when I began hairdressing school and worked at Armondo's Beauty Salon."

"And after you returned to Rhode Island, when did you see Stephen again?"

"In '86 and '87, I seen him."

"And how often did you see him in 1986?"

"About twice."

"And did you have any other means of communication?"

"Just telephone. He called a few times."

"Both you and he were in Rhode Island?" asked Judge Sheehan.

"Right," said Elodie.

"Did you know that Stephen was having a relationship with Kara Lynx?" Cicilline asked.

"Yes, I did. I had also seen them together."

"I want you to look at this telephone record for October 13, 1986. Can you tell me how long that phone call was for?"

"It says twenty minutes."

"Was there anyone other than you living at your parents' house who had a relationship with Stephen Rosati?"

"No."

"So can you recall whether or not that call was made to you?"

"Yes, it was."

"Is there any doubt in your mind?"

"No."

"Now, referring to this exhibit, which is the phone bill for October 12, 1986, I would ask you to take a moment to look at that. What do you recognize that to be?" Cicilline asked the crucial question.

"Oh, I remember spending the Sunday with Stephen, Sunday night, and he called me the next morning on the thirteenth, I believe it was, because it was Columbus Day weekend. I remember Sunday him calling me. He had gotten into a fight with Kara, and he wanted to get together with me, so we did. We went out, had a few drinks and a bite to eat, and then we went out later on."

"Do you remember specifically that he called you before you went out with him?"

"Yes, and he called me the morning after."

"Can you tell positively that it was October 12 and October 13?"

"I can tell positively."

"With no question in your mind?"

"No question in my mind."

* * *

As White had done with every other witness, he presented the governor's warrant from Florida, which was the first step in sending Stephen Rosati to the electric chair, and opened it up to a photograph at the back. "Who is depicted in this photograph?" he asked.

"Steve, Steve Rosati."

White asked a series of questions concerning the exact months that they drove down to Florida, the type of car Stephen drove, the name of the first apartment complex that they lived in, and so on. After nearly an hour of what seemed like nonessential questions and a series of objections by Cicilline, the judge cut in.

"Where are we going with this?" he asked the prosecutor. "How is this pertinent to the issues before the court; that is, to the material issues in front of me? Was the petitioner in the demanding state at the time of the alleged murder, period? That's all I'm interested in."

"It's not beyond the scope of direct examination. I'm just following the trail that began in 1983," White said unflustered, and then he continued to have Elodie discuss every detail she could remember about her time in Rhode Island when she lived with Stephen and about her five months with him in Florida. White asked if the house in Watch Hill had heat. He asked how many nights in Florida Stephen spent with her after their breakup. She said about two. He asked what month she returned to Rhode Island, and so on.

Finally, he reached a germane point. "Do you know Kara Lynx?"

"Not really. I saw her one night at the club with Stephen."

"Did you ever see Kara and Stephen together in Rhode Island?"

"No."

"How did you know they were together in Rhode Island?"

"Stephen told me. I hadn't seen or heard from him until sometime around 1986, and he called me at my parents' house. He told me that he had moved home with Kara."

White went on. "And when was the first month that you saw him in Rhode Island?"

"In October."

"Did you ever spend a night with him in Rhode Island?"

"No."

"When was the first time that you saw the phone record?"

"Last week, when Fran Martin showed it to me, and I told him what happened."

"Do you know what Stephen is accused of?"

"Yes. I first found out when Lieutenant Martin called me."

"When was the last time you spoke to Stephen before that?"

"In '87, [three years ago] Stephen called me." Her eyes lit up. "He had gotten into a fight with Kara."

"Where did you go on October 12, 1986, with Stephen?"

"To a Chinese restaurant at the Lincoln Mall," she said simply. "I remember I was in school and it was a holiday weekend, and I didn't see Stephen so often, so I remembered. We drove around. I went and seen houses they were building in Warwick."

Intently, White continued, "Did you ever spend a night with him in Rhode Island?"

"Asked and answered," Cicilline interjected.

"No."

"Where was Kara October 12?"

"They had gotten into a disagreement. I don't know where she was. She must have went out with friends or something. I don't know."

White wanted to know how Elodie knew that the phone bill was from 1986, and she said she was certain that it was because she was in hairdressing school at the time, and she remembered the 1986 holiday weekend.

Facing an ironclad alibi, White attempted to suggest that there was more to this story than met the eye.

"Do you remember my asking you if you would be willing to speak with me?" White said, referring to Elodie's previous visit to the court on a day she didn't testify.

"Yes."

"Do you remember what your response was?"

"They told me not to."

"I have no further questions," said Mr. White.

A master of understatement, Cicilline passed on redirect.

"I'm a builder, a framing contractor," the burly Josh Essex said after being sworn in. "I've known Stephen since '85, used to see him at the nightclubs, sports activities. We'd go fishing together, work out at his club. Then I started to work for him."

Josh then testified that during the month of October, he saw Stephen just about every day. He'd come to check the job and make sure everything was going okay. Essex then described the fishing trip that he, Rosati, and two other guys went on in late September. They left on the twenty-seventh of the month.

"Here's a picture of Steve and the other guys," Josh said, examining the photos that Cicilline had laid out for him to review.

Cicilline asked about Essex's purchase of Stephen's Corvette, which coincidentally took place the very weekend of the murder.

"Was there anything unusual about the exterior of the car?"

"No, nothing."

"Bullet holes?"

"No."

"Do you know whether or not you saw him during the holiday weekend at all?"

"Yes. I picked up the car on Thursday or Friday, because I wanted to use the car, you know, before I finally purchased it to make sure it was okay, and then I saw him on Saturday [October 11] at the gym because I used to go every Saturday to work out and I saw him."

"Would you also socialize together?"

"Yeah, we'd go to the Rusty Scupper and to bars at night."

"Was there ever a time in October of 1986 that you became aware, as a result of your relationship with him, that he had left the state to go to Florida?"

"No."

"That's all," Cicilline said, as White stood up for the cross.

White asked if Essex recognized Stephen in some bodybuilding photos, and Essex said that he wasn't sure.

"What time did you see Stephen on Saturday, October 11?" White asked.

"Probably between noon and 1:00 p.m."

"Did you see him on October 12 or 13?"

"No, I didn't. But I saw him on the fourteenth because that is when I returned the car to him. I only had it for the weekend because it still wasn't my car."

"I have no more questions," said White.

"Okay," Cicilline said on redirect. "Why are you so able to remember returning the Corvette on October 14th, the Tuesday after the holiday?"

"I had a date that I promised somebody that I was going to take her in the new car, and I wanted her to see it so she'd know I wasn't bullshitting her. Oh excuse me."

"Father, can you give him dispensation for that," said the Irish judge in brogue. I smile rippled through the crowd.

Cicilline asked for the girls name and showed the witness a final payment check for the car dated October 24, 1986. Essex verified that it was his signature on the back. "Nobody has a signature like me," he said.

Stephen's sister, Carlyn Benkhart, took the stand. She looked over at her kid brother, love welling in her heart, her look triggering a reciprocal feeling in the accused. She said that she had been in Europe working on a photo shoot for William Simon, the secretary of the treasury for the first ten days of October.

"Bruce and I returned to Rhode Island on October 11, changing planes at JFK for Green Airport, and my brother, Stephen Rosati, picked us up and took us home where my mother was babysitting the house. It was sometime in the evening."

The statement caused a pregnant pause throughout the crowd and a perceptible change in the demeanor of the judge. With his eyes looking straight ahead so as not to disrupt the proceedings, Carl whispered to Esther, "Judge Sheehan looks very uncomfortable."

Then Cicilline entered in Carlyn's passport as evidence. The date of entry, October 11, 1986, was stamped in the appropriate place.

On cross-examination, Randy White pointed out that Carlyn was present during the beginning of the proceedings and wanted to know why she had not been sequestered. She said that as soon as she learned that she would be a witness, she sequestered herself. The court agreed that she had not violated the rule. White then asked an endless number of questions about her other trips abroad. He also explored the possibility that Carlyn might have used her father's gas credit cards in 1986, but she said that she hadn't used her father's cards for over ten years.

"I have nothing else," said White.

Carlyn's husband, Bruce Benkhart, was called back to the stand, and he also stated that Stephen had picked up he and Carlyn at the airport October 11, 1986. White wanted to know how he could be so sure, and Benkhart said because it was the only time Stephen had ever picked them up. He further stated that Stephen dropped the couple off at Carlyn's parents' house.

"Esther [Carlyn's mother] was babysitting the house," Benkhart said.

"When you characterized the mission of Esther in your absence in Newport as babysitting, [she was] babysitting a house, not a child, correct?" White asked.

Benkhart said they had a dog. "We talk about babysitting a dog, babysitting a house."

For some curious reason, this term irked the prosecutor. "Had anyone suggested to you in any way, whether anybody else in this hearing had referred to babysitting with respect to the house in Newport?" White grilled.

Benkhart thought about it and agreed that it was very possible that his wife might have also used that term. "If you knew how my wife felt about the dog . . ."

He left the sentence unfinished, which brought a laugh in the courtroom, but this did not deter Mr. White. For some odd reason, he hammered on this term for another twenty-five minutes before letting it go.

Detective Coyote had told Randy White that Rosati was definitely in Florida that same Saturday, the day before the murder. It was a tense moment between the two as White returned to his table. Detective Coyote would intimate that Carlyn was simply lying to protect her brother. "It's the most natural thing a family member can do," he whispered, reassuring White that everything was still on track, but the Rhode Island prosecutor did not dismiss this testimony so easily.

Cicilline's investigator, Fran Martin, was called back. After checking with the airlines, he was able to determine that there were no morning flights into Rhode Island on October 13, 1986, only evening flights. In other words, it would have been essentially impossible for Stephen Rosati to have made a 2:00 p.m. phone call to Elodie on Sunday, October 12, from the Rhode Island office, flown down to Florida, killed Joe Viscido at midnight, hopped back on a nonexistent middle-of-the-night flight to Providence, Boston, or Hartford, and been back to the Rhode Island office by ten the next morning to call Elodie once again. Still, White could speculate that it wasn't impossible. Further, there was no definite proof, other than Elodie's testimony, to the supposition that Stephen Rosati made these phone calls. The defense rested. The next witness, Broward County Sheriff's Detective Bobby Coyote, would be for the prosecution.

* * *

Stephen slept with Kara in their Rhode Island condo like a married couple every night for that entire year, but he did see Elodie on the side that evening. But like every night, he came home at the end of the date, way before midnight.

"We weren't getting along so well," Rosati explained. "Kara was going out on the sly herself, with that guy from Barry's Disco, so I called Elodie from the office to her home in Woonsocket. The phone records place the time at precisely 2:20, and then later I picked Elodie up. It was about 7:30. We drove over to the Lincoln Mall for Chinese food and then went parking. I had my Bronco truck instead of the Corvette because I had lent it to Josh Essex, my framer, who was thinking of buying it."

While I was working on this book, I once asked Rosati why he didn't just tell Randy White on the witness stand that he had cheated on Kara that day, and he told me that the reason he replied the way he did was because Cicilline wanted this to come from Elodie.

"Jack thought that it would be more persuasive," Rosati said.

In retrospect, Cicilline conceded that maybe he could have played it differently and had Stephen reveal his affair with Elodie on the stand, but that might have appeared as collusion. It would have made Stephen look like a philanderer, and so he decided to have Stephen stay silent on this issue.

Randy White argued that Kara could have had a key to the office and could have called Elodie to see if Rosati was going there.

"That was absurd," Stephen countered, "because, number one, she didn't have a key to my office, and number two, she would have called from wherever she was. Unlike me, she had no reason to come to my office to do this."

CHAPTER 39:
The Hearing: The Right of Confrontation

Day Eight, Continued: February 13, 1991

Detective Coyote had been on the case since May 1990. He had read through Chevy McNeil's entire 1,000-plus pages of investigations, had interviewed most, if not all, of the key players, and had generated quite a file himself on follow-up inquiries. The detective was not a man who liked to lose, and he knew how to exploit the system. Coyote's goal was simple: strap Rosati over his saddle and bring him down to Broward County. He knew he was on the winning side. No one beat extradition, especially when half a dozen Florida eyewitnesses, including one of the other perpetrators, placed Rosati at the scene of the crime.

Lanky, easily six feet in height, Detective Sheriff Robert R. Coyote pushed his chair back and stepped toward the witness stand. Unlike the day when the Rosatis first met him, when he came up initially to arrest Stephen, the detective was not adorned in gold chains, and his snake ring was also gone. Rather, he was dressed quite handsomely in a brown suit and displayed a certain rugged charm. With his dirty blonde hair combed back behind his ears and hypnotic stare, the detective walked in a jaunty fashion, with arms and legs moving in slightly different directions. Wiry and composed, his skin was unusually light, given that he lived in a southern state, but appeared a little jaundiced. In his early forties, Detective Coyote couldn't help but emanate the air of a cowpoke.

Vigorously, White launched into the foundation of his case.

"In anticipation of your appearing as a witness, did you complete some charts or illustrative materials to assist the court in understanding your testimony?" the prosecutor inquired.

"Yes, sir," Coyote responded with a touch of pride for this work accomplished. "They're right here in this box."

"May I see them?" asked Cicilline.

"I ask that these be marked for identification," said White routinely.

"Judge," Cicilline barked, surprising the prosecutor and much of the audience, "I object to Your Honor seeing these. I object to their being used."

"I don't know what you are objecting to, Mr. Cicilline, so I can't rule," responded Judge Sheehan.

Cicilline glanced at the opposition and took center stage. "I will tell you. The officer has summarized the testimony that he plans to give on these charts. I know of no system that permits [this kind of] testimony to be submitted to the trier of fact, particularly in the prejudicial way that this material is assembled."

White countered, "Your Honor, if I may be heard. The court will recall a series of exhibits including a summary from a computer printout about some testimony received from Mr. Benkhart that I would submit is in no shape, manner, or form any less or more prejudicial for the purposes of this hearing than the demonstrative evidence that the state submits would be helpful to both Mr. Coyote in putting forward his testimony and the court in understanding it."

"Let me show the court Mr. Coyote's Exhibit 5," said Cicilline.

"You're sure I can look at it now?" teased the judge.

Cicilline began with a flourish, "It's entitled 'Homicide Joseph Viscido.' The second suspect is listed as Carl Stephen Rosati, and this is what it says: 'directed by Roussonicolos to rip-off victim Viscido on the night of the homicide.'" Glaring at White, "I know of no circumstances by which testimony of this nature has ever been permitted into a court of law. I mean this is like a final argument being typed up for the jury to read. Certainly these exhibits could be used by the witness to refresh his memory."

"You can rest assured that they are only in for identification," offered the judge.

"That's what I'm concerned about," continued Cicilline. "I'm also concerned about the press's attention that's beginning to center around this case as to how someone interprets this to be evidence."

"It's not evidence, not as yet anyway," said the judge.

"Then I'm satisfied," said Cicilline.

"Your Honor," White jumped in, "has the court ruled with respect to my being able to assist the witness and the court with these exhibits?"

"I'm not paying any attention to those exhibits. If Sheriff Coyote wants to use them to aid his testimony, fine, but they aren't in evidence; they look like total hearsay from the one I saw."

"Your Honor," White said in equal vigor to Cicilline's counterstroke, "I further [my] argument with respect to Rule 101 (B) 3, which exempts extradition hearings from the rules of evidence. I would ask that these exhibits be marked for identification, and as Detective Coyote discusses them, I would ask that they be presented on the easel and then moved into evidence."

"I object," shot Cicilline.

"Sustained," cracked Sheehan.

"Judge," White continued, unabated, "we are not asking nor would we ever expect the fact finder to accept these lock, stock, and barrel— nor would we expect the fact finder to accept the computerized summary, which was accepted into full evidence lock, stock, and barrel."

"Let me see No. 5 again." Judge Sheehan glared down from on high. "Mr. White, you think I can accept straight hearsay now at this point that there's been an absolute denial by the petitioner? I'm not faulting you, but do you think Sheriff Coyote can stand here and have me accept that Pete the Greek, I can't pronounce his last name anyway, set up a drug rip-off with reference to the victim? How in the world does he know that other than through straight hearsay? What good is that piece of information for me?"

"That will come, Your Honor. He's barely begun to testify."

A long discussion ensued regarding the link between the term "clear and convincing evidence" to "beyond a reasonable doubt," which were seen to be comparable terms.

"As far as I can tell," White canvassed, "the burden remains with the defendant. It's not whether his evidence is clear and convincing. It's whether after hearing ours, you remain clear and convinced. It doesn't matter if ours comes in by affidavit or it comes in through the testimony of—"

"That's where you and I part company," interrupted the judge. "Let us not make the petition for habeas corpus just a sham. After reading Mr. Cicilline's memorandum—and I'm not making a final ruling— but it seems to this court that once there's a denial under oath by the petitioner there must be evidence produced, competent evidence, not affidavit, that can be cross-examined by defense counsel."

"But Rhode Island has never spoken on what Mr. Cicilline would like you to adopt as black letter law, Your Honor. It's not a test of is it live or is it Memorex. This isn't a contest of who can bring in the most witnesses live. I suggest that if we put in the extradition warrant and he put on live testimony, we may well expect to lose because that would create the situation that the court fears, and that might be a sham. [But] we have a witness, and that witness you will hear from will tell you he has personal knowledge from having been involved in the investigation. He will tell you about how he talked to virtually every person on that list. He's empowered to in the state of Florida. He has sworn statements under oath. Notwithstanding the artful arguments that Mr. Cicilline advances, there's no case that stands for the proposition that once live testimony comes in there's a requirement that live testimony must be produced."

The judge continued to disagree, referring to "a precedent case cited by Mr. Cicilline which does indeed raise the point of the need for cross-examination."[1]

"But Detective Coyote would be subject to cross-examination," White said. "He will offer testimony in which he will tell you that several witnesses, including eyewitnesses who were at the scene of the murder on October 12, have given sworn statements through a photographic lineup conducted by Detective Coyote. And he can be cross-examined about that. Then it is up to the court to decide whether he has convinced you. It is clear and it is convincing."[2]

"I understand if there's merely contradictory evidence, he goes back, but I must weigh the credibility of the witnesses," rebutted the judge.

"May I say something?"

"Yes, Mr. Cicilline."

"First of all, based on precedent cases, it seems to me that the use of affidavits would be permissible. But the Supreme Court of this state said in critical areas hearsay is not permitted. I submit that Officer Coyote's testimony about what other people had to say is not competent evidence subject to cross-examination.[3] And since the bulk of officer Coyote's testimony, I expect, is directed to the hearsay statements of others, I don't see any point in proceeding any further until we know what the law is that the state is going to cite to support the admissibility of that testimony."

The judge agreed and called an afternoon recess.[4]

CHAPTER 40:
The Hearing: A Decision

Day Nine: February 19, 1990

The judge began the morning boldly, "Ladies and gentlemen, I am about to make a decision." Catching everyone's eye, Judge Sheehan went on. "It will be a preliminary decision, not a final decision, based on the evidence that I have heard so far. I don't want anyone's hopes high or low because of it. I find after reviewing the evidence that the petitioner has sustained his burden by clear and convincing evidence that he was within the jurisdiction of Rhode Island and not within the jurisdiction of the demanding state at the time and place aforementioned."

The crowd rustled as Esther grabbed Carl's hand and squeezed hard.

Blocking any possibility of an outburst, the judge continued, "I must caution you that this is merely a preliminary finding." He stared at Detective Coyote and then at Randy White. "The state of Florida has a right to rebut, and quite frankly their rebuttal does not have to be that strong."

The judge cited *Galloway v. Josey*, a Florida Supreme Court case, which stated that "the burden then shifts to the state to produce competent evidence discrediting the petitioner's proof to such a degree that it ceases to be clear and convincing. While the court may receive any evidence it deems proper, affidavits and other hearsay not based on firsthand knowledge are insufficient to meet the state's burden on the issue. . . . [However,] I want counsel to understand that this ruling places but little burden upon the demanding state because our decision requires only slight evidence to support a rendition warrant."

Judge Sheehan noted that issuing a warrant in itself would not make the petitioner a fugitive. "I can tell you now," the judge continued, "that Detective Coyote's exhibits will not be introduced in this courtroom unless someone convinces me to the contrary. Mr. Coyote," the judge cautioned, "I remind you that you are still under oath."

"Yes, sir," said Coyote who was back on the stand, forthrightly reaffirming his oath to God. "I received this case from Detective McNeil of Deerfield Beach when the Sheriff's Office took over the police services there. That was in May of 1990."

"Had any arrests been made at that time?" asked White.

"No."

"Did the file contain documents and exhibits from which you were able to ascertain the facts alleged with respect to the death of Joseph Viscido?"

"Yes."

"What did you learn?"

"Objection. Hearsay," said Cicilline.

"I'm going to allow it subject to striking it after cross-examination," said the judge.

Coyote described the murder, the creation of the composite drawings of the killers, his discussions with Detective McNeil, and his questioning of various witnesses, such as Michelle Arrieta.

"She said that . . ."

"Objection."

"Hearsay?" asked the judge.

"Yes, Your Honor," Cicilline said, "on a critical issue."

"I don't know what the issue is. I will hear it."

"She was present at the time Viscido was shot," Cicilline offered.

"I haven't heard that," said the judge.

"I'm offering that to the court," said Cicilline. "I don't think the state disputes that."

"I will hear it subject to striking it," said the judge.

"Michelle indicated to me that she was present at the time the victim was shot. She indicated to me that . . ." continued McNeil's report.

"Objection."

"According to precedent cases, I may accept hearsay, Mr. Cicilline, at least in a limited way, but it's this court's opinion that I can take the testimony and give it no weight if I feel it's just rank hearsay or entertain a motion to strike. I mean, there's no jury here and I will listen to it."

"I understand that," said Cicilline, "and I don't want to belabor this issue. However, from *Morrissey against Brewer*, which our court has adopted, it is indicated that at least in the absence of some extraordinary justification for the absence of the witness being present, hearsay should not be admitted on critical issues. I stand to make these remarks now, in the interest of saving time, that I'm going to be objecting to all his statements concerning what other people told him and that relates to a central part of this case."

Seizing the moment, Cicilline went for the jugular. "They can bring Michelle Arrieta here. They can bring Peter Dallas. They can bring Vic Giordano. They can bring Chris Jones. Those are all the critical witnesses about whom this witness will testify. Particularly in a case of this nature, the state should be required to put before you the kind of credible evidence necessary for them to overcome the clear and convincing standard the petitioner has met. It is for this reason I would object to the detective testifying about what she had to say or what any other witness had to say."

Jack Cicilline had seen manufactured cases before. But, in his opinion, this case took the cake. And if he could get a stab at these witnesses in Rhode Island on his own turf before it all had to go to Florida, so much the better.

Randy White, on the other hand, knew that all he needed was a mere contradiction, barely a minimal creation of reasonable doubt, and so he countered in a comparable manner. White cited four cases that supported his contention that the rules of evidence were not as strict in an extradition proceeding. Nevertheless, the judge said that the defense was still entitled to due process and the right of confrontation. The bickering continued for some time until the judge cut in.

"Let's get to the meat of your case," he said to White.

"Fine," said White, thinking that by the nature of the question he had finally won his point. "I'm simply responding to Your Honor at this point. All the evidence comes in and it's a question of weight, after the facts, as to whether the slight burden placed on the state is met or not. To expedite the process, as Mr. Cicilline suggests, there's a long story to tell, and [if he] objects to every other question . . ."

"Well, if the long story to tell rests solely on what someone told Detective Coyote and not what he discovered himself, then I can tell you right now, I'm not going to extradite him."

White was stunned. Stephen felt himself smiling for the first time in a long time. It seemed clear. If Florida would not bring up a direct eyewitness, he could win this case! The energy in the room shifted.

White wanted it back. "Your Honor," he began, "you will learn, and I'm making an offer of proof now, that there are sworn statements by Mr. Giordano, Mr. Danny Ek, Mr. Jeffrey Bloom, Mr. Cory Franco, Mr. Peter Dallas, Mr. Kit Finch, Mr. Victor Merriman, Mr. Calvin Fredrick, all administered under oath in Florida by this witness, Detective Coyote."

"Where's the right of confrontation?" asked the judge.

"There's no right of confrontation in an extradition hearing. That's fundamental!" said White, finally stating his position succinctly.

"That's where you and I totally disagree," said Sheehan.

"Well, I . . ."

"There's a right of cross-examination."

A short recess was called.

When they returned, Judge Sheehan made no further statement, and Detective Coyote once again took the stand.

"On May 29, 1990," the detective began earnestly, "I showed this Men in Motion photo to Michelle Arrieta. She immediately pointed to [Stephen Rosati] and said, 'That's the guy' who came barging through the victim's door on the night of the murder."

This case was being followed daily by the local news media, and now Jim Hummel, the reporter for the *Providence Journal* had his lead: "Fierce courtroom drama . . . Murder witness identifies Cranston man."

"Other witnesses on the scene were Vic Giordano and Chris Jones. I took a sworn statement from Mr. Giordano on September 3, 1990,"

Detective Coyote said. "This was taped and made into transcript."

Recess for lunch was called. During this time in chambers, the judge read through Giordano's declaration.

In the afternoon session, White moved that Giordano's statement be marked for identification.

"I object, Your Honor," said Cicilline.

"Sustained," said the judge.

"You note my objection to the court's ruling, Your Honor," White replied unhappily.

"So noted."

"Thank you, Your Honor, and I rely on the arguments previously given and what I believe is the overwhelming weight of the authority in the country," said the prosecutor, taking the high ground.

"I understand," Judge Sheehan replied.

White continued his questioning of Coyote. Cicilline objected to hearsay testimony, but Coyote was able to get on record that Giordano had pointed to Rosati in a police lineup.

"Did you in the course of the conversation with Mr. Giordano have occasion to ask him the degree of certainty he had with respect to his selection of the photograph?"

"Objection," said Cicilline.

"I'll allow it," said the judge.

"On a one to ten scale," Coyote stated, "Giordano indicated to me when he looked down at the picture that it sent shivers down his spine, and that he would indicate a ten."

"Move to strike everything but 'he indicated a ten,'" requested Cicilline.

"'Sent shivers down his spine' is not material to this hearing," said the judge.

"Mr. Giordano also identified Peter Dallas the same way, through a photo spread," said Coyote. "I'm almost sure his degree of certainty for Dallas was also a ten. 'Ten seconds, I knew it was him,' Mr. Giordano said. 'He was quieter, didn't do much talking.'"

"Let the record reflect that I have not been furnished with those statements," said Cicilline, knowing he had not read this in the discovery.

Moving in for the kill, White nimbly offered into evidence the photo lineups signed by Giordano, and then asked Detective Coyote, "What did Mr. Giordano say that he observed that night?"

"Objection."

"Sustained."

"Withdraw the question, Your Honor."

Detective Coyote described Jeff Bloom's sworn testimony. Unwavering, he said, "And I showed him a photo lineup, and he chose picture No. 5, and I said, 'who's that?' and he said, 'Steve Rosati.' Bloom indicated that he knew Mr. Rosati before this incident, knew him by name, and that's contained within the statement. His house is about four miles away from Joe Viscido's house. On October 12, 1986, he indicated he was with Steve Rosati, Peter Dallas, and Peter Roussonicolos."

"Also known as Pete the Greek?" asked the judge.

"Yes, sir."

White asked if any other persons were present at the safe house, and Cicilline tried to object, but Detective Coyote put on record that Danny Ek, Skip Bloom, the victim of a homicide, and Cory Franco were also present.

Returning to Jeff Bloom's statement, Detective Coyote said, "Jeff Bloom had originally scouted out Viscido's house to make sure that there was something to rob for Pete the Greek. On the night in question, Steve Rosati left the house with Peter Dallas and Pete the Greek. They left in a small white vehicle with no doors, with Pete the Greek going in a separate vehicle. 'You two guys are going to be going into the house,' Pete the Greek said. 'Rosati, you're first.'"

Coyote related that Skip Bloom got an "eight ball" of cocaine from Pete the Greek a few days earlier and that Stephen Rosati was also present.

"Can we fix that date?" Cicilline grilled.

"That would be the day before," Coyote said firmly.

"The eleventh of October?" asked the judge.

Coyote, who had not been sequestered, speedily responded, "The twelfth. I stand corrected. That would be the twelfth."

"All right," said the judge uncomfortably, as he considered this nimble recalibration.

"There's some testimony earlier by this witness stating that this meeting took place two days before," Cicilline began, "and, Judge, I initially objected to the witness testifying and you said you would admit it subject to a motion to strike, or something to that effect. My position now is that the information on these exhibits are before you, so that you ought to look at all the exhibits, all the sworn statements."

Due to the detailed nature of his cross-examination, which was to follow, Cicilline calculated that, at this juncture, it would be best for the judge to see the various witness affidavits, as their inconsistencies would become apparent when they were matched against the detective's interpretation of their contents.

Coyote's testimony resumed. He said that both Dallas and Rosati were armed when they left Bloom's house on the twelfth. "Bloom indicated that Rosati had an automatic and Dallas had a spinner-type revolver."

After a recess that lasted until the afternoon, White brought up the testimony of Chris Jones, the third direct eyewitness, who had fled to Canada. Coyote testified that Jones had picked Rosati out of a police lineup in June 1988. No proof of this deposition has ever been provided, and such a statement cannot be found in the police logs referring to Chris Jones.

The detective then related that he questioned Danny Ek and Cory Franco. According to Coyote, both said the same thing: Stephen Rosati and Peter Dallas left the Bloom compound that Sunday night in the car with no doors. Pete the Greek left in his Porsche, and all of them returned an hour or two later with cocaine, an automatic weapon, an ominous brown paper bag, and a jacket that looked like one Joe Viscido owned. Both men, he said, also picked Rosati out of a police photo lineup.

Coyote moved to Kit Finch, "who had contacted the father about six weeks after the incident occurred with a description of one or both of the suspects . . ."

"I object to this," said Cicilline. "It's my understanding that Chris Jones, Vic Giordano, and Michelle Arrieta are in the house where the killing takes place, and Cory Franco, Danny Ek, Jeff Bloom, and Skip Bloom are at another house on the same night. Finch is nowhere near these premises, so any identification by Finch is irrelevant, especially if it is based on a description given by Michelle Arrieta. I move to strike the testimony of Kit Finch."

"It may be stricken," said the judge, who had heard about enough anyway.

CHAPTER 41:
The Hearing: Detective Coyote Continued

Day Ten: February 20, 1991: Morning Session

Painting with a broad stroke, Detective Coyote continued his testimony, describing a series of peripheral witnesses who placed Rosati in Florida in 1986, such as Victor Merriman, who had worked with Joe Viscido at his father's car dealership; Calvin Fredrick, who stole Stephen's Corvette when he was ripped off in a drug deal gone bad when Stephen was still living at Lighthouse Point with Kara in Florida; and Sweetie Sartucci, Rob Newman's girlfriend, who gave a party where photos were taken of Peter Dallas and Michelle Arrieta.

According to the detective, Sweetie saw Rosati sometime in the middle of 1986, with his Mercedes, at Gee Willikers and also at the Brigadoon Apartments, where Pete the Greek had lived and where Peter Dallas had been sighted. And so, another hole was punched into Rosati's claim that he had never been in Florida in 1986 (even though

Rosati would not take possession of the Mercedes until several months later).

"Detective Coyote," Mr. White continued, "the name of Peter Dallas has arisen. Did there come a time in the course of your pursuit of this investigation that you were in his presence?"

"Yes, at the Monterey Shock Incarceration Facility near Elmira, New York. I was with my partner, Frank Puccini. We interviewed Mr. Dallas about his personal knowledge of the events of October 12, 1986, in Broward County, Florida."

"Do you recognize this document?"

"Yes," Detective Coyote said solemnly, "This is a transcribed copy of the sworn, taped statement I had taken from Peter Dallas on September 6, 1990. Not only did I swear him in, I also advised him of his rights due to the nature of the questioning. On September 19, 1990, Peter Dallas pled guilty to second-degree murder. He should be sentenced in April.

"Dallas," the detective continued, "had lived at the Blooms' for several weeks prior to the incident. In the photo lineup, he picked up picture No. 5, which he identified as Steve. He indicated that he had left with Carl Stephen Rosati at approximately eleven on that evening en route to Joe Viscido's apartment."

With the crowd in amazement, Cicilline cut in. "Your Honor," he said, "I'm asking that the state be compelled to bring Dallas forward. The court's ruling on that will bear upon my right to confront the witness."

"Mr. White?"

"Your Honor, there's no authority which the state is aware of that there is a requirement on the state's rebuttal for an eyewitness from the demanding state."

"This isn't an eyewitness," said the judge, "this is an accomplice."

"Understood, Your Honor," White countered, spouting six precedent cases, including one by the Supreme Court to support his contention that the defense did not have to have a right of confrontation. The extradition clause, White argued, was to prevent two trials. A precedent will be set to show that "there's a premium on running to Rhode Island, because if you run to Rhode Island, you will also get a trial in Rhode Island, and that simply is not what the extradition clause is about. . . . He's only going back to Florida to be tried there; and there, he will be afforded the constitutional guarantees that arise only in a trial, not in an extradition hearing."

Having spoken for a considerable period unabated, White was interrupted by Cicilline.

"I recognize that the role of the court in an [extradition] hearing is a very limited one. But I submit to you that the testimony you have heard so far is to some extent misleading and on a very critical issue. To permit the [prosecution] to suggest to the court that by requiring the state to produce that witness would make us a haven for outlaws I think does a disjustice not only to this court but to the system generally, and I think, in fact, what we should be more concerned about is the higher interests of whether or not Stephen Rosati is, in fact, a fugitive from justice." Cicilline paused to let his words set in.

"Detective Coyote's testimony from witnesses who he claims have identified this man I think is not credible evidence. Credible evidence would come from someone like Dallas, and I submit that's the way to resolve this case. Bring Dallas here!"

In recognition of the many onlookers, Cicilline whirled, "Bringing him here can restore integrity in the system, because whether the court feels that they play any role or not, all these people who are seated out here are citizens who are expected to maintain respect for this system, and we don't maintain respect when we permit the state willy-nilly to deny the defendant his right to confrontation in this kind of a critical proceeding. There's no reason why they can't bring Dallas here except that they are concerned that that person would not identify this petitioner as his accomplice."

"Your Honor," Randy White retorted, "If I may."

"Be as long as you want." Judge Sheehan sat back.

"Peter Dallas talks freely about his involvement in a killing and robbery."

"Why does he talk freely about it?" asked the judge.

"That's an issue for trial," said White.

"An issue of credibility for me," said Sheehan.

"His credibility, Your Honor, is before the court on a very limited basis. Did he select the petitioner as someone that he saw in Florida?" White asked rhetorically.

"Then why didn't you stop there?" queried the judge, shaking his head. "I don't know how many times I can try to lead you without doing damage to the petitioner. I said that your proof [need be] very limited. You have three eyewitnesses. What more do you want? Now you have created an issue [by insisting that you do not have to bring any one of them here]."

White thought quickly. "Your Honor," he said, "the only issue for resolution before the court is whether the affidavits of Peter Dallas should be admitted."

"No." The judge leaned forward and placed both palms on the bench. "That's not true. Mr. Cicilline made a motion for me to order Mr. Dallas here." He turned to defense counsel. "That's I assume what you are saying?"

"That's what I said, Your Honor," said Cicilline.

Esther squeezed Carl's hand, and they chalked up a point for defense. The judge called a short recess to see White and Cicilline in chambers. Upon their return, the judge announced that Cicilline was willing to defer his motion until after cross-examination of Detective Coyote.

CHAPTER 42:
Tainted Witness

Ten days short of Christmas, 1987, Detective Sergeant Chevy McNeil drove out once again to the Bloom residence to interview Jeff. No one was there, so he left his calling card. McNeil knew who the Bloom boys were. Heck, every cop in Broward County knew how Detective Dustin screwed up royally when he shot the boys' father, Herbie Bloom, in the back two years prior, when Herbie ran out onto the lawn in his underwear in a drug raid—on this same house—when no drugs and no weapons were found.[1] And now his kids were in deep shit. McNeil recorded this trip and their absence in his daily logbook.[2] Upon his return, he was surprised to see a message on his desk to call Hilliard Moldof, the criminal attorney, about these very same Bloom boys.

Moldof said the Bloom boys would be willing to cooperate if they were granted immunity. Reluctantly, McNeil agreed and set up the first of three depositions with Jeff Bloom for January 12, 1988. Chuck

Morton, Broward County's assistant attorney general, was also called in. It would be the first time that any of the witnesses had used a lawyer.

McNeil began by displaying his compilation of photo pack lineups.

"Sure, that's him. That's Peter Dallas," Jeff said as the tape player rolled. Attorney Moldof sat by in silence.

"And this sheet. Do you know anybody here, Mr. Bloom?" McNeil asked.

"There, that's Pete the Greek."

Detective McNeil dutifully wrote in his file, "Pointed out suspects in presence of witnesses without any hesitation."

"The tape is rolling, Mr. Bloom."

Jeff Bloom told the detectives that his brother, Skip, had owed Pete the Greek money and that the Greek had come into their house with a baseball bat and "scared Skip shitless." About the same time, Skip had purchased cocaine from Joe Viscido. This alerted Pete the Greek that there was a possible target for a rip available. Supposedly, Jeff drove Pete the Greek to Joe's apartment a few days before the murder, probably as a way of paying off the debt that his brother owed.

"You're saying Pete the Greek, Peter Dallas, and another guy went to the Viscido house?" the detective asked.

"Peter Dallas didn't have anything to do with that part. He was at my house, and after Joe died, Peter Dallas kept on having coke."

"It wasn't Peter Dallas?" the detective asked.

"No, Peter Dallas was at my house." Jeff spoke in no uncertain terms.

"Did Pete the Greek ever make any admissions to you that he had robbed Joe Viscido and killed him?"

"No, sir."

"Anybody else ever tell you that Pete made such statements?"

"Statements like what?"

"I killed or we killed Joe Viscido," the detective said.

"Peter Dallas said something like that at my house—'Joe's done with', or some shit like that." For the police, this Dallas observation, which was also heard by Cory Franco and Danny Ek, became an admission of guilt.

Bloom then shifted gears to say that Pete the Greek had threatened him.

"Just six weeks ago, I went out to the Greek's truck and saw a gun on the floor. I told him that the police were questioning me about

Viscido's death. 'You just better keep your mouth shut, or you'll be dead too,' he said to me. And then he took out his finger like it was a gun and said, 'Pow.'"

Bloom sat back and received a pat of encouragement from his lawyer. He might have stopped right there, but Jeff was now in the spotlight and protected, no matter what he said. Pissed at Michelle Arrieta for ratting him out to begin with, he just rattled on.

"Michelle told me that Peter Dallas was the trigger man."

This blatant contradiction hit the police like a bombshell. Something was terribly wrong, and McNeil wondered if Michelle could be lying. He shot back. "Are you aware that Michelle was not able to pick Peter Dallas out of a lineup?"

Bloom was stunned by this information. "No."

"Well, what do you make of that?"

Caught in a lie, Bloom decided to do the smart thing and bolster it with an even bolder lie.

"I don't make anything of it," Bloom countered. "Giordano told me that same thing. He said that he was almost sure it was Peter Dallas."

"Mr. Bloom, are you aware that Vic Giordano also did not pick Peter Dallas out of a police photo lineup?"

"What do you want me to say?"

"The truth, Mr. Bloom, the truth."

"I'm telling you the truth."[3]

From this discussion, Detective McNeil negated Bloom's first statements that exonerated Dallas, concluding incorrectly in his signed summary report that "Jeff Bloom did in fact admit that the subject Peter Dallas had made a statement to the effect that while at Bloom's home that he had in fact killed Joe Viscido, Jr. Bloom, however, stated that he could not remember the exact wordage that was used."[4]

The following day, Mr. Viscido came to the precinct with yet another solid source of corroboration in Kit Finch. A self-employed mechanic, Finch spent most of his time either at the gym, his brother's saloon, or at the Bloom apartment. Frequenting strip joints, Finch boasted of having a girlfriend who was a stripper, and he also knew a number of the male dancers. One of Joe Jr.'s closest friends, Kit had helped Mr. Viscido clean up the bloodstained apartment after the murder.

"I want you to look at these composites, Mr. Finch, and tell me if you recognize either of these people," Detective McNeil said.

"The big guy. I know him," Finch reported. "It's Stephen Rosati."

Finch described Rosati and the Greek as tight. "Guy's a bodybuilder, big time, practically lives at the gym. He's got another name, like Conan or something. Dances on the strip with a group called the Men in Motion. They're usually at Rosebuds or Gee Willikers. I think Sweetie Sartucci's boyfriend, Robbie Newman, also said the big guy was Rosati."

Finch described Rosati as six foot or six foot two, 220 pounds, black hair, big shoulders, and twenty-five to thirty years old. "I think he's from New York."

Within a few days of this interview, the intelligence unit of Fort Lauderdale secured a promotional eight-by-ten glossy of the Men in Motion that was three years old. There, standing among five bare-chested studs—dressed in black tights, white suspenders, and formal tuxedo bowties—was the former muscle man Stephen Rosati. The pieces of the puzzle finally began to fall into place.

"Yeah, that's him," Kit Finch said under oath, pointing at Stephen Rosati. "And he's not just a dancing stud. He's known for drug rip-offs too."

"You mean besides Viscido?"

"Shit, yeah. Ripped a guy named Fredrick in a deal down at the Point, and he beat up another guy, I think it was a cop who shot his car or something like that. He and the Greek used to run around in combat fatigues, like they were part of the fucking Mod Squad. Jeff Bloom didn't know him by name, but he knew the big guy that hung around with the Greek with the bullet holes in his car."

"Do you know what kind of car?" McNeil asked.

"Black Corvette."

"Did Rosati ever exhibit any other propensity for violence or carry a gun?"

"He was cocky, you know. Definitely had an attitude, but I personally never saw him carry a gun."

"And when Michelle described the shorter guy?"

"She said he had bug eyes," Finch said, completing McNeil's thought. "That's Peter Dallas. That's what we called him."

"Bug eyes?"

"Bug eyes."

"At any time, did you ever see Rosati and Dallas together?"

"No, sir."

"Let me ask you this, Kit. At any time when you talked to Michelle, did she in any way ever indicate to you that she knew who these people were?"

"No, not really. She never really . . . She acted like she was in a daze, but . . ."

"But what?" McNeil queried.

"These things, they . . . they just don't add up."

"Why's that?"

"Well, it's just . . . a lot of people assume that Peter Dallas was one of the people involved, and it just didn't seem right that he was at Robbie Newman's party with Michelle about a year ago."

"They were together! At a party!" McNeil erupted.

"Yeah. It's all there in the photos. Not too long after Joe was killed. Jeff and Skip Bloom were there too. I don't even know if Michelle knew who Dallas was."

"You saw pictures?"

"Sure, Sweetie has them."

Armed with these new leads, Detective McNeil swung by Rosebuds, one of the more famous strip joints where Rosati was known to have danced. The manager was less than cooperative. However, he did paint a picture of Stephen Rosati as "an arrogant bodybuilder type, you know, self-involved, and a real ladies' man. Stephen was one of the top strippers we had. But I haven't seen him in, shit, easily a year."[5]

The manager went back to his office and produced a photograph of Men in Motion, which Sergeant McNeil had already seen, and also a few color postcards. When he returned to the station and called the FBI, Sergeant McNeil learned that the correct legal name for Stephen was Carl Stephen Rosati. The FBI faxed over a report concerning a West Palm Beach arrest. It involved an altercation Rosati had with Paul Brown, a former gun-crazy cop who was fired from two police forces for fights and a possible rape.

"Look at this," McNeil said to Sergeant Kenny. "Kit Finch was right. This Rosati kid drives a Corvette. He took it to Sal's Auto Body to get the bullet holes fixed. Now where's a guy like that get the money to drive a Corvette?"

CHAPTER 43:
Hidden Agenda

Detective McNeil finally got a real break in the case when Peter Roussonicolos, aka Pete the Greek, lost an unrelated case and was put behind bars at the Coconut Creek jail. The detective rushed to the Coconut precinct to interview the infamous Pete the Greek.

Pete sat before Detective McNeil in handcuffs but nevertheless radiated an aura of confidence. "I will be happy to cooperate in any way I can. However, I will have to have my attorney present."

Pete's attorney, Richard Rendina, informed Detective McNeil that his client would not answer any questions without a subpoena for use immunity.

"I'll discuss this possibility with the Broward County State Attorney's Office Homicide Division," McNeil told Rendina. But he knew nothing would happen because to give Pete the Greek immunity would undermine his primary goal; namely, to nail him for the homicide. Additionally, the Broward Police Department did not want to yield to the attorney, because Rendina was an outspoken critic of McNeil's boss, Sheriff Nick Navarro, who ran the Broward Police Department from 1985 through the mid-1990s.

Dauntless, Navarro and his crew had been trying for years to nail Roussonicolos. With 3,000 employees and a $200 million operating budget, Navarro and his underlings were confident they had the resources to prosecute even the most difficult criminals. The last thing they wanted was to give Pete the Greek immunity. Additionally, they knew that such a plea agreement could serve to protect him from other charges as well, and that was out of the question. From their point of view, they finally had the rogue exactly where they wanted him: behind bars.

Richard Rendina's skirmishes with the Broward County Police Department went back over a decade, when the charismatic lawyer stunned the country by arguing that Broward County policemen were busting drug pushers and then reselling the product, mostly cocaine, to other pushers that they had in their back pocket. This stained the integrity of the Broward Police Department nationally, and it also made Rendina a target in a formidable power struggle.

One case involved two well-known drug runners and a half-million dollars worth of high-grade cocaine that they had smuggled by private plane from Colombia. When the case came to trial, as reported in the local headlines, the smugglers and Rendina accused Sheriff Navarro's men of stealing half the product, a quarter-million dollars' worth, so they could redistribute it themselves.[1]

Rendina's other case, even more damning, was covered by Geraldo Rivera on his TV show and also by Harry Reasoner on *60 Minutes.* Nelson Scott, Jr., a Bahamian drug pusher, "implicated a handful of deputies in drug smuggling and other crimes when he was arrested" in 1986.

The *Miami Herald* reported, "[Scott] told prosecutors that several deputies were involved in drug dealing. He said he was given a key to a sheriff's district office near Pompano Beach and sat in on deputies' meetings. He also said he provided deputies with cocaine and prostitutes and sold cocaine for deputies who ripped off smugglers during drug busts."

According to this story, Scott was their liaison on the street. This information was turned over to Internal Affairs at BSO, but they dismissed the case.[2]

"It was a whitewash," said Rendina, Scott's attorney.[3]

"While Scott was waiting for a new trial, federal investigators contacted Rendina saying they wanted to arrange an interview with his client . . . [as] a cooperating witness."

Scott's sentence was reduced considerably as federal prosecutors began their own investigation of corruption inside Sheriff Navarro's Broward County Police Department. Sheriff Navarro, with a brilliant counterstroke, accused Rendina of accepting cocaine as payment from Scott for his defense. Now the media perceived Rendina as a possible drug user himself. This charge was still pending when he defended another nemesis of the Broward Police Department, Pete "the Greek" Roussonicolos.

Because of the bad blood against Rendina, Detective McNeil ceased the interview with Pete and left the Coconut Creek jailhouse empty-handed. McNeil didn't really need Pete the Greek's testimony. The detective just had to corroborate the breakthrough deposition of Cory Franco. Pressure would be kept on Rendina, and a few years later, his license to practice law would be revoked because of drug allegations raised by the Broward County Sheriff's Office.

According to Pete, when Rendina began to negotiate for immunity, the police refused. Apparently, Rendina challenged McNeil to "go and indict Pete. He's innocent, so we'll just prosecute you for false arrest." Pete remembers McNeil becoming so angry during this phone conversation that he slammed down the phone and screamed, "We got you nailed, you son of a bitch. You're going down."

Thus, we see that the murder of a small-time drug dealer, Joe Viscido, Jr., was linked directly through Pete the Greek to his defense lawyer, Richard Rendina, a man thoroughly despised by Sheriff Nick Navarro. Ironically, had Pete the Greek had a different lawyer; he would not have been so large a target.

According to Pete the Greek, shortly before Joe was killed, Jeff Bloom made a phone call to Joe pretending to be Pete the Greek and threatened to come over to rip him off. Jeff was mad at Pete because Pete had threatened his brother, Skip, with a baseball bat for not paying his debts. To get back at Pete, Jeff Bloom called Joe Viscido, a rival dealer, and tried to stir up a hornet's nest.

When Pete found out what Jeff had done, he called Joe immediately. As he told this interviewer, he wanted to smooth things over. Having never met Joe Viscido face-to-face, Pete assured him that he had no intention of ripping him off, and Joe invited Pete over to the apartment.

"I didn't want to go," Pete remembered, "because Joe had an Uzi, and I thought he might try to shoot me. Joe was killed a few days later, and that's how my name got attached to the investigation."

Pete knew right away he was a suspect, even though, according to him, he had never met Joe. They did have common friends, however, and through these connections, during the very height of these investigations, Pete was able to meet Michelle. He assured her he had nothing to do with Joe's murder. Using his charms, Pete invited her to dinner at his father's restaurant. Soon after, they became lovers. Pete knew, of course, that the closer he got to Michelle, the less likely she would be to testify against him.[4]

Clearly, Pete the Greek bedding Michelle shortly after the homicide injured her credibility and also lent support to Detective McNeil's supposition that Michelle was in cahoots with Pete the Greek and Peter Dallas. Together, it was hypothesized that they set up her boyfriend and killed him for his stash.

* * *

The case was coming together, and another witness would help considerably. After four months of hard time, sleeping at Pompano Correctional Institute at night but out during the day on work release at World Jet Aviation Center, Vic Giordano was a transformed man, off drugs and without the bleached Mohawk. Sergeant McNeil noted that Giordano's appearance was the difference between night and day. McNeil wrote in his log, "Giordano will cooperate fully with the investigation in all attempts to identify the individuals responsible." In return, McNeil agreed to attend a parole hearing.

At World Jet, Giordano ID'd Stephen Rosati for the first time. Two weeks later, the ID was made official at the police station. When questioned as to why he had not identified Rosati in the same lineup six months ago, Giordano said, "I was too upset because I was going to the Florida State Prison System the following day. But that's him. That's the big guy." Having had two weeks to think about his recent success, Giordano added, "This picture sends chills down my spine."

Giordano's spine, however, did not tingle when presented with the photos from the lineup of the supposed shooter, and so he did not ID Peter Dallas that day. His parole hearing was postponed and he was returned to his cell.

A few weeks later, Detective McNeil drove back to the Correctional Institute, and Giordano was called out again to see if he could be more successful in pointing out the little guy.

"When we showed you this lineup, did we indicate to you who was a possible suspect at all?" Detective McNeil asked, the tape rolling. McNeil failed to point out that there were only six pictures on the page, and Giordano had already missed picking Dallas from this sheet on two separate occasions. But Giordano was getting yet another try.

"Did you make any indications as to who possibly resembled one of the subjects?"

"Five, and as I look at it again, maybe No. 2."

"Okay, anybody else?" The detective wanted to be fair and not leave anybody out.

"Could it have been No. 4?"

"Okay, so basically as far as that particular lineup goes, you're not able to make any identification?"

"No, not yet."[5]

Dallas was sitting in the No. 3 spot.

"Well, at least we got the big guy," Detective McNeil said to his partner after Giordano was taken back to his cell. "Let's come back another day and see if he can ID the Greek." However, when they did return a few weeks later, Giordano was unable to pick out Pete the Greek.

If the detective couldn't get Giordano to pick out Dallas, maybe Michelle could. Yet, when he dialed up her mother's house, Michelle refused to come in again. Sergeant McNeil asked the assistant state prosecutor from the Broward Attorney General's Office, Chuck Morton, to subpoena Michelle Arrieta and sit in on her testimony. She was tracked down at her new boyfriend's apartment.

An African American attired in a freshly pressed suit and rimless glasses, the refined Chuck Morton was a fellow who lent an air of class to ongoing police procedures. Featured on Dan Rather's TV show *48 Hours*, Morton, an assistant attorney general, was on his way up and within a few years would be in the running for a judgeship. Having already sat in on the Jeff Bloom testimony, he decided to participate in the questioning of Michelle along with Detectives Chevy McNeil and Jeffrey Burndt.

Morton spoke in a sincere tone of quiet authority. After granting her immunity and establishing that she could still be prosecuted if she lied, Morton let the police take over. They ran once again through the entire sequence of events.

"Were you held against your will? Would you have liked to have gotten up and walked out of that apartment?"

"Yes, I was very scared."

"Now what happened?"

"So the big guy was sitting there telling Joe that he was messing with his baby sister, Carrie." Allowed to smoke, Michelle extended her cigarette between her first and second fingers and arched her palm outward for the full effect. "'Excuse me,' I said to the guy, 'but Joe and I are married. He hasn't been with anybody.' And the guy didn't say nothing, not a word. But the little guy was in the bedroom. And then he comes back in and says, 'Where is it?' referring to the cocaine. And so the little guy, at this point, took Joe into the bedroom.

"Then, all of a sudden, I was on the ground, and the big guy was standing over me. Then I heard a fight break out, and Joe said, 'You motherfucker.'" Michelle took a long drag and crushed the cigarette out in an ashtray. "And as soon as the fight started, the big guy ran in there. That's when I went for the front door and heard the gun go off. When I got outside, I got under a car, and I heard the guys, like, running on the walkway. And that was it."

"Prior to Joe's death, had anything been said by anyone to Joe about Pete the Greek?"

"Yes, Jeff Bloom told him that the Greek didn't like him, that he might rip him off—something like that. And Joe told Jeff to tell the Greek to 'Come on, he'd be ready for him.'"

"So, what you are saying is that Jeff Bloom was the liaison between Joe Viscido and Pete the Greek?"

"Yes. And this all happened about a week before his death."

"After this homicide, at any time, were you ever approached by or did you make contact with Pete the Greek?"

"Yeah. I had called Robbie Newman's, and he said someone wants to speak to you. Pete the Greek got on the phone and said that he was sorry to hear about my fiancé, and I said . . ."

"Did he sound sincere or was he joking?" Detective McNeil interrupted.

"He sounded sincere." she said, "And then he told me that he wanted to talk to me. So he came over to my house and told me that he had nothing to do with it, and he was sorry about my boyfriend, and then a few weeks later he took me to his restaurant for dinner."

Michelle went on to say that she had never known or seen Pete the Greek before Joe's murder and that she was aware that people were coming forward giving information to Joe's dad. Michelle was then shown photo lineups.

"Okay," Detective McNeil said. "I want you to concentrate back to that night and be honest with us today. You're under oath. If you see individuals here, I expect you to identify them."

"That's Pete the Greek," Michelle said, looking at the first set of six.

"For the record," Detective McNeil said into the tape, "Michelle has identified Peter Roussonicolos, aka Pete the Greek. Okay. Let's go to the smaller guy."

"I can't sit here and be sure," Michelle began, "but between five and six, I can't be sure."

Chuck Morton interjected, "She can't be positive, but she says that [the small guy] looks similar to No. 5 and No. 6. Let's see, that's Scotty Hogan and Pulli Nosalgad. Peter Dallas was still sitting in the No. 3 slot. Okay, let's go to the big guy."

Sergeant McNeil put the Dallas lineup away and pulled out the one that held the picture of Stephen Rosati.

"I don't see anyone here," she said, as she wrote on the sheet in large letters: NO ID.

"Michelle," Sergeant McNeil said, "I have some photographs that were taken at a party that took place a month or so after Joe's death. Do you remember that party?"

"Yes. It was a birthday party for Robbie Newman."

"So you recall being at the party, and you recall that pictures were taken there?"

"Yes."

"Did you know all the people at the party?"

"Just about everybody."

"Was Jeff Bloom at that party?"

"Yes, and Skip, and Sweetie Sartucci. That's Robbie's girlfriend."

"That's your picture, correct?"

"Yes," Michelle responded, unconsciously patting her hair.

Chuck Morton leaned forward, adjusted his glasses, raised his eyebrows, and placed his chin back in the crook of his closed palm. He was staring so intently that he looked like a statue of *The Thinker*. Detective Jeffrey Burndt pressed in, as Detective McNeil edged Michelle to the crucial next phase.

"I'd like to show you about four or five pages of these pictures," Detective McNeil said, "and I'm going to show you one page in particular. I want you to stand up because there is a glare here a little bit, and I want you to see. Do you know most of these people?"

"Yes," Michelle said, looking over the pictures from the photo album.

"This subject here. Do you know him?"

"No."

"Have you ever seen him before?"

"No."

"Here, again, he's in this picture."

"Don't know'm."

"Does he look familiar? Do you recognize him at all?"

"Nope. Nope."

"Who'd he come with?"

"I have no idea."

"Do you know his name?"

"No."

Detective McNeil hit her with the one question, the only one he really cared about out of the hundreds he had asked that day.

"Is he one of the two individuals that entered the apartment that night?"

"No."

"You're positive?"

"Yes."

"You can say with all certainty that's not him."

"No. That's not him."

The police continued to pressure her, but she remained adamant that the man in the photo was not one of the killers. Finally McNeil hit her broadside.

"Have people told you that's the guy? I'll bet you've done more investigation in this case. And that he was your boyfriend. What do you take me for?"

"I don't know who that guy is!" Michelle shot back. "I've never seen him in my life." She stood and placed both hands on her hips. "Who is that guy?" she demanded, only to see six blank eyes staring back. "Is that . . . I guess that would be Peter Dallas. Is that who that is?" She stared directly into the detective's eyes.

"Is that who that is?" Detective McNeil echoed. Chuck Morton and Detective Jeffrey Burndt leaned closer.

"I've never seen him in my life," Michelle concluded.[6]

This interview was over, but Detective McNeil was not finished with her.

CHAPTER 44:
The Hearing: Cicilline Moves in for the Cross

Day Ten: February 20, 1991

"The crime you investigated took place about three-and-a-half years before you became involved in the case. Isn't that correct?" Cicilline clipped in his characteristic deep no-nonsense voice.

"Yes, sir. Sergeant McNeil led the investigations along with Detective Burndt," Detective Coyote said, readying himself.

"And from your review of the documents that were turned over to you, I take it you concluded that Sergeant McNeil interviewed a number of witnesses in connection with this, isn't that right?"

"Yes. However, I believe that Peter Dallas was not interviewed by Sergeant McNeil."

"Did you talk to people who lived in the area of Viscido's apartment or any other witnesses?"

"No, sir, I did not."

"And that was because you knew that these other people that had been interviewed never said Stephen Rosati was the person that they saw either going into the house or coming out, isn't that correct?"

"The statements I reviewed, none of those people ever indicated, no."

"Now in addition to interviewing witnesses, I take it you looked at physical evidence in the case as well?"

"No, honestly, I didn't. There wasn't very much of it."

"Is there anyone more familiar with this case than you are?"

"Detective Chevy McNeil."

"But you don't talk to him?"

"I spoke to him maybe three times, but not often."

"Do you know if Stephen Rosati's fingerprints were found in the apartment?"

"They were not found there."

The questioning continued on details of the crime. Cicilline discussed the bloody sneaker print that was found on the floor. White objected to this line of questioning, as this was not brought up on direct.

Judge Sheehan stated, "So the record is abundantly clear and counsel on both sides are clear. I will set forth once more my duties as far as this particular case is to determine whether or not Mr. Rosati was in the demanding state on October 12, 1986. I am not here to decide whether or not Stephen Rosati is guilty or innocent. And if I find there's conflicting evidence, contradictory evidence, I am duty bound to send Mr. Rosati to Florida. Everyone understand what I said?"

"I'm not certain how it relates to the question I'm asking."

"It doesn't, Mr. Cicilline. I'm just setting ground rules once more. Objection overruled."

"Was this sneaker print ever compared to Mr. Rosati's foot?"

"No, sir, it was not."

"Was the blood that was found ever compared to Mr. Rosati's blood?"

"No, sir, it was not."

"And you said in your direct examination that you had some evidence that Rosati was living with or associated with a Bob McNeil at the King Neptune Motel?"

"Yes, sir. Sometime in 1987."

"So, you reopened the case in May 1990 and had it to the grand jury by September?"

"That is correct."

"Did Mr. Viscido help you?"

"If I needed help, I did obtain records from him at times."

"In fact, he gave you Mr. Rosati's name, targeted it for you, didn't he?"

"No, he did not. I got the name from the original case files," Detective Coyote said, to Cicilline's disappointment.

But without skipping a beat, the lawyer continued. "Now, I take it you also learned that there were a number of other suspects over the four- or five-year investigation." Cicilline listed a number of them, such as Joseph McBridey, Steve Crotzer, Glenn Bloom, and Mike DelBono.

"The last name sounds familiar to me, but I honestly can't recall if these were principal suspects."

"So you are not disputing me. It's just that you don't recall?"

"I am not disputing you. That is correct, sir."

Cicilline listed another half-dozen names from the investigation, such as Donald Phelps, an Israeli named Tony who drove a Datsun 280Z, and a guy named Nordie. Coyote had not interviewed any of these people.

"Incidentally, at any time during the course of your investigation, did you go to either Rosebud's or Bogie's to determine what employment periods Steve Rosati had at these places?"

"I did not personally go there. I know I did talk to somebody on the phone."

"Did you make an audiotape of every sworn testimony of every witness?"

"Yes, sir, I did, so the State Attorney's Office has documentation."

"Now, you said at some point in your direct examination you did the work that you did to gather the truth, something to that effect. Do you remember saying that?"

"Correct."

"And that's what you are interested in, in this case, isn't that so?"

"That is correct."

The full command of Cicilline's unwavering gaze drilled into the witness. "And you wouldn't attempt to mislead the court about anything?"

Steadily, Coyote replied, "No, I wouldn't."

"Your answers have been full and complete about the things that you have been asked about?"

"That is correct." Beads of sweat began to appear on the detective's forehead.

"And that's because you don't want to hide anything?"

"Correct."

"You certainly wouldn't be putting words in the mouths of witnesses that you were interviewing, would you?"

"No, sir."

"And, in fact, you wouldn't be telling witnesses that man's name is Steve Rosati?"

"If you are referring to some of the statements I know exactly, yes, sir, I did. Some people didn't know him."

"Who didn't know him [by name]?" Cicilline said, almost shouting at one point, so angry was he with the witness. The judge requested that Cicilline speak "a little quieter."

Like pulling teeth, Cicilline managed to get Coyote to agree that Cory Franco and Danny Ek didn't know Rosati's name. "Peter Dallas, I believe, knew his name was Steve," said Coyote. "He didn't know his last name: Rosati."

"This is his pal, the fella he went on a murder with; he didn't know his last name?"

"That is correct."

"Objection."

"He already answered."

Turning to Michelle Arrieta, Cicilline continued, "You told this judge that on May 29, 1990, Michelle identified Stephen Rosati from a photo lineup."

"That is correct."

"Show me *where* Michelle Arrieta's statement is where she identifies Rosati!"

"As stated in the affidavit, I did not take a taped statement from her because she did not [review] that photo lineup." Coyote said that she identified Peter Dallas.

"Where is that transcript?" demanded Cicilline.

"I probably have it someplace up here." Coyote hedged.

"Let's get it. We'd like to mark it as defendant's exhibit," said Cicilline, as the judge called for a recess.

When court convened, Cicilline continued.

"For the record, Detective Coyote, I must remind you that you are still under oath."

"Yes, sir."

"You found the statement of Michelle Arrieta for May 29, 1990?"

"Yes, sir, I did."

"I will ask that it be marked," said Cicilline. "And it's on that date that you indicated that Michelle Arrieta picked out Stephen Rosati from the Men in Motion photograph. Is that correct?"

"That is correct."

"Show me *where* in that statement where that identification is made."

"It is not contained within that statement," Coyote countered.

"Do you have another statement that shows that she made that identification?"

"No, sir, I do not. I did not record that statement because it wasn't from an official photo lineup."

"So, here it is; Michelle Arrieta, the girlfriend of Joe Viscido, present at the time of the murder, and you don't show her a mug shot photo [with] Steve Rosati?"

"No, I did not show her a mug shot photograph of Stephen Rosati [because] I didn't have one [at the time]. She had indicated to me from what I can recall that Deerfield Beach had shown her a photo lineup. She got into an argument with them because she felt that they were more concerned with the drug involvement than the murder of her boyfriend, and she was unable to identify anybody due to the fact that she did not want to."

"By that, do you mean she had been shown photographs of Steve Rosati a number of times in a photo spread and was never able to identify him, is that what you are saying?"

"From what I can remember, she was shown a photo lineup one time by Sergeant McNeil."

Cicilline entered into exhibit Michelle's first police statement made October 14, 1986. "Can you tell us how much she said the man weighed," Cicilline asked, handing Coyote the report to read from.

"Two hundred and eighty pounds."

"This is two days after the incident, isn't that correct?"

"Yes, sir, that is correct."

"Now two years later, on October 10, 1988, and on October 14, 1988, she's brought to a photo spread, isn't that correct? She picked out Steve Rosati on October 10, 1988?" Cicilline queried.

The detective read over his photo lineup spread sheets. "No, sir, she did not," conceded Coyote. "She said No. 5 might be close, but that's not him."

"The photo was of a Mr. Craig Konieszka. Isn't that right?"

"I don't know. I wasn't there," the detective replied coyly.

"Do you think we should bring Michelle Arrieta in to explain that to us?" Cicilline shot back.

"No sir, I do not," the detective answered icily.

"Objection," shouted White.

"He's already answered," said the judge.

"And she doesn't say anything about Steve Rosati, who is in picture No. 6, did she?" Cicilline drummed.

"No." The detective tried to dab the beads of sweat off his brow, but new ones quickly replaced them.

"So, we have here at least on two occasions her making no photo identification of Steve Rosati, is that fair to say?"

"Yes, sir."

"What is it that you brought with you when you came up to Rhode Island?"

"I brought as much as I could take. There's boxes and boxes of information."

"Are you telling me you didn't bring the former statements of any of these witnesses?"

"No, sir, I did not."

"So you didn't bring up any photo lineups where no identifications were made?"

"That is correct."

"So, if she is looking at a photo spread the week after the murder took place, or the month after, and she makes no identification, you don't bring any of those?"

"I do not have those. No, sir."

"As a matter of fact, the first time Michelle Arrieta starts to identify anyone is when she gets into your hands, isn't that right?"

"No, sir." However, Coyote acknowledged that it was the only time she began making, in Cicilline's words, "positive identifications."

"That is correct."

"Let's talk about Vic Giordano. Did he identify anyone when he was talking to the Deerfield Police [before you took over the investigation]?"

"Yes, he did. He identified Stephen Rosati," said Coyote. "I believe it was in August of 1988. He did a full photo lineup affidavit at that time."

"But four months earlier, in March of 1988, Giordano was shown the same photo spread with Stephen Rosati's picture in it, and he says he can't identify anybody. Isn't that correct?"

"That is correct."

"And if we go back to October 13, 1986, the day after the murder, he tells under sworn testimony to another official of the state of Florida that has the same power that you have that Joe Viscido never offered him any drugs and that he doesn't know about Joe Viscido being involved in drug dealing."

"That is correct."

"And he's lying, isn't he?"

"Yes."

"Sure he is, because he knows Viscido was a drug dealer, and he's bought drugs from him."

"That is correct."

"Isn't it a fact that Chris Jones actually bought some drugs that night as well?"

"I believe so. Yes, sir."

"Objection."

"He's answered," said the judge.

"I move to strike," said White. "He's asking him as though he's Giordano or he's whoever it is about whom he is questioning."

"I agree with my brother," Cicilline said to White's surprise.

"Well, that's a first in these proceedings," said the judge, raising his eyebrows.

"Your Honor," Cicilline continued, "if he wants to bring up all the witnesses so I can ask them directly, I will be happy to do that. In the absence of that, there's nothing else I can do. If he's willing to do that, I'm willing to sit down." Defense counsel gave the judge a sardonic smile.

"I've heard enough of that," the judge barked. "Continue."

Cicilline resumed hammering away at details about Giordano's testimony concerning the possibility that he might have recognized the smaller guy.

"On March 25, 1988, your policemen go down to the prison to interview Giordano to show him another photo spread."

"I honestly can't recall," said Coyote, unhappy with the way things were going.

"Giordano is shown this photo spread: six pictures," defense counsel said, hitting the nail on the head. "Rosati's picture is in there.

Can you identify anybody who was at the house on October 12, 1986, and he says no, I can't. Isn't that what happened?"

"That first occasion. Yes, sir."

"But now *you* are involved, right?"

"That is correct."

"Does Giordano get, *like*, some eye care between the time the Deerfield Beach Police show him Steve Rosati's picture and the time you show it to him?"

"He had identified Steve Rosati long before I got involved in this case."

"My question is," defense counsel growled, "did he get some eye care in between?"

"I don't understand."

"Objection!" White shot back.

"You don't know what eye care is?" demanded Cicilline.

"No, sir," Coyote responded, temporarily thrown for a loop.

"Argumentative," said White.

"He's answered it," said the judge.

"And when Giordano was in jail again, the police go to see him, hoping he will cooperate?"

"I can't say that."

"Well, why do you think they went there?"

"To talk about the case."

"This is a good time to break," said the judge.

CHAPTER 45:
The Hearing: Cicilline on Cross, Continued

Day Eleven: February 21, 1991

The house was packed again the following morning, not only by the Rosati contingency but also by an extra crowd aroused by the daily front-page coverage in the *Providence Journal*. Conflicting headlines appeared each day reflecting the case for both prosecution and defense:

February 18: Extradition Fight, Fierce Drama
February 20: Murder Witnesses Identify Cranston Man
February 21: Witness Failed to Pick Rosati in Photo Lineup

Whenever a headline would seem to lean in Rosati's direction, Randy White had no qualms about calling the *Providence Journal* to blast the reporter.[1]

"He would literally yell at me on the phone," reporter Jim Hummel recounted.

To his credit, Hummel—later a local TV reporter for ABC News—accurately portrayed the dialogue, including Detective Coyote's testimony and the clashes between prosecution and defense. Having left out interpretation, Hummel relied on the ambiguity of the issues to drive his headlines. Presenting the Rosati scenario as a possible case of mistaken identity, Hummel—along with the local TV reporters—billed the event as "a murder mystery of the first order." A standing-room-only crowd overflowed the courtroom with the hope that the mystery would soon be solved.

Jack Cicilline continued his cross-examination as if the nightfall had never occurred. "Let's go back to Vic Giordano for a minute. You acknowledged that Vic Giordano was one of the people inside the Viscido house the night of the shooting?"

"That is correct."

"Now, on March 25, 1988 [a year an a half later], Giordano is shown a photo spread with Stephen Rosati's picture in it; is that correct? And he says he can't identify anybody?"

"That is correct."

"On September 3 of 1990, he's now in your hands."

"Yes, sir."

"And where did he tell you he got the name Rosati from?"

"That was the second time he identified Steve Rosati," said Coyote.

"Can you answer my questions, or do you need to add something to them every time?" Cicilline said testily.

"Objection!" White barked.

"Well, I object," defense countered. "I move to *strike* the answer, and I ask the witness to be instructed to answer the questions and not to be volunteering what he *thinks* this court wants to hear!"

"And likewise," said White with comparable verve, "I ask Mr. Cicilline to have enough *courtesy* not to *argue* with the witness."

"Gentlemen," said the judge in a way that called to mind his wise Irish background, "don't mistake kindness for weakness. I'm telling you. Next question please."

"I asked him, 'did you hear the name Steve Rosati,' and he indicated from a few people after the investigation started," Coyote continued.

"So it was not that he knew the name, is that correct?"

"Yes, that is correct."

"And when he says the man is six foot three or four, 220 pounds, in your mind, you're thinking of a fairly huge person, aren't you?"

Cicilline asked.

"I honestly didn't think anything. I just asked him the question, and it was in the statement."

"Is it fair to say that Vic Giordano could not identify Pete the Greek?"

"I honestly don't believe he did."

White began objecting to various questions because they assumed that Detective Coyote had firsthand knowledge of the situations. "He wasn't there. He can tell you what the paper says," said White.

"That's all he is asking," said the judge. "Obviously, I know Detective Coyote wasn't there."

"Judge," Cicilline interjected in a lighter vein, "may I take this opportunity to commend Mr. White for so gracefully avoiding using the words 'this is hearsay,' making his arguments all around it and never saying it."

"All right, all right. I don't need an education here. Continue."

"Yes, Your Honor. Does this document indicate that Giordano picked Dallas out of a photo spread?"

"No, sir, it does not. He didn't identify him at that time."

"Now, let's go back to November 30, 1987. In the second photo spread, who does Vic Giordano pick out?"

"He says," Coyote responded, reading the affidavit, "not sure, but looks like No. 6."

"And who is No. 6?" Cicilline wanted to know.

"A gentleman by the name of Joseph Bagley," said Coyote.

The judge wanted to know if Rosati was also in the lineup. Coyote answered that he was not. Cicilline asked if the Bagley lead was followed up, and Coyote said it wasn't.

Turning to Chris Jones's testimony, Cicilline cited the phone call Jones made from Canada to McNeil a few days after the killing. "And in that first conversation with Sergeant McNeil, he said I don't remember faces, isn't that correct?"

"I honestly don't recall."

Cicilline offered the phone call transcript as evidence. Coyote read from it: "One and five seem like they have similar stereotypes, but I'm not sure if I recognize them from the scene of the crime or anywhere else."

Coyote had the "impression" that Jones indicated Rosati because he was in the No. 5 spot, and Cicilline argued that this statement was too ambiguous to take that position. Cicilline turned to the topic of

Peter Dallas.

"Can you tell us the nature of his agreement with the police [in exchange for his testimony]?" White objected, but Judge Sheehan let it in.

"From what I recall," said Coyote, "the plea is second-degree murder, or a reduced charge of second-degree, which would fall between the guidelines of seven to twenty-five years or something to that effect with a recommended guideline of twelve to seventeen years. I also do know in the agreement he would agree to testify in any future court proceedings in reference to the other subjects. But any agreement would have been with Chuck Morton of the State's Attorney Office."

"So, it's your view that Peter Dallas was one of the actual intruders into the house, is that correct?"

"That is correct."

"And is it September 6 of 1990 that he was interviewed by you?"

"Yes, sir, by myself and Detective Puccini."

"And do you remember during the course of that interview where the plan had been devised to do this?"

"At the Bloom house," said Coyote.

"Did Dallas ever tell you whether or not when they went inside that they were looking for a girl named Kerry?"

"I honestly don't recall."

"Go to page 12 [of Dallas's affidavit]."

"I think you're asking me to look for something that's not there. I didn't ask him that question."

"But all the other witnesses had told the police that when there was a knock at the door, the people inside heard the intruders ask, 'Is Kerry in there?' Isn't that correct?"

"Some of the witnesses indicated that."

"And Peter Dallas never told you that, is that right?"

"From what I recall, he asked, 'was there a female in there?' but I can't say for sure," Coyote offered.

"Well, where are you getting that from, your memory?"

"From my recollection."

"Why don't you look on pages 12 and 13 again before you answer that question?"

"He has already answered that question, Your Honor," said White.

"May the witness address himself to pages 12 and 13?" demanded Cicilline.

"All right," said Judge Sheehan.

Coyote read the transcript: "'how many people were there?' His response, 'I can't really remember.' I said, 'Was there a female?' He said, 'I can't—I can't.'"

"Stop right there. He said, 'I can't remember.'"

"If you will allow me to finish," said Coyote adamantly.

"Read anything you want, Detective." Cicilline knew his man.

"'There was more than one?' 'Yes, sir.' 'Was there a female?' 'I can't—I can't, if I answer yes, I will be lying.' I stated to him," Coyote said, reading his reply on tape to Dallas, "'I don't want you to lie.' Dallas stated, 'I can't remember. I cannot remember.' I said, 'Okay, there were several people?' and he indicated 'two or three or maybe even four people.'"

"But initially he said, "I can't remember. Right?"

"Initially, yes, sir." the detective replied, regaining composure.

"And then you started him with: 'Well, there had to be more than one?'"

"That's not what I said."

"Well, what did you say?"

"I said, 'there was more than one?' Forming it as a question."

"So you were feeding him the answers, weren't you?"

"No, sir, I was not."

"Objection."

"He's already answered," said Sheehan.

"Your answer is no, I wasn't feeding him the answers?" Cicilline scrutinized.

"I said no, sir, I wasn't."

"You knew Michelle was there, so you asked him, 'Was there a woman in there?'"

"That is correct."

"What did he say?"

"He said, 'If I answer yes, I will be lying. I can't remember.'"

"So he doesn't remember anything about a woman being present?"

"That is correct," Coyote said, adroitly reversing his testimony from a few questions earlier.

"Now, the people in the house were all put on the floor. Did Dallas know where they were put on the floor?"

"I believe I asked him that question. I can't recall his response."

"Try page 15."

"Thank you," Coyote said reading over the transcript. "I said to him, 'Now, Steve Rosati was there holding these three people on the ground?' and he said, 'I tell you the God's honest truth I wouldn't be able to answer that. I can't remember if he had them down like over here.' I said, 'You're pointing to just by the tile floor and the carpet?' He said, 'Yes, sir.' And I said, 'In the living room area?' and he said, 'At the time when we came in they just dropped right where they were, you know, when he told them to drop.'"

"So he couldn't tell you where the people were either, could he?" asked Cicilline.

"He pointed to me where he thought," said the detective.

"And that's in this transcript?"

"Yes," he said, and continued reading: "'You're pointing to just by the tile floor and the carpet?' and his response was 'Yes.'"

"I take it you're not telling him anything, is that right?" asked defense counsel.

"Whatever I told him is memorialized in the statement."

"If you weren't in the Viscido house when this was going on, how is it that he told you where they were?"

"I had photographs showing him," the detective revealed.

"Do you have those photos here?"

"No, sir."

"And he describes the seizure of a half kilo of cocaine in the transcript. Where does he say it was taken from?"

"I believe he indicated from Joe Viscido's bedroom."

"You show me where it says that," demanded Cicilline.

"If you would allow me to go through the whole thing, I will look and see if I can find it. Here," he said, and read: "'Somewhere around that. I can't—' and I said, 'Now just beside—for the record, you are saying it was next to the scale on the desk.' He then describes money that was taken, and the picture that I was showing him was a picture of the bedroom."

"Michelle Arrieta said that marijuana and jewelry were also stolen. Did Dallas say that marijuana was taken?"

"I can't recall."

"Well, take a moment to see."

Cicilline gave Coyote time to read through the transcript as he turned and looked at Esther and Carl. His facial expression gave them the equivalent of a thumbs-up. The crowd and, of course, Stephen were riveted to the testimony.

The detective read that Dallas said, "I don't recall anything about marijuana [or jewelry]."

"Did he tell you where Viscido was shot on his body?"

"I honestly can't recall."

"Page 21."

"I asked him at one part on this," the detective said, reading, "'Did you see where he had been shot?' and he said, 'No, sir.'"

"So he didn't see any shooting: that's his testimony to you?"

"Correct."

"Did he tell you where he went after the shooting took place?"

"He stated that he jumped over the body and exited and went back to the Bloom residence."

"Is that in any statement?"

"I honestly can't recall."

"I'm not asking you to editorialize." Cicilline was in total charge. "See page 23."

Coyote complied and began reading. "He indicated he went to—'I don't remember if we stopped off at the house where we usually meet on U.S. 1 right near Pompano Beach. I can't remember the name exactly.'"[2]

"And you expected his answer to be the Bloom house, didn't you?"

"He indicated to me that he lived at the Bloom house." The detective squirmed, avoiding the question.

"Objection, Your Honor," White said, popping out of his seat.

"Ground?"

"Your Honor," White moved to deflect, "my objection is to the line of questioning, [and its] relevance to the proceeding. What Mr. Cicilline is trying to suggest is that a man, about whom testimony has been given, has pled to second degree murder and sits in a jail awaiting the possibility of years in prison wasn't the person who was there because there are discrepancies in his testimony. I can't see what other relevance it might have to this proceeding as it relates to whether Carl Stephen Rosati was in Florida on October 12, 1986."

"Well, let's take a case scenario," suggested the judge. "Let's assume Mr. Dallas was not there. Then what do I do with the credibility of Peter Dallas and his identification?"

"Fine, Your Honor, if you are ruling," White said, calling his bluff.

Flustered by the challenge, the judge retreated. "I'm not ruling anything. I'm just—I just said a case scenario. I didn't say—I don't know what's in Mr. Cicilline's mind."

"It seems to me, Your Honor, that he seems to be trying to show that Mr. Dallas is not as candid as he might have been or might be, and doesn't know as much about the incident as he might."

"I will make no bones about it," proclaimed Cicilline, pausing for full measure as he regained the high ground. "My position is that Peter Dallas was *not* there! And I will prove that *conclusively* before this hearing is over."

This declaration stunned the crowd. *Slam* went the gavel as muttered voices expounded, "Incredible!" "Unbelievable!"

Jim Hummell had his closing for his *Providence Journal* saga titled, "Rosati's Lawyer Clashes with Florida Detective at Extradition Hearing." *ProJo* readers, which included just about everyone in the state, were now hooked to see how Dallas really stood in this multifaceted local story, which was enhanced visually at 6:00 and 11:00 p.m. with the continuing TV press coverage as well.

Gritting his teeth, yet again, Detective Coyote surveyed the room. Loosening his neck muscles, with armpits soaked, and avoiding the stares of the Rosatis, he positioned himself for the next series of questions; however, the judge looked at his watch, let him off the hook, and announced a lunch break.

"Prior to our recess," Cicilline began when they returned to the courtroom "you were about to tell us about your initial inquest with Peter Dallas at Elmira Prison and your drive to Syracuse airport and on the plane flight to Florida with Dallas. Was there further discussion with him about the events of October 12, 1986, at that time?"

"I just couldn't recall. I believe we discussed quite a bit."

"Has any record been taken of this discussion?"

"No, sir, but from what I can recall, I believe he did make an identification [of Rosati]."

"And Dallas said that he had known Steve Rosati for several weeks prior to October 12 and had seen him [quoting from the transcript] three, four, or five days prior to October 12?"

"I believe so. Yes, sir."

"And that would be the seventh, eighth, and ninth of October, 1986, wouldn't it?"

"It all depends, six or seven days before. I do remember him saying that he had seen him there several days before."

Cicilline pointed out that two days before the shooting would be Friday. Coyote reluctantly agreed. "So from the reading," Cicilline said, "is it fair to say [Dallas places] Rosati in Florida on Friday, October 10, and sometime between the seventh and the ninth?"

"From the reading, yes, sir."

"Well, you don't have any reason to disbelieve?"

"Again, it's going from my memory." Coyote positioned himself for some wiggle room. "I do remember Dallas saying something about he had seen Rosati several times. I remember him saying something about a phone call that was made. I believe he indicated he thought to Mr. Joe Viscido. He indicated," the detective rumbled, "Steve was not there during that time. He thought he was there earlier that day. I asked him, 'Could he have gone out of state?' and he said, 'Yes, to take care of business.'"

Flashing one of those looks that said, *sure buddy*, Cicilline continued. He found out that Coyote gave Dallas the "out of state" idea because Coyote had, in fact, presented to Dallas a license photo ID of Rosati from the state of Rhode Island. "Tell me what purpose you [had to do that before Dallas was to go to the grand jury]?"

"No purpose at all. He had already identified him as far as I was concerned."

"Weren't you concerned that this was a man who said I don't know the man's last name? [Or that] he couldn't describe a lot of things that were taken out of Viscido's house that everybody else said had been taken? Weren't you starting to wonder about him?"

"No, sir. I didn't think too much of it."

"Since Mr. Rosati has testified in this case, have you gone back to Mr. Dallas to ask him about some of the things that were said here?" Cicilline inquired.

"No, sir, definitely not."

"You have not talked to Mr. Dallas?"

"I believe Mr. Dallas has called my office from prison on several occasions, but I don't believe that I have spoken to him. No, sir."

"Did you ever ask him how could Steve Rosati be with you on October 10 when four or five people said he was in Rhode Island signing checks. Did you ever ask him that?"

"Sir, I honestly couldn't recall ever talking to him [although] he did call my office every once in a while."

"You haven't spoken to him?"

"I have spoken to him before Mr. Rosati testified. I can't say when, but before I have."

Cicilline took this information in and paused to review his notes. Carl took the moment to whisper to Esther that Detective Coyote had just contradicted himself. Esther nodded her agreement.

"Well, you knew before Mr. Rosati testified that there were other witnesses who had come into this courtroom and said, 'I received my paycheck October 10,' for example," Cicilline continued.

The judge interrupted to ask Coyote, "Did you ask Dallas about those things?"

"No, sir, I did not. I have discussed some of the testimony with Mr. Morton, and a couple of times Mr. Dallas has called, and I always had him contact Mr. Morton."

"All right," said the judge.

"Well, I don't understand that." Cicilline cut to the bone. "Was Mr. Morton asking Dallas these questions?"

"No, Mr. Morton is a prosecutor in the case and I talked to him about it, and I don't believe he talked to Dallas about it."

"As far as you know?"

"As far as I know."

"All right. There are a number of people that were involved in the Bloom house, is that correct?"

"That is correct."

Cicilline asked if Skip Bloom had identified Rosati. Coyote couldn't remember. Cicilline had Coyote review a January 27, 1988, sworn statement by Skip's brother, Jeff Bloom, where Jeff says that the Greek was *not* at the Bloom house on the day of the murder or the day after. In this interview, Bloom identifies a friend of Pete the Greek, "a crazy guy" who drove a Datsun 280Z. Coyote tried to intimate that Rosati had been associated with that car. Cicilline asked him to find the spot in any transcript, but Coyote was unable to.

"You simply want to say things that you think are going to help the state's case, isn't that true?"

"That is totally untrue."

"Objection!"

"Well, I will let that answer stand," said the judge.

"You have no interest in the outcome of this case?" asked Cicilline.

"I'm just doing my job. I have no interest in the outcome of this case."

"Why is it that throughout these transcripts we find you giving witnesses the names of people?"

"Because that's the way I formed my questions at that time."

"You wouldn't consider them to be suggestive at all?"

"I would not, no."

"Do you realize that some of these witnesses in the very beginning had no idea what the big guy's name was, but by the time you had finished with them, they were calling him Steve Rosati?"

"I don't agree with that statement."

"You don't? Well, we will get to that in a minute, detective."

"Please, Mr. Cicilline, no editorializing," said the judge.

As he continued to hammer away at Detective Coyote's recounting of the testimony of the other witnesses, Cicilline was able to establish that Jeff Bloom had said that a man by the name of Antonio was the one who drove the black Datsun 280Z with the bullet holes in it. "Bloom also told people that Dallas was not involved in the killing at all, isn't that correct?"

Coyote agreed but countered, saying that at other times Bloom did implicate Dallas.

Cicilline established that "the tall man with the mustache," presumably Rosati, was present at the Bloom house on Saturday, October 11. "Isn't that correct?"

"Yes," said Coyote.

"Now, you heard the petitioner testify. You heard his sister testify that he picked her up at the airport in Rhode Island on October 11."

"That is correct."

"You don't know any way he could have gotten down to Florida after picking up his sister and be able to be at this meeting, do you?"

"My response to that would be if he picked up his sister," Coyote fired back.

"So you don't believe his sister?"

"Objection!" White shouted.

"Sustained!" barked the judge.

"Is that it?" Cicilline asked, dumbfounded, trying to end the case right then and there as one of mistaken identity.

"Sustained! Sustained!" the judge repeated, now measurably uncomfortable with the entire scene.

"Do you have any evidence that his sister didn't arrive into the United States as she said she did?"

"Objection!" White countered. "There's a time for final argument in a case."

"Mr. White," said the judge, "if I want argument, I will ask you. You know that."

"No, sir, I don't," Coyote said to Cicilline's question—the last before a needed recess.

When all were back from the recess and seated in the courtroom, the bailiff announced, "All rise," as Judge John F. Sheehan reentered the courtroom.

Raising one eyebrow, he caused all whispering in the audience to come to a halt. "For the record, Detective Coyote, I must inform you that you are still under oath. Don't take offense at that. I just have to do it for the record."

"I understand, Your Honor."

Cicilline moved on to the testimony of Cory Franco during his second deposition of June 2, 1988, whereby Detective Coyote had portrayed Franco as being at the Bloom residence the night of the murder and the night before on October 11, 1986.

"What does he tell them?"

"He indicates that on that Saturday, Pete the Greek, Peter Dallas, and the big guy—who I believe he identifies as Steve Rosati—were at the Bloom house."

"Does he ever refer to the big guy as Steve Rosati while he's describing all of that?"

"I do not believe so. No, sir," said Coyote.

"He keeps calling him the big guy, isn't that right?"

"I believe so."

"He also refers to him as the big fat guy too, doesn't he? And when he's looking at the photograph lineup where he points out Rosati, does the photograph show how tall the person is?"

"I don't believe it did, no."

"Well, you know it doesn't. It's from the neck up," Cicilline said sarcastically.

"That's correct."

"If we can just get right on to the issues," the judge said throwing Cicilline a stare.

"Judge, please, with all due respect, I am not taking any shortcuts to do what I need to do with this man."

A shudder rippled through the courtroom. "I'm not asking you to take any shortcuts," the judge said.

"I prefer to ask the questions I prefer to ask," Cicilline persisted, clearly disgusted.

"And I will rule on them the way I want to rule on them."

Defense counsel paused. It was not the judge he was piqued by. "That's the way it should be," Cicilline conceded, and then he returned to his questioning.

"And when you asked the man's name, what does he say?"

Coyote read from page 3 of the deposition. "Giordano, I guess that's his name."

Coyote continued to read his own interrogation in which he told Franco that "Giordano is just a name I threw out before . . . If I told you his name was Carl Rosati, would that," and he answered "Carl Rosati. I don't know. No. 5 is him."[3]

Cicilline then discussed Victor Merriman, the fellow who worked at Mr. Viscido's car dealership who described "two unpleasant people with dirty blonde hair [who] show up in a green Oldsmobile or Chevy with Michigan license plates at Mr. Viscido's garage looking for Joe."

"Did you ever stop to think, gee, the people that killed Viscido might be the people that he was informing against [when Viscido was arrested by the DEA in Ohio]? What did it mean to you as a police officer? Would it mean—here are some people with a motive?"

"A possible motive, yes."

"What did you find out about those people in the Michigan car?"

"Nothing, because I relied on Sergeant McNeil's investigation."

"So, at that point you had already decided how this case was going to go?"

"I would not say that. No, sir."

"Well, you had decided there was no need to look for the people with the motive, isn't that true?"

"I decided that there was no reason for me to look at that."

Cicilline moved on to Calvin Fredrick, a drug dealer who stole Rosati's Corvette after a drug deal gone badly when Stephen was living at Lighthouse Point with Kara in 1985.

"When Detective McNeil interviewed Fredrick, he said that 'he wasn't perfectly sure if Rosati had set him up on the drug rip-off.' So we agree, he wasn't specifically sure?"

"He uses those words, yes, sir."

"Now, that was November of 1988. You get him in '91, and now he's positive?"

"I can't recall exactly what I said," Coyote hedged. "He believed that Rosati had set him up. That's what I recall."

Cicilline hammered away on the difference between Fredrick's uncertainty when Deerfield interviewed him and his certainty when Coyote got him. "Will you concede that here is another instance where evidence got a little better?"

"I would not say that, no."

"Well, we went from a possibility to him now being positive."

Cicilline moved on to Sweetie Sartucci, who looked at the composite of the big guy in 1987 and said that it resembled Billy Edwards. White objected to further inquiry about Sweetie Sartucci.

"What difference does it make? Sweetie Sartucci is never mentioned with respect to the incident of October 12."

"The difference it makes," defense rebutted, "is that the state contends that in the summer months of 1986, she identified a person that she says is Steve Rosati, and she said, no, it looks like Billy Edwards."

"All right," said the judge, irked by the bickering between defense and prosecution. "Continue."

"Did you ever look for Billy Edwards?"

"No, sir, I did not," said Coyote.

Cicilline paused for a long time to look over his notes.

"Do you have much more, Mr. Cicilline?" Judge Sheehan asked after a lull.

"I have nothing further."

"You're sure? I don't want to rush you," Sheehan teased.

"I apologize, Your Honor," Cicilline said. "It's warm in here and Mr. White has been beating up on me for several days."

"Hmm," said the judge. "Mr. White, I'm going to give you overnight to digest."

CHAPTER 46:
The Hearing: White on Redirect

Day Twelve: February 22, 1991

"Good morning," White said to his star witness. "Detective Coyote, is it fair to say that Peter Dallas acknowledges in sworn testimony having been both at the Bloom house and the Viscido residence on October 12, 1986?"

"That is correct," Coyote said.

"Was there ever a time that Peter Dallas claimed to you that he had lied about the things that happened that night?"

"After he was in custody, he indicated that he had lied to somebody, yes, sir. I believe it was a week or two after Mr. Dallas was incarcerated in the Broward County Sheriff's Office Jail. It was a frantic phone call from Mr. Dallas in which he stated to me that he had just been contacted by two gentlemen who identified themselves as attorneys. He said, 'you told me that you were going to protect me.' What he meant was that he was afraid of being transferred to the same facility where Pete the Greek was. But they were separated. I had taken care of that. One was on one floor, and the other on another floor. He had crossed paths with Pete the Greek when two attorneys pulled them both out, and so Dallas was extremely upset. He indicated to me that he was afraid for his life."

"What did you do?"

"Within seconds," Coyote said, dutifully, "I called Chuck Morton of the State's Attorney General's Office. He indicated that Dallas had lied, and he indicated that Dallas feared for his life. I feared for his life. That shouldn't have happened. Mr. Morton obtained a court order, and we moved him under a fictitious name to another jail."

The court order was shown to Judge Sheehan with Dallas's new name and location "blacked out" to protect his safety. After the revelation of this cloak-and-dagger maneuver, White turned the witness back to Cicilline for recross. A few questions were asked and answered, Detective Coyote stepped down, and a short recess was called.

CHAPTER 47:
Closing in

Honest detective work had helped in finding one of Stephen Rosati's last addresses, Wright by the Sea Motel. The date was October 17, 1988. Sergeant McNeil requested from Chuck Morton that Rosati's phone records from the motel be subpoenaed and copied, and they were. The sergeant failed to note that the phone calls did *not* correspond to anyone involved in the case. Kit Finch's former girlfriend, Tiffany Bryant—a local stripper who also knew Pete the Greek—was contacted. Kit Finch was the first person to point the way to Stephen Rosati. He was Joe Viscido, Jr.'s best friend and had helped Mr. Viscido clean up the blood from the apartment. He was also the one person who could tie Rosati to Pete the Greek because he saw them together at nightclubs and, more important, when Rosati and Pete the Greek drove over to Finch's trailer either in Stephen's Corvette or, possibly, in Pete's Porsche sometime in 1985.

Tiffany recognized Rosati, who she knew as the male dancer

Conan "with the big muscles" who came to Finch's trailer with Pete the Greek.

When asked by McNeil if Kit thought Rosati killed Viscido, Tiffany replied, "He definitely thinks it. If you're looking for a big guy, you don't have to look any farther than this guy."

* * *

A big break for McNeil finally came when Jeff Bloom was called back for another interrogation, even though he was a witness who could contradict himself three times in one sitting. It had been two years since the homicide, and it would be his third deposition. The statement was taken in the presence of Bloom's attorney, Hilliard Moldof, and the prosecutorial team of Detectives McNeil and Burndt and Assistant Attorney General Chuck Morton.

"During the interview, Jeff Bloom . . . was inconsistent and changed his version of what happened," Sergeant McNeil reported, "[However, Bloom] did now admit that he had shown Pete the Greek and another subject where Joseph Viscido, Jr., lived on either the Friday or Saturday night before he was killed. The second subject was subsequently identified as Carl Stephen Rosati."

Some believed that Bloom's inconsistencies were linked to his wish to protect his brother Skip.

"Did Dallas ever make any statement in your presence that he had robbed and killed Joe Viscido? And when I say killed, I say in any terminology or phraseology, 'I wasted Joe Viscido,' 'I did Joe Viscido in.' In any manner, shape, or form?"

"No, sir. If so, I would've said. I would've went to the police or something. I would've known for sure who did it 'cause Joe was a good friend of mine." [What Jeff had said in the first deposition was that Dallas stated a fact; namely, that "Joe's done with."]

The police were not going to let go of this crucial point, though. Detective McNeil soon asked him, "The night that this statement was made about doing away with Joe, you know—you can remember Dallas being to your place at that time, correct."

"I—I really—I don't remember."

At this point, Chuck Morton, the prosecutor, interrupted. "Jeff," Morton said, "how do you remember such a statement: that Peter Dallas said that he did away with Joe?"

"From Officer McNeil," Jeff Bloom said to their amazement. "He said that he has other people saying that they heard it said in my house, and I was there. I don't remember that being said. But I guess

I may as well say it, because if he's got other people saying that they heard him say it . . ."

"If you don't remember, you don't remember," Morton obliged.

"No, I don't," said Bloom.

Trying to calm his witness, McNeil continued, "You said that you made the statement that you heard Peter Dallas say that he had done away with Joe Viscido because I told you to say it. That's not the case. You know you heard the statement. I saw it in your face. I saw it in your eyes. I saw it in your total body reactions, your emotional condition. And I understand that, Jeff. I understand that you're deathly afraid. That's correct, isn't it?"

"Yes, sir."

"But I don't want you to put it off on cocaine."

"Yessa."

"Excuse me?"

"Yes, sir."

"So, I don't want you to say it because I'm telling you, because I'm not telling you to say it. You know you heard it, but you're scared to death."

With Bloom's attorney silent as a mouse, the witness nodded his head. "Right?" Detective McNeil asked, trying to clarify the situation once and for all.

"Yes, sir. I can't exactly remember exactly how he said it, though. But I vague—I can remember him, like you're saying."

"'Joe's done with and through with?'" the detective asked.

"I don't know exactly how it went," Bloom concluded, "but I heard something, 'Joe's dead. He's gone.'"

A year later on December 12, 1988, during the third taped interview, Bloom's testimony shifted again. "Prior to the taking of your statement here today, I have indicated to you that I had statements that indicated that you had not told us the truth. Is that correct?" Sergeant McNeil asked.

"Yes, sir."

Bloom said that he had been at Pete the Greek's restaurant.

"Pete started bragging about people he had ripped off and stuff. He said to me, 'Do you know anybody who's got any shit?' I said, 'Yeah, Joe Viscido.' He says, 'You want to show me where he lives?' I said, 'Okay.' So, me and Pete and some other guy, a tall guy with a mustache—I don't remember his name—drove over in a car, went by, and I said, 'There, it's on the corner.'"

"How many days before the shooting was this?" Chuck Morton asked.

"About a week."

"Can you describe the other guy?" Sergeant McNeil asked.

"Tall, mustache, big guy, stocky."

"Would you consider him to be a weight lifter?"

"Yes, sir. Could be this guy." Bloom pointed to Stephen Rosati.

This correlated with two other positive IDs of Rosati, by Cory Franco and Vic Giordano. The ID contradicted previous testimony when Bloom failed to identify Rosati in a photo lineup. Now he was saying that he had seen this big guy the night after Joe was killed and that he had seen him *since* that time as well.

"What kind of car did this guy drive?"

"He was in a black 280ZX [Datsun] with bullet holes all in the side of his car."

Chuck Morton asked, "Could it have been a black sports car?"

"It had bullet holes on the driver's side on the fender," Bloom said, not addressing the issue of whether or not it was a sports car.

"What's this guy like?" the detective asked.

"Weird—the way he talks. He'll, like, scare you."

"You don't know his name?"

"No, sir, I don't. It's a weird name. Totally baffled about his name."

"But you think this is his picture?" the detective said pointing again to Rosati in the lineup.

"Shoo."

"Is that a yes?"

"Yes, sir."

Not letting it rest, Detective McNeil decided to stir the hornet's nest. He read a statement from another witness, probably Cory Franco, concerning Jeff's brother, Skip, going to Joe Viscido's house to obtain cocaine the night of the murder.

"When I first heard about this," the voice on the tape said, "it was from Jeff Bloom. He said he set up Joe Viscido for a bust. Pete the Greek got there and they killed Joe Viscido."

With his lawyer, Hilliard Moldof, by his side, Jeff blasted back. "That's a fuck'n lie. That's the God's honest truth; that is a lie. I'm not lying a bit. Put me on a polygraph, that's a lie."

"So it was coincidence that your brother went over and got this cocaine."

"My brother had nothing to do with this."

"Don't you see, in our position, where that looks clearly like a *recon*?"

"I don't understand."

"Like reconnaissance," Sergeant McNeil explained. "When you go out on a scouting mission to see about the enemy so you can attack?"

"That I understand, but Skip had nothing to do with this."

Although Jeff Bloom's testimony was inconsistent, Detective McNeil felt that they now had enough to go to the Broward County grand jury. First, though, he interviewed Jeff's brother Skip Bloom for possible corroboration. In early May 1989, McNeil drove out once again to Deerfield Beach to speak to Skip. The interview took place on the doorstep of the Bloom house.

"Yeah, I purchased cocaine from Joe Viscido in the afternoon of the very day of the murder," Skip said straightforwardly.

"We have witnesses said you were there that night," the detective replied.

"No, I did go back, but one of Joe's runners brought it out and gave it to me behind the Winn-Dixie. That must have been around five, six at night."

"And then the next day Pete the Greek came after you with a baseball bat?"

"No, that was a couple of weeks later. He scared the shit out of me 'cause I owed him eighty-five bucks."

"It wasn't the day after?"

"No."

"I want you to look at these photos and see if you can pick out one of Pete's friends."

Skip looked over the Rosati lineup but did not pick him out. "I don't see anybody."

"So you don't remember Pete going over to rip Joe off and then return to your brother's place?"

"That's all bullshit," Skip said. "Jeff's blown it all out of proportion 'cause the Greek came at me with a bat one day when I didn't finish paying him. For some crazy reason you're trying to frame these guys, and, I'm telling you, they got nothing to do with it."[1]

CHAPTER 48:
Ambush

Joe Viscido, Sr., warned his wife. Fearful that his own life might be taken and willing to risk it in any event, Viscido kept his .357 Magnum handy as he put on another disguise.

"Your wig's practically on backwards!" Rose tried to keep up a good face as she adjusted the wig, kissed her husband, and said, "Be careful."

Mr. Viscido headed over to Pete the Greek's father's restaurant, Little Athens, to stake it out. He passed the open fruit market and nailed another set of flyers of the composites of the two killers to the telephone poles, along with a picture of Joe that mentioned the $10,000 reward. He hated ripping down signs of other wanted men and lost kids, and he vowed to start a group for families of missing and dead children as soon as he nailed the rats that killed his son. He had also purchased newspaper advertisements, which displayed the same information. Everybody in Pompano Beach would know that

Joe Viscido, Sr., loved his son. Viscido pulled his car into a shady spot under some low-hanging trees—and watched.

When he saw Pete the Greek, he wondered if the big man with him could be Rosati. His heart pounded as he reported into his tape recorder what he believed to be a cocaine deal going down by the restaurant. He spotted Joe's gun, the Uzi. Viscido jotted his speculations down in the daily log that he kept of all his meetings on this investigation.

"We need more, Joe. The Assistant AG wants more," Detective McNeil said, reluctantly, referring to Chuck Morton, the point man at the Attorney General's Office who would oversee this entire case.

"What do you want me to do? Go in there and arrest them myself? The Greek's carrying, you do something about it! And what the hell's with Dallas? Do you mean to say you can't find one SOB with a record as long as my arm? You got an FBI file, don't you? Give me something, Chev!"

"You know I can't do that," the cop responded.

"Can't?" Joe yelled, causing McNeil's fellow officers to glare in their direction. Viscido was undeterred. "The hell you can't! This ain't a one-way street. I gave you leads, and you're dragging your ass."

Completely disgusted, Viscido stormed upstairs and chewed out the chief of police as well. Although the cops would not give Viscido photographs or transcripts of the depositions they had already collected, they did give him the address of the New York jail where Peter Dallas was incarcerated. McNeil also suggested Viscido swing through Ohio again as he had been there once before.

"Ohio's bullshit, Chev, and you know it," Viscido said. "You put the pressure on, and Jeff Bloom is going to crack. Mark my words. I've been to Bloom's house a dozen times. He and Cory are going to come through. They're in this on the back end. On my own, I practically already got their confessions in the bag." With a touch of pride, Mr. Viscido patted the tape recorder in his chest pocket. "I'll be back in a month."

He unloaded a roll of film, his collection of surveillance tapes, and another possible address for Stephen Rosati, slapped them on McNeil's table, and headed out the door.

"You take care," Chevy McNeil said. He placed a concerned arm around the distraught man and walked with him to the parking lot. "These men are dangerous; they're killers, Joe. I don't have to tell you. You find anything, I want a promise you won't move on your own."

The detective placed a heavy hand on Viscido's shoulder and waited calmly until Viscido conceded a nod. "You find anything, anything at all, Joe, you give me a call."

So moved by the gesture, Mr. Viscido nodded again as he held back tears and drove off.

Before he left town, and unbeknownst to Detective McNeil, Joe Viscido, Sr., stopped at a local gun shop. Even though he already packed a pistol, he considered other options, examining rifles and scopes. After a time, as Viscido later told the *Sun-Sentinel,* he opted for "three more guns, hundreds of rounds of ammunition, and a set of binoculars."[1]

Consumed with his quest, there was absolutely no doubt in his mind that he wanted to kill the shooter who he assumed to be the big guy. He hired two more detectives to try and find Rosati, but the leads kept coming out at dead ends. Thus, he turned his attention to the mastermind and driver, Pete the Greek.

"I want that man dead," Viscido told his wife, to her horror.

"Joe," she said, "I can't handle this kind of life. You're going too far. Look at yourself."

"I am looking, Rose. Our son's dead, and I have to live with myself."

"Don't you think I hurt too?" she cried. "But this is crazy. You've got guns. You're becoming like them! If you don't put those things away, I won't be here when you get back." When Joe Viscido, Sr., strapped on his weapons, Rose packed her bags and walked out of her husband's life.[2]

Viscido had put on his best disguise: a wig, a set of false teeth, wire-rim glasses, and a chest plate to change the shape of his body. He got into a rented car, as Pete the Greek had already spotted Viscido's own vehicle, and then he headed out once again for Little Athens. He considered changing the license plates to further hide the identity of the vehicle, as he reviewed for the tenth time his escape route. He knew it wouldn't be easy to carry out a murder and considered a single headshot as his best option. Viscido dropped behind the Porsche, leaving two, sometimes three lengths between the cars. He followed it all evening.

Pete delivered a package to Oakland Park, had a beer at Scalley's Saloon, and shot the breeze with some of his buddies outside in the parking lot. Viscido patted his shoulder holster and checked the chamber for the umpteenth time. Beads of sweat poured from his brow as an unbridled vengeance tore through his heart. Every time Pete the Greek laughed, a knot in his chest drew tighter. "That man is going to die," he chanted as he waited and tried to review once again his alibi. It was after midnight before his opportunity finally arrived.

Mr. Viscido pulled in behind Pete the Greek's car at the Pompano Beach 7-Eleven and readied his mind for the attack—swift and clean. Wrapping his fingers around a .45 caliber pistol stuffed in his pocket, he got out of the car and waited.

Pete was inside, eyeballing the junk food aisle. *Why can't the cops pick up this guy?* Viscido thought as he tried to stop his hand from trembling. Mr. Viscido had already spent a solid year doing police work, following leads, and making the case. *We have this guy dead to rights.* He ruminated about his son, the daughter-in-law, and grandchildren he would never have, and about the death of his hopes and his dreams. *My Joe was going to go straight. I know it. He just needed a little more time.* Mr. Viscido was a proud man. He had built up a serious car dealership, which he had hoped his son would have taken over, and now every ounce of his being was invested in one thing: revenge. Pete turned toward the window; Viscido dropped his head.

"Please God, give me the strength to blow his brains out," Viscido chanted softly. He watched the Greek reach into his wallet and pay the cashier. Mr. Viscido's whole body trembled as the grieving man moved closer to get a better shot, as he went over again and again his getaway plan.

A punk with a cigarette pack stuffed like an extra bicep in his shirtsleeve absentmindedly tapped the hood of the rented car as he sauntered into the store. Viscido's heart felt heavy and his breath grew short. *Did that guy see me? Would he remember the car? Would I have to kill him too? My God, another man's son.* Crazy and conflicting thoughts raced through his mind, and panic began to overtake him. His armpits were soaked, his palms were sweating, and his mouth was dry.

Pete nodded to a chick by the magazine rack, exited the store, and glanced his way, without a tad of recognition, as he continued forward and brushed right beside him. Viscido reached for his gun, which was soaking wet. Pete placed his thumb on the door handle and opened the door. Viscido had his chance and had to act. Pete ducked his head as he sat behind the wheel, and Viscido moved forward. Pete turned the key in the ignition, checked behind him, placed his right arm over the passenger seat, and drove away without ever knowing that Viscido was there.

Having chickened out in this admitted second attempt on Pete the Greek's life, Viscido went back to his empty house, apologized to a photograph of his deceased son, and cried like a baby. His only consolation, he reasoned, was that Pete was not the actual triggerman. Viscido redirected his anger once again toward the big guy as he packed his gear and headed north.[3]

McNeil finally received a photo of Rosati from Bob Whiting of the FBI, which was taken after Rosati got into a fight with an ex-cop. Now, in May, the grand jury met to indict Pete the Greek, Peter Dallas, and Stephen Rosati. Unfortunately, the news was unfavorable. Highly distraught, Mr. Viscido drove over to the police station to discuss the situation.

Dealing with Joe Viscido was not Sergeant McNeil's only concern. There was also the embarrassment of letting a big case dissolve. The Broward Sheriff's Office didn't like to lose, and McNeil was now looking like a loser. Deerfield Beach had been a small outpost, and to the top brass, members of their crew were considered novices when it came to homicide investigations.

"I'm sorry," was all Detective McNeil could muster.

Viscido was completely taken aback.

"They simply didn't have enough proof to indict," McNeil explained.

Tears began to flow as Viscido raced out of the precinct house and wheeled out of the parking lot before Detective McNeil could reach him. Rose, who had reluctantly returned home, tried to console Joe, but he pushed her away and left the house. He bought a pack of cigarettes for the first time in quite awhile. Deeply depressed, Joe realized the only way out for him was to get back in the saddle and finish what he set out to do.

A few days later was Mother's Day. Rose drove out to the cemetery to spend the day at her son's grave. When she returned, her husband was gone. He left a note saying he was going to New Jersey because that's were he thought the big guy was living.

Detective R. T. Fitzgerald of the Palm Beach County Sheriff's Office notified Sergeant McNeil that Skip Bloom had been found shot to death along with his dog. The bodies were found on a road in Boca on May 22, 1989.

"Somebody'd have to be pretty angry to shoot a dog. What kind of gun was used?" the detective inquired. "Let me get out there and go over this with you. This guy's death may be related to the Viscido case

I'm working on. Skip would have been a key witness to help straighten out this mess."

Sergeant McNeil drove to Palm Beach the following day and reviewed the Viscido case with Detective Fitzgerald.

"The Greek's in jail, so it can't be him. Do you know anything about the big guy, Rosati?"

"Yeah, he's a dancer from the Palm Beach area," Fitzgerald said.

Sergeant McNeil couldn't believe it. "I've been looking for this guy forever. How'd you find him?"

"On the computer. I think he might be living in the Fort Lauderdale area now," Fitzgerald replied. "Yeah, here, look at this." McNeil leaned over to get a better view. "Rosati had a speeding ticket in February down in Pompano Beach. That's how he popped up. He's driving a Mercedes with a Rhode Island registration."

"Rhode Island? What the hell is he doing with a Mercedes from Rhode Island?"

"That must be why you missed him," Fitzgerald said.

"Out of state," McNeil said reflectively.

"Bingo," Fitzgerald cut back in. "We've got him at the Port Royale apartments in Fort Lauderdale."

"I'll grab Hernandez—he's a big guy—and go down and stake out the place ASAP. We'll see if we can pick him up."

Joe Viscido, Sr., checked his hidden tape recorder and drove out to Jeff Bloom's home. "Jeff," he said, the tape rolling, "why don't you just admit you set up my son, and that's why he got killed. You took Dallas, Rosati, and the Greek right over there, pointed out where he lived, and the next thing you knew, Joe was dead."

"That's a crock, Viscido, I don't even know who Rosati is. And I never did this. You're whacked out man. You're out to get me, and my brother's dead. Fuck'n coincidence, ain't it? Get outahere." Bloom began to sob. Joe Viscido, Sr., turned away and then shut off his tape machine.[4]

Three days after Skip Bloom was found murdered, Sergeants McNeil and Hernandez knocked on Stephen Rosati's door. It was lunchtime and Rosati was there. According to the sergeant's report he read the suspect his Miranda rights and then interviewed him at the apartment.

Although Rosati admitted to knowing Pete the Greek, "he denied that he had any involvement in any type of drug rip-off which involved Joseph Viscido. Rosati appeared quite nervous about having an interview."

Sergeant McNeil asked Rosati to come down to the police station, and Rosati said that he would after he took a shower. The sergeant waited about an hour and a half and then called Rosati back. Rosati said that he tried to call the sergeant to tell him that he had changed his mind because he wanted to have an attorney present. Phone records confirmed this.

An hour later, an attorney representing the Rosati family in Florida called to discuss whether or not Stephen should talk to the detective. As it turned out, the lawyer denied permission.

At this point, Sergeant McNeil would be taken off the case. Because of a reorganization of precincts within Broward County, which caused his jurisdiction to change, the case was transferred to seasoned undercover detectives Bobby Coyote and Frank Puccini. They would set out to reinterview the key eyewitnesses, solve the problems outlined by the grand jury, and follow through on the arrests of Peter Dallas, Pete the Greek, and Carl Stephen Rosati.

CHAPTER 49:
The Hearing: Private Eye

Day Twelve, Continued: February 22, 1991

The subliminal buzz that generally hovered between testimonies dropped to dead silence when the next witness entered the courtroom. This man and the one to follow could shatter the prosecution's case. Apparently, most of the people in the audience sensed it, and White tensed in anticipation.

An imposing figure of football-player-sized proportions, William Venturi, of Geller and Venturi Associates, lumbered in. A licensed private investigator for the state of Florida and a former detective with the Metro Dade Police Department of Miami, Venturi was now honorably retired. Venturi was a seasoned pro with seven years experience in homicide. Pete the Greek's attorney, John Howes, had hired Venturi to investigate the Peter Dallas connection. With the approval of a Florida court, Venturi, along with his partner, Jeffrey

Geller, interviewed Dallas at the Broward County Jail on September 27, 1990. This was shortly after Rosati had been incarcerated.

"Did you make a request to see Roussonicolos [Pete the Greek] on the same date?" Cicilline asked.

"I don't believe so. I had been seeing Mr. Roussonicolos on a steady basis, but on that date, we were there to see Mr. Dallas. We pulled Dallas out about 2:00 p.m. The jailers brought Mr. Dallas into a large room. They turned him over to us, and then we went into an interview room."

"Was Roussonicolos there?"

"No, sir."

"And what did you do?"

"I told Mr. Dallas that we were private investigators working for attorney John Howes and that we represented Peter Roussonicolos. We were with him about an hour and a half."

"At any time, did Mr. Dallas say he wanted to leave?"

"No. I told him that I noticed that there was no attorney representing him. He told us that he was told by the clerk's office that he would be appointed an attorney at his hearing, and he said that he *did* want to talk to us."

"Did he tell you how he was transferred from the New York prison to Florida?"

"Yes. He said it was not voluntary."

"What did he say about Stephen Rosati?"

"Said he didn't know him, never met him." The judge looked over at Detective Coyote, who did not return the gaze. Venturi went on. "He said that he was first shown [photos of Rosati] by the Broward County detectives when they came to see him in New York. They told him that he was involved in a murder case and that he was facing the electric chair. He said at that particular time, he panicked when he heard the words *electric chair*. Says they interviewed him for quite some time, showed 'em photographs of the home where the murder took place and a composite sketch of Mr. Rosati, and he says they talked to him for quite a while. His words, I believe, and I quote, were, 'They wrote a book and they wanted me to fill in the blanks.' He said, 'I was scared to death.'"

"Was he afraid of the police personally or afraid of something else?"

"No, the police he wasn't afraid of. He'd been around a long time, had beaten a similar rap in New York. 'I had a good lawyer protecting me,' he said. 'I went to trial and I won.' He said, 'I've been around, but when it comes to the electric chair, and I know I don't have the money for a good lawyer to protect me, I'll do anything not to go to the electric chair, and I told them anything they wanted.'"

"And he said that he didn't know Rosati?" Cicilline repeated for clarification. Spellbound, the crowd waited for the answer.

"Never met him."

The judge's gaze was enough to stifle the buzz that began to erupt throughout the courtroom.

"Did he acknowledge any involvement in the Viscido murder?"

"He knew *nothing* about the murder until the police played tapes for him and read transcripts of witnesses that implicated him in the murder."

"What happened after that?"

"Well, it was an extensive interview. My partner had numerous notes that we wanted to just go over. I felt that this man was scared and I believed him, but, anyway, I went back to my office, and when I get there, I got a call from an individual claiming to be Peter Dallas's brother. He was calling from New York. He said that . . ."

"Objection."

"Ground?"

"Ground?" White repeated to the judge sheepishly.

"Yes," the judge challenged.

"I withdraw the objection."

"All right," said the judge. "You didn't want to use that dirty word *hearsay*."

"No comment, Your Honor," White spoke wisely. The judge stared him down. White responded, "Instinct."

Cicilline broke in, stealing the moment. "Instinct. That will be a new exception to the hearsay rule."

He returned to the witness. "And what did he say?"

"The brother said that Peter felt that I could be trusted and that the family was going to try and raise the money to get an attorney that would represent him properly, and then he would come forth and tell the truth."

"That is all," Cicilline said, whirling around. "Your witness."

White stepped up for the cross. "During your seven years as a police detective, how many homicide investigations would you estimate you have been involved in?"

"About a thousand."

The number staggered the prosecutor. Shocked, but buying time and trying not to show it, he improvised, "A thousand homicides, is that right?"

"Yes, sir," Venturi said.

"When you were in the police department, was Howes a prosecutor or a defense lawyer?"

"I didn't know John Howes then." Since then, however, Venturi said that he had worked on as many as forty cases for Howes.

White wanted to know if Venturi was aware of possible criminal activity associated with Pete the Greek. Cicilline objected on the grounds that these kinds of questions might be a violation of attorney-client privilege. The judge agreed.

"Did you read Roussonicolos's case file?"

"Never had a chance. No, sir."

White asked when Venturi began working with Geller, and he said "About two years ago, sometime back in '88." Geller was also a former police officer. White droned on for nearly an hour on these topics before asking about Dallas.

"What was your reason for going to see Peter Dallas on September 27?"

"I [wanted] to see what he had to say about the case."

White asked numerous peripheral questions on why Venturi was working for Howes and how many files were involved. If Venturi was not allowed access to the files, how did he know that Roussonicolos, Dallas, and Rosati were linked? Venturi answered that it was spelled out in newspaper articles. These kinds of questions continued for what seemed like an eternity, amid Cicilline's objections, before a recess was called for lunch.

White came back from the break with a copy of the prison logbook, which showed that Venturi had signed out Pete the Greek and Peter Dallas at the same time on September 27.

Venturi explained that maybe he did see Pete the Greek the same day but just didn't remember. It had taken White nearly three hours to reveal this finding. Cicilline acknowledged the revelation in two sentences.

"I have conceded the point," Cicilline said. "At one point he did say no, and on reflection, he later said that maybe yes, he did see them both on the same day."

Venturi said, "I don't remember seeing him that day, but if we pulled him out, then we talked to him. [However,] we saw Dallas alone, and if I saw Roussonicolos, he was alone. They did *not* see each other. I did *not* have them together."

White hammered away again on the logbook entry showing simultaneous requests for access to Dallas and Pete the Greek for nearly another half hour. According to Venturi, Geller thought that they had seen Pete the Greek on the same day, and White wanted to know why Venturi's testimony had been discussed with Geller during lunch break. "He's my partner," Venturi said.

"When you first visited Peter Dallas [five months ago], did you know beforehand that you would be a witness at this hearing?"

"No."

"Did you know Mr. Cicilline as of September 27?"

"The first time I heard the name was when I spoke to [Fran Martin] on the phone last week. I never knew I would be a witness in this hearing until last week."

Shocked that there was no prior relationship between Rosati and Venturi, the prosecutor did his best to hide his surprise. "You didn't have a statement from Roussonicolos on the twenty-seventh when you went to see Dallas?"

"Sustained," said the judge anticipating Cicilline's objection, who nodded to him in synch. "He's already testified he had."

"Respectfully, Your Honor," White persisted willfully, "I ask respectfully that the witness be allowed to answer the questions on cross-examination."

"Now listen," the judge said angrily, having endured White's obdurate strategy of staying on a single point, the logbook discrepancy, for an entire day. "Let's get one thing straight: I will run this courtroom, and I will ask questions I want, and I will make any comments! If you don't like it, there's a seventh floor, and you know what you can do up there."

"I understand, Your Honor."

"We will take a short recess," announced the judge.

When court resumed, Judge Sheehan cautioned, "From now on, if I want comments on objections or anything else, I will ask for them. Mr. White."

"Thank you, Your Honor," White nodded, and then he continued. "Mr. Venturi, how long did you spend with Peter Dallas on September 27?"

"About an hour an a half. Geller was with me the whole time."

"How did the conversation go?"

"I told him that we were working for John Howes, who was representing Peter Roussonicolos. I asked him right off if he had an attorney, and he told me he saw someone his first day in court, but that person was not appointed to him, and he didn't know the person's name."

"Did he tell you that he had signed a plea agreement?"

"Not at that point. Maybe an hour later."

"Certainly then you knew he was represented by counsel, correct?" asked White, back on target.

"At that point he told us that he had made a deal with a black guy named Chuck from the State Attorney's Office. And I said Chuck Morton, and he said yes. I said, I thought you told me that you didn't have an attorney. He says, 'Well, I don't even know if this guy's my attorney.' He says, 'If I had money to get a real attorney I wouldn't have done this,' and he just went on and on. At that time I stopped the conversation and found the log, which listed his attorney. It was Tom Gallagher, who's a public defender. I said, is Tom Gallagher your attorney, and he said that he didn't know his name."

"Did you do anything once you found out that he, in fact, had counsel and that Chuck Morton was involved?"

"Normally, I would have called counsel, but he agreed to continue to talk. He wanted to talk, and maybe we talked to him for another five or ten minutes, and at that time I terminated the conversation and attempted to call Mr. Gallagher at the Public Defender's Office."

"When you finally reached Mr. Gallagher, did you tell him what Dallas had told you?" the prosecutor wanted to know.

"No. I was calling to basically apologize for, you know, going ahead and talking to his client, and he said he appreciated that, and he [also said] he knew about the conversation and that basically it was our conversation."

"I take it," White began portentously, "that as a professional, both working in the homicide division for the prosecution and now for the defense, your ultimate interest is the ends of justice, correct?"

"Yes, sir," Venturi said.

"And Peter Dallas told you, among other things, that he wasn't there?"

"Yes, sir."

"And wouldn't it be fair to say that that's something that is absolutely critical to the defense of his case?"

"Yes, sir."

"And you didn't tell Mr. Gallagher what Dallas had said?"

"He seemed kind of short on the phone. He wasn't listed as the attorney of record, and now we found out he was the attorney. We were calling him to advise him that we did speak to his client and that was it."

"You knew that Carl Rosati was a co-defendant then, and you had not by then had any contact with his defense team?"

"None, whatsoever. . . . This file has been laying dormant for a long time. I ran into Richard Rendina [one of Pete the Greek's attorneys] down in Miami. He had [seen] a copy of a statement I had taken, and he said it might help the defense up in New Jersey. I said, well, they never contacted me, and I said, I'm not going to contact them, and then I got a call from Mr. Martin."

"You mean New Jersey or Rhode Island?" asked the judge.

"I'm sorry, Rhode Island."

"You're saying that you knew that Peter Dallas told you that he did not know Carl Stephen Rosati and that he had not participated in the murder, and it's your testimony that upon learning from Mr. Rendina that someone in Rhode Island was interested in a statement you had taken from Dallas, your response was, 'let them call me, I'm not calling them?'"

"Yes, sir."

"You testified before that your ultimate objective as a private investigator and a homicide detective previously was the interest of justice."

Like a pulling guard in a football game, Cicilline moved to block. "Objection," he belted out. "The law enforcement officer performs one function, a private investigator performs another. Statements, as the court well knows in these kinds of circumstances, are often kept as secrets so law enforcement officers don't get an opportunity to rehabilitate a witness. It doesn't mean because he didn't call up the police or call me because this evidence was favorable to me, that he's misperforming in some way or abused public office."

The judge continued the line of reasoning: "He has no obligation as a private investigator to notify anybody if he doesn't want to."

"That's the point of my objection," Cicilline said, nodding to his star witness.

"Sustained."

"Did you memorialize the statement?" White asked.

"Yes, sir. My partner, Jeff, was taking notes."

"Why didn't you use a tape recorder?"

"Because Mr. Dallas said, 'No, I'm not taping anything.' 'Why not?' I asked, and he says, 'If you want to talk to me, take the tape out of the machine,' at which time I did."

"How many times did you speak to Dallas?"

"Just that one day."

"How much longer, Mr. White?" the judge asked, concerned about the Florida Attorney Driscoll catching his Miami plane.

"Not very much longer," White replied.

White asked Venturi five more times if he ever spoke to Dallas again, and five more times he said he didn't think so. Finally, White produced a log, which showed that Venturi had called down Dallas on September 26. Venturi agreed that that was his signature, but he didn't think he saw him that day. "Maybe he didn't come down," Venturi said.

"I don't have anything else," White said.

CHAPTER 50:

The Hearing: Monterey Shock

Day Thirteen: March 7, 1991

It would be two weeks before Venturi's associate, Jeffrey Geller, would take the stand. Cicilline took that time to compare Detective Coyote's statements against the depositions of the Florida witnesses taken by Coyote and his predecessor, Detective McNeil. Fortunately for Detective Coyote, he wasn't there.

"I thought Coyote would be here today, and I would have called him to impeach him with his testimony concerning Michelle Arrieta. He says something that is very inconsistent," Cicilline boldly announced.

"As you know," the judge said, "I have the transcript of Mr. Coyote's complete testimony."

"I have nothing further," Cicilline said.

"And by the way," the judge added impartially, "I have everyone else's testimony. I didn't single out Mr. Coyote."

Jeffrey Geller entered, and dead silence once again pervaded the courtroom. A younger man than Venturi, and somewhat smaller, Geller had an air about him that gave people the impression he was a straight shooter. As he had only been to Broward County Jail once in his life, he said, without a doubt, that on September 27, 1990, he and Venturi saw both Pete the Greek and Peter Dallas. He also said that he had a difficult time convincing Venturi of this because Venturi simply did not remember that this had occurred on the same day.

"We did not see Dallas and Roussonicolos at the same time, however."

"Was Dallas notified that he was not required by law to speak to you?" Cicilline asked.

"Yes. As a matter of fact, we asked if we could tape the interview, and he wouldn't allow that."

"What was it that Dallas said to you about Carl Stephen Rosati?"

"He said that he never met Stephen Rosati and actually used the name Carlos Stephen Rosati."

"Carlos?"

"Yes."

"And did he say where he had first heard the name?"

"From the police."

"And will you describe the procedure whereby he heard information about this case from the police?"

"He indicated to us that he had been incarcerated at a place in New York called Monterey Shock Incarceration Facility and had been interviewed by two detectives from Broward County, one being a detective by the name of Coyote and the other he knew only by his first name, Tommy. He indicated that they talked to him about the case and showed him statements, played tapes for him, showed him pictures, and basically told him all about this murder, and then interviewed him at that time about his involvement. He said he had no idea what happened and did not take part in anything."

"Did he say that he knew anything about the Viscido homicide?"

"He said that he confessed to the police his involvement along with this Carlos Stephen Rosati because they threatened him with the death penalty."

"And tell us what happened with respect to the photographs."

"He indicated that he had been shown a photograph of the crime scene, and when he didn't recognize it, the police had a problem with that. So Dallas indicated to them that that's how he remembered the crime scene, even though he hadn't been there, and during this entire interview, you have to understand, he just kept saying I wasn't there. I didn't do this."

"Did he discuss with you his need for a lawyer?"

"Yes, he wasn't happy with the representation he was getting. If he had a real lawyer—that is how he said it, a "real lawyer"—he would tell the police and the state the truth. But as long as the guy that was representing him at that point kept telling him to cooperate with the police and the state, he wasn't going to tell anybody the truth."

Randy White jumped up for the cross. He wanted to know what Geller knew about the case before he interviewed Dallas. "What did Venturi tell you?"

"That Dallas was going to testify against Peter Roussonicolos."

"Isn't it true that you knew before you got there that you were not only to see Dallas but also to see Mr. Howes's client, Mr. Roussonicolos?"

"That's correct."

"And Dallas never disclaimed knowing Peter Roussonicolos, did he?"

"Oh, absolutely not. He's known him for years."

"Isn't it a fact that on September 27 the idea of yourself and Mr. Venturi going to see Dallas and calling Roussonicolos at the same time was intentional [so that] Roussonicolos [would] see Dallas, so that Dallas would be scared about what he was going to say?"

"Objection. I object to this calling down business," said Cicilline.

"I know it," said the judge. "He's a very seasoned police officer. I think he can handle himself on the stand."

"I'm sure," said Cicilline, "but I think Mr. White, who probably doesn't have the experience that we do about how you get into a prison—I mean that's the way it works, you know, you sign all the names when you go in. You don't keep running back and forth to see different prisoners."

"The witness can answer that. Certainly after your helping him," the judge quipped.

"I had only just met Dallas. He did not seem afraid of Peter Roussonicolos to me when I met him."

"But he was going to testify against Roussonicolos about a murder?"

"It happens every day in Dade County," Geller said. "It doesn't mean they have to be afraid. Some are, some aren't."

On redirect, Cicilline asked, "Is it fair to say at this moment you are representing Roussonicolos and not Rosati?"

"Right."

"You had no interest in Rosati?"

"I didn't even know who Rosati was."

"Did you ever ask Dallas flat out, do you know Carl Stephen Rosati?"

"Yes."

"And what did he say?"

"Dallas didn't know Rosati," Geller said. "Never heard of him."

"The petitioner rests," Cicilline said.

White requested the option of putting on extra testimony, and the judge said that the court would give him two weeks. Stephen winced. "At that time," Sheehan continued, "if there's no further testimony, then both sides will be prepared to argue."

CHAPTER 51:
State of Terror

The judge had given Florida two weeks to come back with a witness. Esther, feeling confident that they would not, had a party catered. It was her first and only moment of celebration since her son had been incarcerated six months earlier, and now she expected him home any day.

"This testimony was electrifying," Esther said, "and all of us thought, at that moment, that we had won our case. We invited Venturi and Geller back to celebrate."

During the meal, Geller became serious. "Mr. Rosati," he said to Carl, "I don't want to burst your bubble. However, it is imperative that you realize that even if Stephen beats this extradition hearing he is not going to be safe."

"What do you mean, he won't be safe?" Carl shuddered. "Why is that?"

Geller put down his knife and fork and turned squarely to face the man. "Because they will stalk him, and they will find him. And then they'll bring him down to Florida, no matter what."

"Are you serious? Who? Coyote?"

"Not Coyote," he said in a dismissive manner. "Professionals."

"Professionals?"

"Bounty hunters. That's what they do for a living. And don't think that fences, guard dogs, deadbolts, or alarm systems will stop them. These guys are animals. Your only recourse is to hide Stephen in a place where they will never find him."

"You mean out of the state?"

"I mean out of country. It would be best if even you did not know where he is."

The investigators then painted a foreboding picture. Venturi elaborated, "You may think that your son is big, but he's small in comparison to the guys I know they'll send. These men who'll come up will be as large as mountains. They'll kidnap Stephen—for sure—chloroform him, stuff him in a trunk, and, just like that, drive him in that condition across state lines. And the next time Stephen wakes up, he'll be in a Florida prison. They don't mess around."

"It was crazy," Esther recalled. "If we had won extradition, and this seemed certain after Venturi and Geller's testimony, Stephen would be a free man within the borders of the state of Rhode Island. However, if he was outside these borders, for any reason, it wouldn't matter. He would be a fugitive from justice. In other words, these bounty hunters could be legal kidnappers, as long as they got their catch past the state lines."

The Rosatis now had good reason to be frightened because now they knew that if they won, their son would have to be put in some type of safe house. Furtively, they sought out a friend who was in the Knights of Malta, a secret religious order with monasteries throughout the world. This individual agreed to help in the event that Stephen won the hearing. The plan was to put him in an underground enclave in Canada, North Africa, or Europe—a location that the Rosatis would not even know.

"I realized now that I was not living in a free country," Esther imparted somberly. "You could win a legal battle, fair and square, and then have kidnappers run free reign. There was nothing we could do."

The law is vague here. Bounty hunters can legally kidnap people and take them to the requesting state. Although their actions would be illegal within the state where extradition was successfully blocked, once Rosati was outside state lines, he would be considered a fugitive from justice and could be legally hauled back to Florida.

"We were opening the door not only to a legal nightmare," Carl said, "but also to a political potboiler between the states of Rhode Island and Florida. Constitutional questions involving states' rights were now involved."

"It was ludicrous," Esther said, "to think that Stephen would be free. We could win but still lose. They would get their man no matter what the outcome."

Likening the Florida police and the Rhode Island prosecutor to "a dark force that had sunk their talons into us," Esther recounted, "We couldn't tell Stephen this. He was frightened enough as it was in jail, while we, outside of jail, were living in a state of terror of our own. We had a former police officer with the experience of 1,000 homicides under his belt telling us, "They have their own code of justice."

"Yes, Mr. Venturi," Carl said, "Justice, Broward style."

CHAPTER 52:
Good Cop—Bad

Michelle Arrieta was later questioned by John Aguero, Florida's assistant state prosecutor, with several other attorneys about the very deposition she gave that Cicilline and Detective Coyote had discussed at the hearing. This was in a separate investigation involving the murder of Joe Viscido, Jr. Michelle read over her transcript with Detective Coyote, whereby she picked Peter Dallas out of a photo lineup.

"Do you remember that?" Aguero asked.

"Uh-huh."

"Was that the guy?"

"Yeah."

"All right. Did Coyote prompt you in any way or tell you, 'I'd like you to pick No. 3'?"

"I don't even know which picture or which guy you're talking about right now," Michelle said.

"Right, right. I'm listening. I'm just looking for something," Aguero said, trying to gain her confidence. "But when you looked at it back then with Coyote, and Coyote left you—whenever that was—did you think, you know, this guy really made me do something I didn't want to do, or did you think everything was aboveboard? You know what I'm saying?"

"My personal feelings about that?" she asked.

"Yes."

"I just—they arrested me that day. They had me for eight hours, and I was crying my eyes out."

"Eight hours?" Aguero was astounded.

"Yes. And in all that time, they wouldn't even let me go to the bathroom. It was like, *get out of here.*"

"Who's this?"

"Tommy Puccini, whoever else. I don't ever want to see him again, and I haven't since that day."

"The statement says it's taken by Coyote."

"Oh, he was there."

"So was this identification something you didn't want to do, or was it something you did want to do?"

"I wanted to do it, but I wanted to be sure it was the right guy, you know. I don't want to put nobody that's innocent behind bars for the rest of his life."

"So when you're saying in here that No. 3 is the small guy, is that what you were thinking was the right person?"[1]

"That's what I was thinking, yeah. Basically, it was the right person, and the thing is that the picture didn't look like him, but they went over it a million times and they were—I looked at the person, certain points, and I said, yeah, that's him, because I think the guy he showed me had tons of acne and everything was different. But then they went over and told me like people really, really, really change, and so, I mean . . ."

"Was there ever a time when you and Coyote and Puccini didn't get along?" another attorney interrupted.

"Bobby Coyote and I, we always got along. He was very nice to me. He saw, you know, that I was a good girl, an honest girl, and that I wasn't lying to them, but it was that one day they called me into their office. He had heard through the grapevine that I was going to be arrested. People on the street told him they were going to arrest me, and sure enough, they [did]."

"What do you mean they arrested you?"

"'We're arresting you for lying to us,' they said. They came to my house. It was early in the morning. I was sleeping. So I threw myself together and went with them. They had me in this room for eight hours screaming and yelling and telling me you're lying and lying, and I was crying, and they were flashing pictures in front of me of Joe's death and of him, you know.

"And then, well, 'We're putting you under arrest for lying to us.' I was, like, what?! I can't believe this. They put handcuffs on me. And they took my purse out of the office. So I'm sitting there, and then they came back in and said, well, we have good news and we have bad news. We're not arresting you for lying, but we're arresting you for a warrant you had with your license from nine months ago, which I never knew I had. I thought I had cleared all that up.

"So they arrested me for that, and they drove me with that Puccini in the back seat with me, and they were acting like it was a big joke, ha-ha laughing."

"Do you think they were just trying to get at who killed Joe, though, or was it just that they were evil?" another attorney inquired.

"I'm sure that they were trying to get something out of me that I couldn't tell them. I mean, I took a polygraph and I told Bobby Coyote I'll talk to you, I'll deal with you, but I don't want to see those guys anymore because if they can't see that I'm honest, I have nothing to hide."

"Okay, so getting back to the photo ID, and you picked No. 3, Peter Dallas. So at that point, did you know what Dallas looked like?"

"Oh, yeah, I knew. I hadn't seen him in person, but I'd seen tons of pictures of him. I've seen enough pictures to know Peter Dallas by that time."

"Who showed you a picture of him and said this is Peter Dallas?"

"The Deerfield cops."

"That's the only way you knew what his name was?"

"Peter Dallas was supposed to be at this party I was at, and that's another reason they said I was lying. Now, I'm supposed to stop and shout in the middle of the party, there's the guy who shot Joe! First of all, I never saw him, and they were a little confused because they got this picture of him at this same party."

Aguero thereupon showed Michelle the photo lineup once again. She reached over to No. 3 and said she knew that was Peter Dallas. And then she said, "It's so confusing. I mean, isn't there any way you could bring these guys in front of me so I could see them. These pictures do nothing."[2]

CHAPTER 53:
Final Arguments

Day Fourteen: March 20, 1991

It had been a fortnight since White and Cicilline had battled for the life of accused murderer Stephen Rosati. Judge Sheehan waited for the prisoner to be unshackled and seated comfortably in his chair beside defense counsel before proceeding. Not wanting to avoid responsibility on any level, the judge looked over to acknowledge Rosati's parents before proceeding. They nodded back.

"As I recall last time, Mr. White," the judge began, "you wanted to wait until today until you rested your case?"

"That's correct," White said dutifully. "I would like to submit as a full exhibit an affidavit of Charles Morton, assistant state attorney in Florida, a plea offer of Peter Dallas dated September 19, 1990, and a transcript of that offer."

"Any objection, Mr. Cicilline?"

"No, Your Honor."

"I have no other offerings at this time," said the prosecutor, referring to Peter Dallas's admitted involvement in the Viscido homicide, "and the state rests."

"Mr. Cicilline, anything further to offer?"[1]

"No, Your Honor."

"Mr. White, I will hear your final arguments."

Randall White entered center stage and unfolded his brief. Having lost recently to Cicilline on appeal on an unrelated murder trial, he did not want to lose again. This was a high-profile case, and this was the culmination. White had worked overtime to use his eagle eye to handle every detail. Reminiscent of an Ivy League law professor, with his fine, prematurely gray, shoulder-length hair, freshly pressed suit, and confident air, he began his discourse.

"Thank you, Your Honor. As everyone in the courtroom is well aware, this proceeding has been a long one. It has been hotly contested at times. It's been exhaustive, and we come to a point now where the decision will be yours. I will attempt to sum up the state's case, and the court and Mr. Cicilline have shown patience throughout the proceeding."

"Sometimes, Mr. White," the judge interjected to the amusement of the audience.

"And I would respectfully ask that the patience be given me again."

"So everyone understands," the judge continued in a more serious vein, "this case is extremely important to the petitioner and it is extremely important to the state of Florida and the state of Rhode Island, so you have all the time you want. We have today, tomorrow, and then we can start again Tuesday if we have to."

"Thank you, Your Honor," White replied. "This case is complicated by its length, by the fact that the proceedings have been adjourned from time to time, and by the fact that there are nearly one hundred exhibits from both sides to consider, eight separate volumes of transcript, and other multiple exhibits.

"In due respect to the court, and as it has been stated off the record on a number of occasions, this is, for all concerned, unfamiliar turf. I think it is conceded among myself, Mr. Cicilline, and perhaps even the court that a contested extradition hearing, let alone one of great length, is a rarity, and for that reason I think it appropriate to look again before reviewing the facts at what the state submits is the controlling law with respect to extradition."

Referring to a previous memorandum submitted, White continued. "First and foremost, the state urges that the court keep in mind as it reviews the testimony and documentary offerings by both sides that we are involved in a habeas proceeding, not a criminal proceeding.[2]

"[Let me] quote from the United States Constitution, Article 4, Section 2: A person charged in any state with treason, felony or other crime who shall flee from justice and be found in another state shall on demand of the executive authority of the state from which he fled be delivered up to be removed to the state having jurisdiction in the crime.

"Now, the courts [have said] that the purpose of the extradition clause was and is to perfect and maintain the Union among the states. This isn't a question of, in the classic sense, a criminal trial, [or] a matter of defendant's rights. While those rights must be in some measure observed, and the court must be sensitive to their existence, the extradition clause primarily sets forth the proposition that if one state says that they have an accused against whom a trial is sought, then the state in which he is found, called the asylum state, must give him up.

"Now, in this particular case, the state of Florida wants Carl Stephen Rosati. They have charged him with murder and robbery, and they want him back for trial. Not 'we want you to try him.' Upon receipt of the demand from Governor Martinez of the state of Florida, Governor DiPrete of our state said, okay, here he comes. It's a mandatory provision in the extradition clause of the United States Constitution. That is the point and the limited point at which this proceeding is invoked.

"The extradition clause wasn't and isn't self-executing. . . . And that's where and how a body of law has developed to figure that out. . . . The habeas court may consider whether or not the petitioner is a fugitive. That is, was he in the demanding state at the time the crime is alleged to have occurred, and is he now to be found in the asylum state?

"What Carl Stephen Rosati through his counsel is contesting is that he wasn't [in Florida] on October 12, 1986, [and now he] bears the burden. Usually, it is the state that bears the burden, but states vary in the nature of what quantum of proof is required to meet the burden. Some states use the standard 'clear and convincing.' Some have called it 'beyond a reasonable doubt.'"[3]

Quoting from *Muncey v. Cluff*, a 1905 case, White read, "'When it is conclusively proved that no question can be made that the person was not within the demanding state when the crime is said to have been committed . . . the court will discharge the defendant. [However, if] there is merely contradictory evidence, [then the petitioner has not met his burden and he goes back].' In other words, [their argument has] to be clear. It's got to be convincing. And the burden is on Carl Stephen Rosati to show he wasn't there. And if after review of all the evidence of both sides a question remains as to whether or not he was there, then that question must be resolved in the denial of the application for release under habeas corpus.[4]

"Now, having said all that as backdrop, I have urged that this is a matter ultimately of state's rights. Otherwise, to set up a burden of less than the one I have described would be to have an asylum state afford a petitioner greater rights than he would have if he were found and apprehended in the state that is demanding him, and that simply would defeat and undermine the clear meaning and effect of the extradition clause as it was adopted. . . .

"Although the temperature differs between here and Florida, and they have palm trees and we have icicles, one thing we do have very much in common is the United States Constitution. All that Florida is asking is to send him back so we can afford him at trial the same rights that you would give someone if the situation were reversed. This case does not involve a consideration of sending Mr. Rosati to a foreign land, a land whose laws may shock and disturb us. This is Florida. This is the United States, and at trial Stephen Rosati will, I'm sure, be afforded the full panoply of rights available to him by the United States Constitution when issues of guilt or innocence are being addressed. They're not and should not be addressed in this proceeding."

"I don't mean to interrupt you, Mr. White," the judge said, "but if I find that petitioner has, in my opinion, by clear and convincing evidence established that he was not in the demanding state, then the burden shifts—and if you don't agree with me, please tell me—the burden then shifts to the demanding state to produce competent and substantial evidence according to the cases you just gave me. Now, what if I believe both?"

"It would then be a situation where contradictory evidence existed, and then the extradition clause would be in order," White said.

"Thank you," said the judge.

White then proceeded to review the testimony of each of Rosati's witnesses: owner of the condominium, next-door neighbor, bookkeeper, people at the gym, Stephen's friends, and other associates—none of whom could say that they knew where Stephen Rosati was on October 12, 1986.

"Sure, they saw him in 1986, maybe even in October of 1986. But that was five years ago. Air travel hasn't advanced much, if at all. You know, I know, Mr. Cicilline knows, everyone in the room knows that the distance between Florida and Rhode Island, while perhaps fifteen or sixteen hundred miles on land, is but a matter of hours in the air. Stephen Rosati could be seen at breakfast in Rhode Island and lunch or dinner in Florida," White said. "What it boils down to is the few people who did address themselves to the critical date or dates.

"Now, you have on October 11 Mr. Rosati's well-intended sister and brother-in-law. Did they go to Europe? Did they photograph William Simon's yacht? I don't know, but I'm not sure that accepting the fact that they did is necessarily dispositive of whether Steve Rosati picked them up at the airport on October 11, 1986. And even if he did, it's not dispositive in any measure of his presence or absence from Rhode Island or Florida on October 12.

"Now, to the meat of the petitioner's case and whether or not it makes the grade: whether it passes muster with respect to being clear and convincing. The people who talked about October 12, 1986, primarily were three people: the petitioner, his sometime girlfriend Elodie Vanderpyl, and his live-in girlfriend Kara Lynx. What did they say about October 12, 1986?

"You heard from Kara Lynx at some length: her relationship with Stephen, how they had come back and forth to Florida, and how they lived together up here between December of '85 to the end of '87. Her claim was, 'He was with me every night, every single night, except for the fishing trip, he slept in his own bed.' His date with Elodie would have had to have been 'midday, morning, or early evening.'

"I submit that the thrust of what Kara Lynx is claiming is that Stephen was home with her on that night the way he had been faithful for the two years of cohabitation here in Rhode Island. That's not what Elodie Vanderpyl says. Elodie Vanderpyl says that on the night of October 12, the one you have to worry about, she says she went out to eat with him and had a few drinks. Well, whether Kara Lynx and Elodie Vanderpyl had independent recollections of the night of October 12, 1986, they couldn't both be right in a clear—in the clear context of what they had to say. He couldn't have been both home and eating out at a Chinese restaurant with Elodie."

White then moved to the crux of the issue. For Cicilline's unquestionably brilliant defense, it was his weakest link. Cicilline sat with his client pensively and listened to White continue.

"What does Carl Stephen Rosati say about this? He's the one on the hook. He's the one that's been detained since September. He's the one that was startled by the accusations, hinted at in May of '89 when police officers came to his door in Florida and shocked again in September when Detective Coyote showed up and arrested him. He's the one who searched his mind and his soul because this thing upset his life and turned his life upside down. And he doesn't tell you anything. He never utters a word about where he went that night. He talks about a phone call.

"I ask the court to recall and review the testimony of Carl Stephen Rosati with respect to that phone call. Does Stephen Rosati realistically remember that the call was twenty-two minutes long? In any event, we pressed on. He's searching his mind and soul and he's decided that it was, because they were planning to meet. He doesn't give you where they met, where they went, what they did. He offers nothing on that. And in that regard, I suppose he remains consistent with both Elodie Vanderpyl and Kara Lynx, but in the court's consideration of whether that evidence is clear and whether you are convinced about where he was the night of October 12, 1986, the night witnesses in Florida say he was in the Bloom residence and later the Viscido residence at the scene of the murder, it tells you nothing. It's not clear, and it's not convincing. Not by a long shot."

Carl and Esther Rosati looked on with deep concern in their eyes. White had decisively struck a nerve on a key point: Why hadn't Stephen simply admitted that he had met with Elodie that Sunday? Certainly under counsel's advice the accused had decided to be evasive on this issue, and White exploited this hole in his story to the maximum.

After a short recess, White proceeded to present the state's case.

"Mr. Rosati was willing to suggest falsely to the license authority in Florida that he lived somewhere where he didn't live in order to rent a car on his trip to Florida in January 1988. [He deceived a landlord in 1984, when he stated that he was married to Elodie Vanderpyl in order to obtain a lease.] The point being, Stephen Rosati has, in those circumstances, shown a willingness to shade the truth to meet his ends. What effect does that have on the weight of his testimony concerning where he was on October 12, 1986?"

Since Rosati had flown down to Florida two times in 1988, White wanted to know if there were there other times and challenged the court to decide.

"Sweetie Sartucci suggests she saw Stephen in Florida in 1986 at a restaurant with Pete the Greek and then saw him again in 1987."

To White, Sweetie's story "was very compelling." For all anyone knew, White intimated that Rosati could have commuted to Florida on a regular basis and that Kara Lynx had possibly gone out of state in May 1986 to visit her sister in New Jersey.

White reviewed Detective Bobby Coyote's testimony. Through Coyote's review of his numerous affidavits from Michelle Arrieta, Vic Giordano, Danny Ek, Cory Franco, and Jeffrey Bloom picking Stephen Rosati out of police photo lineups, White stated that within the limited context of an extradition hearing, the state had met its burden of providing contradictory evidence. Michelle Arrieta's initial reluctance to pick Rosati out of a police lineup, White contended, was due to the fact that "she was angry with the Deerfield Police, and that, I think she had a phrase for it as some kind of contest [she said "pissing contest"] about whether or not they were interested in the murder investigation or perhaps something else like a drug investigation." According to White's summary, she did, however, pick Rosati out of the Men in Motion photo. "Now, I'm sure there would be argument made by Mr. Cicilline about the credibility of all these witnesses. Without belittling the witnesses, a lot of them have jail in common."

White contended that there might have been cross-talk between them, perhaps even while they were in jail.

"Does that impeach them? Of course it does. But is it fatal? No! Mr. Cicilline will contend, I believe in good faith, to suggest [that their statements] were the creation of the fiction of Bobby Coyote, who wanted it to come out right. That's not what happened at all. What happened was that ultimately all these people with their various concerns against penal interest finally came around. Perhaps not Chris Jones, because he never makes a positive ID, but as to Arrieta and Giordano, who with Jones were at the scene of the crime, they ultimately aired the truth.

"The same with the people at the Bloom house. Look how they track Dallas and Rosati leaving the Bloom residence, disappearing, and coming back with that baggy Danny Ek talks about. Dallas talks about that too. Of all the things Mr. Cicilline pointed out that Dallas supposedly didn't know about the crime scene, that's the one thing he does talk about: that conspicuous baggy that Rosati and Dallas end up with back at the Bloom house. Those things underscore the veracity of Bloom, Ek, and Franco as to the fact that they saw Carl Stephen Rosati on that night in Florida, October 12.

"Now, ultimately, you have Peter Dallas, who was the subject of much contest in the course of the hearing, and you have Venturi and Geller. Did they intentionally, or perhaps even subconsciously, create a situation where Dallas is intimidated by either the sight of or the prospect of Peter "Pete the Greek" Roussonicolos? [Look what happens] after these two guys came to see him," White says, "Dallas's name was changed and he was relocated to another prison.

"Was it imagination, or was it real? Dallas ties the whole thing together by identifying Rosati first from a composite, not because Coyote is itching to have him do that but because it's the truth, because what does he do? He tells you that Giordano and the other people who identified him and Rosati were right about me. They were right about me, Peter Dallas, and they were right about Stephen Rosati because I was with him, and he's the one that was with me on October 12 in Florida.

"Think about the circumstances. Think about the fact that this guy now is awaiting sentencing, facing multiple years in jail on a plea of second-degree murder. Isn't that the ultimate waiver of impeachment? His being an accomplice and a co-defendant, and suggests of motive with respect to who did what at the incident. Isn't that ultimately the admission against interest to say under oath that those facts that were set forth by the assistant state's attorney [Chuck Morton] in Florida are true?

"In spite of your previous ruling [that Rosati had presented evidence that he was in Rhode Island in 1986], that it was clear, that it was convincing," White summed up masterfully, "we say no! At the very least, there has got to be contradictory evidence. We submit that it is even more than that, but we don't have that burden, and in that light, the state respectfully submits that the habeas petition should be denied, and the respondent should be returned to Florida for trial."

"Mr. White," the judge said, "that was an excellent presentation. You obviously did your homework on it. We will recess until 2:15."

After the recess, it was finally Jack Cicilline's turn to present his case in defense of Stephen Rosati. If ever a man was born to be a lawyer, it was the steely-eyed tough guy from the street-smart section of Federal Hill, Jack Cicilline. Unlike his preppy counterpart, Jack didn't have a bevy of paralegals to do the legwork. He did it himself.

For two solid weeks Jack went back to his academic roots, the halls of the law library. And that is where Cicilline, the scholar, prepared his defense. With glasses perched above his eyebrows, ready to drop when the type got too small, and his deep voice resounding, the defense counsel approached the bench to begin his summation.

"Mr. Cicilline?"

"Thank you, Your Honor. I think it is helpful for us to look back at the history of the rendition [extradition] statute in deciding what the court needs to do today. Long before rendition became a part of the American Constitution, [nations] were extraditing people from one country to another. In fact, in this country in 1643, under the provisions of a rendition statute between the commonwealth of Massachusetts and the colony of New Plymouth, a person who was a fugitive from one colony would be brought back to the other colony if he was an escapee, if there were affidavits signed by chief magistrates in the demanding state."

"Much like a habeas petition," the judge suggested.

"These are predecessors," Cicilline corrected. "The point is, long before habeas corpus came into vogue, these various colonies had other kinds of protections to ensure that it wasn't simply on the word of an ordinary policeman. The chief justice or the magistrate, or in this case the reviewing body, would examine the question of whether the person ought to be extradited." Cicilline moistened a thumb and turned a page.

"Before the actual rendition language was written into the Constitution of this country, there were twelve drafts, and following that—in the first years of the nation—there were a number of cases that were decided which made it clear that the purpose of the rendition statute was to ensure that the states mutually supported one another. As Chief Justice Taney said in *Kentucky v. Denison*, unless there was adherence to this principle, this new experiment in government— namely the new United States—would fail.

"But at the same time that this was all going on, rendition was generally a matter left to the governors. The governor would decide, without interference of the courts, whether a fugitive ought to be returned. In 1790, the matter had become of such concern to the nations that President Washington asked his attorney general to write an advisory opinion on the rendition language in the U.S. Constitution.

"At that time, the governor of New York refused to extradite a man to Massachusetts because he found that the man was not a fugitive from justice. The Supreme Court made it clear that a fugitive from justice is entitled to insist on proof that he was within the demanding state at the time it is alleged the crime was committed.

"In 1842, the governor of Illinois refused to send a man back to Missouri when that governor demanded him. In 1876, the governor of Illinois refused to extradite a man to Wisconsin after reviewing his situation and decided he wasn't a fugitive. I mention these cases so that you understand that from the beginning, rendition in America involved the exercise of discretion by judges—I'm sorry, governors—who after hearing the facts of the case make a decision about it. It's not a question that it simply calls the demanding state, files its papers of requisition, and the person automatically is sent back.

"Now, while I recognize that later decisions by our own Supreme Court seem to say something different than that, the reading of the statute is plain. No demand will be recognized unless the accused was present in the demanding state at the time of the commission of the crime. The courts [therefore] can inquire of [this] by route of habeas corpus."[5]

Cicilline cited a Montana case from 1983 that involved the cashing of a check, a phone call, the lack of available plane flights to Missouri, and the testimony of people who placed the witness in Montana within and around the actual day that the crime was committed.

"And the court in that case said he had met his burden of establishing by clear and convincing evidence his absence from the demanding state on the date of the crime."

Judge Sheehan asked if the case was appealed, and Cicilline said he didn't know. This was key to the judge, because he did not want to rule in Rosati's favor if he knew it would be overturned on appeal. A discussion ensued concerning the "shifting of the burden of proof" from Rosati to the state, now that the judge had stated that Rosati had established his case.

"But what if I'm convinced of both arguments?" the judge asked.

"If you have some question in your mind, he goes back," Cicilline said.

Cicilline, however, couldn't see how this could be possible. The judge had to weigh each argument to see where he stood.

"If, after integrating all the evidence, you are clearly convinced that he was in Rhode Island, then he doesn't go back."

"Is there any law?" the judge asked. "I have looked high and low. Is there any law to that effect?"

"I think" Cicilline offered objectively, "what they do is they generally end up [considering] whether they are clearly convinced that the petitioner was in the asylum state. But if you go through the analysis and you say, look he offered some witnesses, and the state offered some, and its unclear to me where he was, he goes.

"Where I think some problems come in is in the second stage of analysis concerning the credibility of witnesses. In other words, when you are deciding, you [need to] consider such things as was the testimony live? Did the prosecution rely only on affidavits? I think Mr. White conceding, said that affidavits were not to be considered in the same fashion that live testimony would be."

Confident in his position, the strength of the plea, and the citing of two hundred years of precedent cases, Cicilline gave John Sheehan everything he would need to legally allow the judge to block Rosati's extradition.

"Let me cite several cases in which it says it is almost a requirement that live testimony be furnished to overcome a very strong case presented by the petitioner," Cicilline said, adding, "and the ones I refer to are Florida cases. *Clark against the Warden of the Baltimore Jail*, for instance, used the phrase, 'consider all the evidence on balance.' The court is permitted to consider whether the witnesses are live or by affidavit. *State against Macreadie*, a Florida case from 1936, suggests that affidavits do not constitute competent proof to controvert a prisoner's live testimony in a habeas corpus proceeding.[6]

"What I'm saying is that the Florida cases say in the absence of live testimony you never overcome a compelling case. I submit our case is very compelling. It's impossible to reach the conclusion that he's in the state of Florida. We have documentary evidence to show that he's here. We have live witnesses. October 12 was the only significant date originally, but we learn through witnesses they were saying 'I was with him on the eleventh.'

"Now, I don't have to remind the court that there are three witnesses who have testified during the course of these proceedings that this petitioner was in the state of Rhode Island on October 12 of 1986: Elodie Vanderpyl, Kara Lynx, and the petitioner himself. There are three other witnesses who testified that he was present here on October 11. They are his sister, his brother-in-law, and his father. Then we also have Jacqueline Palozzo Bahra saying that she believed that he was in the health club on the twelfth. She wasn't absolutely certain, but she certainly gave some credence too—so it's another fact.

We have other witnesses who place Rosati in Rhode Island on the tenth [the bookkeeper and one of Rosati's workers at the health club who received his Friday paycheck on that day].

"Now, the state has suggested that he could not be with Elodie Vanderpyl and Kara Lynx on the night of October 12."

"Well, the way I view that," said the judge, "quite frankly, is that he certainly can have dinner with somebody, and then go home." White stifled a frown.

Cicilline, of course, agreed. "But in addition to the live testimony, and now I'm talking about six witnesses who put him here at a critical time, the eleventh and the twelfth, we have two phone calls, twenty-two minutes on the twelfth and twenty-one minutes on the thirteenth. And these phone calls could not have been made in such a way for him to go to Florida after the first and return before the second. The state may suggest that that doesn't prove that he was talking to Elodie Vanderpyl, but they haven't offered evidence in contradiction to show that it was somebody else who was making those phone calls.

"In addition to the phone call documents, there's the matter of the gas slip made out on October 11 by the petitioner, and the state has done nothing to rebut that.

"I submit to you that before you even get to the Coyote aspect of this case, you have got to say to yourself, in order for me to have evidence to overcome Carl Stephen Rosati getting on that stand and saying I was in Rhode Island, and here's the proof of it, here are the documents, you have got to say to yourself—any normal person would say—I want to hear from Michelle Arrieta. I want to hear from Vic Giordano. I want to hear from Peter Dallas. I want to hear because how [else] can I rationally make this work in my mind?"

"Do I have a right to demand these witnesses be brought up?" asked the judge.

"No, you don't have the right to demand that, but the state has the obligation because of this contradiction of a fairly solid case."

Taking in the abstract the position of the judge, Cicilline summarized what Sheehan could be thinking: Detective Coyote is telling me that witnesses have said this. Cicilline tells me that they are lying. At an earlier time, they gave different descriptions. How can I honestly rear it up in the absence of those live witnesses? Cicilline turned to face his frequent opponent.

"What you really ought to be saying is, Mr. Attorney General, if you want this man extradited, it's your obligation to put before me the kind of evidence that waters down what he said, and the only way in my mind imaginable to do that is to bring those witnesses here. Then, if you are convinced at the conclusion that his clear and convincing status no longer exists, then he gets sent back to Florida."

Here was Cicilline at his finest, using critical thinking and punching holes in his own argument to show his objectivity, because he was so sure he was right. And because Cicilline felt he knew the truth, he was also sure that any witnesses that Florida brought forward would have to be manufactured, and thus their testimony could be demolished on the stand.

"Why do you say I can't demand [Dallas] be brought up here?" asked the judge.

"That would be partisan. I think your role is a neutral and detached officer. That's [White's] burden. Clearly, you can indicate to him, your case is sliding and you probably ought to do this. But maybe in the interest of justice the court can do anything it wishes, you know, including presenting witnesses on its own behalf, and I had a case in which Judge MacKenzie called a witness over objection of the state and the defendant, and the Supreme Court said he was perfectly within—"

"I don't think I have the power to do that, but I have the power to orally issue an interstate subpoena. That's what I would be doing. And, frankly, Dallas disturbs me. You have a motion on that."

"Yes, I did."

"I haven't ruled on that yet."

"I understand."

"Go ahead, I'm sorry. I didn't mean to interrupt."

"That's all right," said Cicilline. "There are several important things that you have got to consider about Coyote, and the first is that he never sought the help of a fellow police officer. He never went to the crime scene. He never reviewed the tangible evidence in the case. He never took the time to examine the scores of other suspects whose names were developed over the course of the investigation—names I asked him about. He never went to the places where Stephen Rosati said he lived and worked in those time periods to [check his facts]. He took witnesses who had no knowledge of what the petitioner's name was and gave them a name to use.

"Detective Coyote said two things to this court which I consider significant in your assessment as to how cavalier he was about the truth of any situation. He swore under oath by affidavit that Michelle

Arrieta had picked out a photograph of Carl Stephen Rosati from a photo spread and that she positively identified him. Yet on October tenth and fourteenth of 1988, she's given photo spreads, which include the petitioner's picture, and she makes no identification. Then he tells us that on May 29, 1990, she picks out the petitioner from the Men in Motion photograph, but nowhere in her statement [that day] does it indicate that she identifies anyone. She also never signs the back of the photo.

"And this most significant [so-called identification] is not even reported by him until six months later! The question is, is the court to believe at this juncture that Michelle Arrieta has, in fact, identified the man who sits here today? He's certainly not [six foot four, and he's certainly not] 280 pounds.

"More recently, Detective Coyote told this court that Dallas would be sentenced on schedule and that there was no connection between his willingness to testify and the outcome of these proceedings. We now learn from Mr. Morton, who's the prosecutor, that Dallas will not be sentenced until the other trial is over."

Cicilline also reviewed Giordano's inability to initially pick out Dallas from a police photo spread but instead picked out Joseph Bagley. Then, after being in jail, his ability to ID witnesses changed.[7] Chris Jones, Cicilline added, also made no identification.

"The three survivors of this event said that the intruders who came to the door were asking for someone named Kerry. Dallas had no recollection of anything along that line. Dallas was asked if there was a female in the house where Joe Viscido was murdered, and he said, I don't know. Was marijuana taken? I don't know. Were there people on the floor? I don't know. Where was Joe Viscido shot? I don't know.

"It seems to me when you weigh those kinds of answers up against the fact that Michelle Arrieta and Vic Giordano, in the first three years of the case, after having been shown Dallas's picture repeatedly, never pick him out, the court ought to question whether this man was ever there.

"Here's a man [Dallas] who says I was with Rosati several times before the events of October 12, I was with him on the seventh, I was with him on the tenth—the day everybody knows he's writing checks in the state of Rhode Island. I was with him on the eleventh, the day he's picking up his sister and brother-in-law and sees his father in the state of Rhode Island. I was with him on those days. I don't think you can assign any credibility to the testimony of the affidavit of Mr.

Dallas. Dallas's testimony, it is just unworthy of belief. . . . I think you have got to say—somebody has got to hesitate and say—is it possible that this man was not there?"

"He's facing the electric chair and potentially I can see where someone would cop a plea to take seven to twelve or twelve to seventeen," said the judge.

"Well, while you mention that," said Cicilline, "it's also significant to point out that in the affidavit provided by Mr. White this morning, there is nothing certain about what Dallas's sentence is going to be. Mr. Morton makes it clear that we are going to see what happens after he has testified. And that's on the record."

Staying the course, Cicilline was implying that Dallas's sentence might be predicated upon how he would testify in the Rosati case, and thus it could be even shorter. By inference, defense counsel also called into question the entire procedure of use immunity (promising immunity in exchange for testimony) and the possible pitfalls and misuses of such a procedure.

The Jeff Bloom affidavit was dissected, whereby Bloom described the big guy as stocky, whereas Stephen Rosati was muscular and trim. Bloom also said that he was with the big guy on October 10 and 11. Cory Franco said during his first interview that he wasn't even at the Bloom house on the twelfth.

"Franco tells us that Jeff Bloom had looked through the window and witnessed the crime. That's totally inconsistent with what Jeff Bloom is telling the police, and further Franco describes the fellow as a big, fat guy. Danny Ek, who picks out the petitioner on June 26 of 1988, says, 'I don't know where I know this guy from Adam,' but this is portrayed as a positive ID when Coyote represents it."

Cicilline faulted Coyote's investigation of Victor Merriman, who picked out Rosati as one of the people who came to the car dealership he was working at looking for Joe Viscido a few weeks prior to the murder. Cicilline's criticism was that Coyote completely ignored both the Michigan license plate lead and the fact that Viscido had been arrested by the DEA in Michigan and had ratted on some people up there.

"But I think a moron would have said to themselves, God, there's got to be some relationship [to the Michigan incident], but when you question Coyote, he is indifferent to that lead because of an alternative personal conclusion he had already formed in the case."

That Dallas was put into protective custody because of his fear of Venturi and Geller was "just incredible to believe." Cicilline reasoned that these two investigators received a call from Dallas's brother shortly after the interview. The brother was looking for help for Dallas in locating a lawyer.

"Dallas told these people the truth, and there's no way in the world that this court can conclude that Venturi and Geller went in there to threaten him."

As Cicilline headed into his close, the judge interrupted. "If anyone thinks I'm going to render a decision now, don't get their hopes up. I'm not. I'm trying to get in my own mind the law I should apply."

White reentered the discussion. "Your Honor . . . I'm not conceding that the law in Rhode Island should be that there be a requirement for live testimony. [However, we have] had live testimony of a police officer: the state's case had Detective Coyote. That is sufficient for cross-examination."

"Well, to put your mind at ease," the judge understated, "I think that Mr. Cicilline effectively cross-examined every one of the affidavits provided by Detective Coyote. So I'm not ruling that it is a requirement [for you to bring up some witnesses], I'm saying, I would much prefer it."

This was a staggering statement by a judge to a prosecutor; namely, to completely dismiss the substance of the testimony of his only witness. However, the judge was also suggesting a possible lifeline by announcing that he might not rule after final arguments.

Concerned about setting a precedent by deciding in Cicilline's favor, Judge Sheehan apparently had little compunction in setting another precedent: moving the goal posts in allowing White an essential do-over. Cicilline certainly was aware of this unorthodox tact. However, he saw an advantage; namely, to question a key witness in his home state of Rhode Island, knowing that if he were successful, Stephen would be a free man.

After thanking Mr. White and Mr. Cicilline for their fine presentations, the best he had heard in thirty-one years, the judge decided to address the parents of Stephen Rosati on the record.

"This has been a long ordeal," the judge said, "but in my good conscience, I cannot rush this decision. I hope and pray that it will be right whatever I decide, but I'm going to read all the cases that have been or will be supplied to me, and I'm going to read every bit of the transcript, and then I will render a decision, which I think will be based on the law and on the dictates of my conscience. And that's all I can promise anybody. I know one side will be unhappy and one side will be happy, but I'm not here to run a popularity contest. I'm here to do what I think is right under the law."

CHAPTER 54:
A Witness Comes Forth

Court would be recessed for over two months, and for those sixty days Stephen Rosati continued to sit in jail. Judge Sheehan had stated that when he was a defense counsel, he "died a little bit" during every trial. Now, as judge, he would die a little bit more.

During that time, it became crystal clear to Detective Coyote and Randy White that in order to make sure of a win they would have to bring up a witness. White and his silent Florida counterpart Driscoll wanted Dallas, but Coyote told them that he feared for Dallas's life. If Pete the Greek got to him, or if the Rosatis were Mafia as he suspected, there was no telling what might happen. Detective Coyote appeared amenable to having Dallas interviewed, but he had to keep the whereabouts of his star witness a secret at all costs.

White realized the seriousness of the situation, particularly if Rosati was as dangerous as Detective Coyote said he was. If anything were to happen to Dallas, it would look bad for the state of Rhode

Island. All they needed was contradictory evidence. Thus, any eyewitness would do.

Meanwhile, Detective Coyote turned the screws on Michelle Arrieta. He had her confirm, once again, the Dallas photo, but she wouldn't budge on Rosati. Since Giordano was in jail on a cocaine charge and had already identified Rosati on two previous occasions, he seemed a better bet. Coyote also considered Jeffrey Bloom, Cory Franco, and Chris Jones, but Jones, still in Canada, seemed impossible to locate.

On April 22, 1991, James B. Harpring, a public defender for Vic Giordano, entered a formal motion with the Broward County Sheriff's Department to modify Giordano's sentence of cocaine possession, hoping to commute the last ten months to the two months' time already served. Detective Sheriff Robert R. Coyote supported this recommendation in writing because Giordano had proved to be "a key witness in [the] first-degree murder case" of Joseph Viscido, Jr., a month later. Acting Circuit Judge James B. Balsiger signed the "Order Modifying Sentence" freeing Giordano. This decree placed Giordano on three years' probation and suspended the balance of the one-year incarceration to time served, which was about two months.

As the weeks dragged on, White became more concerned that he could lose this case. Dallas's life had to be protected, which was a key concern. White appealed to Judge Sheehan that he needed more time. The requested delay, however, pushed the judge to the brink. Having waited six, seven, eight weeks, it didn't look like he would wait any longer. In the interim, the judge conferred with Florida prosecutor Jeffrey Driscoll about Dallas, and Driscoll also talked with Jack Cicilline. Finally, on June 4, court was reconvened.

The judge began. "I specifically asked Driscoll if Mr. Peter Dallas was the person who was the one being questioned. Can you, Mr. White, or you, Mr. Cicilline, shed any light on this?"

"Your Honor," White began, "I have spoken to Mr. Driscoll on a daily basis, sometimes three or four times daily." The prosecutor thereupon proceeded to produce long sentences about the situation that drew no conclusions. The upshot of his contribution was that Driscoll had sent a man to interview Dallas, but no interview had taken place!

This was astonishing, as court had been delayed nearly two months for the express purpose of getting Driscoll to interview Dallas for clarification.

"Thank you," the judge said, still clearly dissatisfied.

However, what White did not say—and perhaps did not know—was that fully a month earlier, on May 1, Dallas had called Chuck Morton's office to recant his testimony. This caused great confusion at the Florida prosecutor's office. Dallas was supposed to take a polygraph, but he was not given one at that time. He was afraid, and that led him to believe that his life or the lives of those in his family might be in danger from the Rosatis or their supposed Mob affiliates. And so Dallas waffled and apparently recanted his recantation. Yet Jeffrey Driscoll kept a poker face when he returned to Rhode Island and did not disclose these series of events.

No matter what, Judge Sheehan still felt that Rosati was entitled to the right of confrontation. "Florida law," the judge said, "indicates that the defense counsel should be entitled to live testimony that could be cross-examined."

The affidavits provided by Detective Coyote did not meet that criterion.

"The court is not ordering the state of Florida to bring up live witnesses. The court is requesting the state of Florida to bring up live witnesses. I will continue this case for testimony of those witnesses. I will hear you, Mr. Cicilline, on bail."

"Bail is a matter of right, notwithstanding the provisions of the Constitution which seem to say otherwise: that in proper circumstances the court may exercise its discretion and admit a defendant to bail in circumstances like this. I believe that the nine-month period [that Mr. Rosati has been in jail] is simply one circumstance that warrants your exercise of discretion to admitting the defendant to bail."

Cicilline went on to state that although Rosati had one infraction years ago in Florida, "he has lived a worthwhile kind of life. He was gainfully employed here, had substantial ties, roots in the community, and a home, and his parents own a substantial business."

Cicilline was willing to put up $400,000 worth of unencumbered property for the Rosatis.

White argued against bail because "the offense with which the prisoner is charged is shown to be an offense punishable by death or life imprisonment under the laws of the state in which it was committed: murder and robbery."

Hearing both sides, the judge made his decision.

"After viewing the witnesses for the petitioner and viewing the affidavits submitted by the state, I feel that one more day of incarceration is too much for Mr. Rosati, and, therefore, I'm going to grant bail. The court will grant bail at $300,000. That will not be 10 percent. It will be property belonging to the family or to Mr. Rosati himself."

"Giving Florida the benefit of the doubt," Sheehan gave them until June 25 to produce a witness or witnesses. If they did not bring witnesses up, he would make a final ruling based upon live witnesses brought forth by Cicilline versus affidavits and Detective Coyote's hearsay evidence for the state, a decision that arguably should have been made months earlier, right after "closing" arguments.

Since the Rosatis had proven their case, the judge finally came through on a bail hearing. "I was elated," Carl said. "Esther was elated. This was an important sign. Throughout this entire process, since we always knew the truth, and we knew we had right on our side, as terrible as things were, we still were confident. And at this juncture, we were as sure as we could be that we were going to win extradition. Stephen was pumped up; we all were."

Unfortunately, White's appeal to withdraw bail was supported by the higher court, and Stephen was forced to stay in jail. The months dragged on until Cicilline finally called to say that he had a contact in Florida.

"It looks like the prosecution wants to delay. Now this information is confidential, and what it means is they might be getting ready to fold. Mum's the word."

This information was discussed between Esther, Carl, and Red Gooseberger, who had been with them every moment along the way. However, as Esther recalled, as soon as Cicilline's call came in, "the first thing Red did was call Sallie Hughes, the reporter from the *Miami Herald* who was covering the story for Florida. In previous reports, she had appeared sympathetic to our plight, but, still, he had no right to call."

"What are you doing? Jack told us to keep quiet!" Carl told Red.

"Don't worry," Red retorted. "I just want to see what she knows."

"And then he told her exactly what Jack told us!" Esther said. "We couldn't believe it. We were speechless."

"You big mouth!" Carl blurted out. "Jack told us not to tell anybody!"

Having been unofficially in charge of the Rosatis' publicity campaign, Red said simply, "We can trust her."

"But of course, we couldn't," Esther recalled bitterly.

The following day, Hughes wrote an article on the delay and slanted the story in favor of Viscido's father. "She simply took what Red had given her and slapped him in the face with it," Esther recalled. "Our Florida lawyer was furious. Chuck Morton was furious. Jack was keenly disappointed. They might have backed off, but this destroyed any chance." The thought that Stephen could actually get convicted loomed again as a real possibility.

Esther and Carl drove to the ACI.

"Stephen looked worn," Esther recalled, "but still in good shape. We told him that the delay by the judge was not a good sign. I could see his spirit fading. We discussed that if he ever got convicted, we would help him commit suicide. I would have helped him, and then I would have committed suicide myself."

With his long dirty blonde hair—even though he was dressed in a fine gray suit—to Esther Rosati, Detective Coyote still "looked like a thug." She said Coyote had a hypnotic quality and was even quite affable to the people that surrounded him. Seen as cocky and arrogant, Esther surmised that the detective gained his position of power "through a direct infusion from the top: from Broward County supreme chief Sheriff Nick Navarro."

After weeks and weeks of stalling, Detective Coyote entered the courtroom with his secret witness. Carl and Esther thought it would be Peter Dallas, the person the judge also hoped for. However, Cicilline thought it would be Jeff Bloom, the fellow who ran the supposed safe house. They were all caught off guard when they found out it was Vic Giordano.

There are 3,000 employees under Sheriff Navarro, and all of them and their families voted for him, year after year. A refugee from Colombia, Navarro ran his county "like a little dictator." Carl and Esther had seen pictures of the sheriff giving awards to Detectives Coyote and Puccini, and they thought of this duo, particularly Coyote, as Navarro protégés.

As the Rosatis saw it, the Broward Sheriff's Department had a hidden agenda. They were after Pete the Greek's attorney, Richard Rendina, a brash criminal lawyer who had uncovered a hotbed of corruption throughout Navarro's entire little empire. One of Rendina's clients, Nelson Scott, a known drug trafficker, stated to the press and to *60 Minutes* that the Broward police force had cops on the take. After they would bust a drug pusher, according to Scott and Rendina, Scott would resell the drugs and share the profits with the police. As the attorney who brought this scandal to light, Rendina had to be taken out, and the way to get him was through Pete the Greek.

According to Esther's assessment, Stephen and Dallas were merely pawns. Broward was building a powerful case against a made-to-order "big guy" and a made-to-order "little guy." The fact that they didn't even know each other or that Stephen was living 1,500 miles away from the scene of the crime or that he had two eyewitnesses, corroborating evidence, and a half a dozen other ways to prove his whereabouts meant nothing to them. This didn't faze them. As prosecutors linked to the attorney general, with the overt and tacit backing of governors, judges, the U.S. Constitution, and policemen from two states, the Broward Police force had essentially unlimited power and unlimited funds.

"As private citizens," Esther lamented, "we were no match."

Esther watched as Stephen walked into the courtroom flanked by armed policemen, handcuffed as if he were the deranged murderer they made him out to be. "It was outrageous, surreal," she recalled. "We were helpless, except for the fact that we had the truth on our side and they had a pack of lies." As powerful as truth was, it was obviously not enough, and Esther was forced to face the reality of what her family was up against.

"Once I began to comprehend the magnitude of what was happening," Esther recalled, "I realized that I had stepped into a world of darkness, an evilness that was palpable. You could touch it and feel it. I also realized that all the criminals are not behind bars. The criminals were the system. There was nothing left that reflected sanity. Goodness and righteousness had died. Where was the sanity? With our case, we were threatening an entire system, and I set my sights on toppling it.

"The reporter for the *Providence Journal* Jim Hummel was a nice enough guy," Esther recalled, "but ultimately, he was incapable. The truth was so blatantly on our side, but he kept writing the story from a supposed vantage point of objectivity. One can't be a passive bystander when such a massive injustice is occurring. My son was facing the electric chair. More adamant than ever, Randy White tied himself closer and closer to Detective Coyote. Unable to see that he was playing the fool, like a young buck following the lead, he kowtowed to Detective Coyote and provided him with a cab to pick him up at the airport and another cab to take him back. Essentially, Randy White became the urbane counterpart to Coyote's sleaziness. Although he was an educated lawyer, Randy White wouldn't know the truth if it smacked him in the face in neon lights."

CHAPTER 55:
The Hearing: I Accuse!

Day Fifteen: June 25, 1991

Like a maître d', wearing his best suit, Red Gooseberger led the Rosatis to the front row and then moved away to schmooze with Jim Hummel, the reporter from the *Providence Journal*. Three television stations had their cameras rolling. As the media moved around, rumors spread in hushed tones that underneath it all organized crime was involved. Today's events would cover the next day's front page and would make both the six o'clock and eleven o'clock news on all three networks. This was a big day.

Jack Cicilline thought that the best way to combat the testimony of one of the only three direct eyewitnesses was to get one of the others on the stand. Since Chris Jones had never been in Coyote's hands and Michelle Arrieta had, the plan was to bring Jones in. Further, Jones had never ID'd Rosati. Cicilline's investigator, Fran Martin, took the next plane to Canada to locate him. Fran wasn't feeling well, so he asked Red Gooseberger to join him.

A husky young man with short, cropped hair, wearing jeans and a short-sleeve shirt rolled up at the biceps was led into the courtroom. The young man sneered at the accused, as he stood off to the side ready to take the stand. Detective Coyote, who was in the building, was nowhere to be seen.[1]

The gavel cracked. "No one will be allowed to stand in this courtroom other than authorized personnel," Judge Sheehan boomed. Stragglers took their seats.

Randy White ruffled his mane as he stepped forward. Jeffrey Driscoll, the Florida prosecutor, sat silently.

"Your Honor," White proclaimed, "pursuant to our last session, at which time you had asked the state of Florida to present further evidence, the state has brought forth a witness today which we'd like to present." White paused to feel the energy of the packed house and positioned himself for a good shot in front of the cameras. "I call Vic Giordano to the stand."

"All right, all right," Judge Sheehan said, calming the crowd, as electricity flew between Rosati and Giordano. "Any of you troopers want to stand up here, you can," the judge suggested. Giordano was sworn in, and the prosecution went first.

"Directing your attention to October 12, 1986," Randy White said, "do you know where you were in the late evening?"

Giordano said that he was in Joseph Viscido's apartment. "Joe was a friend from childhood," the witness added. "Michelle Arrieta and Chris Jones were also there."

"Describe what happened."

"There was a knock at the door. Michelle approached, looked through the peephole, didn't know the two guys. I looked through the peephole, and I couldn't identify them either. 'Joe,' I said, 'I don't know these guys. You better check it out before you answer the door.'"

"What race were they?"

"White males. One guy was taller than the other. Joe opened the door and they yanked it out of his hands and forced their way in."

"And you had a direct view of the taller man?"

"Yes, a direct view. The taller guy had a gun, and he spun around, twisted his arm and took Joe's gun and started telling everybody to put their hands up. And the other man was in there too, but the bigger guy was doing the talking."

"Did you raise your hands?"

"Yes, I did. And then they told everybody to lay on the floor. Then they threw Joe to the ground. The bigger guy had his knee on Joe's back."

"And you were on your stomach?"

"Yes."

"And you picked your head up to get a view of the taller man's face?" White suggested in question form.

"Yes. The guy was hitting Joe, kicking Joe, yelling at Joe. He wanted the clips to the gun, and he was also saying something about a girl named Kerry. So they beat up Joe a bit, and then the smaller guy took him into the bedroom. The larger guy was by my side. Then a fight broke out in the bedroom. I could hear bouncing off the walls, off the dresser. Then the bedroom door got slammed closed. At that time a gun went off or a shot was fired, and then the taller guy that was next to me crashed through the bedroom door, and at that time, I looked up and saw Michelle and Chris run out the front door and I proceeded to follow them out."

"And during that period of time when you were in the same room as the taller man, did you get a good look at his face?"

"Yes."

"And the lighting was good?"

"Yes."

"Can I ask a question, sir," Judge Sheehan inquired. "When the shorter man went in and you heard a fight, you heard a shot?"

"Right."

"And that's when you say the taller man went in and crashed the bedroom?"

"Yes."

"Did you hear any other shots?" asked the judge.

"Yes, I heard a second shot," Giordano said as defense counsel winced, for Rosati had graduated now from being an accomplice to being a triggerman.

White asked if Giordano had identified the big guy from photo lineups, and Giordano said he had, for Sergeant McNeil and then later for Detective Coyote. White showed the witness his signature on the various lineup sheets, and Giordano verified his signatures.

"Were you certain of your selection?"

"Yes, I was."

"Did any person whether from law enforcement or any other

311

person tell you which picture to pick when you identified No. 4 as the big guy on August 23, 1988?"

"No."

"Had anyone ever told you, hinted, suggested, demonstrated in any way who it was or what picture you should select as the taller man or the big guy on September 3, 1990?"

"No."

"Can you identify the taller man that you saw that night if you were to see him again?" White asked.

"Yes," Vic Giordano said as he, again, nervously curled his lip.

"Now, I would ask you to look around the courtroom here and tell the court whether or not you see the person who was the taller of the two persons who entered Joe Viscido's apartment on the night of October 12, 1986."

"Yes, I see him," Giordano said, looking at the defendant, sitting next to Jack Cicilline. "Right there," Giordano said. "He was the bigger of the two guys."

"Why don't you step down," the judge said, for reasons difficult to comprehend, "and step within three or four feet of that table and point out?"

Vic Giordano stepped down from the witness stand, as *Eyewitness News* cameras captured the entire sequence. Reluctantly, but with a sense of resignation, he moseyed over to where the defendant was sitting, limply flipped up his arm, and gestured with a weak forefinger directly to the accused. "This guy, here—gray suit, tie, white shirt."

The local TV station, Channel 10, had its six o'clock lead.

Stephen Rosati felt like he'd been hit in the solar plexus with a sledgehammer. "Liar," he mumbled loud enough for Giordano to hear, daggers of hate spitting between the two men.

"And may the record reflect," Randy White echoed, "the witness has identified the petitioner, Carl Stephen Rosati."

"The record may so reflect," Judge Sheehan acknowledged.

"And you are sure of this?"

"Yep," Giordano said, "positive."

"I have no other questions."

"Court will recess for five or ten minutes," the judge announced.

Judge Sheehan was the first to speak when they returned from the recess.

"All rise," cried the bailiff. "You may be seated."

"Mr. Giordano," the judge glared down at him, "I will remind you, for the record, you are still under oath."

"Yes, sir."

Cicilline moved in for the cross, as he approached the stand set up for his notes and looked them over. Calmly removing his glasses, he turned his eyes on the witness. Giordano backed away, ever so slightly, and the *Providence Journal* memorialized the moment with a photograph. Cicilline asked the man about his present state of employment. Giordano said that he was the manager of Little Caesars. He had been a roof painter and a builder of swimming pools before that.

"You have been convicted of several crimes during the same time period you discussed with us, isn't that correct?"

"Right."

"You were convicted of the crime of possession of marijuana in April of 1983 and possession of cocaine in August of 1990. Is that correct?"

"Yes."

"And what sentence did you receive in that case?"

"County jail time."

"What's that?"

"That's two months, and I'm on three years' probation."

"And in March of 1988, for possession of cocaine, what sentence did you receive in that case?"

"Thirty months."

"And of that sentence you served how long?"

"Eight months."

"So from March until, what, November of 1988, you were actually incarcerated, is that correct?"

"No, I got out in August. I was in work release in August."

"But you were incarcerated?"

"I was at the Community Pompano C. C. [Police Center in Pompano Beach]."

"Until when?"

"I believe the first week in September."

"So at least part of the time that you were talking to the police was while you were in the custody of the county jail, is that correct?"

"Well, that's—you want to call it work release, yes. I had a full-time job, and I just went back to the center at night."

"How many times do you estimate it was that you spoke to policemen in connection with this case?"

"I don't know—fifty, a hundred times."

"And you gave them a statement every time?"

"No, not every time. I made about four formal statements. I would call them back; sometimes they came to my house."

"And . . ."

"And they would just talk to me, ask me what I was doing, if I was staying out of trouble—stuff like that."

"How many times would you estimate that you were shown photographs of different individuals?"

"Maybe four or five times."

"That's all?"

"Uh-huh."

"And when was it that you were first able to make any identifications?"

"August 23, 1988."

"But you had seen photographs before that?"

"Yes, a couple of times."

"Now, going back two more years to October 12, 1986, for a moment. You told us that you arrived at the house at approximately eleven o'clock? And, in fact, you were brokering a deal with Chris Jones to sell thirteen ounces of cocaine, isn't that right?"

"Right."

"All right, and the cocaine was going to be sold for $800 an ounce, is that right?"

"I don't remember the price."

After an objection was raised, Cicilline moved to paint his portrait of the witness. "You were a drug dealer?"

"Right."

"And dealing in ounces of cocaine was something you customarily did?"

"Yes."

"This wasn't the first meeting you had with Viscido about drugs either, was it?"

"No."

"Viscido was your supplier?"

"One of them."

"Who were the others?"

"Sustained," said the judge, anticipating an objection by the prosecutor. After further jousting between the lawyers, Cicilline bore in on Giordano's credibility. "Did you tell anyone that you and Chris were going there?"

"No."

"Did you have the $10,400 with you?"

"No."

"Why not?"

"Chris couldn't get the money."

"Okay, Joe was upset about that, isn't that right?"

"He was mad."

"Sure he was. He didn't like the idea of keeping thirteen ounces of cocaine in his house for any long period of time, isn't that right?"

"Right."

"And you were five or six hours late for the meeting?"

"Right."

"And strangely enough, someone else knows that the cocaine is there, isn't that right?"

"Right."

"You didn't tell anybody to set up the deal?"

"No."

"You're sure of that?"

"Positive."

"So you're in the apartment in Joe's bedroom, what for?"

"Getting some coke."

"So you're not only a dealer, you're a user?"

"Right."

"How long had you been using cocaine?"

"Five years."

"How much cocaine did you use per week?"

"I don't know, an eight ball."

"A what?"

"Three and a half, four grams a week."

"So you were buying a small quantity to resell part of it to support your drug habit?"

"I bought it for a friend of my girlfriend."

"In any event, do you see the thirteen ounces of cocaine?"

"Yes."

"So it's there in the house. There's no question about that?"

"Right."

"So there's a knock at the door, and you could really see the big guy, is that fair to say?"

"I could see them."

"You could tell what they looked like?"

"Right."

"They bust in, there's a struggle—ten, twenty seconds?"

"Maybe twenty, thirty. You know, it happened pretty quick."

"And you say the taller of the men is on top of Viscido, kneeling over him. You're lying on the floor?"

"Right."

"And you can see this man?"

"Yes, I'm looking straight at him."

"So is it fair to say that you saw him for about twenty seconds in the hallway, ten to thirty seconds when he came inside, and a minute after. Is that correct?"

"Right."

"So at that time, you got a really good opportunity to view his size?"

"Yes."

"How tall are you?"

"Five foot nine, five foot nine and a half."

"How tall do you think I am?"

"Five foot ten."

"And what do you think I weigh?"

"190, 200 pounds."

"So if I told you that I was five foot eleven and I weighed about 220, you'd recognize that you thought I was smaller than I actually am?"

"A little bit," Giordano agreed.

"The man that you looked at that night. I take it you gave a description of him to the police?"

"Yes."

"And do you recall how you described him then?"

"I think six foot one or six foot, 200 to 210 pounds."

"And that was because you had a good opportunity to look at his size?"

"Right."

"Six foot one, any more than that? Any more of a description than that?"

"A mustache, dark hair—black hair."

"And you described him as being a big guy?"

"Yes, he was big."

"Now, bearing in mind that you tend to underestimate—as you

did with me—the height and weight of an individual, would you now say that he might have been even a little taller than that?"

White objected, but Cicilline noted that Giordano had, at another time, estimated the big guy's height to six foot four.

"Yes, up to six foot four," agreed Giordano.

"So?"

"That was a couple of years later."

"Because, in your mind, he was a very big person?"

"Well, can I say something? Back then I weighed 120 pounds. So anybody was big to me then. He was big, yes."

"You knew the difference between how tall you were and how much taller this other man was, didn't you?"

"Right."

"You're how tall?"

"I'm like five foot nine and a half."

"So this man that you were talking about was at least what?"

"Three, four inches taller than me," Giordano said.

"Or five. Are you sure of that?"

"Yes."

"There's no question in your mind?"

"Yes!"

"And that was because you were looking at him way above you?" asked Cicilline.

"Not way above—four or five inches higher than me."

"Could we have the petitioner stand by the witness?" Cicilline asked.

Accompanied by a trooper, Vic Giordano stepped from the stand and stood by the defense table. With TV cameras still glued to the front of the courtroom, Stephen Rosati got up from his seat and walked over to face his accuser. They stared eyeball-to-eyeball and looked like two pit bulls about to tear each other apart.

"That's enough, that's enough," the judge shouted. "Let's get back."

Tensions continued to run high as Cicilline continued, "You're five foot nine, he's five foot ten. Does that affect your judgment of him in any way?"

"No."

Flabbergasted, Cicilline went on. "Wasn't the man you were looking at, three, four, or five inches taller than you?"

"That was the man I was looking at," Giordano retorted, evading the question.

Angered, Cicilline fired back. "You concede he's not three, four, or five inches taller than you?"

"Yes."

"And the man you saw you said weighed 220 pounds."

"200, 220."

"Do you know how much Rosati weighs?"

"No."

"About 175 pounds."

"Objection," White chimed in.

"There is testimony about this, Your Honor," Cicilline shot back.

"Please, please. If I want an argument, I will ask for it. I realize that people's weight can fluctuate over a five-year period," Judge Sheehan responded.

"Excuse me," Cicilline said, still dumbfounded by Giordano's response. "It's not whether he was reduced in size. I was talking about his height."

"Well, you said, 175 pounds," the judge said.

Not wanting Cicilline to complete his thought, White interfered quickly. "My objection, Your Honor," White said, "is in the counsel's dialogue with the witness."

The judge nodded to Cicilline, signaling him to move on.

"Now, I understand you took an oath this morning to tell the truth, is that right?"

"Yes."

"And you understand the importance of telling the truth?"

"Yes."

"Can you recall the last time you lied to anybody?"

"Oh yeah, I lie. I'm human."

"About anything important?"

"Not recently."

"Well, let's take October 13, 1986. Your lifelong buddy has been killed, and you give the police a twelve-page report that you went to your girlfriend's home to change your shirt. You lie to the police, don't you?"

"I did that night."

"You don't say a single word about your drug-dealing activities, do you?"

"Not that night."

"Did you tell the truth the next day?"

"No."

"How many years was it before you began to tell the truth?"

"Not years—a couple of months."

"You lied about what happened at that house that night, didn't you?"

"Objection."

"He can answer yes or no," said the judge.

"I lied about not being there to buy drugs, right."

"Everything else was true?" Cicilline asked.

"Yes."

"And they asked you if Joe Viscido was selling drugs, isn't that right?"

"Right."

"And you said no?"

"Right."

White objected, and a verbal altercation broke out between prosecutor and defense. "Please, please, let's go on," said the judge.

"You were asked if you knew what kind of drugs Viscido was using, and you said you didn't know. Isn't that right?"

"Right. I lied about the drugs. I was on probation. I'm not allowed to hang around with people that deal drugs or use drugs."

"So, in addition to violating the terms of your probationary period, which was a promise by you to keep the peace and be of good behavior, you lied to the police, isn't that right?"

"About drugs, right."

Cicilline moved on. He tried to punch holes in Giordano's statements concerning his ability to get a good look at the taller guy and then requested that Giordano describe the shorter person. White objected on the ground that it had nothing to do with Rosati, but Judge Sheehan allowed the line of questions because it related to Giordano's observational abilities.

"He was about five feet and weighed 130 to 140 pounds, with his face scarred," Giordano said.

"And you thought that you had seen him sometime before?" Cicilline asked.

"He looked familiar," Giordano responded.

"Were you ever able to identify him?"

"In September of 1990, I did."

"But you recall having been shown his photograph on three separate occasions and not being able to identify him?"

"Objection."

"I'll allow it," said the judge.

"I don't know," Giordano said.

Cicilline showed Giordano two photo lineups that he viewed in 1988 and that included Peter Dallas's picture, though he did not identify Dallas. Cicilline showed Giordano a picture of the composite photograph that the police constructed based upon his description. Giordano said that the drawing was created with the help of Michelle Arrieta, and Cicilline asked that Michelle Arrieta be brought up to testify. The judge called a sidebar and deflected Cicilline's request.

"First of all, I wouldn't order the state of Florida to bring anybody up, but based on this testimony, I'm not even going to request that they bring her [or any other witness] up," the judge said to the astonishment of Jack Cicilline. "Remember, the issue here really is, I have found that the petitioner by clear and convincing evidence has proven to this court's satisfaction that the petitioner was not in the demanding state. Now Florida comes back with a witness who absolutely identifies this petitioner as being there. I don't think anyone will disagree that as contradictory evidence, I must extradite [Carl Stephen Rosati]. It's up to the trier of fact to find guilt or innocence of this petitioner, not of this court. I'm not shutting you off," said the judge.

It seemed, however, that he had already formed his decision before Cicilline completed his cross-examination of Vic Giordano.

Cicilline asked if Giordano had spoken to Joe Viscido's father with regard to the investigation. Giordano said that he saw Mr. Viscido once at the wake. "He was crying. He just couldn't believe that his Joe had died over drugs," Giordano said. "And I saw him once more when he was following me, and I told him I had nothing to do with it. That's all I said, and I said I would help."

"And you saw Mr. Viscido later?"

"Just that once. He was following me, spying on me. I guess he thought I was involved. And I told him that I wasn't."

"On March 25, 1988, Detective Burndt came to the jail and showed you a photographic pack with a picture of Mr. Rosati, is that right?"

"I didn't look at the photos. I refused to look."

"Well, but you told Burndt 'I didn't see anybody in the lineup'?"

"I turned my back and asked to go back to my cell."

"Well, weren't you the guy who decided back in December you were going to start to tell the truth, and you were going to do whatever you could to help?"

"Right, until I got the thirty-month jail sentence. I was pissed. Excuse my language."

"So, when you got pissed, you did what you wanted?"

"At that time, yes."

"In other words, you figured out in this system that there are ways to get ahead?"

"No."

"No?"

"I was just mad at Deerfield for the long sentence because I was hoping I would get probation again."

"So you're on probation?"

"Right."

"So you made a deal with the police?"

"There was no deal made."

"But you're a witness because you have been helped, isn't that right?"

"No!"

"You got no help?"

"No, I haven't."

"What have you been promised in return for your testimony here?"

"Zero."

Cicilline continued to try and crack this witness, but several approaches did not work out, so he returned to the question of identification.

"Let's get back to the photos. On November 30, 1987, you are shown a photo spread, and you pick out Joseph Bagley, who is six foot, 210 pounds, and choose him as the big guy."

"Rosati's photo wasn't in that spread," Giordano said.

"You said, 'Looks like No. 6.'"

"Yes, not that it was him, but that it looked like him." Giordano wasn't budging an inch.

After a short recess, the questioning continued.

"Mr. Giordano," Cicilline asked, "you were arrested on August 20, 1990, and you gave a statement identifying Stephen Rosati on September 3, 1990, in front of Detective Coyote?"

"Yes. Just me and Detective Coyote."

"And you also picked out Peter Dallas as well after you had been shown three packs with Dallas [and never ID'd him before]. How is that possible?"

"I don't know. I just for some reason picked him out that day. I

321

recognized him that day."

Cicilline went through each of the previous times when Peter Dallas was passed by. "Had anyone said anything to you about Peter Dallas between September 1988, when you did not pick him out, and September of 1990, when you did?"

"No."

"Was the name familiar to you? Did you know he was a suspect?"

"No."

"You hadn't talked to Michelle or Jeff Bloom?"

"No."

"On September 3, you refer to the big guy as Rosati. How is that you knew his name?"

"Well, talk on the street was that his name was brought up."

"Was Dallas's name brought up?"

"No."

"Who had you talked to about this?"

"All the local drug dealers."

"Told you what?"

"That drug dealers had been ripped off even before and the talk was that it was Rosati, but I hadn't seen his picture and didn't connect the name to the picture," Giordano replied, holding his own.

Cicilline had the witness read his transcript of the affidavit where he describes the big guy as between six foot two and six foot four, 220 pounds, black hair and a mustache. "That's all," Cicilline said, and Giordano stepped down.

"Your Honor," Cicilline said, "I may be producing further witnesses, and I am not sure of your schedule."

"I have six and a half years to go," said the judge.

He had reason to feel chipper. With Vic Giordano's testimony, Sheehan was off the hook. The road to Florida had now been paved.

CHAPTER 56:
The Hearing: Judgment Day

Day Sixteen: June 26, 1991

Rumors that Carl H. Rosati was a Mob chieftain, or worse, that Judge Sheehan was in his pocket, began circulating. Their source was difficult to pin down. First off, any high-profile crime case in which Jack Cicilline is involved can carry potential Mafia baggage. That was one of the worries the Rosatis had when they initially hired him. Then there were allegations of Mob ties from Florida. Both White and Cicilline were concerned not only about these persistent baseless contentions but also by the tactics of the press.

Rhode Island had followed the case for nine months with continuing coverage on all three local TV networks, and there were over twenty articles in the *Providence Journal*. It was a living soap opera, and now the supposedly impartial daily was going to choreograph a fantastic conclusion: Stephen Rosati on his way to a death sentence in Florida.

On the day Giordano testified, June 26, 1991, the *Providence Journal* ran a nonstory above the fold on the front page linking Judge Sheehan to the Mob! The piece was adorned with a full-color spread of a mansion belonging to the alleged mobster Ken Guarino next to a picture of a scantily clad bimbo from a skin magazine. The second lead, also on page one, was the key Giordano testimony. Coincidence could not explain the juxtaposition.

"Police know Kenny Guarino is a pornography kingpin," the article said. "Mafia bosses know him as a man they can trust. . . . He and his wife were married in a private ceremony last year by Superior Court Judge John F. Sheehan." Stephen Rosati's picture also appeared on page one underneath the byline "Witness Puts Rosati at Scene of Slaying."

Inside the newspaper on page six was a gallery of portrait-sized photos that included Judge Sheehan one slot over from New York crime boss John Gotti. Jack Cicilline could be seen questioning Vic Giordano a few pages later. The juxtaposition of the prominent images of Judge John Sheehan next to the most notorious mobster in the country, the "Teflon Don," John Gotti, and the placement of a front-page article linking Sheehan to an alleged porn king on the very day the paper was also covering the culmination of the high profile Rosati extradition hearing was not the *Providence Journal*'s most shining hour. What the *Journal* had done was serve to perpetuate the myth that judges in the state of Rhode Island were in the pocket of the Mob and, further, that the Rosati family might also be Mob connected. This contention also unnerved Florida Detective Coyote, who had, from the start, theorized that this was so.

This was judgment day. Cicilline had real hopes that Judge Sheehan would rule in their favor because Cicilline believed that the judge was convinced of Stephen's innocence. But after Jack took one look at the paper, he knew that the odds for a win had dropped to nearly zero.

"Eight months of work were overturned by forces working feverishly, blindly, to sacrifice my son," Esther said chillingly.

Jack Cicilline requested extra time to locate additional witnesses, including a person who was at the Chinese restaurant when Stephen and Elodie had dinner five years earlier.

"Given Mr. Giordano's testimony, what bearing would that have?" the judge asked, knowing that he now had the establishment of contradictory evidence with a prosecutor's witness that was cross-examined. Another Rhode Island witness for the defense could not offset this. However, Cicilline was also negotiating with Chris Jones, who was no longer in Canada but back in Florida. Without revealing his identity, however, Cicilline said that if this second witness were to testify and not ID Rosati, "that would go directly to the Giordano issue."

Esther felt this was their last chance to combat Giordano's testimony. Having flown from Canada to Florida, Fran Martin finally called with the good news.

"Mrs. Rosati," Fran said, "Chris's parents are willing to have us meet with him." The Rosatis waited for the meeting, but Chris never showed. Esther dialed the father's number.

"Mr. Jones, we badly need your son's testimony. He knows my son did not do this terrible thing, and he can save him."

"If your son is innocent, then let God take care of it," Mr. Jones replied.

CHAPTER 57:
The Hearing: Copping Out

Day Seventeen: June 28, 1991

The court came to order as Judge Sheehan asked if Jack Cicilline was ready to present his next witness, Chris Jones.

"I'm standing to tell you that I am not ready," Cicilline said reluctantly.

Cicilline explained to the judge that he had spoken with Jones on the phone on five separate occasions, and he simply refused to meet his appointments. He would not come up to testify.

"Based upon this, I would respectfully request a further continuance until we are able to secure some definitive statement from Jones and ultimately his production here to testify."

"Well, Mr. Cicilline, I'm not saying you should agree with me, but," the judge argued, "suppose Jones does not ID Rosati. Wouldn't that merely be contradictory evidence which is up to the trier of fact, when I'm not the trier of fact in this case?"

"I don't think that it goes to the issue that Your Honor must resolve, and that is whether or not the petitioner has shown clear and convincing evidence and whether that has been overcome simply by the [contradicting] evidence of two [Florida direct eye] witnesses," Cicilline summed up cogently.

Noting his "awareness of the seriousness of these proceedings," the judge countered, "I am not inclined to grant any further continuances. I am going to decide this case today."

"Please note my objection," said Cicilline.

In White's final arguments, he noted the following:

"It is the petitioner's burden to show that he wasn't there on October 12, 1986, and to show that conclusively. The burden is a substantial one. It is a significant one. Some courts have framed it in terms of 'beyond a reasonable doubt.' Rhode Island framed it as 'clear and convincing.' The court must decide that the evidence was clear, and the court must be convinced in light of all the evidence that he was not in Florida on October 12, 1986. Otherwise he's not entitled to release and he has to be sent back.

"Carl Stephen Rosati has an alibi. He presented several witnesses, but the only people who really talked on the point of issue of October 12, 1986, are himself and his two former girlfriends, Elodie Vanderpyl and Kara Lynx. Each of them says he was here on October 12. Against that evidence through Detective Coyote's testimony were five people interviewed in Florida, each of whom identified through pictures Carl Stephen Rosati. You heard from one of them, Vic Giordano. Michelle Arrieta and Vic Giordano say through Coyote, and Giordano to this court in person, that they saw him in Deerfield Beach on the night of October 12. Jeff Bloom told Coyote. Danny Ek told Coyote. Cory Franco told Coyote. And their affidavits are part of the case records.

"Carl Stephen Rosati does have an alibi, but in light of all the evidence that alibi does not clearly and convincingly establish his absence from Florida on the night of October 12, 1986. The strength or weakness of the [conflicting] alibis is something that should not be measured in Rhode Island. The court simply can't as a matter of law decide to choose one story over the other. Under the circumstances, Carl Stephen Rosati must be rendited, and I urge the court to deny his writ of habeas corpus."

"Mr. Cicilline," the judge said.

"Your Honor," Jack Cicilline began, "the petitioner was required to establish by clear and convincing evidence that he was not in the demanding state on October 12, 1986, and to do that he offered some twenty-odd witnesses in support of his presence here in the state of Rhode Island. The state countered that evidence with two witnesses.

"The first witness was Detective Coyote, whose testimony was affidavits of prior testimony of other witnesses in this case, witnesses who did not actually come here to testify.

"We know, for example, that Michelle Arrieta described the taller of the two men as having sandy hair and weighing 280 pounds. Jeff Bloom said he was big, tall, and stocky. Cory Franco said he was a big fat guy.

"Finally the state put on Vic Giordano. And when you cut away all he is from what he said, the description Your Honor is left with is that when he first makes an identification he describes the taller man as six foot one or six foot two, weighing between 200 and 220. And then two years later he has him at six foot two to six foot four with the same weight. We also know that when first shown a photo spread, which contained a photograph of Stephen Rosati, he did not make an identification. However, [now] he comes into this courtroom and he says that's the man.

"Now, the question is, are we to just take that evidence and suggest that it puts the state over the edge? We know, for example, that the court can consider whether or not the witness has been convicted of a crime, and he has. The court can consider whether or not the witness has used drugs, and he has. We can consider whether or not at another time he gave testimony that was inconsistent with what he said here, and we know that he has done that too. Does the law in its wisdom suggest that all those factors which can be used in any other case, and which traditionally are [used] in trial courts every single day, be set aside because [this proceeding is an extradition hearing and not a trial]?

"The court must be satisfied that the evidence that is presented by the state is credible and substantial. And no case suggests simply because the state offers a witness who places the petitioner in the demanding state that all else ends. . . . Because if that were so," Cicilline said, putting his finger on the heart of the matter, "there would be no need to have a judge to hear a habeas petition.

"In order for this court to deny the petitioner's petition for writ of habeas corpus, it must find that Giordano's testimony was so compelling that the testimony of the twenty-odd witnesses presented by the petitioner has been overcome."

The judge cut in. "Not to interrupt you, Mr. Cicilline, but would you agree with me that it's not my function to judge the guilt or innocence of this petitioner?"

"Absolutely," Cicilline replied.

"All right," said the judge.

"But," said Cicilline, "what I am saying to the court is you take the evidence presented by the petitioner and you weigh it against the evidence offered by the state. If after you do that you still conclude that he has established by clear and convincing evidence that he was here, notwithstanding what the state has said, then the writ must be issued. If you have in your mind that there's a question, I don't know whether he was here or there after you hear the state's evidence, then the writ should be denied.

"Now, I know I do not need to repeat for the court the testimony of the individual witnesses, nor do I need to remind you of the physical exhibits that we introduced during the course of this trial. But I can't think in my mind what there was about Giordano that overcomes what Kara Lynx had to say when she said, 'He was not away from me one day of his life while I was living here.' I don't know what there was that Giordano had to say that overcomes what Elodie Vanderpyl had to say when she said, 'I was with him on the night of October 12, 1986.' I don't know what Giordano had to say that overcomes the testimony of the petitioner himself when he took the stand and he said, 'Judge, I was not in Florida. I didn't do this on October 12, 1986.'

"And I could go through the balance of the other witnesses, but even if I wanted to pass them off to say that they were mistaken, or they somehow had the wrong time periods in mind, how do we account for the physical exhibits presented to this court?

"We have checks that were issued and signed by him and cashed by him in and around the time of this event that lock in the time frames. Things that he couldn't create or anyone create later on. But most importantly, how do we overcome those two telephone calls that were made from the Rosati office to Woonsocket, the home of Elodie Vanderpyl, on October 12 and October 13? What was there that Giordano said that can cause the court to say, I have got a question in my mind whether he was in Rhode Island or in Florida on October 12? What was there that can destroy the probative force of those telephone records? I submit there was nothing. I submit that you just can't sweep all that aside.

"The easy road, of course, is to say the evidence is in conflict and the petitioner should be returned to Florida and his case should be tried there. That's the easy road, but the road of courage is to say I have listened to Giordano and my experience as a trial lawyer and my experience as a judge tells me that witnesses in these kinds of circumstances very often make mistakes. The reported cases on eyewitness identifications are replete with reference to the caution that everyone should take in the area of eyewitness identification."

"I am well familiar with those cases," agreed the judge.

"I'm certain you are, Your Honor," Cicilline said as he moved in for the close. Summoning up all his power, Cicilline hit the judge broadside with a challenge of conscience. "But it seems to me," Jack said unflinchingly to this colleague he knew so well, "the real issue is, can you, in your heart and mind, say that the testimony of Vic Giordano was so compelling that it can cause me to set aside twenty witnesses? I heard from the witnesses that swore under oath who knew Carl Stephen Rosati that he was here at the critical times: his sister, his father, the investigators, all the people, and if you are capable of saying that that has been overcome by the testimony of a drug-dealing witness who has a criminal record and about whom any judge at another time might say this man is not worthy of belief, if you think that testimony rises to that level, then you certainly should deny the writ for habeas corpus. But if after you consider all of that, you say that it just doesn't reach that level, I can't say that because I still believe that this man was in Rhode Island, then under those circumstances, Your Honor, it's your duty to grant the writ, and I ask you to do that."

A long pause followed while the Rosatis, Jack Cicilline, Randy White, and the Florida prosecutor, Jeffrey Driscoll, waited for the judge to make his ruling. More than six months had passed since the hearing began, and in a strange way the group of combating opponents and the judge had become like a family unit.

"All rise," said the bailiff as Judge Sheehan returned to his seat. With a pensive look he flipped back his robes. "Please be seated," he muttered and then he planted himself in his chair.

"You make a very compelling argument, Mr. Cicilline," the judge began forebodingly. "And while I do not say that I am heartless, I feel that I have to rule from my mind rather than my heart.

"The issuance of a rendition warrant regular on its face is prima facie evidence a fugitive is wanted and is sufficient to justify his arrest, detention, and delivery to the demanding state. I find that the warrant is regular on its face, that it has been signed by the governor of Rhode Island, that a crime of murder has been committed in Florida, and that Carl Stephen Rosati was indicted for the crime. The only issue before this court is whether or not Mr. Rosati is a fugitive and whether or not he was in the demanding state at the time of the alleged incident in October of 1986.

"I made a preliminary finding at the end of the petitioner's case that he had satisfied by clear and convincing evidence that he was not in the demanding state, that he was in the state of Rhode Island.

"I have not changed my opinion on this regard and will go a step further. I will find beyond a reasonable doubt that at the end of the petitioner's case he had established to this court's satisfaction that he was not in the demanding state."

The judge went on to state that Detective Coyote's testimony could not carry any weight because it was based on "a piece of paper," and that had to be compared to the twenty-two eyewitnesses Rosati had supplied.

"I requested a live witness to be cross-examined, and the state of Florida acceded to my request. They did, in fact, bring up Vic Giordano. I might say, at this time, it is this court's opinion that Mr. Giordano will never get Citizen of the Year in Broward County. Nevertheless, at the crucial point of his testimony, he unequivocally pointed out the petitioner to the court.

"As I previously mentioned, it is not this court's function to prove the guilt or innocence of this petitioner. It is this court's function to abide by the dictates of the United States Constitution and the Rhode Island Constitution and the agreement between the states concerning rendition. I find contradictory evidence. I find that Mr. Giordano, his drug-related record notwithstanding, positively identified Carl Stephen Rosati as the individual who participated in the crime that occurred on October 12, 1986, in Deerfield Beach. Therefore, this court feels that it is faced with contradictory evidence that must be resolved in the state of Florida. That is a constitutional mandate that this court finds it must follow.

"I think I have sufficiently placed on the record how I evaluated the petitioner's witnesses, but it is this court's strong feeling that I do not have the right to test the guilt or innocence. That is up to the state of Florida. I have personally tried cases in the state of Florida, and I am sure Mr. Rosati will get a fair trial there. I will not comment on what I personally feel the outcome of that trial might be. It's not before me." Stifling quickly remonstrations by family members and friends, the judge concluded, "I would hope there will be no outburst in this courtroom."

After the decision, the judge left open the door for Mr. Cicilline to make a motion for a hearing before the supreme court of the state.

"They will not pass judgment on whether I made an error or not," the judge said. "They pass judgment on what they feel the evidence is that has been submitted by the petitioner and by the state of Florida."

That night, the TV announced the long-awaited decision. Channel 12 began with an interview and a quote from Stephen, dressed in his prison garb at the ACI. "People can watch me tonight," he began, "and they can make up their own minds, but I'm an innocent man."

Interviewed by TV reporter Tom Magair, Judge Sheehan, dressed in his robes and half-moon reading glasses looked drawn and somber. "I have no other choice but to deny the petition for habeas corpus."

"And with that," Magair said, "Stephen Rosati has lost his extradition hearing."

"They know I had nothing to do with it," Stephen said before the cameras. "They will have their time in court, but worse than that, they are going to have to face God. They are going to have to face Him. I've been living in a nightmare for nine months, and it's still not over."

The scene then shifted to a press conference held in the boardroom of the Rosati Group. NBC Channel 10 and CBS Channel 12 both attended.

Channel 10 covered Carl: "These charges are trumped up," Carl said directly into the camera. "Florida will go to any lengths to get this case resolved in their favor. But that's not justice, and we're concerned about it."

On Channel 12, well-known anchorwoman Karen Adams said for *Eyewitness News*, "Stephen Rosati's parents made a public plea stating their son's innocence."

"I am outraged at the intentional fraud of the Broward Police!" Esther proclaimed. "They said they would fry my son in the electric chair! This is more than shoddy police work. It's intentional fraud." Starting with a bang, Esther ended with her voice cracking on the last word.

After Judge Sheehan ruled to extradite, Carl and Esther requested a meeting. The judge met with Stephen's parents, Jack Cicilline, and the sheriff; the court stenographer was also present. Since the ordeal had lasted nearly ten months—seventeen actual days in court—the judge had the dubious honor of having presided over the longest extradition hearing in the history of the state and probably the country.

"I know that your son is innocent," the judge said, "and when he goes to Florida, he will be exonerated. However," he went on, anticipating their next question, "an extradition hearing is not based upon whether or not a person is innocent or guilty. That is for a court to decide."

From this statement, it was clear to Carl that the judge had merely found a way to send Stephen down. "That is why he gave Florida two full months after closing arguments to complete their case," Carl noted. "This was unheard of."

Without direct eyewitness testimony from the prosecution, the judge would not have had a clear-cut basis for supporting Florida's case. Further, Judge Sheehan didn't want to interfere with relations between states. Essentially, he had said to them, "If you don't get someone up here, I am not going to send him down." This delayed the trial from April until June.

A few days after the hearing, the Rosatis obtained the Florida court order commuting Giordano's prison sentence to time served in exchange for him testifying against Stephen.

"This is enough for the judge to change his mind," Carl calculated.

"I don't know if he will," Jack replied, "but he should,"

The judge reviewed the document carefully and returned it to Cicilline. "I've made my decision," Sheehan said, referring to a ruling that, according to Cicilline, would end up plaguing him to the end of his days.[1]

From the Rosatis' point of view, this was a situation whereby "the judge did nothing and the prosecutor, Randy White, allowed a known perjurer to be the centerpiece of his case. That's fair-minded justice for you!" Carl exclaimed. The Rosatis had no choice but to appeal to the higher court.

CHAPTER 58:
The Supreme Court

The Rhode Island Supreme Court was presided over by Justices Weisberger, Fay, Shea, and Kelleher. Cicilline established Judge Sheehan's ruling that Rosati had "proven beyond a reasonable doubt" that he was in Rhode Island at the time the murder was committed. He established that Sheriff Coyote's testimony had been discounted because it was hearsay, and he presented the court with the document verifying that Giordano had made a deal for his testimony but had refused to admit that such a deal had existed when asked about it in court.

With bravado, the assistant attorney general stepped forward. "Your Honors," White proclaimed, "This case is a prosecutor's dream." The issue was simple. It had nothing to do with whether Stephen Rosati was innocent or guilty but whether there was contradictory evidence allowing for an extradition to take place.

The Rosatis waited for the judges to come back and give a ruling, but were dismayed when they found out that a clerk had written up the decision, which began, "This court is forbidden to try the guilt or innocence of the accused . . ."

Concerning the allegation that Giordano's testimony was perjured, the court begged the question by stating, "It is not unusual for prosecutorial authorities to obtain testimony from those accused with criminal conduct under the expectation, whether expressed or implied, of favorable treatment." Contradictory testimony that could be cross-examined had occurred; therefore, "the petitioner has failed to prove either by clear or convincing evidence or certainly beyond a reasonable doubt that he was not in the demanding state at the date of the alleged crime."

"Judge Sheehan did not rule on the evidence," Esther explained. "He knew Giordano was lying. It would have taken a man of character to have the courage not to extradite. It was Florida that was corrupt, but because of the insinuation that Rhode Island was corrupt, the judge was afraid to rule according to the truth."

Esther addressed the judge. "Your Honor, it is your responsibility to bring justice into your courtroom."

"I only have to follow the law," the judge replied.

The hearing had taken ten months. Esther was disgusted with him. "Thank you for your endurance," was all she could muster, because that was something that she could thank him for.

This event reminded Esther of Pontius Pilate and the presentation of Jesus in his courtroom. Supposedly, powerful and ruthless Pontius Pilate washed his hands and let the blood be shed someplace else. "Take and do what you want with him," he said of Jesus. "Fearful of pressure from the high priests, he evaded responsibility."

No one could save that man," Esther said, "but we were not going to let this happen to our son."

In their quest to overturn the supreme court ruling, the Rosatis launched a two-pronged attack. First, they held a press conference that was covered by the three local TV stations, and then they appealed to the new governor, Bruce Sundlun. Esther sent a telegram to the governor, which was published in the *Providence Journal*, whereby she accused "the Broward County Sheriff's Office [of] . . . intentionally fram[ing] her son," and requested that the governor "protect our son."

She also got the idea to arrange a meeting with Margery Sundlun, the governor's wife, at her office in downtown Providence on South Main Street. [For Rhode Islanders who remember Mrs. Sundlun, at a later date she became severely injured and brain damaged when a car hit her while she was jogging.] Mrs. Sundlun, an elegant lady dressed in a fashionable skirt, matching silk blouse, and jacket, her silver hair tied neatly in a bun, greeted Esther Rosati who was also fashionably attired. Mrs. Sundlun put down the French poodle that was forever in her lap and shook Esther's hand.

Though skeptical, Mrs. Sundlun agreed to read the case. In the interest of saving time, Esther highlighted the passage in the 1,400-page transcript whereby Judge Sheehan stated that Stephen had established his innocence "beyond a reasonable doubt." Mrs. Sundlun called Jack Cicilline to review these passages and also argued back and forth with Esther to debate details.

Esther made her appeal from one mother to another.

"Margery, you are my last resort. You must get your husband to review this case. My son is innocent, and the judge has admitted it."

Mrs. Sundlun said that she did speak with her husband and, as a result, was able to set up a meeting with Sheldon Whitehouse, legal counsel to the governor and, later, the U.S. senator from Rhode Island. However, rather than review the case himself, which would have been the objective way to ascertain the situation, Whitehouse simply set up a meeting with the prosecutor. Naturally, Randy White devalued the defense's case.

Concerned with the legal ramifications for the governor if he did not comply with the extradition request, Whitehouse complied with the prosecution. Since the previous governor, Governor DiPrete, had signed the original extradition papers, Whitehouse had a neat reason why Governor Sundlun could not override.

The Rosatis were aghast. From their point of view, Governor Sundlun, through his "spineless" legal counsel, was allowing their son to go to Florida to face the electric chair when he, himself, was aware that there were improprieties in Judge Sheehan's decision. Rather than truly studying the case from the perspective of potentially sending an innocent man to the gallows in another state, Whitehouse simply deferred to the prosecutor. For such a serious situation, and considering that the judge had ruled that Rosati had made his case "beyond a reasonable doubt," Whitehouse's actions were lame.*

---

*   Interestingly enough, Lincoln Chaffee, present governor of Rhode Island, recently attempted to block extradition to a Federal prison of accused murderer Jason Pleau because Pleau's possible sentence would be an execution, and Rhode Island does not have a death sentence, "Death Penalty Watch, Rhode Island and the Rest of the World," by Andrew Rosenthal, *New York Times*, 12/22/2011. This defense simply was not thought of during the Stephen Rosati extradition hearing, which occurred twenty years earlier.

Having failed in their attempt, the Rosatis wrote compelling letters to Senators Chaffee and Pell, Congressman Reed, and U.S. Attorney General Dick Thornburgh. The buck was passed to John R. Dunn, assistant attorney general from the U.S. Department of Justice Civil Rights Division. The response to their letters was disappointing:

Dear Mrs. Rosati:

After a careful review of [your] report, we concluded that this matter lacks prosecutive merit, and we closed our file. Accordingly, we intend to take no further action. Thank you for bringing this matter to our attention. This division is dedicated to the enforcement of federal criminal civil rights statutes. We appreciate your cooperation in our effort to achieve that goal.

"I was appalled to realize that I was confronted with idiots," Esther concluded. "We were not dealing with rational or logical people. There was a fallacy in the system. In this country, you are supposedly *presumed innocent*, but we were always coming from a position of guilt. Detective Coyote said that he didn't know about Giordano's plea bargain, but [the private detective] Venturi told us that was impossible: 'How could anybody sit where he is sitting,' Venturi said, 'and pretend he didn't know about it?'

"Judge Sheehan knew that Stephen was in Rhode Island at the time of the murder, but he did what was simply convenient for the state and for himself. Even though Jack provided him with an extensive list of precedent cases where judges ruled not to extradite, he still wouldn't budge.

"Randy White entirely discarded every one of our witnesses, not one of which had a criminal record. These were people of integrity. He also discarded, with a flippant wave of his hand, the documentation: verified stamped and dated checks, credit card receipts, and telephone records. It was astonishing. "My whole realization was that these people were not profound thinkers. We were locked into a device where they simply followed a narrow interpretation of the law. Their decisions were politically motivated and were not based on the evidence. The state, and even the country, had now become our foe.

"The only outstanding person in all of this was Jack Cicilline," Esther concluded. "He stood alone as a noble man. The rest of them were all wimps. Jack fought this case with perseverance and constant strength. He never gave up and never left a stone unturned. While we were fighting extradition, if I felt that there was another person out there who could help us, Jack was with us. He kept saying, over and over, 'We need time,' because he knew that their case had holes in it and that at any day a witness could flip."

The strongest thing for the Rosatis, even when they lost the extradition hearing, was that the fight was going to continue. Esther revealed that "there was panic, terror, and fear," but because truth was on their side, not for a single moment did Carl and Esther Rosati consider giving in. "Winning became the overriding thing."

Many Rhode Islanders concurred, and they rallied behind Stephen Rosati. Outraged at the travesty of justice they had witnessed through reading Jim Hummel's ongoing and astutely written reports in the *Providence Journal,* they voiced their opinions in print. On Saturday, July 27, 1991, the newspaper published a number of letters to the editor, all in favor of freeing Rosati:

Maureen Smith from Westerly wrote: "What a shameful commentary on the judicial system of Rhode Island, which throws innocent victims to the wolves."

Susan Ann-Latz of Westerly wrote: "It appears to me that this delay allowed a witness of questionable reputation from Florida the time to fabricate false testimony and point a finger at an innocent man. It is time to stop this travesty of justice now."

William Castelluccio and Margot Walton added their thoughts regarding the outcome:

"From all written accounts, there seems to be substantial evidence indicating that Mr. Rosati was in Rhode Island at the time the Florida crime was committed. We believe that his implication in this crime is, at best, a matter of mistaken identity, and at worst, a criminal attempt to exonerate the guilty and incriminate the innocent."

CHAPTER 59:
Railroaded

Rosati, still at the ACI, was becoming increasingly forlorn. He had spent nearly a year fighting to stay out of Florida, and now it looked like he could be going down. Detective Coyote had really scared him. Stephen feared that he would either be snuffed out on the way there or possibly murdered once he was stuck in a grim Southern jail.

"I was waiting any day for them to take me in the middle of the night," Stephen painfully recalled. "You see guys leave the prison in the middle of the night all the time.

"Judge Sheehan couldn't even look me in the eye when he said, 'Mr. Giordano would not win the Most Honorable Man in Broward County Award, but I can't dispute this on an extradition hearing.' You could see on his face what the judge was really saying: 'I know Giordano's a lying sack of shit, but I'm a weak prick, and I'll send Rosati down to Florida, so now I'm off the hook.'

"But Judge Sheehan, if he was a real judge, could just as easily have said, 'this kid proved his case. He's staying here.' That's if he had had any courage, which he didn't have. Sheehan knew I was innocent, and just as much told us so even on the record. His argument simply was, it wasn't for him to judge. A jury had to do this in Florida. At least, that's what he'll tell you in public. The truth is the *Providence Journal* had just ID'd him at a Mob wedding,[1] and he was underneath it all, shitting in his boots, or should I say his robes, from the bad publicity, so he caved. That's my opinion."

Rosati now found himself both angry and depressed. His parents had spent a year fighting, and now he realized that he was still going to have to wait probably an additional year just to go to trial. Smoking even more, he began to suffer from the ravages of anxiety. He figured that if they could nail him in his own state with almost a dozen witnesses on his side, he wouldn't stand a chance on their turf.

He reconsidered suicide. "If I get convicted and get a life term, then maybe I'll do it." He definitely preferred the electric chair to life in prison. "The thought of spending a lifetime in prison—you might as well just kill yourself."

The captain of the Intake Center came to his cell. "Steve, I hate to be the bearer of bad news, but Florida is here to get you." It was August 7, 1991, eleven months since the day he was first arrested.

"I packed my stuff," Stephen recalled. "I had my mind prepared. I could either break down or keep my composure and handle this like a man. I was scared out of my mind, but I also said, 'Fuck this whole thing. You've taken everything away from me. The only thing left is death.' The captain took me to the changing room."

Carl and Esther stated expressly that they did not want Detective Coyote taking their son down to the Broward County Jail. They just didn't trust him. "But there he was, with another cop ironically named Steve. And this guy was big, easily 265 pounds."

"Oh no, not you," Rosati said disgustedly as he changed into street clothes. "I was incapable of showing him any respect." The police shackled their prisoner with a fancy knee brace, which allowed him to walk but would lock if Rosati straightened his leg to shift into a run.

"I hope you don't take this personal," Coyote said to Rosati's astonishment, "but I didn't put this thing together. It was the Deerfield Police Department. I know your family hates me, and everyone hates me, but I didn't put this together."

What did he want me to say? Stephen thought. "In his own screwed up way, he was apologizing to me. Coyote was actually scared that day.

I could hear his voice quivering. I just kept my mouth shut. I'm the one facing the electric chair, and his voice was breaking down."

They drove Rosati right by the Providence Airport, actually located in Warwick, just two or three miles from the Rosati Group offices. Now Stephen was terrified. "What the fuck is going on?" he asked, quite fearful that they would make the whole drive by car, and if that were the case, there would be no telling what would happen. As everyone knew, a drive to Florida from Rhode Island took at least two nights.

Before they got to the airport, Coyote had the driver turn off the highway, and they parked the car by a house. Leaving the prisoner handcuffed and locked in the back seat, they disappeared into the building. Now, completely terrified, Rosati searched for a way to escape. This move struck him as too bizarre.

The two cops returned and continued their sojourn, down the interstate, through Connecticut, into New York, over the Throgs Neck Bridge, and all the way to LaGuardia Airport, nearly four hours out of their way. Apparently, their reason was to avoid the TV cameras set up at T. F. Green Airport in Rhode Island, where all three networks had been positioned. Ironically, at the beginning of the ride, Stephen pointed out a sign in Richmond right by Route 95 that read "The Rosati Group."

"I was going to build a hotel there, a Comfort Inn," Stephen told the detective.

"You'll be out in six months," Coyote responded.

Now why, after all this, would he say that? Rosati ruminated, and then later reasoned, *Because he already knew by then who the real killers were! And this guy's on the police force in the state of Florida in the United States of America, land of the free, home of the brave. What bullshit. And he didn't just set me up. He set two other guys up as well, nailed three completely innocent people, who all don't even know each other, and at the same time got witnesses to lie under oath, to say whatever he needed them to say. And this wasn't just to do time. This was to die. What a disgrace.*

On the plane, the stewardesses were notified that Rosati was a bad guy. "They looked at me like I was a turd and catered to Coyote and the other guy. We were pretty much quiet the whole trip down."

"We'll be the last ones off the plane and take a different exit," the detective uttered when the plane finally arrived. "There will be people with machine guns."

Flanked by three other storm troopers, Coyote's partner, Frank

Puccini, entered the plane. His gun was drawn, and he had a big smile on his overweight face.

"Well, Frank, it looks like you finally got me, huh!"

"Yeah!" Puccini laughed.

Rosati looked out at the landing field to see a full squadron of police cars and six guys with machine guns drawn. "You would have thought I was Manuel Noriega."

Placed in the lead vehicle, Rosati was taken to the prison with an entourage of three or four other police cars.

"Why this incredible overkill? Was it Coyote's attempt to portray me as a Mafia hit man?" Stephen calculated. "That's the only thing that made any sense about this."

At the Broward County Jail Intake Center, the prisoner was forced to remove all his clothes and stand naked before the cameras. The sense of shame and degradation was overwhelming. According to the detective, these photographs of Rosati's nude body were taken to show that he hadn't been beaten up. BSO could say they never abused their prisoner. Rosati was then fingerprinted, given some clothes, and taken to a holding cell, which was a room inside another room with no mattress, just a chair. Here was just the first step in a procedure calculated to strip whatever dignity the prisoner had left before he finally got into BSO's hands. The next day, they took him to maximum security, which was located on the seventh floor.

"There I was in one of the biggest jails in the country with 3,200 inmates, the majority Southern black. Now I have more than just my court case to worry about. I met a couple of white guys that seemed okay, and then I was transferred to a cell occupied by a big black guy who snored so loudly that no one could stand it.

"After a few days of that torture, I was moved into Ice Berg's cell. He turned out to be a decent guy, a big black kid who held church in his room every evening between 4:30 and 5:00. Eight or ten guys would sit around a circle and read chapters from the Bible, a new selection every night. Ice Berg was in for robbery.

"Here he was, my roommate, this big jailhouse-preaching colored guy with a bald head, 'getting down' with the word of the Lord. 'You got to give everything to God,' he'd say. 'You can't keep your eye on the worldly thing. You gotta keep your eye on the spiritual thing. You gotta keep your eye on the Lord.' He'd almost sing it. It was unbelievable, and sometimes he'd make me laugh."

Each evening the prisoners would start with an opening prayer.

"Someday, Lord, we will be free. We pray that we will be judged fairly and that all brothers, black or white, shall get along." Then they would read the verse and end with a closing prayer. Stephen found these prayers comforting, but a lot of these guys were in for pretty tough crimes.

"It wasn't long before another inmate downstairs began his own prayer group, and so there arose a mighty rivalry between the two churches. Ice Berg held his own for a while, but then he'd steal your food and blow his whole credibility."

Naturally, there was a chapel with a traditional preacher as well, and that is where the prisoners would go on Sundays. That's where Rosati saw Pete the Greek for the first time in about five years. Stephen hadn't been in jail two weeks.

"Steve," the Greek said, coming over and giving Rosati a big hug. "I'm so sorry all this happened. I can't believe they even have you associated with this. I don't even know how your name came up. I hardly ever knew you."

"Pete's a very open guy, and I could tell he felt genuinely sorry for what happened to me. It's true he uses everybody he comes in contact with, but he laughs and has a sense of humor, and, generally, he's okay."

Rosati, however, was conflicted about spending time with Pete the Greek.

"He wasn't really a friend of mine, more like an acquaintance. And I felt that if I spent too much time with him, it might look like we were closer than we really were. But we were in this crazy situation together, both accused and imprisoned for a murder neither of us was involved in, so we stayed in touch and kept our meetings short.

"Pete didn't know shit about the case, though. I knew more than he did. He did say that he knew Dallas and said that Dallas had been ripping him off at his Deli, so he threw him out of his life. He said that if he could just get to speak to Dallas, he could get me cleared. 'I know he won't testify against you, if they just let me speak to him.' But like Giordano, they had Dallas by the balls. If he didn't go their way, stick to the tack laid out for him, Coyote would set him up for the electric chair like us. That's the kind of scumbag power Coyote had. But unlike me, Dallas had a record, and even though he had nothing to do with this case, it didn't mean dick. He was going to do what he was told to do. To make sure, Coyote kept him insulated in another prison under an assumed name. Cicilline couldn't even get to him."

At the ACI in Rhode Island, each prisoner could have his own

TV, but in Florida there was only one per mod, "and it became a real pain to watch it with thirty-five other crazy guys, each fighting over what show they wanted to see. At least at the ACI you could spend some time zoned out in your own TV space."

On the other hand, unlike the ACI, at Broward County Jail prisoners were not as restricted to their own rooms. They could walk out of their cells into a day room where the TV was. It was small, but at least it gave the prisoners a little freedom. "Nevertheless, because of all the arguing it usually became a drag." Another difference had to do with overall policy. The guards were much more strict at Broward, and so there were fewer real fights than at the ACI. With all Stephen's fears, which at times had been overwhelming, this came as a pleasant surprise.

"Either way, I was going out of my mind with the boredom and the mental torture. But like at the ACI, working out with weights is what got me through in Florida.

"The routine at Broward was set up just to wear you down. At 5:00 a.m. every morning the alarm bell would go off because that's when breakfast was. Who the hell wants to eat at five in the morning? After that, there was nothing to do but go back to bed until daybreak. We were supposed to have an hour in the afternoon for rec time, but even that was cut short, getting us in late, taking us out early, so that real time was reduced to about forty minutes. Thus, to maximize my time with the weights, I would do my stretching exercises in the cell.

"Many bodybuilders have no idea, but stretching is equally important as lifting. Being limber is the key, and I'm so limber, I can complete a 180-degree leg split. That looks exactly like an upside-down letter T when it's done right. Most guys can't believe it, but all it takes is patience, persistence, and concentration. When I'm in the split, I can't quite explain it, but I feel at one, whole. A certain calmness comes over me, and I'm able to get into the kind of head I need to push the metal."

Rosati's training partner was Rambo, a black fellow who was about five foot nine, 230 pounds.

"If it wasn't for Rambo and the weights, I don't know what I would have done. Three days a week, we'd work out so hard we'd almost pass out. It was the only creative way I knew to absolve myself of the rage I could hardly contain.

"Much to my relief, the guards were really nice to me, probably because I treated them with respect. Not too long after I got down there, I got a job serving lunches to ninety prisoners. The guards felt they could trust me, and I became exactly that, a 'trustee.' It was a six-month stint."

Rosati's parents were now shuttling back and forth between Rhode Island and Florida every week. Like clockwork, they interviewed attorneys and visited their son on Mondays without ever missing a week.

"The Goose came down whenever my parents needed him, and I also got a visit from Bob McNeil, my real estate friend from Texas who stopped by when he was in town to visit me."

Over time, the Rosatis interviewed fifteen attorneys. Most of them were brash with connections to the police. "And you got the feeling," Stephen said, "after listening to their rap that, unlike Jack Cicilline, they had no balls and would sell you down the river if they could come out financially ahead."

On the other hand, there were three attorneys the Rosatis liked: Fred Hedard, who Stephen had met in court; David Bogenshutz; and the one they hired, Jeffrey Harris. However, another one of their attorneys down there, Victor Tobin, the one they had initially hired almost a year earlier, had called Carl and Esther virtually out of the blue to tell them that he had access to information that could get their son off scot-free but that it was going to cost them. He said he had information pointing to the real killers.

Because they had no privacy, and because they obviously could not trust the authorities, Carl and Esther conversed with their son through a code, and they also talked in riddles. They told Stephen in offhanded ways that Mr. Tobin was close to cracking the case, and Stephen began to get his hopes up once again. They also told him Mr. Tobin's fee was going to be $50,000.

CHAPTER 60:
By the Short Hairs

After the Florida sheriffs came to pick Stephen up, the Rosatis left for T. F. Green Airport, the main airport for Rhode Island, in hopes of seeing him off. However, true to his elusive nature, Detective Coyote did not go to where he had told the Rhode Island police he would go. Rather, he drove nearly four hours out of the way to leave from LaGuardia in New York because, according to Carl, he did not want to confront them, and he did not want to confront the press who were expecting him. Meanwhile, the Rosatis ran into Randy White at the airport, who was just as surprised at the switch.

That night, TV stations showed the dejected parents at an empty terminal. As was his style, Carl forthrightly informed the reporters that he was disappointed because he and Esther were unable to see Stephen off on the flight, but he also made a pledge before the cameras to continue the battle down in Florida.

Two friends of the Rosatis, John Gilman and his wife, Ellie, came to support them and had lunch with them at the airport. They offered their condo in Boca Raton to Carl and Esther, so they packed their car and moved to Florida on August 8. Red drove the Mercedes down with Esther on a nonstop run, and Carl flew down a few days later.

Carl told the *Providence Journal*, "If we didn't win extradition, then no one could win it," and if the prosecution, the judge, the governor, and the Rhode Island Supreme Court had to rely on a convicted cocaine addict rather than the testimony of twenty-two upstanding citizens, none of whom have ever had any arrest records, then, from Carl's point of view, there was something wrong with the system.[1]

"I always felt confident we would win," Carl said, "but it was all offset by the fact that Stephen was incarcerated and suffering. We were all consoling each other."

Esther told Stephen that she would be in Florida the day he got there, and so she asked Red to drive her down. They left immediately.

"The system was destroying our lives," Esther recalled bitterly. "It took everything from us: our dignity, our son. I had to be there for him. He was facing the electric chair."

Now, in a new prison situation, without the protection he seemed to have at the ACI in Rhode Island, Stephen's mother feared that his life would be in jeopardy all the more. And Esther was also concerned about Joe Viscido's father. The Rosatis had friends faxing them up articles from the *Miami Herald* and the *Sun-Sentinel* on a regular basis, and several of them raised Esther's antennae.

In April, the *Miami Herald* ran a full front-page article partial to the Rosatis' cause with the title "Did Broward Dad Nail Wrong Guy?" Written by Sallie Hughes, the article explained in detail the case against Florida, Stephen's testimony, and Judge Sheehan's ruling that Rosati had made his case "beyond a reasonable doubt." But this did not deter Mr. Viscido. In this and in a subsequent article published in September, he said he "had no doubt that Rosati is the killer." Mr. Viscido "dismissed the alibis because they did not cover the exact time of the murder. The rest, he said, are perjuries. The phone calls, the paychecks," he said, "were all made up. . . . Tell [Mr. Rosati] for me," Mr. Viscido spoke with a biblical vengeance, "I lost a son. He is going to lose a son. He can count on it."

"Although we were living in this state of continual terror," Esther recalled, "we had to stay rational. The strength of the truth was so strong. We always knew that we would eventually win. It was just a matter of time. But at what price?"

On the trip down, Esther began to feel that Red was becoming manipulative. If Esther brought up any issues related to business or to her husband, Red would later take her words out of context and use them against her. Gooseberger was well aware of how much money was flowing through their hands. He knew they had paid $12,000 for two days' testimony of the private investigators Venturi and Geller, and he knew how much they were paying local Florida lawyers.

"And he began to get greedy. More and more, he talked about the financial ramifications if we were to sue Florida for misconduct," Esther recalled.

"There's billions in this suit," Red would say. But Carl and Esther's son was in jail fighting for his life, and the last thing they were thinking about at that time was some hypothetical situation down the road.

They had put up with the Goose because he was helping. They saw Red as human and capable of making mistakes. However, they had to consider that he happened to be an eyewitness to their son's whereabouts on the day of the murder because that was the day Gooseberger's son was christened. Neither Red nor his wife testified during the extradition hearing, because this simple fact was not uncovered until well into the hearing. Since Red hadn't been sequestered, that became a problem. Also, Cicilline wanted to save that important surprise if they went to trial in Florida. So Red was a possible lifeline for the Rosatis, and in strange ways he began to use it. For instance, he sent Stephen a series of letters that revealed his displeasure at having to put up with Esther and Carl. The letters, of course, were sent to the Florida house of correction where Stephen was being held.

August 21, 1991
Dear Steve:
Before you read this novel, please remember this is between me and you. Let me tell you, it has been a difficult decision whether to mail this out or not. . . .
The bottom line is Steve's in jail and Red Gooseberger and Jack can get you out. So I really don't give a shit if your mother and father like me or not. . . . Hang in there big guy—you'll win this case as soon as the process moves along.
Red

(4:41 AM)
Dear Stephen:
I have been awake since 2:55 a.m. . . . . unable to sleep. . . . My little son is sleeping on the floor in front of me in his little homemade fort. It is unbelievable how much I love this little guy, and it breaks my heart to know that an innocent young man like you, Steve, is in jail for a crime he did not commit.

Remember, you have the best lawyer in the country and with my knowledge of this case and my ability to communicate this knowledge to the right people, it is impossible to lose. I continue to get very upset with your father for his lack of loyalty, because every time I make a move he fucks me again for another couple of dollars. He forgets I not only have put my family aside for your freedom, I have put my "life" on the line when I tell people about the "BSO" police misconduct and the "BSO" corruption. . . .

Stephen, there is one promise I will make you and that is no matter what, I will never stop fighting for your freedom. I am at this very moment (5:40 a.m.) coming up with new ideas for Jack to present.

Well, it is 6:03 a.m. and my little guy just laughed in his sleep. He is such a happy boy. . . . Maybe when you get out you will never be the exact same happy young man, but you can look back and count your blessings that you are a free man. You can also look back and know that Jesus Christ got you through this ordeal, and he can get you through any turmoil in your life. You'll also look back and say Red Gooseberger is a true friend. And Stephen, I love you very much. . . .

Gooseberger kept tacking on addendums, one after the other, extending the letter ad infinitum. One of them said that Carl and Esther had purposely left him without any cash, so that he had to borrow $650 from friends of his parents to pay for his car and hotel bills. The letter also went on to say that Red had "never asked for a penny" from Carl, but he did expect Carl to cover his expenses. During the course of the time he worked on the case, according to the Rosatis, "$25,000 flowed through his hands.

"He knew that we were struggling financially to meet all our obligations," Esther recalled, "and we needed more money to pay for Jack—if he was going to take over the case in Florida—more money for Florida attorneys and more money for investigators. We had lost business because all our efforts were involved in saving Stephen, and all of our liquid assets were gone. We still had substantial holdings in real estate, but they were frozen because the market was down."

Cicilline was willing to take land as payment, which was doing the Rosatis a great favor. But the other attorneys wanted cash. Red knew that they were vulnerable. To cut expenses, Red suggested they hire a public defender and let him take over the case.

"Red," Esther said, "I will never get a public defender. I would rather kill myself and use the insurance money to pay for a proper defense."

Esther went to her mother to ask for help, but she was rebuked. Her mother's concern was that Stephen would be found guilty anyway and the money would be lost. She did, however, loan Esther $5,000, which, according to Esther was more than her other relatives did. Together, she and Carl sought smaller amounts from a larger circle of family members and raised about $30,000, which, according to Esther "we desperately needed if we were going to keep Stephen's defense afloat."

Esther was now living in Florida full time, while Carl commuted back and forth over long weekends so he could run their business in Rhode Island. They visited Stephen every Monday through a glass partition and were allowed to meet him in an open area once a month.

During most of their visits, however, they couldn't physically touch or hug their son. Looking at each other through safety glass was difficult for each to bear. Further, the only way to communicate was through a phone, so Esther or Carl had to take turns speaking to their son. Then there were times they didn't speak on the phone because they didn't know who was listening in. In those instances, they wrote notes and pressed them against the pane.

"Financially, of course, it was very draining," Carl remembered. "I would start a deal but couldn't finish it."

They lost clients. Deals that required Stephen's assistance fell through. A few accounts left because of the association the Rosatis now had with criminal activities, but Carl didn't care. His son's release was his priority. "I would prefer to lose some business than lose my son," Carl said. "It was as simple as that."

Out of the blue, the Rosatis received a call from Pastor Lottie, leader of the Prayer Group from Rhode Island. She chose this time to ask for funds to help build her new church. Esther informed her that they were in Florida and could not help at this time. The pastor "became cold and took Stephen's name off the prayer list. She also canceled the insurance policy she had with us. I took comfort in watching the evangelist Billy Graham on TV," Esther said, "I recalled his statement, 'The strength of our nation resides in the family.' How right he was."

Carl and Esther drove to the new prison. In Esther's assessment, "It was drab and oppressive. The place was so much colder than the ACI, and we could only visit once a week."

The waiting room was filled with cold plastic chairs. Most of the visitors were minorities, and there were many children. When called, Esther and Carl would go upstairs and visit with their son through a glass partition, According to Esther, he always looked in a dismal state, and that tore her apart. Prisoners could not get out into the sun, so Stephen always looked pale.

"The first time I saw Stephen in that condition, I was taken aback," Esther recalled painfully. "I didn't think there were prisons like this. The place was designed specifically to cut off all link to the outside world, and contact visits were only once a month.

"No matter how bad those conditions were, I looked forward to being there, to seeing Stephen. As the weeks plodded on, I could see what was happening to him. He had been lean and fit when he got there, but the place was wearing him down. His skin had taken on a sallow, almost yellowish complexion. The food was bloating him, and we, of course, could not bring him anything to eat. What really shocked me was seeing gray hairs beginning to sprout from his head." He was just thirty-two years old.

Each time Carl and Esther came, it became more difficult for their son. He would ask his parents to leave because he couldn't handle the letdown. "Something was dying in him," Esther realized, "and on a certain level, he was cutting himself off from us. I began to face the horrible truth: my son was becoming institutionalized."

* * *

"Money was going out the door like water from a faucet with a flow that was almost impossible to stop," Carl painfully remembered. "Concerning the big bills for their enormous legal fees, there was no such thing as time payments. This wasn't something you could take a loan out for." Although Carl had considerable assets, he only had so much liquid cash. "If you unload something when the timing is wrong, you lose out both ways. At the same time, of course, we were also trying to protect our assets."

Carl called Victor Tobin, their lawyer in Florida.

"Look, you guys," said Tobin, "you want to talk to me, send me $5,000."

"Victor, we are not even down there yet, and you want all this money?" Carl said.

Thinking Tobin too greedy, the Rosatis' interviewed fourteen other lawyers, finally settling on Jeffrey Harris. Since he was a friend of the prosecutor's, Carl discussed this with Cicilline, but he said this could be a help rather than a hindrance. Since they needed a local attorney in Florida, Harris was hired, although it was always assumed that Jack Cicilline would be their trial lawyer once it proceeded to that step. Harris quoted a fee of $40,000 with a ceiling of an additional $10,000 if circumstances warranted additional work. Considering that the Rosatis received other bids well in excess of $100,000, Harris's fee seemed reasonable.

One curious event involved David Bogenshutz, one of the more expensive attorneys. Bogenshutz said that he knew all about their case and that the real killers had thrown the murder weapon and another gun into a lake. Because his fee was so steep, $100,000 more than Harris's, this statement went in one ear and out the other.

While all this was happening, the Rosatis received another call from Victor Tobin, who said that he had important information concerning Stephen's case that would allow Stephen to be freed within the next thirty to sixty days. "But he also wanted big bucks," Carl said.

Red and Esther met with Tobin. One of his associates, it seemed, had a client that had the information that could free Stephen! Esther called her husband and told him that Tobin wanted $50,000, to which Carl replied, "That's blackmail. I wanted to speak to him myself. I couldn't see how he could justify this gigantic bill.

"Like just about every other attorney we talked to, it was never what they could do for Stephen, but it was always how much it was going to cost. Dealing with Jack Cicilline was a whole different story. We discussed a fee, but I didn't pay him any funds for three months, and once he settled on a fee, he never requested another cent. We had to force more money on him because of the extraordinary amount of work he did. For these fellows, it was the exact opposite. They wanted everything up front before they did a thing for you."

After speaking with Tobin, Carl felt that the most this lawyer could possibly justify was $25,000 to $30,000, but Tobin held firm. "Why do you need $50,000? Because you have us by the short-hairs, and you know we are vulnerable?"

"That's what we require," Tobin responded. "And if you want your son released, then that's what it's going to cost."

Thinking about the amount Bogenshutz had quoted in comparison, Esther said, "We'll pay the fee. Just get my son out." Carl agreed.

It looked as if their son could be freed with Tobin's help and his inside information; however, the Rosatis still had no idea how long it would take. Carl gave Tobin an initial payment of $5,000 and later an additional $10,000, and then he called Jeffrey Harris to try and recoup the $10,000 advance. Harris returned $3,800, chalking up the balance to his expenses. He had been on the case a week.

Now that they were working with Tobin, the Rosatis also met Tobin's associate, Ray Miller, at their law offices. "Mr. Rosati," Miller said, "we know that special agent Michael Breece of FDLE [Florida Department of Law Enforcement] is handling the case. He knows the two real killers, but they could skip town if Stephen is released because they'll put two and two together. FDLE is investigating all of this—the guns, bullets, ballistics, witnesses—and they don't yet have all their ducks in place."

The Rosatis later found out that this had all surfaced June 17, while they were still fighting extradition in Rhode Island! A full week *before* Giordano flew up to testify, Detective Michael Breece of the Florida Department of Law Enforcement notified Detective Coyote that he had the wrong killers. Coyote asked Breece to keep the lid on his investigation. He feared that if the Rosatis found out about the parallel investigation it could have overturned his case in their favor. Simultaneously, during that same month of June, Peter Dallas was threatening to recant his testimony, but this too was kept secret.

"Now, here we were, the last week in August, and all this time they knew that the real killers were on the loose!" Carl exclaimed in disgust. They wanted to keep Stephen incarcerated because they didn't yet have a case against the actual perpetrators. "Dealing with my son's life this way, allowing him to stay in jail day after day, still, in his mind, possibly facing the electric chair. . . . Tell me this is not insane."

The Rosatis also later found out that Ray Miller, Tobin's partner, was representing the actual getaway driver. Carl was elated because it looked as if Stephen would soon be free. Carl even got to like Tobin, as he was a very engaging person with his constant stream of profanity, even in the presence of Esther. That's just how Tobin talked:

"These fuck'n guys, they got the fuck'n killers. You just have to stand put and wait. The FDLE fished the guns out of the fuck'n water, got the fuck'n weapon used to kill Viscido, and even got

Viscido's automatic rifle. The bullets have to be fuck'n matched, so in the meantime, they can't pick up the killers, but they are under surveillance. But you gotta remember, if they fuck'n get wind of this, they could haul ass, and then we'll be forced to go through trial. So let's just sit back and fuck'n wait."

Carl immediately told Stephen that he would be out of jail within the next thirty to sixty days, not knowing that was not the case at all. Both deadlines were passed, and they waited sixty more days. Everything seemed imminent, which at least gave Stephen and his parents hope. At every meeting from then on Stephen would ask, "When is it going to happen?"

Carl and Esther had to respond, "We don't know."

Finally, in September, Tobin met with FDLE Agent Michael Breece, and it was at this time that the Rosatis finally learned that Breece's investigation of the Viscido murder was completely independent of the one put together by Broward County. Detective Breece, they were told, brought a packet of information on the real killers to court. "It was too amazing," Carl said. This information, which the Rosatis had to keep confidential, was in turn sent to another assistant attorney general from Florida, Cynthia Imperato. In the presence of Judge Goldstein, Ms. Imperato forwarded the package to Chuck Morton, the district attorney in charge of Coyote's investigation. The judge asked Chuck Morton to review the material and come back with his findings. He gave him an October deadline; this would be sixty days from the day Stephen was placed in the Florida prison.

Morton, however, thought the case against Stephen was airtight. With the testimony of Giordano as one of the witnesses at the scene of the crime and Dallas as co-conspirator confessing to the murder, Morton did not even open the packet! So the judge gave Morton another sixty days until December 1 to review the material so that he could make his decision.

Since Morton was blocking the investigation, the Rosatis alerted the newspapers. They, in turn, began to pressure Judge Goldstein to release, through the Freedom of Information Act, the contents of Breece's envelope. The judge would do no such thing, at least until new arrests were made, but the newspaper coverage succeeded in putting pressure on Morton to consider FDLE's case against the other men.

Now that Stephen Rosati was finally down in Florida, the local newspapers took full advantage. One of the most compelling pieces was a Sunday edition front-page burner on "Fathers and Sons" in the

Palm Beach Post written by Ron Hayes. "One Dad's Mission Puts Another Dad's Son in Jail," was the headline. The reporter reviewed the entire case and interviewed at great length the two fathers, Joe Viscido, Sr., and Carl H. Rosati:

"I want him dead!" Mr. Viscido said referring to Stephen Rosati. Having made a vow to his dead son to "get his killers," Viscido explained, "I believe in the death penalty."

"The only problem is," the journalist wrote, "Rosati has 22 witnesses and 167 documents that put him in Rhode Island at the time of the killing." Unmoved by this evidence, Viscido revealed that when the case first went before the grand jury in the spring of 1989, when Sergeant McNeil was still in charge and no indictments were handed down, Viscido ran home crying. Tensions reached such a peak in his marriage that he and his wife, Rose, split up for a while.

With characteristic grace, Carl Rosati replied, "I understand the loss, but he has to understand that you have to have the right person."

Viscido responded bitterly, "I hope the Rosatis get to feel the pain that I do."

Esther's ire was raised. "My son is so totally framed," she countered. "They've taken our lives and thrown it into utter chaos. An innocent young man is sitting in jail because Mr. Viscido has had a crusade to create a martyr of his son, who dealt in death."

Both sides were requested to appear on a local talk show and the Rosatis accepted. "When you have the truth," Esther said boldly, "you have nothing to hide."

Mr. Viscido declined to appear on the show and said, "Tell the Rosatis, I'll see them in court."

CHAPTER 61:
Turning Tide

Since Peter Dallas was still a major key to keeping Stephen in jail, the Rosatis kept trying to locate him. Detective Coyote had falsified the prisoner's name and kept him in an unknown location. Gooseberger tried to track down Dallas's relatives. He also kept pushing the idea of putting on a benefit for Stephen to raise money, to cover the costs for his defense, and he even set a date: November 10.

"I was totally against it," Carl recalled. "It wasn't necessary, and in a way it was demeaning." Finally, Carl agreed only on the condition that any monies raised would be put aside to help other falsely accused individuals who did not have the means for defending themselves. It was Carl and Esther's plan that Stephen would oversee this fund when he got out. "Essentially, we did this just to appease Red," Carl said.

"I can't say I ever got along with Red," Carl admitted, "although he certainly was, through much of this ordeal, an integral part of our organization." Actually, they never really started off on the right foot because right from the start Carl saw Red try to take over when Carl was in the hospital. "Red had fetched the discovery, and Red had also found the telephone records with the all-important October 12 date. He was a hero, but he let it go to his head," Carl said.

Even before Stephen went to Florida, Red had already informed the Rosatis that he wanted a third of the money from their civil suit against the state for wrongful imprisonment.

"First of all," Carl retorted, "I don't know if there will be a civil suit. And if there is, this will be Stephen's money, so you will have to discuss it with him."

The way Red approached him turned Stephen off. "I'm the one in jail, and you want my money on a lawsuit, which we don't even have?" Stephen said dumbfounded. It was at this point that Red's attitude began to change.

The Rosatis tried repeatedly to discourage Red from coming to Florida. It was costing them money, and, after a time, it had become unnecessary. Red would come down and spend his nights at the strip joints and his days meeting with attorneys, judges, and business people. The Rosatis felt that they had essentially put Red into a whole different lifestyle. And so he began to see himself in high esteem as an investigator. Finally, they decided to cut him off. Carl told Red that they could no longer afford his trips to Florida.

"But in retrospect," Carl admitted, "we probably allowed much of this to happen, and so we tried to shut him off, but it was practically impossible. So when he asked for the benefit, I gave in."

"I'll arrange everything," Red assured Carl, and he did.

Red made up fancy tickets that read, "Gathering of Friends for Stephen Rosati." Then he booked the Club Sirocco in Warwick. Five hundred tickets were sold at $20 each. Bob and Jayne of Crosby Caterers did the benefit for free, and Blake McFadden provided the club at no charge. Profits ran about $8,000 to $9,000. Two or three weeks later, when the Rosatis asked Red for an accounting of the money, he said that he had spent the balance.

"How could you do that?" Carl was flabbergasted. And then he demanded, "Give us the balance of the money." It was at that point that Red left the office, never to return.

"Why would he do this in the ninth hour?" Jack Cicilline pondered.

From the Rosatis point of view, Red's action struck them as "all so crazy and self-destructive," but, as it turned out, that was only the beginning of the nightmare with Red Gooseberger. He had devoted almost every day for over a year to helping in Rosati's defense. Unfortunately, he was on disability, which meant that it was legally impossible for the Rosatis to form some type of business arrangement with him, as Red would then be cut off from his annual income, which at that time exceeded $70,000 a year. Red was stuck, but he was also angry and felt used.

The Rosatis wanted to go to the police, but Cicilline told them to forget it. "In a way, maybe we owed him more money," Carl said. "So, even though we were embezzled, we let it go."

The following Saturday, Red slipped into the offices of the Rosati Group when no one was there and stole some private papers. A few days later, he sent a letter saying that he would have nothing to do with the Rosati family.

Shortly after that, the *Providence Journal* confronted Carl and Esther, alleging they had ties to the Mafia. Red also sent letters to the Florida police telling them that Stephen was involved in drug running. Letters were sent to a local Rhode Island university where Carl was on the board of directors alleging that he had been involved in kickback schemes, and the Goose sued the Rosatis for $40,000 for supposed expenses for the time he worked the case. Red continued to terrorize and harass the family for many years to come.

In the autumn of 1991, while waiting to return to court for a bail hearing, Pete the Greek's mother, Nina Roussonicolos, invited the Rosatis to a traditional Sunday dinner. A sympathetic woman who was somewhat rooted in the old world, she had no idea how she could help, but she did make it clear that Esther should let here know if she could do anything.

The Rosatis remained frustrated because they were still barred from speaking to Detective Michael Breece and state prosecutor Cynthia Imperato, the two individuals who headed up the independent investigation. However, the Rosatis were able to see them both at the courthouse on December 2, the deadline Judge Goldstein had given Chuck Morton to review Breece's packet. The courtroom was crowded with six rows of people waiting for scheduled hearings. Also present were newspaper reporters from the *Miami Herald*, the *Sun-Sentinel*, and their local TV counterparts. Nina sat next to Esther.

Dressed in a casual suit, locked in handcuffs, and surrounded by armed policemen, Stephen was led into the courtroom alongside a distinguished looking gentleman who wore glasses, had a receding hairline, and exuded a sense of refinement. He also wore handcuffs.

The man Carl thought looked like a professor turned out to be Pete the Greek. The Rosatis' lawyer, Victor Tobin, was present along with Pete's counsel, Chris Pole, the lawyer who had replaced John Howes, his previous attorney, and the one who had passed the discovery (the entire police record of the case) to the Rosatis a year and a half ago. Peter Dallas was still being kept hidden in an unrevealed prison under an assumed name.[1]

Morton had done nothing! Even after Judge Goldstein had directed him for the second time to read the contents of the new investigation, he simply refused. When Tobin made a half-hearted attempt to get bail for the prisoners, Carl could not sit silently any longer. Onlookers talked among themselves, trying to figure out who was arguing with Stephen Rosati's lawyer. They sat in hushed expectation waiting for the moment to play itself out.

Carl looked over at Stephen. There was deadness around him. His face and body were puffed up from the lousy food he was eating. His spirit was in decline. Carl told Tobin that he wanted to speak at the hearing. Meekly, Tobin made the request, as Carl barged through. "Some days I really shine, and that day was just one of those days," Carl remembered proudly. He was determined to give the reporters something to put down in their papers.

"I can't understand this, Your Honor," Carl said. "You have in your possession new information which tells you that Stephen and Peter were not there." At that moment Carl could sense the crowd becoming silent as they began to tune into his plea. "How can you allow these two innocent men who are sitting before you to stay locked up when you know the identity of the real killers? This is not justice. This is injustice! This shouldn't happen. This is America!"

The effect was electric. As reporters furiously wrote their notes and Esther grabbed her husband's hand, Chuck Morton moved forward to block. Placing all ten fingers against each other, almost in a pious manner, the prosecutor paused before he began.

"Your Honor," he opened, "with all due respect to Mr. Rosati's father, I cannot see any reason to grant bail when we have in custody a co-defendant who has testified and signed a confession stating that he committed this crime with Stephen Rosati and Peter Roussonicolos."

The judge looked to Carl like "a lost soul." He didn't know what to do, but the Rosatis knew that with Dallas's confession still hanging over them, it would be unlikely that Stephen would ever get bail. The judge announced a recess and called Breece, Imperato, and Morton into chambers.

Barely able to contain his emotions, Carl left the courtroom to compose himself.

* * *

Carl later found out from Stephen that after his speech, Pete the Greek broke down in tears. Pete told Stephen that he had never seen anyone stand up for him like that before. Like Stephen, every day for a year and a half Peter Roussonicolos had also faced the thought of dying in the electric chair for a crime he didn't commit.

Finally, Esther had a person of like mind to commiserate with. Quickly, she and Mrs. Roussonicolos became very close.

Having been portrayed all this time as some terrible individual, the Rosatis found Pete to be very personable. "No doubt he was a rogue," Carl admitted, "but like Robin Hood, he did not in any way portray an air of evil the way Coyote did, or that sad sack Giordano."

The Rosatis later learned what happened in chambers. Breece and Imperato told Morton that there was a conflict because they had different assassins for the same crime. Obviously, one group had to be wrong. Morton still wouldn't budge. Thinking on her feet, Cindy Imperato suggested that an outside impartial prosecutor be brought in to review both investigations, and she further suggested that to help the situation, she would make a deal. She told Morton that she would take herself off the case if Morton agreed to do the same. Lawton Chiles, then governor of Florida, was contacted. He acted with conviction by appointing the diligent and highly respected John Aguero as independent special state prosecutor to study both the Coyote and Morton case and the one put together by Michael Breece and Cindy Imperato.

Chuck Morton received permission from his boss, Mike Satz— the new head prosecutor of Broward County who had replaced Sheriff Navarro—to abandon the case.

"Meanwhile," Carl said, "Cindy Imperato had simply used a ruse to unload a turkey, as she returned to the case and got back the packet they had given to Morton. The seal on the envelope had never been broken! If ever there was a reason for someone to be cited for contempt of court, this was such a reason, but, of course, nothing happened."

The judge, in turn, ruled to deny bail subject to the findings of the independent governor-appointed prosecutor. Victor Tobin, Rosati's attorney, was essentially in a waiting game, figuring that once the new killers were arrested, the case would fall on its own. He hadn't, however, dealt in any way with Peter Dallas, and that is where the Rosatis stood after the court scene. They called Stephen on the phone that night.

"Dad," Stephen said in the most dejected voice imaginable, "I'm innocent. How can they do this? After all you said. It just didn't matter. They are going to do anything they can to keep me in here."

"Stephen," Carl responded, "You will get out of there. I know it is taking forever, but now they know who the real murderers are, and you will get out of there."

Even though the Rosatis were aware that FDLE was on track with this other case, the agency wouldn't divulge any details. That's all the Rosatis knew. They didn't have names. They didn't even know what the evidence was against the other suspects. They only knew that it was supposed to be strong. So if the assistant attorney general, Chuck Morton, was going to hang onto Dallas, then it was evident that Morton was ignorant about Breece's findings.

"How could this be?" Esther wondered. "Was Morton living in a vacuum?" She tried to reach Dallas but had no way to locate him.

As far back as May, during the very midst of the extradition hearing, Dallas wanted to recant, but he was afraid because Detective Coyote "had scared the living daylights out of him. Simply put," Carl said, "Dallas preferred five or seven years on a deal than the possibility of getting the electric chair. Now he was in a jail that we couldn't get near. And Coyote had the audacity to tell Morton and Randy White that Dallas was being hidden away for his protection from us! This was Coyote's masterstroke in duplicity, but it gave Esther an idea."

At the hearing, she spoke to Mrs. Roussonicolos.

"Nina," Esther began, "you said to me time and again that you didn't know if there was anything you could do to help because you don't have the know-how. But now you can help me. I want you to find your friend, Mrs. Dallas." It turns out that Mrs Roussonicolos and Mrs. Dallas were distant cousins.

"I can't talk to her because she has an unlisted phone," Nina responded.

"You have to find out where she lives, so I can send an investigator over. You must do this," said Esther.

Nina called Esther the following night. By that time the newspaper reporters, particularly those from the *Miami Herald*, had done their homework. Stephen and Pete the Greek's peculiar situation was out of the bag.

New Investigation Casts Doubt on Murder Case
Miami Herald
By Dexter Filkins, Staff Writer

One of South Florida's most celebrated murder cases took a startling turn Monday when prosecutors begged off the case after new evidence suggested they may have wrongly charged three men. . . . The new investigation raised questions about whether the two men indicted for the murder—Carl Stephen Rosati and Peter Roussonicolos—may have been wrongly charged. The two men have been jailed since last year.

[Judge] Goldstein who met privately with lawyers and police for more than an hour, agreed to ask Gov. Lawton Chiles to appoint a prosecutor from outside Broward County. . . .

Victor Tobin, the attorney representing Rosati, said that the parallel investigation confirms prosecutors targeted the wrong men. He said the prosecutors asked to be removed from the case to cut their losses.

"The state is on a ship that is slowly sinking," Tobin said. "They wanted to get off." . . .

Troubling questions have dogged the prosecution from the beginning. . . . The state's star witness against Rosati and Roussonicolos is [Peter] Dallas, who pleaded guilty to second-degree murder and admitted his role in the crime.[2]

Through a niece, Nina found where Mrs. Dallas was living. Esther called Cicilline's investigator, Fran Martin, who called another investigator, and this man went over to Mrs. Dallas's apartment in New York. He told her that Rosati's mother had some information that could possibly save her son, and he gave her Esther's Florida phone number.

"Mrs. Dallas called me," Esther remembered, speaking excitedly. "She spoke in broken English and told me how Detective Coyote had threatened her."

"He tell me not talk," the woman said. "My son, maybe they kill. Detective, he frighten me."

Esther told Mrs. Dallas that she had newspaper clippings containing evidence that their sons and Pete the Greek had nothing to do with the Joe Viscido murder. Esther mailed the articles overnight.

Mrs. Dallas was able to reach her son. She told him that the real murderers had been located. Now he realized that he had a chance to beat the rap by simply telling the truth.

"Just a few days later," Esther recalled, "Peter Dallas called me! He verified that he was being held under an assumed name in one of the prisons. He said that Detective Coyote put him in isolation for his protection because his life was in danger. He had no idea about the newspaper articles and the other case. He was appalled. Dallas was looking for a way to get to his attorney, but he couldn't. That's how deeply Coyote had buried him."

So Dallas wrote a letter to the judge taking back everything.[3] The date was December 12, 1991. "Can you imagine the insanity of all of this?" Esther proclaimed. "Coyote was telling this man that he would be in danger if he told the truth! I finally was able to shut Chuck Morton's mouth because now he had no recourse." It took three mothers operating together to do the trick.

Murder Case Witness Claims He Lied to Police
Sun-Sentinel, **Tuesday, December 17, 1991**
By Barbara Walsh, Staff Writer

A key witness in the Joseph Viscido Jr. murder case claims he lied to police about the murder because they threatened to send him to the electric chair.

Peter Dallas, who has pleaded guilty to second-degree murder for Viscido's death, wrote a letter to Broward Circuit Judge Barry Goldstein saying investigators coerced him to lie about the 1986 murder. . . .

"I have been terrified sitting in jail for 15 months, terrified, not knowing what to do," Dallas wrote. "The officers threatened that they had physical evidence against me that could put me on the electric chair if I didn't tell them what they wanted to hear. . . ." [Judge] Goldstein has sealed all evidence in FDLE's investigation. . . .

"Dallas has been trying to make the statement to several people including the state Atorney's Office for several months now," said [Victor] Tobin [Rosati's attorney]. . . .

"This has been going on long enough," [Attorney Christopher Pole, who is representing Roussonicolos] said. "They have all this new evidence that should be unsealed. You can't have someone indicted for a murder case and withhold information. It's contrary to the Constitution."[4]

It was Christmas. Stephen Rosati was so depressed that he told Carl and Esther that he didn't want to see them. They had raised his hopes because it looked as if he could be released any day, but he was gritting his teeth. Due to the institutional food, the lack of sunlight, and the dreary conditions, the prisoner had become more bloated than ever, and a veil of dullness had taken over his personality.

"In a way," Esther said, "it became unbearable to see him that way, and he knew it. We were exhausted, out of funds, and just simply worn out."

Stephen's release seemed imminent, but the Rosatis had been let down so many times, they were afraid anything could happen. Even with all the signs that he would be freed, the newspapers still reported that "the elder Viscido, whose story attracted national attention, said he is still confident Rosati and Roussonicolos are the right suspects." The Broward Sherriff's Department was also immoveable in their belief that Detectives Coyote and Puccini had arrested the right men, and they continued to put pressure on the independent prosecutor to support their claim.

"Go home. Go see Carlyn." Stephen turned away from his parents.

They took the next plane for Rhode Island.

Right before the New Year, Red called Carlyn. It seemed clear to Esther that Red purposely chose a time when her daughter wouldn't be there so he could leave a message on her recorder. The Rosatis kept it for posterity.

"Carlyn, this is Red," the message began plaintively. "I'm calling from Naples, Florida. The attorney general's office has requested that I come in to discuss Stephen's situation. This is very serious." Red repeated this phrase "very serious" a few times. "It is not about the Viscido murder but about the drug case involving Calvin Fredrick. The police said that guns were involved. It is very important that you speak to them about this."

The call hit the mark. Esther became hysterical. A wail erupted from deep within her that echoed through the house and out the windows. She sobbed so much that Carl became frightened and called a doctor. Just when they were on the verge of triumph, the Goose stuck it to them.

According to Esther, "Red Gooseberger hadn't been in Florida when he made that call." He just wanted to steal their one moment of happiness when they were so close to triumph, so he placed the call in the middle of the holiday season, at the time when it would be the most damaging.

"It was like having the head of a drowning man pushed down under the water after he had finally come up for air," Esther recalled.

* * *

Shortly after Christmas, the Rosatis returned to Florida. It was at this time that they learned from Victor Tobin that the police had the murder weapon. "It was too amazing." Carl exclaimed. "Five years had passed, and this gun was traced to the very man they now ID'd as the actual shooter!"

A witness, the actual driver of the car, had contacted Ray Miller, Tobin's associate who had gone to the FDLE, and they realized that it was the same case involving Dallas, Stephen, and Pete the Greek.

"Since the real killer, the short guy, had threatened the real getaway driver, this driver had stepped forward. That is how the case was finally solved," Carl said. "The real short guy had struck Viscido in the head with the gun and it went off, and that's how he got killed. We never even knew the names of the actual perpetrators until after the judge released Stephen from jail."

Bail was set at $50,000, with $5,000 required up front. The Rosatis put up land they held in Florida as collateral and paid the court a nonrefundable fee of $5,000 in cash. Why the bail was nonrefundable when the man that was out on bail was wrongfully imprisoned was never explained to the Rosatis.

On January 24, 1992, Stephen Rosati was released from jail, and on February 5, all charges were dropped. Rosati was finally a free man. Too late for a flight back to Rhode Island, the family went to a lounge and just relaxed.

"Stephen was so relieved," Carl said, "it was just euphoria. I saw a person who had been changed in those seventeen months from my little boy to a mature man. I was so proud of him because of the way he had handled himself while incarcerated, and the way he handled himself on the stand before prosecutors and judges. I saw an individual of great depth and that made me respect him all the more. At the same time, I felt the greatest love for my son that I have ever had. To me he was now a man of substance.

"My wife just couldn't take her eyes off Stephen, and I saw the relief in her. The pain had subsided, but it would be a long time, before we could ever truly recover. I watched as a beautiful woman became devastated by events that were just incomprehensible. The feelings that she and I were going through were something you can't explain, and you wonder if you will be able to bear it each day. It's something you have to experience to understand; and I certainly do not wish this pain on anyone.

"But I believe that the Good Lord has a way of taking you through each day because, physically or mentally, without his help we would not have made it, and I know that Stephen relied upon him as well. Why Stephen and we suffered all this pain, I can't say. But I'm sure the Good Lord has a reason for what he does. I accept that."

Esther felt that once Stephen was released, "like a bad dream, it would be over. We drove over to the bondsman's office just as he was pulling in with Stephen. Our eyes locked onto each other. We just cried. It was that same kind of sobbing and crying when they first took him away. To hold him again, it was a pleasure unmatched in all my years of living.

"It was all the months and months of waiting, and there you are. It had been hard to grasp the reality that they could just pick him up and do this, and just as fast as it happened, it was over. We were all so happy just to be together. The feeling was, 'Oh my God, this is over.' As quickly as we could, we flew back to Rhode Island."

"Rosati, pack your things," the voice crackled over the intercom. "I both did and didn't believe it." Stephen recalled when he heard it. "I had all this stuff, so I decided to give it away. I chose, of course, the friends I had made: Rambo, the guy I had lifted weights with, and another black guy I worked with on the lunch line. My clothes, my sneakers, a radio headset—I was glad to give it to them.

"I couldn't wait to step out the door, but once I did, I became scared and actually had the impulse to jump back in. I was nervous and couldn't believe the sky was so high, so I ducked. The outside was so big, too big. There was no ceiling anymore, and I had difficulty adjusting to that."

At five the next morning at their home in Scituate, Stephen went for a run. He just wanted to breathe the air. He wanted to open a door and move from one room to another, just to experience that freedom.

"It was as though he were feeling that space—to flow with his environment rather than being cut off from it," Esther said. "To see stone crabs at a restaurant in front of him, he just looked at them, speechless. It was a quieting time in terms of emotion."

Stephen was going from imprisonment to freedom. He had to quiet himself, to move from one phase to another phase. "He just sat," Esther said. "It wasn't exhaustion. It was almost as if he were resting for the first time."

Stephen called Jack Cicilline and thanked him. Jack's mother-in-law passed away, and Carl went with Stephen to attend the funeral. "Jack and Stephen embraced," Esther said. "They were happy to see each other. I don't think Jack could quite believe it. I don't think any of us could."

EPILOGUE

"You may not think much of me, but once you begin to study Coyote's case, you'll see that it will fall like a house of cards."

Statement made by Special Agent Michael Breece to the ardently skeptical governor-appointed prosecutor, John Aguero, on their first meeting.

The Proffer

Detective Michael Breece was a special agent for the Florida Department of Law Enforcement (FDLE), Broward County Division. Independent of Detective Bobby Coyote's investigation, Breece also studied the Viscido homicide. As his case progressed, he worked with Cindy Imperato, assistant statewide prosecutor. Faced with two separate conclusions to the same murder, the governor of the state of Florida, Lawton Chiles, appointed Florida Assistant State Prosecutor John Aguero as independent counsel to oversee both versions. The following account was taken directly from Michael Breece's case files and from extensive interviews with Michael Breece, Cindy Imperato, and John Aguero.[1]

If not for Breece, Stephen Rosati probably would have spent the rest of his adult life in jail or, along with Pete the Greek, he might have even been executed. The FDLE, according to Breece, is to the state of Florida what the FBI is to the entire country. Breece's specialty was smugglers and drug traffickers.

His involvement started during a surveillance episode on another case. Breece became aware of a story stemming from Los Angeles concerning burglar alarms that had gone off at some estate. Rare works of art by Picasso, Miro, Matisse, and Chagall had been cut out of their frames and were missing. Shortly thereafter, Breece recalled seeing an article in the *Miami Herald* about an estate auction in Pompano that was offering works by these same artists.

Sporting white bucks, freshly pressed Dockers, and a silk shirt, the special agent attended the auction undercover. Bon vivant, former millionaire, and suspected drug trafficker Tony Martinelli was running the auction with his associate, Elton Magdaleine. Both were arrested and the art works confiscated. With price tags in the quarter-million-dollar range, Breece attempted to get these works identified so they could be returned to the California estate from where he assumed they came.

"I'm not a man who likes to be embarrassed," Breece recalled. "I'm big on thoroughness and like to cover every base." However, Breece *was* embarrassed when it was discovered that the paintings were all forgeries—painted by Paul Kuz, a Spanish art forger who had a studio in Miami—and were completely unrelated to the works from the California estate. "Kuz was so talented that he could create these forgeries completely from his head," Breece said. He also said that some of Kuz's works have sold for more than $300,000.

Facing at least six years in prison, Elton Magdaleine became an informant. He turned on his boss, Tony Martinelli, implicating him in a Milwaukee firebug case whereby a restaurant insured for $1.5 million was torched. Now, besides art forgery, Martinelli was facing ten years for a variety of other charges, including arson and kidnapping.

On June 1, 1991, Martinelli decided to take a proffer through his lawyer, David Bogenshutz, one of the attorneys the Rosatis had interviewed. Martinelli would eventually tell authorities what he knew about an illegal caper. The prosecution offered no promises in return—only that they would take the information into consideration.

Martinelli, then forty-four, had been the owner of Scalley's Saloon. A budding tycoon, Martinelli had many legitimate contacts. These included Benihana, king of frozen Chinese food; wrestler Big John Studd; and Merv Griffith, to whom he was loosely connected through his wife's girlfriend. Martinelli made his initial fortune in Connecticut in a glass products business, and from there he became part owner of a bank, which he sold at great profit. Then he moved to Florida to take over Scalley's Saloon.

Attorney Bogenshutz was skeptical about going to the Broward Sheriff's Office (BSO), so he contacted Michael Breece, whom he respected, at the FDLE. Martinelli described to Breece a 1986 incident in which he witnessed the aftermath of a homicide. At the time, Martinelli said he was living in a rented lakefront home located next to the Boca Raton Sailing Club with his girlfriend Kelly McCabe and temporary resident Jim Phaedra.

Martinelli's chauffeur Bob Minnow, who moonlighted as a drug smuggler, was able to introduce his boss to a variety of characters, including twenty-four-year-old Kerry Carbonell, a six-foot-one, 190-pound, small-time cocaine dealer, and his five-foot-eight, forty-two-year-old mentor Jim Phaedra, also known as Jimmy Fay, Horace Wilfred (Phaedra)—his brother's name—and Poppa Jim.

Phaedra, a crack addict who always packed a concealed weapon, had a record that stretched from 1978, when he was arrested for possession of a kilogram of cocaine. At the same time, the police had located nearly a quarter ton of marijuana and a live grenade in a locker that Phaedra owned. Although his fingerprints were found about the locker, the case was never prosecuted. Entranced by Phaedra's dangerous tales, Martinelli hired him as a bodyguard and allowed Phaedra to move into the lakeside house along with his girlfriend Barbara Dayku. According to the chauffeur, in late 1986 there was a "shake-up," when Martinelli kicked Phaedra and Carbonell out. Having come to view Phaedra as "a parasite," Martinelli went so far as to move himself into a new residence to rid himself of the thug.

Sometime in late summer or early fall 1986, Martinelli became aware that Phaedra, Kerry Carbonell, and a Boyce Rickenbach were planning to hold up a neighborhood drug dealer. He remembers one evening, at approximately seven o'clock, when he and Kelly went out on a date. Upon their return, he found Phaedra and Carbonell standing in his home. Obviously shaken, Carbonell was wearing a blood-spattered polo shirt. Carbonell took off the shirt and handed it to Martinelli to launder, and then left the residence.

Phaedra, according to Martinelli, stated that Rickenbach had pointed out a residence to them earlier that night where narcotics and money were being stored. Phaedra reportedly stated that he and Carbonell entered the residence and held two males and one female at gunpoint. Phaedra said that he removed one of the males to the bedroom to locate the stash, as Carbonell held the remaining white male and white female at gunpoint in an adjacent room.

At that time, according to Phaedra, the white male he had taken into the back room grabbed for his handgun and a fight ensued. In wrestling for the gun, the .45 discharged, warning Carbonell of the skirmish. Literally breaking the bedroom door off its hinges to get in, Carbonell tried to assist Phaedra, who by that time had been able to free his gun hand. As Phaedra went to strike the subject in the head with its barrel, the firearm discharged again, and Carbonell was sprayed with blood. Phaedra said that the white male "went limp" and fell to the floor.

Phaedra and Carbonell ran from the residence, but not before grabbing a ten-pound bag of marijuana and an Uzi machine gun. The hostages that were being held had run from the scene. In a state of panic, Rickenbach stepped on the gas and drove the trio away in a reckless manner. Phaedra had to yell at Rickenbach to slow down.

When they arrived at Martinelli's residence, Phaedra and Carbonell took the murder weapon and the Uzi submachine gun and heaved them into the lagoon behind Martinelli's home. Carbonell wanted to keep the Uzi for himself, but Phaedra convinced him to toss it.

"You didn't heave the guns right behind my house?" Martinelli asked.

Phaedra stuttered when he answered, saying that he had thrown them in the water by the clubhouse, which, in any event, was nearby.

"The next day," Martinelli continued, "Rickenbach stopped by the house with his family in a car packed with his belongings. Phaedra leaned into the car and said something to Rickenbach, and that was the last we ever saw of him."

According to Martinelli, Phaedra scanned the newspapers

repeatedly for an article about the murder but found none. Martinelli knew neither the dead man's name nor the site of the caper. He thought, however, that Rickenbach might have known the dead man from working out at a local gym. Because he was working on a number of cases, Sergeant Breece filed away this information until he could follow up some of the leads offered by Martinelli.

A graduate of Florida Atlantic University, Michael Breece had been a patrolman in Boca Raton before he was bumped up to the FDLE. Now in his late thirties, Breece had become a pro, having attended seminars on such topics as narcotics, homicide investigation, and fingerprint matching, as well as training on investigating crime scenes. Tenacious and a stickler for details, Breece decided to solve the vaguely told case Martinelli had outlined.

"I just couldn't locate the victim," Breece recalled. "Since Martinelli had targeted August of '86, I checked for six months around the date."

Breece met with medical examiners in half a dozen counties, studied their reports, called seventy-five sheriffs' offices, perused lists and lists of police reports, missing person files, and newspaper articles—anything he could get his hands on concerning drug deals and homicides from that time frame.

The Viscido murder was dismissed as the one in question because the Chuck Morton crew had solved that case with three perps locked up and awaiting trial. With Imperato's help, Breece continued to scour the records, but it was the Viscido case that kept coming up as a match. At the same time, through Rickenbach's sister, Breece located Rickenbach in New Jersey and sent word that he wanted to speak to him.

Two months later, which was three weeks before Stephen Rosati arrived in Florida to await his trial, Boyce Rickenbach called. Although Rickenbach hedged in revealing any information, it became apparent from the way Rickenbach appeared nervous that he knew exactly what incident Breece was referring to. Breece "bullshitted Rickenbach" because he wasn't certain of anything, but at the same time, he advised Rickenbach that he might be able to get him immunity if he came clean. Breece told Rickenbach that if he told exactly what he knew, Breece would present this evidence to a statewide prosecutor to help Rickenbach out.

"I never meant for anyone to get hurt," Rickenbach cried. "Can you keep my name out of it? My wife and my father, in particular, are going to go nuts."

"You are involved in a serious crime, Mr. Rickenbach," the special agent said. "The best advice I can give you is to get a lawyer."

Rickenbach sought out Ray Miller, someone his sister had worked for. Miller was the law partner of Rosati's soon-to-be Florida attorney, Victor Tobin. The following month, Rickenbach agreed to take a lie detector test, which he passed.

Breece notified Detective Coyote and kept him informed about the parallel investigation. "I told him that he might have the wrong people, but Coyote told me to stall."

"It sounds like mine," Coyote said, "but it's going to hurt my case if they [the Rosatis] find out about this before I get Rosati down to Florida. We already have two people in custody, and one of them has confessed."

However, Breece did not want to let it go before he investigated further.

"I figured this had to be a coincidence. Something here didn't make sense. So I continued my investigation. I ran computer programs, checked the FCIC [computer network for the state of Florida] and the NCIC [computer network for the nation]. These list everyone who has ever been arrested. I was looking for missing persons or for an unidentified body. It quickly became clear that it was, indeed, the Viscido homicide."

Breece related what he had found:

"In his taped sworn statement, Rickenbach stated that on October 12, 1986, a Sunday evening, he was at Tony Martinelli's lakefront home attending an informal party and watching football. At about 7:00 p.m., Jim Phaedra and a subject known to him as Kerry asked him if he was aware of anyone who would sell a user quantity of cocaine to them that evening."

Rickenbach mentioned Richard Whistler, a young middleweight boxer from Deerfield Beach whom Rickenbach had been training at one of the local gyms. They met with Whistler at a shopping center about 8:00 p.m., and the foursome drove to Joe Viscido's apartment in Rickenbach's tan 1982 Toyota Starlet hatchback. Phaedra and Whistler went to the door, but no one was home at the time, so they dropped Whistler off, and the three of them returned to Martinelli's apartment.

Later that evening, Phaedra suggested that they return to Joe's place. It was clear to Rickenbach that Phaedra and Kerry were going to commit armed robbery. They arrived about 11:00 p.m., and

Rickenbach parked the vehicle by a five-foot wall on the west side of the complex. Shortly after they went in, Rickenbach heard two distinct gunshots. He held fast and soon noticed two men run from the apartment and leap over some hedges. Five minutes later, Phaedra and Carbonell calmly sauntered from the building. Carbonell carried an automatic weapon at his side, and Phaedra carried a .45-caliber handgun in one hand and a shopping bag in the other. Carbonell got into the front seat, and Phaedra got into the back.

"The guy's dead," Phaedra said. "Let's get back to Martinelli's." Phaedra also said that they had obtained a substantial amount of cocaine that was wrapped in plastic inside the shopping bag. Neither man showed any remorse.

Phaedra sat in the back seat with the gun out, "pointed at the floor in a ready type position." The entire way to Martinelli's, Rickenbach feared for his own life. Upon their arrival, Phaedra and Carbonell argued as to whether or not they should keep the weapons. Carbonell wanted the Uzi, but Phaedra demanded that they ditch them both. Phaedra grabbed the Uzi from Carbonell, walked around to the back of the house, and threw it and his pistol into the lake. The next day, Rickenbach packed up his gear and moved his wife and baby son to another location in Boca Raton.

Phaedra, however, wanted a meeting. Along with Carbonell, he met with Rickenbach and Whistler. "Phaedra and Carbonell said that they would kill us if we ever brought testimony against them," Rickenbach recalled. "Phaedra also said that he would kill my family. There wasn't a doubt in my mind that he would carry the threat out if need be."

"Do you think it's the Viscido case?" Imperato asked Breece.

"As far as I can see," said Breece, "there is only one way to tell."

After giving the statement, Rickenbach agreed to get into a car with Detective Breece and another officer and direct them to the apartment where the murder took place. He drove them directly to Viscido's. Rickenbach also took Breece and company to Martinelli's lakefront home, and he pointed out the approximate location where Phaedra threw the weapons. Then he returned to the police station and picked Phaedra and Carbonell out of police lineups.

"BSO continued to jerk me around," Breece recalled. This had been going on since June or early July 1991. "I'm trying to keep an open mind, but now, with the Rickenbach statements [and the drive-by], I was a hundred percent positive."

But Breece didn't stop there. He sought further confirmation to really convince BSO that they were barking up the wrong tree. For instance, Breece found out that on November 7, 1986, Rickenbach's wife sent a letter of resignation to Palm Beach Middle School citing as a reason "extremely serious family responsibilities." Breece noted that this resignation "was consistent with Rickenbach's assertion that he and his family had left Florida for New Jersey a few weeks after the incident because he had been threatened by Carbonell and Phaedra." It also locked in the Viscido murder as a strong possibility, but Breece and Imperato were going to need even more proof to convince Broward law enforcement.

In late summer 1991, Rickenbach was granted immunity by assistant statewide prosecutor Cynthia Imperato. Just three years out of law school and now a prosecutor, Cindy seemed to be on the side of the underdog, doing pro bono work for women in distress. Both she and Breece called Chuck Morton to invite him to Rickenbach's upcoming testimony. "You need to hear this," Breece said, but Morton did not attend. Breece speculated that there were two main reasons: "(1) Morton did not realize the ramifications of Rickenbach's testimony, and (2) if Morton doesn't hear it, he doesn't have to reveal it."

Detective Coyote was also invited to the interview but, like Morton, he declined.

"Mike," Chuck Morton said to Breece on the phone, "your case is just too pat. We have a confession from one Peter Dallas and also a lie detector test, which he passed."

"Morton thought our case was contrived," Breece recalled.

Imperato and Breece asked to see the results of the lie detector, and Morton sent it over. "Dallas did not pass this test," Imperato realized. "These findings are uncertain. We have to go back to Detective Coyote. He's got to see what you have," she said to Breece.

Breece also decided to hire divers to search for the weapons. Because of the cost involved and the long-shot aspect of finding anything after so much time, the cautious Breece saw this as a big step. In early September, Breece contacted the award-winning Boca Dive Team. Asked to locate guns dumped into a lake six years earlier, they saw this as a challenge. Gathering their equipment, including a metal detection device, they dove into the lake behind Martinelli's former home and began to search for the weapons. Hour upon hour they scoured its mucky underbelly, and by the end of the day, their search was rewarded. They had located Joe Viscido's Uzi.

Breece told them to keep at it. Two very long days later, they found the murder weapon—a .45-caliber pistol registered to one James Phaedra. From their condition and location in the muck, it was apparent to the dive crew that the weapons had been at the bottom of the lake for a number of years.

Breece called BSO homicide detective Bobby Coyote immediately, but he was unfazed. "Mike," he said, "there are half a dozen ways to explain that. You have to speak to one of our witnesses. He was there—in the apartment—when the hit went down, and then we'll see what you really have."

Breece agreed. On September 9, 1991, he met with Detective Coyote, who took him to Coral Springs Corrections Halfway House to interview Vic Giordano. Giordano explained that the short guy took Viscido into the rear bedroom. He remembered two shots being fired, at which time he and another young male bolted from the apartment. Giordano yelled to his friend to leave the car alone and both continued running.

Breece wrote, "It should be noted that Giordano mentioned 'jumping over hedges' when leaving the apartment compound, which was a key detail given to him by Rickenbach. Giordano said that he saw a Toyota Tercel parked directly by a wall facing the west side of the apartment, that it was silver or gray in color and was idling."

When showed photo lineups containing Phaedra and Carbonell, "Giordano could not identify either subject." He also did not recognize the names Phaedra, Carbonell, Martinelli, or Rickenbach. He did, however, recognize the name of Richard Whistler, whom he knew from St. Coleman's Catholic High School in Deerfield Beach, where they had both attended. As time wore on, Giordano simply stood by his contention that his ID of Rosati up in Rhode Island was correct.

BSO conveyed to Agent Breece that he didn't have a thing. "Giordano," Coyote said, "was at the scene, and he's never seen your guys."

"I don't think you're right, Bobby," Breece replied.

The following week he called up Rick Whistler.

"Hello," Whistler said.

"This is Sergeant Michael Breece of the Florida Department Law Enforcement Agency."

"What can I do for you, Sergeant?"

"I would like to stop by your house to discuss a specific serious event which took place in late 1986."

Suddenly nervous, Whistler agreed to the interview. Fifty minutes later, Sergeant Breece was at Whistler's house. That was late September 1991.

"I graduated Pompano Beach High School in 1978," Whistler began, "and have lived in this area for twenty-one years. Sure, I know those names. I've been friends with Joe Viscido, Vic Giordano, and Kit Finch ever since those years. We all got stoned together more times than I can remember. And when times were tough, I have to admit I dealt some dope to help pay the rent. Everyone did. It was no big deal—just a way to get some extra money.

"Since graduating high school, I've worked as a lifeguard in Ft. Lauderdale and Pompano Beach and also spent a little time as a professional boxer. That's where I met Boyce Rickenbach, who became my trainer and over time became my friend."

"Did Rickenbach know you dealt in marijuana?"

"Sure. I sold him an ounce every now and then."

"I don't think we have to beat around the bush, Mr. Whistler. Let's get to Joe Viscido's murder."

Whistler broke down into tears and then continued his story. "Rickenbach wanted ten or twenty pounds of marijuana, so I went to see one of my friends who was well connected, and he directs me to an apartment."

"I understand," the sergeant said.

"So we go to this apartment in Deerfield Beach to arrange the buy. I waited in the car, and Rickenbach returned with a small stash."

"I think he can handle it," Rickenbach said to me, "but we gotta come back in a day or two."

"So a few days later, we scored a little cocaine, and that's when I found out it was an old high school buddy of mine, Joe Viscido, who was supplying. But I didn't see him that day either.

"On the night of the murder, Rickenbach met me at Lighthouse Point with two of his buddies. He was driving his Toyota Tercel. As he had told me that he would only have one friend, I became upset. One of the guys was kind of short, maybe in his forties, and the second man was much younger, but a lot bigger, with shoulder-length, curly hair.

"'Calm down, everything's cool,' the shorter guy said, so I hopped in and directed them to the apartment building and pointed out the room. I thought it was going to be a marijuana transaction. It was at that time that I saw the shorter guy pull out a handgun, and the younger, bigger guy pulled out a police badge. 'I'm a Vietnam veteran and a cop who's done this before,' the big guy said to me, as if I believed that bullshit. This was going to be a rip, plain and simple, and I wanted out. 'You're gonna lose your cut,' Rickenbach reminded me, but I didn't give a shit even if it was a thousand dollars. They saw that it was to their advantage, so they let me go, and I went home.

"'Viscido's dead,' Rickenbach told me the next day when he stopped by the house. 'He got shot in the head during a rip,' he said. 'We got about one and one half pounds of coke and a lot of pot, but something went wrong. A fight broke out and the man got hurt. There was blood.'""Hurt!' I practically shouted at the guy. 'Viscido's dead. Your buddies whacked him. He's out of there. Dead, as in dead as a doornail.'

"Rickenbach stammered, 'I didn't . . . didn't know. We can't say anything about this. Those guys are nuts. You gotta promise me.'

"'Yeah, I promise,' I said. What was I gonna do? He was scared shitless. I helped him move his things, even gave him fifty bucks, and that was the last I ever saw of him."

Whistler swiftly picked out Kerry Carbonell from twelve photos set up in a lineup, and then he picked out Jim Phaedra out of a set of six pictures after a few minutes' deliberation. Sergeant Breece thanked Whistler for his cooperation and told him that he would have to repeat his story in the near future.

Both Breece and Imperato were convinced that once Coyote heard Whistler's testimony he would reconsider his own case. Under her auspices as assistant statewide prosecutor, Cindy Imperato invited Detective Coyote to hear Rick Whistler for himself. Thus, on September 19, 1991, Detective Coyote came to the meeting accompanied by Broward State Attorney's Office investigator Andy Greico.

As with the first recounting, Whistler was overly apologetic, and he openly wept on a number of occasions, consoled by his wife, as he went through every detail once again.

"How did you feel knowing that your friend got killed and the wrong guys were being arrested?" Detective Breece wanted to know. Overcome, Whistler turned away and avoided the question.

After Whistler left, Special Agent Breece turned to Detective Coyote. "Bobby," he said staring the detective directly in the eye, "you've arrested the wrong guys."

Coyote deftly picked apart one or two details that contained inconsistencies and repeated that he had a confession. Shrugging his shoulders, he left with an equally skeptical Greico.

Shortly thereafter, Imperato began to feel the pressure from a rumor that Stephen Rosati's father, a mob leader, was paying her off and paying Breece off as well. "It was so far out," she recalled. Having been put in the hot seat for simply trying to do her job, she and Breece continued to put their case together undeterred.

On September 24, Breece confirmed James Phaedra's signature on the Richmond Virginia application for the .45-caliber pistol found in the lake, and the detective also interviewed Martinelli's former girlfriend Kelly McCabe, who was married now and had a different last name.

Martinelli had often socialized with Boyce Rickenbach, Jim Phaedra, and Kerry Carbonell, McCabe said. Phaedra also lived with them at the lakefront house for a period of time and acted as Martinelli's bodyguard, although she did not know why Martinelli would need one.

In 1986, Kerry Carbonell began to stop by, but according to McCabe, "Carbonell was out of Martinelli's league. He was just a dirt bag."

Nevertheless, one night, which she thought was in September, she saw Carbonell come in with blood on his shoes, and she commented on the sight. McCabe also remembers Martinelli offering Carbonell a clean shirt. She was ordered by Martinelli to go into an adjoining room and not come out until she was told. She broke up with Martinelli shortly after that.

In late 1990, McCabe ran into Martinelli by chance, and he told her what had happened—Phaedra and Carbonell had been involved in a drug rip-off that turned into a murder.

On October 3, 1991, nearly four months into his investigation and just a week after Deputy Sheriff Coyote had sat in on Whistler's live deposition, Special Agent Mike Breece forwarded his findings to Detective Coyote and to Broward County prosecutor Chuck Morton. This was done under the direction of Judge Barry Goldstein, who was presiding over the bail hearing for Stephen Rosati and Pete the Greek.

A few weeks later, Cindy Imperato followed up with a phone call to Coyote. "Mike's case is very strong," she said, waiting for his response.

"Don't worry," Sheriff Coyote answered, "I'll get to it."

"When? You've got guys in jail," she said.

Astounded at what she perceived to be the policeman's refusal or evasion of his duties, Imperato's hopes now lay with Broward County's assistant state prosecutor, Chuck Morton. Breece also called Morton. "Chuck, we've been polite so far, but we are convinced that you have the wrong people! You've got to do something. No matter how you feel, you have to look at both cases." Breece also informed Coyote's overseer, Captain Auer.

Four years later, Assistant Attorney General Chuck Morton recalled the situation in a deposition:

"What I was making a judgment on is not so much who was guilty, but really what could I in good faith go forward with in light of . . . the information that was in front of me. . . . If there was something that BSO was aware of that FDLE was not aware of in their investigation, that might have some bearing, shed some light on their findings . . . and visa versa. . . . I wanted them to share information. That was my primary concern, so that both agencies could make an informed decision as to how to proceed. And so, whether or not I actually read the reports they may have submitted to my investigators . . . I can't say that I read everything that Breece had, because I'm so sure they were sharing everything they had with BSO or the State Attorney's Office. I mean that's just my honest answer there."[2]

A key reason BSO was reluctant to change course was because they were particularly interested in incarcerating a local rogue they finally had their hooks into.

"There had been a big push to get Pete the Greek," Breece recalled, and the Broward Sheriff's Office was happy they got him. "One woman in their office was quite arrogant to me," Breece continued. "BSO was giving me the stiff. Their top boss, Mike Satz, called my commissioner and told him to back off."

But FDLE didn't, and Breece continued to get the support of his commanding officers.

The Governor's Man

On December 3, 1991, Breece went to Judge Goldstein's court with Cindy Imperato to attend the bail hearing of Stephen Rosati and Peter Roussonicolos. Breece and Imperato were sure Chuck Morton had reviewed the material he had been given in October so that bail could be granted to the prisoners. Morton had not, and Breece's investigation was still essentially undisclosed. Since *Brady v. Maryland* demands, "exculpatory evidence that negates the guilt of someone must be given to the accused," Breece informed Rosati's lawyer, Victor Tobin, that the real murderers had been identified. Nevertheless, bail was denied. Morton was taken off the case, announcing on his departure on December 10, 1991, that "Governor Lawton Chiles [w]ould appoint a new prosecutor before the end of the week."

Judge Goldstein had been in a pickle. Morton had simply refused to read Breece's report and Goldstein was not in a position to rule on the Breece material. With a prompting from Imperato, Goldstein turned to Governor Chiles for advice. They sought out a special prosecutor from an area of the state unconnected to South Florida. The name of the state attorney from the tenth judicial circuit, John Aguero, kept coming up. Aguero, whose reputation was "straight as an arrow," was thereby appointed by the governor to decide between both cases.

Aguero began by interviewing each camp separately. Starting with BSO's case, he invited Detective Sheriff Robert Coyote to his offices in Bartow, which is located in the center of the state, about an hour's drive from Disney World. Whereas Aguero looked like a throwback from the 1950s, with a military buzz cut and pant legs so short that his white socks stood out, Coyote, as an undercover cop, looked more like a member of the Hell's Angels. With large muscles, a cocksure swagger, tattoos along his forearms, and long dirty-blond hair, Coyote walked in accompanied by his partner, overweight, unkempt Frank Puccini, and the refined assistant attorney general, Chuck Morton.

Aguero remembers that they presented Carl Rosati, Stephen's father, as "the underworld king of RI." The Coyote-Morton camp painted a dark picture of organized crime in Rhode Island. The Rosatis' lawyer, Jack Cicilline, they reminded Aguero, represented Raymond Patriarca—the head of the mob in New England—and he also had ties to "the boss of bosses," John Gotti. "The Rosatis," they said, "have an unlimited amount of wealth. They could buy off anybody." Their description created the image in Aguero's mind of Carl Rosati as a Mafia don. "Don't you think it's a bit odd that Breece's best witness, Boyce Rickenbach, employs the same law firm as Stephen Rosati?" Morton said. "It looks too shady to me."

The Coyote-Morton camp told Aguero that the Rosatis would do anything to save their son. Aguero remembers that there was even the implication that the Rosatis might have paid Phaedra and Carbonell to take the fall. The guns in the lake could even be a plant! "There's no telling what they'll do or how far their web extends."

If that were the case, Aguero reasoned, then Michael Breece

and even Cindy Imperato could also be in on the take. Therefore, he impounded their bank records to look for possible payoffs, and he also checked for any large purchases. He was going to leave no stone unturned. Then Aguero called each of them in.

Breece remembers being concerned because his wife had received a large Christmas bonus from the biotech firm that she worked for, and he was afraid that Aguero would think it came from Rosati. Imperato was insulted that her honor could be called into question. On the other hand, Aguero's tough-mindedness appeared to them to be the best way to sort out the controversy.

"When I first met John Aguero, he had no respect for me at all," Breece recalled. "'You may not think much of me,' I said, 'but once you begin to study Coyote's case, you'll see that it will fall like a house of cards.' Nevertheless, I sorely resent, even to this day, the innuendo that I was bought by Rosati." Breece even went so far as to check on the Rosati name in connection with organized crime. "Mr. Rosati was completely clean," Breece said. "Absolutely no connection whatever."

Aguero, whom Breece now sees as "a pit bull" and "the sharpest legal mind he has ever met," took his top investigators Tom Spate and Jerry Hill to a hotel for a marathon meeting. Spate and Hill took one case and Aguero the other, and then they swapped. Playing devil's advocate, they tried to tie Rosati to Scalley's Saloon owner Martinelli and then to the actual wheelman, Rickenbach. Morton's suggestion about sharing the same attorney was solved when it was discovered that Rickenbach had gone to Tobin's partner, Miller, because his sister, Carla, had once worked for Miller. Both Spate and Aguero felt that the Dallas confession was bogus. Referring to Breece's case, Spate said, "I don't see how you can get around those guns." Phaedra had purchased the pistol in an obscure town in Virginia. By the time they left the hotel, the Aguero team was leaning in Michael Breece's direction.

Then Dallas recanted his testimony.

Along with the witnesses and physical evidence against Phaedra and Carbonell, particularly the match on the bullets from Phaedra's gun, it became clear that Morton and Coyote had indicted the wrong men. Thus, at the beginning of the following year, Aguero gave the order, and Pete the Greek, Peter Dallas, and Stephen Rosati were set free.

On the day Stephen was released from jail, January 24, 1992, Joe Viscido's father recalled that he "cried like a baby. I was still convinced that that he and Dallas and Pete the Greek had killed my son," Mr. Viscido explained. Not until much later did Viscido see how terribly wrong he had been.

On that same day, Special Agent Michael Breece drove over to King Toyota in Deerfield Beach to interview Kerry Carbonell, who was working as a mechanic at the dealership.

"I didn't shoot nobody," Carbonell yelled at Breece.

"Calm down. You are at a place of business," the sergeant warned. Carbonell had already done time for aggravated assault against a police officer in 1989, so Breece was careful around the big guy.

"You can't put me back in jail just for a simple robbery. I can't go back."

"Would you like to make a statement?"

"I need to speak to my grandfather first. He's a state rep."

According to John Aguero, Carbonell was referring to his uncle, Ron Saunders, who was "equivalent to the Speaker of the House in Florida."

"But I can tell you this," Carbonell said. "I didn't shoot the guy, and I wasn't there when he was shot."

"Don't leave town," Breece warned. He called Aguero, convinced of Carbonell's guilt.

At 9:00 a.m. on February 3, 1992, Breece met with Judge Goldstein to issue warrants against Kerry Carbonell and James Phaedra for armed robbery and murder. Carbonell was arrested an hour later at Dismas House, the drug rehab center where he was living, located in Dania. By noontime he was in the Broward County jail.

"Was the guy who drove us arrested?" Carbonell wanted to know.

"Don't worry, we got him," Breece said ambiguously.

"I know, even if a guy is not the shooter, if you're there, you're just as guilty, but I didn't do it. I can't go to jail for forty years," Carbonell cried. "I can't do the time. I can't do the time. I can't . . ."

As Detective Breece started to leave, Carbonell spoke again. "Sergeant, can I at least see my girlfriend?"

Carbonell had been banned from seeing his girlfriend, a topless dancer from Broward County with a long arrest record for shoplifting and drug trafficking, as part of the deal for his parole. "I'm not sure about that. I'm sorry," the detective said.

"It's not fair!" Carbonell cried. "I can't handle this."

Breece left the cell to speak to the officer in charge. He wanted to make sure the officer was completely aware of Carbonell's police record. Breece especially wanted the officer to know about his violent streak. Known criminal activities had begun for Carbonell when, as a teenager, he worked for the now deceased but locally infamous "Fat George" Canon. By the time he was seventeen, Carbonell had committed armed robberies and numerous domestic break-ins. He ended up in jail a year after the Viscido homicide, arrested for an unrelated cocaine charge. After serving four years, he went on parole but was required to wear an electronic bracelet so his activities could be monitored. Just a few months later, Carbonell was arrested again.

The following day, Breece traveled with another officer up to Richmond, Virginia, where they met with the State Police Fugitive Squad. At high noon, they drove over to Jim Phaedra's home in Hopewell and arrested him. Phaedra gave no resistance, was read his Miranda rights, and said that he understood. While being booked, he waived extradition, saying he had full knowledge of his actions.

"I just want to get this over with," he said. "I know it's not going to be easy."

"There's a lot of evidence against you," Breece said.

"I know, I know."

"You are the one with the greatest problem."

"I know."

"Do you want to make a statement concerning the events of October 12, 1986?" Breece said upon their arrival in Florida.

"What I want is to see an attorney," Phaedra responded.

"Because you requested legal counsel, it is best that you not respond, but we want to tell you that we have recovered the guns from the lake."

Phaedra nodded, conveying that he understood. By the end of the day, he was secured in Broward County Jail. With Kerry Carbonell, Jim Phaedra was indicted by a grand jury for first-degree murder and armed robbery on February 13, 1992.

Coincidentally, Phaedra's attorney was Hilliard Moldof, the same lawyer who represented Jeff Bloom, the owner of the supposed safe house. Since Moldof had been present at all of Bloom's sworn affidavits, he knew the scenario that Rosati, Dallas, and Pete the Greek had committed the crime. Thus, that would be Phaedra's defense. Breece went over Bloom's statements with Chuck Morton and Detective Coyote. They remained unconvinced that Rosati, Dallas, and Pete the Greek were innocent. Detective Coyote intimated that Rosati was linked to the mob.

"I'm telling you, Mike, I was scared for my life when I was up in

Rhode Island," he told Breece. "That guy's connected, and he paid off Dallas to get him to recant."

The best way to sort this out was to speak to the other primary suspects. In late February, Breece met with Peter Roussonicolos. Still in jail facing an unrelated charge, which he was later cleared of, Roussonicolos said that a fictional scenario had been cooked up, making him the driver and Dallas and Rosati the armed robbers. Roussonicolos figured that Jeff Bloom, Danny Ek, and Cory Franco had collectively misinterpreted events. He also suspected that the Broward police were out to frame him because he was a thorn in their side, but he didn't tell Michael Breece that.

"Dallas had never even met Steve," Pete said, "and Steve wasn't even in Florida on the night of October 12, 1986. I met Steve in '84 or '85 at Rosebuds, where he was working as a dancer. We became friends and saw each other a couple of times, but I hadn't seen him for years, up until a few months ago right here in jail. I couldn't believe he was even pulled into this thing. Dallas, of course, is a totally different story. I'm embarrassed to say he's my cousin. The guy's extremely screwed up and constantly in a drug haze. My girlfriend couldn't stand the guy, so I told him to take a hike, and that was way before October of '86."

"Thanks," Detective Breece said.

As he turned to go, Pete the Greek stopped him. "One more thing," he said.

"What's that?"

"The car with no doors."

"What of it. Was it yours?"

"Yeah, but the cops impounded it months before Viscido bought the farm. Coyote made a big thing of it, but I got the proof. And if we didn't get freed when they caught the real guys, that was going to be our ticket out."

* * *

In March, Detective Breece and Cynthia Imperato flew up to Rhode Island to interview Stephen. They brought along John Aguero and Detective Spate. Breece wrote in his notes that his investigation "has since proven [that Carl Stephen Rosati] was wrongfully charged in the murder of Joseph Viscido, Jr."

"That guy, Rosati, is squeaky clean," said Aguero on the plane ride back to Florida.

How could the Deerfield Police investigation go so wrong? Breece wondered. In reviewing Sergeant McNeil's files—the extensive case that was put together before Bobby Coyote took it over—the detective noted a reference to the case of Jay Prince and Terry Malone, wherein Prince had told McNeil that Kerry Carbonell and a guy called Poppa Jim committed the crime. Breece also noted that Prince *had* picked Carbonell out from a police lineup. He called Jay Prince.

"Yes, Sarge," Prince said, "I remember the whole thing. It was back in '87, when me and my buddy Lunchmeat [Terry Malone] were beseeched by Kerry Carbonell to join him in committing drug rip-offs of some of the local drug dealers. It was at that time that he related the entire incident. Carbonell told us that they liked to go in with fake police badges pretending they were cops. 'That shit works all the time,' he said. Poppa Jim was the one who shot the guy, and Carbonell was so close when it happened that his face was scarred with powder burns. The sergeant has the whole thing on tape."

"What sergeant? What are you talking about?" Breece and Imperato wanted to know.

"McNeil. He and some other cop bugged me up, and then I went in to speak to Lunchmeat. I had already told McNeil everything, but he wanted confirmation."

Imperato called Sergeant McNeil. "What's this about an audiotape?"

She was astounded that when McNeil had turned over his files to Breece, he had neglected to include this audiotape. Reluctantly, McNeil admitted that the tape was somewhere around and that he would look for it. It was clear to Imperato that if Jay Prince had not mentioned the tape's existence, she or Breece would never have known about it.

On his second interview, Jay Prince was even more vocal. He described Poppa Jim as head of a group they called the Zoo Crew. Prince told Breece that Carbonell would sometimes cry because of the murder he was involved in. Poppa Jim, however, was an entirely different type, "a bad motherfucker, cold-blooded, stone-cold killer. He told me he's killed about thirty people, and I believe him."

Prince then related how he tried to tell Sergeant McNeil about Poppa Jim back in 1988, when he had worn a wire and gone to speak about the crime to Terry Malone.

"First I told Detective Brennan, and since he knew that there was an ongoing investigation of the murder, he sent me to McNeil. I know Lunchmeat was scared and didn't say too much on the tape, but it's on there."

In June, Breece met with Special Agent Ken Brennan, who substantiated the fact that Prince had spoken to him about these events. Brennan described a meeting with Deerfield Detective Jeff Burndt and his overseer, Detective Sergeant Chevy McNeil.

"Sergeant Brennan was frank in his appraisal that he became frustrated with the Deerfield detectives' immediate discounting of the information provided by Jay Prince. The Deerfield detectives were apparently certain in their convictions that Peter Roussonicolos had committed the Viscido homicide."

Brennan told Breece that he was surprised that the Deerfield detectives were not more thorough or assertive in their investigation of Prince's information, which Brennan described as seemingly "right on the money." After he turned Jay Prince over to Deerfield, Brennan said that he did not participate any further in the investigation. Sometime later, Brennan followed up and contacted Sergeant McNeil, who told him that the Prince information on Kerry Carbonell and Poppa Jim had been discounted. McNeil's statements surprised Brennan.

A week later, on June 22, 1992, Breece met with Sergeant McNeil to retrieve the Prince/Malone audiotape along with some others, which had also been excluded from the official police files. He also listened to an interview of Joe Viscido, Sr., and Jeff Bloom that was taped when Viscido was wired.

"Viscido Sr. asked numerous times if Peter Dallas, Pete the Greek, or their associates had ever admitted to killing or participating in his son's murder. Bloom's repeated answer was a confident or positive no." Bloom did later state that Dallas had said at some point, "Joe's done with."

Bloom told Mr. Viscido that he did not know Stephen Rosati but proceeded to describe Rosati as a muscular weight lifter. Bloom then concluded that Rosati must be "the husky dude" involved in the killing. Michelle Arrieta was then interviewed to find out why she ID'd Rosati and Dallas in 1990.

"Arrieta advised that in the months prior to that ID, Deerfield Police Department investigators had made it clear to her that Peter Dallas was their suspect, and in prior photographic lineup sessions showed great annoyance at her lack of identification of Dallas. In addition, Ms. Arrieta related that Vic Giordano and Joseph Viscido, Sr., displayed anger toward her and were pressuring her for not identifying Peter Dallas as the perpetrator."

Michelle was direct in telling Breece that she could not identify Dallas because she did not recognize him as the smaller of the two perpetrators. She told them that she received threats of arrest from the Deerfield Police Department because of her inability to ID Dallas.

"In fact, at one point, Ms. Arrieta stated that she was arrested after one of the photo lineup sessions and placed in a holding cell for several hours. She stated she was unexpectedly released but re-arrested a short time later for an old traffic warrant."

Detective Bobby Coyote showed her Dallas's photo lineup, and by this time she knew what he looked like and picked him out. Breece wrote:

"She made the identification of Dallas under duress and is emphatic to state that she truly could not identify Dallas as the actual perpetrator. Michelle further reasoned that if the Deerfield and BSO investigators seemed so certain as to Dallas's guilt, she would just make the ID to be rid of the situation.

"At a later time, she stated that she was shown an advertisement displaying six male dancers and asked if she could ID any of the males as a perpetrator in the homicide. Michelle advised she could not identify any of the dancers; however, she remembered pointing to one advising, 'He looked like the larger perpetrator,' but discounted it because she was certain the larger perpetrator had light brown or medium brown hair. The detective told her that the man could have dyed or bleached his hair. She also thought Rosati was too short, as the larger perpetrator was bigger."

On August 21, 1992, Kerry Jay Carbonell was found hanged in his cell at the Broward County Jail. A recurring disciplinary problem, Carbonell had been under daily psychotherapy for depression and had been prescribed antidepressant drugs. That afternoon he had gotten into a quarrel with guards over the dosage of his medication, and he was moved into a solitary maximum-security cell designed for inmates in danger of hurting themselves or others.

At about 8:00 p.m., Carbonell tied one end of a twisted bed sheet to the wall side of his bunk bed and the other end around his neck allowing for a sitting motion to create a chokehold. When the big guy sat forward in a leaning position he simply hanged himself. Jim Phaedra's attorney, Hilliard Moldof, was suspicious of the death, but it was ruled a suicide. Betty, Carbonell's common-law wife and mother of his seven-year-old son, told him the day before that she was leaving him.

388

"Unfortunately, suicides are very common in jail," Cindy Imperato commented.

For the record, another suicide was associated with this case. On January 3, 1993, Danny Ek, one of Jeff Bloom's friends, died from a self-inflicted shotgun blast to his chest after a dispute over divorce and child custody with his wife. He had called her four times threatening suicide. He left three suicide notes, saying suicide was "the only way."

The last suspect from the BSO investigation, Peter Dallas, was the most troubling. In April, Breece tracked down one of Dallas's prison inmates, James Boughton. He told Breece that Dallas had broken down, claiming he had implicated two other individuals in a murder that they did not commit. Dallas said that he was in prison in New York when Florida detectives tricked and pressured him into giving false statements. For these statements he was promised a lighter sentence.

Boughton, a former Coca-Cola executive and U.S. Army intelligence officer imprisoned for cocaine trafficking, said that Dallas was "very stressed and remorseful over his false accusations." However, Dallas made it abundantly clear that he was going to "save his own neck first" by continuing the ruse of his confession to the Viscido homicide. Although he was innocent, he still believed that the Broward police could put him into the chair if he didn't play their game.[3]

In June 1993, the trial of Jim Phaedra began. John Aguero would be the lead prosecutor accompanied by Cindy Imperato. Phaedra's defense essentially was the same as that of the Broward County Police Department: Pete the Greek, Peter Dallas, and Stephen Rosati did the crime. All three came down to testify.

Traveling with his father to Florida, Stephen had mixed feelings about meeting with Mr. Viscido, the man probably most responsible for putting him on a fast track toward his possible execution. Reluctantly, he shook Mr. Viscido's hand as they discussed the case.

Mr. Viscido admitted that he had almost assassinated Pete the Greek on several occasions. The two of them embraced and laughed about it before newspaper cameras. Off camera, Pete the Greek grabbed Peter Dallas by the throat and yelled at him because he was the reason that they were almost fried. Mr. Viscido's wife, Rose, revealed to Carl Rosati that it had occurred to her that her husband might have the wrong men, but she was too afraid to confront Joe with her thoughts.

Phaedra's defense attorney, Hilliard Moldof, adeptly attacked the

389

testimony of prosecutor Aguero's three key witnesses: Scalley's Saloon owner Tony Martinelli, wheelman Boyce Rickenbach, and the fellow who pointed out Joe's apartment at the outset, Rick Whistler. Moldof's defense for Poppa Jim Phaedra rested on the supposition that Stephen Rosati, as the big guy, and Peter Dallas, as the little guy, entered the apartment, and Pete the Greek waited outside with the car running. A problem Moldof ran into was that Detective Coyote's investigation of Rosati and Roussonicolos, to a great extent, was inadmissible because of the hearsay rule. But Dallas's confession was not hearsay and thus was admissible. Therefore, this confession became the focal point of the defense.

On the stand, the two policemen who took the deposition, Coyote and Puccini, contended that Peter Dallas's confession was a true accounting. This cast doubt on Phaedra's guilt. Puccini was adamant and said, "I thought we had the right people when we arrested them, and I still think that."[4]

The prosecutor, John Aguero, countered by answering for the jurors a question: "Why on earth would a person confess to a crime that he or she did not commit?"[5] Relentlessly, Aguero cross-examined Detective Puccini first and then Sheriff Coyote. "I went through the entire Dallas confession line by line," Aguero said. "Puccini got the worst of that." Remembering back, Aguero re-created a small part of his cross-examination:

"On line two of the Dallas confession, you tell Dallas that he and Stephen Rosati went in there."

"That's right," Puccini replied.

"Well, didn't you just tell him?"

"Yes."

"It got very heated. I showed how they fed Dallas every answer. It made him look like an idiot," the prosecutor said.

Cindy Imperato, Aguero's co-counsel, reported that Detective Puccini's testimony came off as weak, whereas Detective Coyote was much more composed. After Aguero asked the detective why he interviewed Dallas for a full hour before he started rolling the tape, Coyote said that maybe he had made a mistake there and perhaps he should have done it differently.

"Then I put Dallas on the stand," Aguero said. "Dallas said these guys had threatened him with the electric chair. They told him that they had his bloodstained footprint in the room. They told him that they would reduce his death sentence to seven years and he'd be out in three."[6]

Aguero explained that when Dallas first gave that confession he was serving a two-year jail sentence in New York State. By doing a concurrent sentence of three years, it meant that Dallas would have to serve only one additional year. They gave him a choice: twelve more months in jail or life in prison ending in the electric chair. "They just intimidated him," Aguero said, "[essentially the same] way they intimated Stephen Rosati and Michelle Arrieta."*

To prompt Dallas, "Puccini and Coyote said on the stand that they had only played short portions of tapes [by Vic Giordano, Jeff Bloom, Cory Franco, etc.], whereas Dallas said they were with him for over two hours and that they played long portions. Dallas was," in Aguero's words, "just a punk hoodlum."

He did tell Aguero that he was sorry he got Steve and Pete in trouble, but this did not come out on the stand at all and was not the point of his testimony.

Aguero stated that even with Moldof's deft cross-examinations, Tony Martinelli, Rick Whistler, and Boyce Rickenbach all performed well. Aguero was particularly impressed with the testimony of Martinelli and the wheelman, Rickenbach. "They were excellent witnesses," he said.

When Stephen Rosati and Pete the Greek testified, Moldof tried to get Pete to plead the Fifth Amendment, implying that if he didn't keep silent, the Pandora's box of his illicit past would be opened. But the Greek didn't comply and did well on the stand. Moldof tried to intimate that Stephen Rosati was in Florida in October 1986, but Rosati went through a detailed discussion of his business operations during that period, and then Kara Lynx was called to the stand.

"Dressed to the nines" and "a stunner," Kara was a very credible witness. As before at Stephen's extradition hearing, Kara verified that she was living with Stephen on a daily basis in Rhode Island throughout the whole of 1986 and would certainly have known if Stephen had left for a few days, which he did not. Carl Rosati also stated succinctly that he was in daily contact with his son during that same period because of the many business dealings they were working on together.

Then Aguero put Michelle Arrieta on the stand.

"You have to remember," the prosecutor recalled, "none of the

---

* At Rosati's extradition hearing, Detective Coyote intimated that Dallas would be in jail seven to twelve years when, in fact, his deal with BSO could get him out in one!

three primary witnesses ever really identified Phaedra or Carbonell from the photo pack."

Aguero explained that he showed over forty photos to Michelle, Giordano, and Chris Jones. Some of the pictures were different views of Phaedra and Carbonell and other possible suspects. Giordano was still convinced that Rosati was the guilty man. Michelle told them that it had been over five years since Joe's death. She needed to see live witnesses. Jones, who was "scared to death" because of his fear that the BSO were really involved in the drug rip-off, did, in fact, pick Phaedra out along with one other person as looking like the killers. But he was not definite, and so Aguero did not want to go with the weak ID.

"When I put Michelle on the stand, I took the biggest chance in my entire legal career," Aguero admitted. Since she had not definitively ID'd Phaedra from the photo pack, he was not certain what her testimony would be. "I could see her eyes looking at Phaedra, and Cindy said that she 'could see it all coming back to her.' She nudged me and so I took a chance," Aguero said.

A gal with spunk, Arrieta looked directly at the person who murdered her boyfriend, James Phaedra, and said without any doubt in her voice, "That's the man." And that was that.

During closing arguments, defense attorney Moldof put up an excellent summation, saying, "Dallas confessed to the crime. Jim Phaedra did not." However, Moldof could not overcome the physical evidence, which included the murder weapon registered in Phaedra's name and the corresponding witness testimony, and Aguero won the case. On July 1, 1993, Jim Phaedra was sentenced to a life sentence with a minimum term of twenty-five years.

Finally vindicated, Stephen Rosati and Peter Roussonicolos sued Florida for wrongful imprisonment. Peter Dallas had a suit as well, but for obvious reasons, he is in a different category.

Aguero felt that Chevy McNeil was a good cop who simply had "tunnel vision." Once he keyed in on Rosati, Dallas, and Pete the Greek, he could not be persuaded to consider an alternative possibility. Aguero was angry with McNeil, however, for taking so long in presenting the Prince and Malone audiotape implicating Kerry Carbonell and Poppa Jim. On the other hand, he felt Detectives Coyote and Puccini were incompetent. They were "overzealous," but he did not see malevolent intent on their part. His greatest criticism centered on their inability to consider the possibility that they might have been wrong.

"When Michael Breece came to them, they should have opened their mind to a different possibility," Aguero said.

Cindy Imperato's greatest criticism of Coyote, Puccini, and their prosecutor, Chuck Morton, was in their decisions to not read Michael Breece's reports. This was simply incomprehensible to her. She also noted that Detective Coyote had told her on at least two occasions that he had not read Breece's reports, but on the witness stand, when asked if he had, he said yes. She and Aguero noted that Coyote may have perjured himself, but they let it go. Imperato was also critical of Sergeant McNeil, who dismissed the Prince and Malone audiotape implicating Carbonell and Poppa Jim. She was most upset that the existence of the tape was never revealed to her or Breece until after Jay Prince spoke of its existence. Prince's proclamation came as a total shock to them.

"Coyote should have looked at the big picture," Breece reflected. "You don't browbeat witnesses. His manner was wrong, and what they did is inexcusable—90 percent of it. He's just incompetent, and he's certainly paying the price now. Morton is unprofessional. He has said that he was never apprised about Rickenbach, and that simply is not true. Homicide is serious business. You get the electric chair or you can get life, and you have to be very careful."

Because of the blown Dallas confession, both Michael Breece and Cindy Imperato have been called to testify against Detective Coyote on several occasions. Usually, Imperato's testimony about the case is barred, but her presence does carry some weight. Now a judge, she has maintained friendly relations with Detective Coyote and Chuck Morton and sees them in the course of her work throughout the year. She states that they are unshakable in their belief that they were right. As late as January 1, 1995, Chuck Morton, Bobby Coyote, and Frank Puccini still contended that Peter Dallas's confession was an honest one.

Detective Coyote, Imperato said, stayed in homicide until an injury from a car accident forced him to retire. As reported by the *Sun-Sentinel*, "With two dozen screws, pins, and rods holding his lower spine together, a vertebra removed, two others fused, atrophy of the muscles in one of his legs, and a morphine pump implanted into his stomach to ease his pain, Detective Coyote stated, 'Now, I kinda walk crooked.'"[7]

One of the reasons BSO backed Coyote, Imperato speculated, is that his division probably believed his story. Lieutenant Fantagrassi and the head of the homicide unit, Sergeant Richard Scheff, accompanied Detectives Coyote and Puccini to the Phaedra trial to lend their full support.

"If they had moved Coyote off homicide, it would imply weakness on their part, and they do not want to look weak or be wrong," Imperato concluded.

The issue remains, however, whether incompetence, tunnel vision, or overzealousness can truly explain the ability to craft a detailed comprehensive case that choreographed six eyewitnesses, their carefully prepared taped depositions, a bogus confession, and the arrest of three entirely innocent suspects, where two of the men didn't even know each other, and one was 1,500 miles away at the time the crime was committed. How does one tie together two men who have never met?

Wrongful imprisonment is not new. In the 1990s, the introduction of DNA tests enabled upwards of seventy-five men who were on death row to be set free. Local law enforcement has the ability to hold a person's life in their hands by a simple say-so.

In this case, if it weren't for finding the actual guns, according to John Aguero, "Stephen Rosati would probably have spent the rest of his life in jail." Aguero's investigator, Mike Spate, stated that although he had seen bad cases made against a single individual, in his thirty-two years as a police investigator he had never seen a wrongful case made simultaneously against three individuals. Neither had Cindy Imperato.

How did Detective Coyote's boss, Captain John Auer, head of Investigative Services for the Broward County Sheriff's Office, react to the verdict of Jim Phaedra? Referring to Rosati, Auer told the *Tampa Tribune*, "Most people in jail are going to say, 'I didn't do it. I was somewhere else.' Had we gone to trial [against Rosati and the others], I think we would have gotten a conviction."[8]

What does Stephen Rosati say to this? "They can make anybody look guilty."[9]

AFTERWORD
Eleven Years Later

"Shoot my good side."

> Judge Ilona Holmes to photographers
> during the Rosati trial against the
> Broward Sheriff's Office for wrongful
> imprisonment, September 2003.

In 1996, Carl Rosati died in a hospital two days after heart bypass surgery. The funeral was a lavish affair held at one of the old churches on Spring Street in the heart of the historic district of Newport, Rhode Island. The chapel was filled with mourners. After the service, the funeral procession wound down Bellevue Avenue past the great Newport mansions and then turned right after the Tennis Hall of Fame to drive along the scenic coast. After Second Beach, the procession moved inland through a lush rural byway of manicured

395

estates and horse farms to a cemetery that had no headstones. After the burial, the procession returned the same way to Carlyn's home off Cliff Run. It sat just a street away from Senator Pell's place and several blocks from Jackie Onassis's Hammersmith Farm and the overlook to Narragansett Bay and Newport Harbor.

Carl's passing was a deathblow in every sense of the word to the Rosati Group. Nearly twenty years earlier, Carl had suffered a pair of heart attacks. He had come close to death in 1990 when Stephen was first arrested because his heart valve had become infected. But he recovered and thus was able to continue to run his real estate and insurance business during the entire eighteen-month ordeal. However, it took a toll on his health and on the business he had founded.

In 1993, the Rosatis began their civil suit against the Broward Sheriff's Office for false arrest. Stephen sent thank-you notes to Michael Breece and John Aguero for all they had done. In the case of Cindy Imperato, on July 14, working to compose the letter with his parents, he wrote:

Dear Cindy,

Having known you for a while now, I feel like you are part of my family. I just wanted to write to tell you: Thanks for the Truth!

Thank you for struggling with this case for these past few years, and for coming through in the face of adversity. Thank you for using your ingenuity to have the final outcome of the truth come forward. Your actions were directly responsible in saving three innocent lives. Words cannot express the feelings that I have for you as a person.

Your work and your integrity in bucking the system should be commended. All too often, people in bureaucratic situations look the other way, and thus allow injustice to take place, but because of people like you, in this instance, this did not happen.

It is heartening to know that there are officers of the law like you, John Aguero, and Mike Breece protecting the rights of citizens. I will always be grateful.

Your friend forever,
Stephen Rosati

Since Jack Cicilline was a criminal attorney, he handed the case over to the able civil attorney Michael Avery, who began the long task of deposing witnesses. These included in-depth grilling of Sergeant

Detective Chevy McNeil, Detective Sheriff Robert Coyote, the Florida assistant attorney general Chuck Morton, and Peter Dallas.

Jack's son David Cicilline, a Brown graduate and also an attorney, was called in. He worked with Avery to set a date for trial. I had testified as a handwriting expert for David when he was first starting out on an immigration case, and I was impressed with his skills as an attorney. For his summary, he created large placards that outlined the strength of the case. However, unlike his hard-as-nails father, on first meeting David came across as genteel. But during trial, surprisingly, he was razor sharp.

Much like his father, David became a fixture at the superior courthouse up on Benefit Street. It seemed that every time I testified at superior court, I would run into David. Son of one of the most well known lawyers in the state, David was fast making a name for himself. Having run for local office, he soon gained a local House seat representing Providence's posh East Side. Simultaneously, the Rosatis' court dates kept getting delayed.

Several years later, Avery was offered a position to teach at a university. He abandoned the case, and so it was put completely into David Cicilline's hands. Although he flew down to Florida a few times, David was finding it impossible to obtain a date for the court trial. On top of that, Esther was unable to run the business on her own, and Stephen was too distraught from the trauma of his incarceration to be of any real help.

The income from the Rosati Group had disappeared, and the dot-com crash ate up additional assets. Yet still there were calls for more cash outlays for endless trips to Florida to deal with the Rube Goldbergian maze of courtroom blind alleys and false promises by opposing attorneys and judges who kept passing the buck. Stephen had trouble dealing with his sense of guilt for being responsible for the entire calamity. Unable to fill his father's shoes in business, Stephen turned to his one source of success, bodybuilding. He began entering competitions full time. Major regional meets were held just once or twice a year.

To prepare himself, Stephen consumed massive amounts of food on a daily basis. In short order, he bulked up to an enormous 270 pounds. In order to win, the excess weight is shed weeks and days before the competition. If done right, the muscles are drawn taut, and the person looks like dynamite on the day of the meet. This is a lifestyle for a young man, not one in his late thirties or early forties. After several gut-wrenching disappointments, Stephen succeeded in stunning fashion by winning Mr. All New England in the heavyweight division in 2001. He looked perfect. This was a terrific athletic achievement, but the price paid for this win came shortly after when Stephen suffered a heart attack and a corresponding nervous collapse.

At his lowest point, Stephen hit the depths of hell. Trying to pay back the family, he sought get-rich schemes. At Foxwoods Resort Casino in Connecticut, he lost the ransom of kings. With his life in shambles, he took to drinking. Finally, he turned to therapy sessions, where he realized that one of the reasons he gained all that weight was literally to build a wall around himself for protection from the fears that plagued him: his ordeal in prison and the loss of his livelihood and reputation.

Esther's only salvation was the case. Taking on a lawsuit like this is not a part-time occupation; it is all-consuming. She found herself thinking about nothing other than the case and her dilemma, as Stephen held on by a thread.

Michael Avery was gone, and David Cicilline was setting his sights on the mayor's office. Buddy Cianci had been the mayor of Providence for over a quarter century. Easily the most flamboyant character in the state, everybody knew Buddy. Most often flanked by one or two very large, armed policemen, his average day could include a spot on *Imus in the Morning*, short speeches at any number of parades, local gatherings or specialty conferences, obligatory appearances at various funerals, night spots on local TV—even *60 Minutes*—and dinner at any one of the "in" places downtown or on Federal Hill.

Involved in kickback schemes, Cianci's fall was a stunning turn of events. Much like a modern-day Boss Tweed, he was found guilty and, almost overnight, was sent to prison. David literally waltzed into the office in a surprise landslide victory.* Now that he was the new mayor, the Rosatis needed a new attorney but did not have the funds nor the energy to hire or educate another one. There only recourse was to go back to the new mayor's father, Jack, who already had a full schedule. Although he had been out of the case for a decade, to Jack's credit, he agreed to take on the civil suit, even though he was a

---

* David Cicilline would end up serving two terms as mayor of Providence—eight years—and is now in his second term as a member of the U.S. House of Representatives. A popular figure in the state, ironically in 2012, David won a hard-fought battle to retain his House seat against his worthy opponent, Brendon Doherty, former head of the state police and contender for governor. Doherty, who trained at Stephen's health club, was the first Rhode Island policeman to arrest Stephen so many years earlier in 1990.

criminal attorney. It would be a stretch, but without him or Esther's resilience and overwhelming financial sacrifice, the suit would have died.

In February 2003, Jack Cicilline located Judge Ilona Holmes, who agreed to schedule the trial for September 22. Eleven years of seemingly daily work on the suit had elapsed since the case was first set for trial.

In August, Dan deVise of the *Miami Herald* called asking to do an article on Stephen and the impending trial. Dan spoke to Stephen on the phone for an interview. He wanted to bolster the article with a photo, so he called me to see if I could arrange for one to be taken here in Rhode Island. It had been about eight months since I had last seen Stephen, although we spoke from time to time on the phone. We set up a rendezvous with a photographer from the *Warwick Beacon*, a local Rhode Island newspaper. The location was a health club near Stephen's apartment not far from Knight Farms, the prestigious housing development that his father built in the 1960s.

When I arrived at the club I couldn't believe my eyes. Although dressed in a suit, Stephen was looped. I did not know this at the time, but he was on antidepressants and had made the mistake of having a drink to take the edge off. The result was that he could barely stand up. He had just recovered from his heart attack and looked like a withered old man, even though he was dressed in one of his thousand-dollar suits. I was dumbstruck.

The photographer, sensitive to this unusual situation, had Stephen pose in front of the weight machines. Considering the situation, the photograph came out rather well.

"What are you doing these days?" the photographer asked Stephen, just making conversation.

Stephen had no reply. He was so out of sorts from the combination of the alcohol and antidepressants that he simply broke down. It was a very awkward moment. I went back with him to his apartment.

The place turned out to be a gloomy lower-level one-bedroom flat tucked under a raised ranch located at the edge of a desolate field. Ironically, it was within walking distance of Knight Farms, the elite neighborhood in which he had grown up. Esther had been forced to sell her Knight Farms house just a year before. The assets of the Rosati Group had been sold, and their revenue stream had ended. To continue the fight, Esther needed to shelter at least several hundred thousand dollars. On top of that, she was covering the cost of Stephen's residence, so she needed to find an inexpensive place of her own. She chose an apartment complex for retired people in Newport.

Stephen feared he had ruined his name. "I didn't know what to say when that guy asked me what I was doing," he sobbed, referring to the *Warwick Beacon* photographer.

I had never seen a person so unhappy. Even though I am trained in psychology, I was overwhelmed. Leaving Stephen alone was out of the question. I waited for Esther to arrive.

"You are working this case," I said with conviction.

That simple statement put matters back into perspective, and this moment became a turning point. Dealing with this lawsuit now became a full-time occupation. Stephen had avoided the case because, in his own words, he "lived it," but now it was business. From that day on, Stephen turned his attention to learning everything he could. He stopped combining liquor with antidepressants and thus began to get his life back on track.

In January 2003, Cindy Imperato called Esther to inform her that Governor Jeb Bush had appointed her to a judgeship of the 17th Judicial Circuit Court in Broward County. Two years earlier she had been nominated and, at that time, had asked Stephen to write a letter on her behalf. From time to time, she would fax appropriate articles on the continuing climate of corruption, meet with Avery when he was down to depose witnesses, or speak to Esther directly as the suit against the Broward Sheriff's Office waxed and waned. She also swapped Christmas cards with the Rosatis every year. When Carl passed away, she called Esther to give her condolences.

A graduate of Virginia Polytechnic Institute, class of 1979, Cindy obtained a master's degree from Florida State University and then enrolled in their law program. She received her doctorate of jurisprudence in 1988. Advisory member to the Broward County Crime Commission on ethical issues—a post she shared with the state attorney general, Broward County chief of police, and dignitaries such as Congressman Foley and Alexander Haig—Cindy was also an adjunct professor at Nova Southeastern University, where she taught criminal pretrial practices.

This was tremendous news because she was one of the good guys. From what Cicilline could gather, all the Broward Sheriff's Office would have in their arsenal would be three cops of dubious reputation, who Cicilline was going to put on the witness stand anyway, and the drug dealer who was at the scene of the crime, Vic Giordano, who was still willing to testify that he thought the "big guy" was Stephen. The Rosatis, on the other hand, would have the governor-appointed statewide independent prosecutor, the FDLE detective who cracked the case, and not one, but two judges. Cicilline opted not to have me testify as a handwriting expert because the bookkeeper who co-signed Stephen's payroll checks was living in Southern Florida, and she could verify the bank checks instead.

On August 29, 2003, I contacted one of my expert witness colleagues, Ruth Holmes, one of the country's leading professionals in jury selection, whose resume included two nationally publicized assisted suicide trials of "Dr. Death" Jack Kevorkian, which he won. Even though he was later convicted, Holmes's work had been duly noted. She also appeared on national TV, including *The Barbara Walters Show*. Holmes discussed the case with Esther and Jack.

"This is a tricky proposition," she cautioned. "You are seeking a person who will give sympathy and remuneration for Stephen on the one hand, and yet on the other hand also have within them the capacity to move against the establishment. This is a double-bind situation. You want jurors to be emotional, generous, and sympathetic to Stephen from whatever profession they come from but also enraged by the system that betrayed him."

Ruth went on to discuss how Jack should present his final arguments using colorful poster boards with archetypal images. These would include a symbol for Stephen's home and one for his office, a telephone to indicate telephone records, a gas station for the credit card receipts, a bank for the salary checks, and a poster of a church to represent the christening Stephen attended the day of the murder. The idea was to present these powerful symbols portraying Stephen as a church-going Rhode Island businessman to the brain's right hemisphere, which reacted to more subconscious visual and emotional stimuli.

"Your presentation," she concluded, "needs to empower the jury to support law and order and also to hold it accountable."

Not only did Jack have to worry about the mix of the jury, but he also needed to try and discern whom the dominant one or ones would be. This was the centerpiece of Ruth's argument: to not only find sympathetic individuals, but also to locate ones strong enough to combat an opposing point of view and at the same time influence fence-sitters, such as the timid and conventional types who are incapable of appreciating how merciless these law enforcement officials could really be.

Jack minimized Ruth's assessment. There was no possible way Jack Cicilline would use poster boards in any final summary. However, he did factor in some of what she said and proceeded to deal with the difficult task of selecting a jury with Doug Bates, Pete the Greek's attorney. Potential jurors were warned that this case could take a month or more to be resolved. Cicilline and Bates felt fortunate that they were able to load the jury with women, who they hoped would be sympathetic.

On September 21, 2003, the trial began. It was covered almost daily by writers who were well familiar with this case from both leading Southern Florida newspapers, Paula McMahon of the *Sun-Sentinel* and Dan deVise and Wanda DeMarzo from the *Miami Herald*. These three writers, their cohorts, and these two newspapers had long led the charge in revealing decades of corruption in the Broward Sheriff's Office. Most recently, DeMarzo and deVise had begun a series of reports discussing the reason BSO's conviction rate was legions ahead of the national average. According to their analysis, which appeared in an October 7 article on mishandled cases, it was not because BSO was better at solving crimes but because they were better at fixing results.

One well-known case was that of Frank Lee Smith, who went to death row in 1985 for the rape and murder of eight-year-old Shandra Whitehead. Convicted on a "shaky ID" by the victim's mother, Smith was later exonerated when DNA evidence pointed the way to serial killer Eddie Lee Mosley, who by this time was dead.

"Rather than concede the identification was flawed, sheriff's administrators suggested another theory," wrote DeMarzo and deVise. "Smith," BSO concluded, "was in on the crime with Mosley."[1]

Paula McMahon of the competing *Sun-Sentinel* used the same Frank Lee Smith case as her lead-in to the Rosati, Roussonicolos, and Dallas civil trial. Boldly titling her article "Civil Trial Started in Broward Wrongful Arrest," Paula wrote, "If a jury agrees with the plaintiffs, the verdict could come with a hefty price tag."

Like her *Miami Herald* competitors, Paula had been waiting a long time for this botched Viscido homicide case to finally come to a head, and she scored a coup when she interviewed John Aguero, the veteran Polk County prosecutor appointed by the governor to sort things out.

"Dallas's confession was coerced," Aguero declared. "The police acted improperly. They had blinders on and they wouldn't listen to anything that didn't fit in with their theory of the case. It is probably the most disturbing thing that can happen to you as a prosecutor when you realize that police officers are lying to you."

Paula's opening salvo, "This trial is his final hope to remove the taint of trauma of his arrest," ended with a quote from Stephen Rosati.

"It doesn't follow me. It has become me. I was in the prime of my life and they took my best years away."[2]

The article did not go unnoticed.

The Rosatis had settled into a Comfort Inn near the courthouse along with Jack. To avoid the press, they told the front desk to keep their whereabouts private. Since witnesses would be flown in, they kept a series of rooms available. Living arrangements alone would run upwards of $500 per day. Both Breece and Aguero would be arriving shortly. Since Cindy Imperato's office was close by, they stopped in to arrange when she would testify. Her office was just down the hall from that of Judge Ilona Holmes, who would be trying the case.

Cindy stood out because she was a female and, more importantly, because now she was a judge and married with a child. She greeted them cordially. After exchanging small talk, Cindy dropped the bombshell. She was not willing to testify. The Rosatis were taken aback.

"Why?" Esther asked incredulously.

"This is awkward. I have to deal with these policemen all the time. You have Breece, and you have Aguero. It would be overkill anyway; you really don't need me."

Nor would either of Stephen's former girlfriends agree to testify.

Stephen had been out of contact with both of his girlfriends for over a decade. Elodie Vanderpyl was perhaps Stephen's most important witness because she could verify that she had been with him in Rhode Island the day of the murder. There was a distance in Elodie's voice when Stephen finally reached her. She said she'd get back to him and called back a few hours later to say she wanted money. The Rosatis saw this as unethical, and Jack felt they didn't really need her. As for Kara Lynx, who had been such a strong witness for both the 1990 extradition and Florida trial, she made it clear that she had a new life and in no way would she come. She had left that past long behind. Trying to force her was out of the question. Dejected, Stephen put down the phone. It was a telling blow.

Jack was still confident. He had Aguero; he had Breece; he had Stephen's Florida lawyer, Victor Tobin, now a judge; and he had Mrs. Salvadoro, the Rosati's bookkeeper, who co-signed all of Stephen's paychecks in his presence throughout that entire period

To my mind, Elodie's testimony was crucial even if it had to be paid for. Since I was writing this book, I thought it best not to testify and offered to prep a Florida handwriting expert to verify Stephen's signatures at the crucial times, but experts are expensive, and most of this was trumped by the bookkeeper's testimony. Jack decided to emphasize other aspects, although I stayed on the witness list. He was holding quite a number of trump cards.

The trial began on September 22, 2003.[3] It was held at the Broward County Courthouse on South East 6th Street, located in the heart of Fort Lauderdale just blocks from the high-end district, which ran along New River, a large meandering waterway that fed into the Intracoastal Waterway. The nine-story building was filled with courtrooms. It also abutted a massive jailhouse.

Detective Frank Puccini arrived on opening day, overweight and dressed in full uniform, gun included. Detective Sergeant Chevy McNeil opted to wear a suit. The lynchpin, Sheriff Bobby Coyote, however, was nowhere to be seen. Still injured from a car accident, Coyote had been forced into disability retirement. Now under heavy medication due to chronic back pain, gimpy, and walking with a cane, he had submitted a medical note to the judge to be excused from testifying. The rumor circulated that if Coyote attended at all, it would be on a gurney.

Stuart Michelson headed the defense representing Detective Sergeant Chevy McNeil and Bruce Jolly represented Detectives Bobby Coyote and Frank Puccini. This was a new twist for the cops, because up until now they were almost always part of the prosecution. Now they would feel the sting of being the victim.

"Michelson is skinny," commented Stephen, "with that horseshoe of hair circling his bald spot, and a squinched face. Jolly, on the other hand, is a plump Irishman, with his gut hanging over his beltline. I can't get the image of Laurel and Hardy out of my mind, but these guys are not in it for the laughs. This is their bread and butter." Collectively, they and their law partners had earned over one million dollars in the dozen or so years they were on the case, and their tab was still running."

Unlike the plaintiff's counsels, who were working on a contingency basis, Michelson and Jolly and their respective firms were each being paid by the state over a thousand dollars a day. They approached the attorneys for Rosati, Dallas, and Pete the Greek. The number of

$500,000 was tossed out to Rosati and $175,000 was mentioned as a possible figure for Dallas and Pete the Greek. Stephen and Esther had not spent a dozen years fighting for their day in court to settle in a pretrial arrangement, particularly when their out-of-pocket expenses and business losses were four times the amount of that figure.

Dallas decided to settle. He was the bad guy in this tale, and he knew it. He took the money and counted his blessings. Peter Roussonicolos was a different breed altogether. He owned a Porsche, and $175,000 was not a lot of money to him, particularly when a third of it would go to Bates. Hoping that his twenty-odd convictions could be kept out of court, Pete the Greek decided to ride Rosati's coattails. He too had been maligned and sent to prison for a year and a half for a crime he had nothing to do with.

Since Stephen's situation was so radically different from that of Pete the Greek's, Jack Cicilline tried to get the case separated, but Judge Holmes would hear none of it. She was not about to have an entire trial be repeated for two individuals who had been arrested together, right or wrong, for the same murder.

"All rise," the bailiff announced.

In full robes and with a commanding presence, Judge Ilona M. Holmes entered. A large, attractive African American who enjoyed the oddity of wearing multicolored spiked heels beneath her robes, Ilona had advanced to a judgeship at the mere age of thirty-six and been promoted just three years later by Governor Lawton Chiles to the prestigious 17th Judicial Circuit Court in Fort Lauderdale. Glossing over her relative lack of experience, the governor pontificated, "Ilona has done a stellar job as a county judge and is deserving of elevation to the circuit court."

Holmes is just the fourth black judge appointed to the Broward County judgeship since Florida became a state. In comparison, it took John Sheehan, the judge who ruled on the Rosati extradition hearing, a number of bitter years of turndowns before he obtained his judgeship, and by that time he was well over sixty, with more than thirty-five years' experience as a prominent trial lawyer.

Now forty-four years old, Ilona gave the impression of a woman who knew what she was doing. Aware that this was a high-profile case, Ilona made no bones about telling the newspaper photographers on more than one occasion to "shoot my good side."

Esther looked up in appreciation. Had it not been for Judge Holmes, this case might never have gotten to trial. But Judge Holmes also had a capricious side. For reasons difficult to comprehend, she barred from testimony such key witnesses as Boyce Rickenbach, the actual wheelman in the Viscido homicide; Mrs. Salvadoro, the Rosatis' bookkeeper who co-signed salary checks with Stephen during the time of the killing; Lawrence Copp, the accountant who charged $15,000 to study the Rosatis' books and verify business losses in excess of $800,000; and Carlyn Benkhart, Stephen's sister, who he picked up at T. F. Green Airport in Rhode Island the day before Viscido was killed.

Since Rosati and Roussonicolos were the plaintiffs, they would present their cases first. Cicilline decided to start off with perhaps his biggest gun, Peter Dallas. Esther was well aware of the irony. She had written out the checks to cover the plane flight and hotel bill for the man who knowingly lied by accusing her son of murder, recanted, and then settled for a hefty sum out of court.

Since Dallas had taken a lie detector test in a closed-door session, Michelson argued that it should not be admissible, and Judge Holmes concurred. She stated that lie-detector testimony would not be permitted.

"Fine," conceded Cicilline.

Bruce Jolly, arguing for the detectives, gave an opening statement. Pointing out Rosati and Roussonicolos as if they were cohorts, Jolly began, "If these two men were not the killers, the evidence we will present suggested that they were the killers. As we will show from their actions, these were better than good subjects."

The counsels for the plaintiffs presented two somewhat different scenarios. Jack Cicilline had not changed much in the dozen years between the extradition hearing and this culminating civil action. A large stocky man of imposing stature, Jack was dead-on serious. He painted a terrifying image of misguided detectives who would go "to any lengths" to imprison their targeted suspects even when confronted with overwhelming evidence that pointed them in another direction.

Doug Bates, Pete the Greek's attorney, was physically much smaller than Cicilline. With black hair slicked back, a moustache, and humorless demeanor, Bates argued that his client, Peter Roussonicolos, was targeted by the Broward Sheriff's Office because he was a perennial irritant due to his previous arrest record and the minimal ability of BSO to make anything else against him stick. "This is a case of egregious police misconduct, a vendetta pure and simple, because they wanted him," he pointed to Pete, "and they wanted him," he pointed to Stephen, "two innocent men, to go to jail for a crime neither one of them committed."

All witnesses would have to be sequestered. This meant that Esther would have to stay in the hallway during the rest of the trial, an action that could take a month or more. Naturally, she was not happy. In fact, this was the key reason why Esther did not testify at Stephen's extradition hearing thirteen years earlier. She wanted to sit in the courtroom to support her son. Resigned, she moved into the hall as Peter Dallas took the stand.

A scruffy man, now forty and barely five foot five, Dallas opted smartly to wear a suit. Unlike his old wild days, his hair was cropped short. A high school dropout, he now had a job working for a builder in the Midwest. Dallas had testified on several occasions over the last decade, called in whenever a defendant needed to show how BSO had intimidated witnesses. He thus was well tested on the stand. He sat confidently and stated that he had been terrorized and threatened with the electric chair by Detectives Coyote and Puccini if he did not confess to the murder of Joseph Viscido, Jr., even though he told them he had nothing to do with it.

"And why was that?" Cicilline asked.

"I was desperate. I had no power, no money. They made me think the only way I could escape the electric chair was to sign on. They brought me to tears, so I played along."

Puccini squirmed in his seat but tried to look dignified as Dallas pounded the table in a re-enactment of how Detective Coyote slammed his fist on photo after photo of the crime scene, to force Dallas to say exactly what they wanted. Scott Andron, writing in the October 3 issue of the *Miami Herald*, caught the flavor of his speech.

"When I couldn't answer no questions, they made me listen to those tape recordings—saying 'Peter Dallas did this and Peter Dallas did that.' Detective Coyote was like, 'This is what we want you to say.'"

Not to be outdone, Paula McMahon filled in more details for the *Sun-Sentinel*. She wrote, "Dallas was simply browbeat into implicating his cousin, Pete the Greek, who he knew was innocent, and Stephen Rosati, a man he admitted now he had never met."

"They said, 'No. 5 is the guy you were with, right?' pointing to Carl Stephen Rosati," Dallas recalled. "Right," Dallas replied. "And then later, when I tried to change my statement, they just threatened me again and again with the death penalty."

The jury sat captivated as Dallas's body shivered.

"Did you eventually recant this testimony?" Cicilline asked.

"Yes I did. I'm sorry. This was the worst mistake of my life."

In a subsequent article, the *Sun-Sentinel* revealed that Dallas had settled out of court and that Rosati had been offered $500,000 by the BSO but had turned it down. Stephen had given Paula McMahon this information, but he had assumed naïvely that it had been said in confidence. Paula revealed all to Stuart Michelson perhaps because the source was obvious, or for another reason.

Michelson argued, "This act by Stephen Rosati was a breach of confidence on a detail of mediation under Florida law. Although my brother is from Rhode Island," Michelson continued, referring to Stephen's lawyer, "he should have known better in counseling his client. I am asking that Rosati be sanctioned from talking to the press and, further, that this case be dismissed."

Needless to say, Jack was not happy with Stephen's action. Stephen took it out on Paula McMahon, letting her know over the phone that he felt that she had betrayed his confidence. It was a tense time that night at the Comfort Inn.

"Jack, you're making me insecure."

"Esther, you'll never be insecure," Jack responded characteristically.

That Friday, Cicilline outlined the grave issues involved in this case.

"We are alleging that these Florida detectives conspired to coerce eyewitnesses to give false statements, that they hid evidence which pointed to other individuals, and that the constitutional rights of my client have been violated." Cicilline was not against sanctioning the Rosatis from speaking to the press, but, "looking at the entire case on balance," he argued, "this is not grounds for dismissal."

Judge Holmes returned with her ruling. She would not drop the case.

Wanda DeMarzo and Dan deVise, the two reporters for the *Miami Herald*, had been waiting a decade for this case to reappear. They would use this trial as a showcase to reveal other wanton actions by the Broward County Sheriff's Office. That Sunday, September 28, 2003, the *Miami Herald* highlighted a laundry list of misbehavior: groping inside the underwear of a teenage girl by a BSO deputy; pulling a driver out of his car by his hair (it was later determined that the man was a surgeon); sexual misconduct with a female cadet from the Police Youth Auxiliary; and moving a car-mounted video camera to hide the beating of a suspect. Michelson and Jolly were feeling mounting pressure to settle, but Stephen and Esther felt they had the winning cards and turned down another offer above the million-dollar mark.

The next witness to testify was Tony Martinelli, the tycoon and owner of Scalley's Saloon, who turned informant after being arrested for selling forged paintings. Martinelli had told Breece what he knew about the Viscido homicide in exchange for the possibility of obtaining an early release from prison. On the stand, Martinelli opted to wear a silk shirt open at the neck with tailored pants and alligator shoes. He explained how Carbonell and Phaedra returned after the homicide and threw Viscido's Uzi and the murder weapon into the lake behind his house. Martinelli described the bloody shirt of Kerry Carbonell that he helped launder and other details that made it clear that Carbonell and Phaedra were the real culprits in this case. Stephen commented that Martinelli had made an excellent witness.

Michelle Arrieta came next. Now in her late thirties, she recounted precisely in grim detail what she had gone through and told the court that she had not recognized anyone in the photo lineups but that her denials were seen as lies. She described how Coyote and Puccini had arrested her for an old traffic violation and kept her imprisoned for over eight hours with no access to a bathroom. She said that she broke down in tears and was very intimidated.

Michelle testified that at that interrogation she ID'd Pete the Greek as well as Stephen, though she knew, like Stephen, Pete had nothing to do with her boyfriend's death. She admitted that she did this "because I wanted to get the heck out of that tiny room and I wanted them to leave me alone." She recalled that Sergeant McNeil browbeat her into identifying Peter Dallas as one of the perpetrators after she told him repeatedly, "That wasn't the guy." This false identification occurred while assistant attorney general Chuck Morton looked on. Michelle ended on a high note, salvaging her reputation by letting the jury know that when she finally did see photo-pack lineups containing Phaedra and Carbonell, she picked Carbonell out and then picked Phaedra out at his trial.

Michelson and Jolly wanted to introduce Michelle's polygraph test into evidence, which she had passed. The implication supported the contention that Detectives Coyote and Puccini had every right to believe that Michelle's ID's of Rosati and Pete the Greek were legitimate. But Judge Holmes was firm in blocking this strategy. She would not allow such evidence to be presented.

"Lie-detector results are not admissible in criminal trials," the judge said in a side bar. "Further, they are rarely admissible in civil trials as well because they are not considered scientifically reliable evidence."

What Judge Holmes didn't know was that this lie detector test never contained any questions concerning Michelle identifying either Rosati or Pete the Greek. She passed the test because she was never asked a question that she had to lie about!

"I call Detective Chevy McNeil to the stand," said Cicilline.

McNeil looked haggard. He had made a severe blunder in this case, and it had already made the press and been discussed by the plaintiff's attorneys in their opening statements. During the height of his investigation into the Viscido homicide, DEA agent Ken Brennan had approached McNeil from Fort Lauderdale. Brennan had located a witness whose information seemed "on the money." The witness, Jay Prince, had told him that Kerry Carbonell and one Poppa Jim had perpetrated the Viscido homicide. Prince had also told McNeil that Carbonell and Poppa Jim often posed as Broward police officers to carry off their rips, so the MO matched as well.

After Michael Breece cracked the case, he noticed in BSO's records that Prince's admission to Sergeant McNeil, plus his identification of the real killers, was put on tape. When confronted, the detective sheepishly admitted that the tape did exist and that it was still in his possession.

Pete the Greek's attorney, Doug Bates, did the grilling. After asking Sergeant McNeil about his education and expertise, Bates was able to paint a picture of McNeil in 1990 as an inexperienced detective who coerced his witnesses into identifying men who had nothing to do with this murder by feeding them false information and then pressuring them into saying what he wanted them to say.

McNeil's greatest error was to not put Carbonell in a photo lineup that he could show Michelle Arrieta and the other witnesses. On the stand, McNeil admitted that he made a mistake when he typed in his official log that Michelle and the other witnesses were unable to identify Carbonell in such a lineup.

"And why didn't you hand this audiotape to Agent Breece when the second investigation was under way?" Bates asked McNeil.

"I just forgot about the tape entirely," McNeil responded weakly.

"Well, where was it?"

"I kept it in my athletic sock drawer at home along with a few other tapes," McNeil answered.

"Why the sock drawer?"

"Because I didn't want my wife or son to tape over it by mistake."

"And that's the reason you let it sit in your drawer—I mean your gym sock drawer—for eight months!" Bates asked incredulously.

"I already admitted I forgot it," McNeil retorted, adding lamely, "I mean, I didn't try to hide it." Because he had a leg injury, McNeil wasn't jogging anymore. That is why he said he had forgotten about the tape.

The Associated Press, numerous newspapers, and TV stations throughout the country—in particular, CNBC's *The Final Countdown* with Keith Olbermann—had fun with its lead: "Florida Officer Had Evidence in Sock Drawer while Suspects Sat in Jail."

The next day at trial, McNeil said that he didn't think of the tape as evidence because the transcript existed.

"You did ask for a receipt when you handed it over to Breece, didn't you?"

"Yes."

"And did Detective Coyote know about this tape and interrogation of Jay Prince?"

"Yes," McNeil admitted.

Called to the stand, Michael Breece, the man most responsible for saving the lives of three innocent men, discussed the great rift that occurred between FDLE and the Broward Sheriff's Office when it came to light that his investigation clashed with theirs. He explained how he cracked the case by finding Boyce Rickenbach, the actual wheelman, who told him about the guns in the lake. Breece told how he invited Chuck Morton and Detective Coyote to his offices to show them his evidence and to allow them to interview an important witness [Richard Whistler, a friend of Rickenbach]. But they ignored Breece and dismissed or minimized his work entirely. Breece also explained how the governor called in John Aguero to sort things out and how his side eventually prevailed. Jolly and Michelson were ineffectual in offsetting the implications of what this detective had to say.

The next witness was Victor Tobin, Stephen's lawyer while he was in Florida. When he took the stand, Judge Holmes made it clear that the jury should understand that Tobin was not testifying as a judge but as a lawyer who had defended Stephen Rosati at the time when this event took place. Nevertheless, Tobin was a judge, and it made a difference. To Esther, Jack, and Stephen's utter surprise, he turned out to be their best witness.

Coming on the heels of Breece's stinging testimony on the stand, Tobin continued the assault.

"I was unable to get their attention. They wouldn't listen or respond," the judge in the witness box said, captivating the jury, as he stared unflinchingly at Detectives McNeil and Puccini. He paused full measure before continuing. "The reason these detectives are sitting here today is because they had tunnel vision. They wouldn't listen to anything!"

Tobin had reprimanded the defendants in no uncertain way. Not only had they not listened to him, they had brazenly ignored other solid leads and withheld evidence that could have set Stephen Rosati free. It was a stunning moment, and Jack rushed out on the break to tell Esther.

"This is going to turn everything," Jack said, grinning. "Tobin has made a very big impression in the courtroom. Things couldn't have gone better."

The next day, Stephen and Pete took a tour of the jail with the full jury. Both local papers carried photographs of this dramatic excursion. Michelson and Jolly had tried to block the outing, but Judge Holmes allowed it. This act of seeing where Stephen and Pete the Greek had been incarcerated made a profound impact.

Cicilline called Chuck Morton to the stand. This was a rarity: Jack Cicilline, defense attorney as prosecutor, and Chuck Morton, assistant attorney general, on the defense. Like Judge Holmes, Morton was one of the few African Americans working in a high position of the legal branch for Broward County. As usual, Morton exuded an air of refinement, but he had never faced an opponent like Cicilline before.

Morton said he never would have sought indictments against Rosati and Roussonicolos had it not been for the confession of Peter Dallas. Then he complained that FDLE was not forthcoming in sending him any details of the case they were building against Carbonell and Phaedra.

Stephen couldn't believe it. "Morton was playing a game of cat and mouse, and Jack got ticked off," Stephen recounted.

Jack's aggression took Morton by surprise. From Jack's perspective, Morton was part of the problem, and Jack was going to try and get it out of him. But he became too aggressive. The judge cracked the gavel, warning Jack to tone it down.

Uncomfortable, Morton shifted in his seat and then continued to justify his position. Since Pete the Greek had been accused of similar crimes involving drug rip-offs in the past, it was reasonable, Morton said, to suspect him.

To prove Morton was culpable, Bates and Cicilline had to show that Morton willfully ignored evidence pointing to the innocence of Rosati, Dallas, and Pete the Greek. Jack reminded Morton that, at the time, Judge Goldstein had requested that Morton open up the case file that Michael Breece presented him while Stephen and Pete the Greek were still in jail. This fact overtly contradicted Morton's suggestion that FDLE had withheld information.

Here is where Cindy Imperato's testimony would have been crucial because she was there during this critical event. She had also been appalled that Morton had never opened up Breece's file, even when given an extra month to do so. Without Imperato, Cicilline improvised.

"Would you like me to bring in Judge Goldstein and have him tell the court that you refused his direct order to look at the Breece file?"

Morton was stuck. He startled the court by admitting that mistakes were made. Jack asked Morton what he thought about Detective McNeil withholding a surveillance tape from Breece. Morton assured the court that had he known about the Jay Prince tape he would have turned it over. He also agreed that the caliber of the witnesses against Rosati and Pete the Greek was not high.

"So all you really had was the Dallas confession. Am I right?"

"Yes," Morton said.

"And aside from that Dallas confession, there was no smoking gun?" Cicilline asked.

"Yes," Morton agreed, "There was no smoking gun."

Jack returned to the issue of the caliber of the witnesses and then asked Morton about the techniques that the police used to obtain their ID's of Rosati and Pete the Greek. Morton acknowledged that it was his function as assistant attorney general "to seek the truth." Jack thereupon got Morton to agree that "some of these witnesses had probably been coerced after lengthy, belligerent interrogations." This was a stunning admission.

"As Morton spoke," Dan deVise reported in the *Miami Herald*, "Bruce Jolly, the veteran attorney representing the police, was heard to mutter under his breath, 'Oh my God.'"

Morton was proving the plaintiff's case. He had refused to open Breece's report even after being ordered to do so by Judge Goldstein on two separate occasions in November and December of 1990. There was no excuse for this. So rather than digging himself into a bigger hole by trying to defend his indefensible position, Morton admitted in a more general sense that mistakes were made. But that tactic didn't work, as it became clear to the jury that, by his actions, Morton had indeed "willfully ignored evidence pointing to the innocence of the victims."

The next witness was Stephen Rosati. He spoke for an hour and succeeded on two fronts. First, he was able to outline the full extent of the business losses accrued by the Rosati Group and the cost of litigation to date. Documented out-of-pocket costs exceeded one million dollars, and that did not count the potential future revenues that were lost, nor did this figure take into account the cost of pain and suffering.

Stephen recalled how when first arrested in Rhode Island, Detective Coyote promised him a lighter sentence if he implicated Pete the Greek.

"He said I would fry in the electric chair if I didn't play along. But since I didn't know anything and didn't do anything, I refused to play along, and that is when I stepped into a world of madness that stays with me to this day."

Fighting back tears, Stephen described his ordeal in prison. "Nobody in this room will ever know the living hell I went through."

Barely able to contain his emotions, Stephen described the difference between the jail in Rhode Island, where physical contact with visitors was allowed on a regular basis, and the Florida jail, where they had to speak into phones through safety glass. Fearful of their conversations being bugged, Stephen said that when the real killers were found, his mother wrote this on a piece of paper and held it up to the window for him to read.

Judge Holmes cracked the gavel and warned the witness that she would not tolerate the use of the term *real killers*. She saw this as prejudicial and let it be known that such terminology could be the cause of a mistrial.

Taken aback by the judge's stance, Stephen collected himself and then continued with his description of what it was like to live in the jail that the jury had toured just a few days before. Tears welled up and he started to cry.

Halting Stephen in midsentence, the judge ordered the jury out. With the court cleared, the judge admonished Stephen for being "overly dramatic" in his presentation.

"Don't say what you think the jury wants to hear," she warned.

"Just give them the facts or I'll stop these proceedings right now."

It had taken Stephen over ten years to get to this point. He truly had reached the edge of his sanity, living through delay upon delay upon delay as this trial was postponed. Stephen had wanted to be a real estate developer and live a normal life. All of that had been taken from him. The jury was spellbound by what he had to say, but Judge Holmes suspected it was an act. Stephen reined himself in and waited for Jolly to rebut.

Jolly pointed out that Stephen had done very little in the world of business for the last five years. Most of the time had been spent working out and gaining and losing weight to compete in bodybuilding competitions. He had not held a steady job, did not have a steady girl, and had no social life. Stephen described himself as simply "paralyzed."

Jolly emphasized Stephen's lifestyle in 1985 when he worked in Florida as a male stripper and got involved in a drug deal gone bad. Jolly skipped neatly over the five years from late 1985 through September 1990, when Stephen was working as a successful home builder and real estate developer, and suggested that Stephen had rested his entire future on the hope that he would cash in with this lawsuit.

"So you have been waiting all this time for this case to make a change in your life?"

"Mr. Jolly," Stephen responded, "My life has been ruined for the last thirteen years."

"I have no more questions," Jolly said, turning back to his seat with an expression on his face that suggested that this was really all just a big scam.

The next day, Esther Rosati testified. This case should have gone to trial in 1995 or 1996, which was nearly a decade before, while Carl Rosati was still alive. But the lawyers for the Broward Sheriff's Office were masters at creating delay tactics. What was Esther to do? Should she have given up and simply dropped the case after BSO arrested her only son and then begrudgingly released him, destroying his life in the process and the livelihood of the family?

Certainly Esther hoped to benefit financially from this lawsuit, to recoup some of the losses that were sustained by the actions of a misguided police force. But that was really not the driving force behind Esther's actions. She wanted the world to understand that cops could be wrong or bad but also that misguided assistant attorneys general can be their dupes and send innocent people to jail or even to the electric chair rather than admit they got it wrong. You judge a person by her actions, not her rhetoric. Esther's actions from the moment Stephen was arrested was to do whatever she could to save her only son. Esther literally sacrificed everything toward that end.

Now seventy-sixyears old but still youthful in appearance, Esther was never seen without a stylish Madison Avenue outfit. She was born into a world of wealth and had lived her entire life at the top edge of society before it all collapsed, shortly after her husband passed away. She can turn some people off by her appearance. She can appear artificial to those who have no understanding. Esther got on the stand and let the horror of the ordeal all pour out. In eloquent prose, she described the nightmare of what had happened to her life. During a pregnant pause, she began to cry.

Stuart Michelson, sitting by Detective Puccini, was heard to mutter loud enough for the entire courtroom to hear, "What a joke!"

"Shut your fucking face, you faggot," Pete the Greek retorted.

Michelson had difficulty keeping a straight face, so Pete continued.

"How dare you laugh at a woman who has gone through all that suffering? You keep that up and I'm going to get you."

Judge Holmes banged the gavel several times and ordered the jury to leave the courtroom. Coming to Michelson's defense, Judge Holmes raised her voice and admonished Esther for displaying excessive emotion, calling her a "drama queen."

Esther couldn't believe it. Did the judge have no understanding of what she had endured to get to this point? Could she have stopped herself from crying?

Michelson asked that the case be dropped and that Pete the Greek be cited for contempt of court because of his threat. Judge Holmes called an adjournment. She would decide the following day whether or not to let the case continue.

Dan deVise interviewed Cicilline and Bates for the October 9, 2003, issue of the *Miami Herald*. "'If this case is dropped,' say his attorneys, 'that would be a shame.'" Although it was debated whether Pete the Greek said, "get you" or "kill you," "they concede Pete made the comments, but they stress that whatever he said came in the heat of painful testimony about a painful topic."

Judge Holmes weighed everything. She cited Peter Roussonicolos for contempt of court but decided on balance that Pete's outburst should not be the cause for dropping the lawsuit. There would be no rebuttal by Michelson or Jolly of Esther Rosati, at least for now.

Jack Cicilline called his final ace in the hole and last witness,

John Aguero, the well-respected, governor-appointed independent prosecutor who had freed three innocent men and put the right guys behind bars. Aguero had been shocked to find out that his partner in this case, Cindy Imperato, was not going to testify. He assured the Rosatis that he could bear the load.

After being sworn in, Aguero reviewed his resume as Polk County and statewide prosecutor for nearly twenty years. He said that he became skeptical of Detective Coyote's case because Coyote hid from him the tactics and amount of time he had actually spent in obtaining his confession from Peter Dallas. Aguero also said that Coyote told him that Carl Rosati was a Mafia leader in Rhode Island and that he had paid fall guys to take the rap for his son for the Viscido homicide.

"This was all proven to be false," Aguero said.

When Aguero mentioned the polygraph test that Peter Dallas had taken, Michelson jumped to his feet.

"Your honor, with the mention of Mr. Dallas's polygraph, we feel that this information has irreparably harmed our clients and we call for a mistrial."

"Bailiff," Judge Holmes directed, "please have the jurors leave the room."

Photographers for the newspapers caught her good side as the judge glared down at the independent prosecutor. "I said I would not tolerate any discussion of polygraphs. Mr. Aguero. You have been around long enough to know, or you should have known, the ramifications of your actions. You may step down."

"Bailiff, call back the jury."

According to Dan deVise and Wanda DeMarzo, writing for the October 10 edition of the *Miami Herald*, Judge Holmes was "bellowing."

"I am calling a mistrial. This case is over."

Like that, without spending even a moment in chambers to consider an action that would stop a suit that had taken over ten years to get to court, the civil suit ended. Standing in her robes and multicolored spiked heels, Judge Ilona Holmes exited the courtroom.

Appalled, Esther would refer to the proceedings in a future letter to the editor of the *Miami Herald* as "a kangaroo court." Stephen was in shock, but Jack said it was a good thing because in his nearly forty years of experience he had never seen such ineptness.

"We're better off without her," he said.

Aguero was stunned. With tears in his eyes, he walked over to the

Rosatis and apologized.

"There is nothing to apologize for," Stephen told the man who had set him free. "It wasn't your fault. It was the judge."

Aguero went up to Cindy Imperato's office to regroup and tell his former partner what had occurred. Soon after, Aguero reported to Stephen and Esther how startled he was to see, of all people, Chuck Morton come out of Cindy's room! It was a very awkward moment.

"We'll get 'em next time," Stephen assured Aguero. They shook hands and parted.

The jurors were taken aback. Several came over and hugged Esther. A middle-aged woman, the owner of a gas station, said in no uncertain terms that they would have awarded the Rosatis a figure in excess of ten million dollars, in comparison to a proposed miniscule award for Pete the Greek, perhaps $95,000.

"It's very unfair what happened to these people," another juror told the *Sun-Sentinel*. "I feel very sad that this [trial] ended now. This was a gut-wrenching, awful thing . . . to put these people's lives on hold once again."

Another said, "She knew [we] only heard about half the evidence in the case, but she doubted attorneys for the Sheriff's Office and the detectives could explain away what happened." Other jurors, who did not want to be identified, nodded in agreement as she spoke.

Esther's out-of-pocket costs for this trial were over $30,000. There was nothing left to do but return to Rhode Island and wait for the retrial. It was set for February 2004. Roussonicolos would be arrested and jailed on the contempt charge shortly thereafter.

Salvage

For the second trial, the Rosatis were advised on how to deal with Pete the Greek. Esther was urged *repeatedly* to get rid of Pete by allowing him a piece of their case. She simply hated the idea of benefiting a person who one way or another had been responsible for what had happened to her son. Stephen took the advice and offered to pay Pete a percentage if he agreed to get out, but Esther opposed this idea. "Jack says we don't owe him a thing," Esther rationalized. There was no changing her mind, particularly with Jack's blockheaded stance. Nevertheless, Stephen persisted, but he couldn't come to an agreement with Pete as to what would be fair, and they argued on the phone.

It was obvious that the Rosatis' position would be legions stronger without Pete the Greek sitting next to Stephen during a new trial, but there was a counterargument; namely, that the jury in the previous trial, knowing about Pete's record, was still willing to award Stephen a hefty settlement. Pete was also myopic. According to Stephen, Pete preferred the limelight to stepping aside and accepting a reasonable settlement from whatever the Rosatis might realize.

Pete's contempt of court trial came up in the interim, presided over by Judge Ilona Holmes. She chose her bright red spiked heels for the occasion. Pete's attorney put the incident into perspective.

"Talk about a mountain out of a mole hill," he said. "We were all there. Mrs. Rosati was crying, Mr. Michelson burst out laughing. In the heat of the moment, Pete lost his temper and yelled something. There is no doubt that Mrs. Rosati has suffered because of the wrongful imprisonment of her son. This contempt trial shouldn't even be taking place."

Judge Holmes was not swayed. Peter Roussonicolos was convicted for contempt of court and sentenced to four months. But his suit against BSO would continue. In total, he spent fifty-one days in jail, one extra day than the sentence called for, counting time off for good behavior. Pete was supposed to be released two days before the upcoming civil action, but Judge Holmes could not be located at the proper time to sign off on the debt. Since the new trial was about to take place, it would greatly hamper the plaintiffs' case if one of them was absent because he was sitting in jail. Obviously, Holmes knew this but delayed Pete's release until the last possible moment. He got out less than twenty-four hours before the new trial was to begin.

Stephen, appearing trim and fitting neatly into one of his thousand-dollar suits, looked like dynamite when he arrived in Fort Lauderdale on February 18, 2004. He had gained confidence due to the overall success of the last trial. On the whole, the Rosatis were pleased with the new judge, Thomas Lynch. An amiable man with a beard and a ponytail, he resembled an ex-hippie. In a prime example of how arbitrary the law can be, Judge Lynch saw nothing wrong with discussing polygraph test results during the trial. He also had no qualms about the use of the term *the real killers* when referring to Carbonell and Phaedra, and he would allow every Rosati witness to testify that had been barred by Judge Holmes.

Another big difference in this trial was the idea that the detectives would be personally liable as well as the Broward Sheriff's Office. It was the same situation in the first trial, but this point came out in more pointed fashion.

Michelson argued that the jury was tainted and an entirely new jury was chosen, one that seemed, in Esther's words, "more upgraded, with more quality."

But they did lose four women who were critical of the police department. Both Jack and Esther were satisfied with the new jury of three women and three men, including a teacher, a builder, and an architect—all college educated. The architect, like the judge, wore a ponytail, which gave him an independent air. With two people on the jury involved in the world of home building, Stephen felt good about testifying. He knew that when he explained the details of his business, he had two jurors who could easily identify with what he would be saying.

At the opening, Cicilline hammered home the idea that Sergeant McNeil kept a tape recording that could have exonerated his client. "He'll tell you that he forgot that it was at his home in his sock drawer, but you'll have to decide whether he's telling the truth about that, or if it's just a cover-up."

Michelson and Jolly took a different approach, as the *Sun-Sentinel* reported, "toughening their legal strategy to discredit Rosati" through his association with Pete the Greek. "Roussonicolos has twenty-two felony convictions, and Rosati socialized with criminals," Michelson said. Because of Pete the Greek's known past criminal activities and because of Rosati's lifestyle, said Jolly, "the detectives were acting in good faith and had legally sufficient reasons to arrest the men."

After opening arguments, Michelson approached Jack and offered his clients $350,000 if they would take Puccini out of the case. The man was afraid he was going to lose his house. It was still up in the air as to whether or not they could get Detective Coyote on the stand, and without Coyote, if Puccini was out, all that would be left would be McNeil, who ultimately was not the man who arrested Stephen.

Jack needed Puccini. The deal was passed up. Michelson then offered a million dollars to be divided between Stephen and Pete the Greek any way they wanted. It was insulting to the Rosatis to lump the two men together as if they were in the same boat. And, of course, there would be no equitable way to split such a settlement. Jack let Michelson know that the Rosatis' accountant would be testifying and that he could verify over $800,000 in lost business and several hundred thousand more in legal fees. These were just out-of-pocket costs the figures didn't include the loss of future business and punitive damages.

"Come back with something realistic," Jack said.

Detective Coyote was questionable because he had letters from doctors stipulating that it would be nearly impossible for him to endure the physical requirements of coming to the courtroom and being on the stand. Stephen got the idea to hire a private detective to tail Coyote and videotape him to see just how handicapped he really was. They chose Jeff Fuller of Out of the Box Investigations.

Peter Dallas took the stand and, once again, explained how Detectives Coyote and Puccini threatened him with the electric chair if he would not agree to say that he did the deed with Rosati and Pete the Greek. The jury watched intently.

Stephen dialed up Cindy Imperato to try and convince her to change her mind and testify, but she had caller ID and would not answer the phone. Esther decided to go to her courtroom, and Cindy met with Esther in chambers.

"All we want is for you to verify that Morton never opened up Breece's pack. That's it."

"I've made my decision." the judge said, a complex look of concern in her eyes.

"This is unacceptable, Cindy. I think I deserve an explanation. You, of all people, know what I have gone through and what we're up against. You've received letters of recommendation to gain your judgeship from John Aguero and from Stephen, who *you* called. And now, Aguero tells me you are meeting with Morton! I find your actions lack integrity."

"How dare you impugn my integrity!" Judge Imperato blasted back. "This conversation is over."

"Cindy, it's taken me more than ten years to get here. Every day is a struggle. You can't just sit there through your silence and enable corruption to continue right here in your county."

"Mrs. Rosati, let me be as blunt as I can. Do not ever say that I lack integrity or I will see you in court. I can understand your anger, but I am not going to testify. Do not ever call me again."

One wonders if Cindy brought up her decision to avoid testifying as a key witness in a wrongful imprisonment case when she met with her colleagues at the Broward County Crime Commission to discuss ethical issues.

Back at trial, Cicilline proceeded to skewer Sergeant McNeil when he got on the stand. He got McNeil to admit that he kept the tape of Jay Prince in his sock drawer and never released it to Detective Breece. He got McNeil to admit that he "made a mistake" in his logbook when he wrote that Michelle Arrieta did not pick Carbonell out in a photo lineup because she never saw this suspect in a lineup. And, in a masterful stroke, Jack even got McNeil to admit that both Stephen and Pete the Greek were innocent of the crime he had accused them of.

"I'd never seen anything like it, the way he destroyed him!" Stephen said.

The next witness was Sergeant McNeil's partner, Jeffrey Burndt. Jack wanted Burndt to support the supposition that McNeil ignored, hid, or tampered with evidence, and that McNeil altered his logbook about the Carbonell matter.

Stephen looked up at Burndt and, as it was alleged, mouthed the words "You're going down."

Nothing was said out loud. In point of fact, Detective Burndt told Stuart Michelson that Stephen had mouthed this sentence but did not say it out loud. This was reported to the judge. Michelson asked that Stephen be held in contempt.

Noah Bierman of the *Miami Herald* interviewed Jack about it and reported the story in the March 10 edition. Cicilline conceded that if indeed Stephen had threatened Detective Burndt with those words that it was grounds for contempt. Jack would not tolerate this kind of behavior from his client, and he let Stephen know it in no uncertain terms.

"I didn't do anything," Stephen retorted. "This guy's a lip-reader?"

Judge Lynch sent the jury out of the room and then reprimanded Rosati. "I'm going to have to sleep on this contempt of court request," he said, adjourning court for the day.

"Oh, this is all bullshit," Stephen spat when they got outside. "These assholes can send me to fucking death row on fake evidence and they're complaining that I may have mumbled something under my breath. Jack, this is insane. I didn't do anything."

Jack was pensive. "Do you understand the judge could drop this case?" He didn't have to say anything more. Stephen did not have an easy night. As he did every evening while the trial was in progress, he took out his Bible and prayed to enter God's tabernacle.

With the jury still out the next morning, Judge Lynch announced his decision. The case would continue. The contempt of court citation would be decided later. Eight months after this case was concluded, Stephen had to fly down to Florida with Jack to face the contempt of court charge. Burndt testified that he read Rosati's lips but did not hear anything. Jack established that Detective Burndt was not a qualified lip-reader. No one else heard or saw anything. Stephen was not convicted.

The day after McNeil and Burndt testified, Jeff Fuller, the private detective, met Jack and Stephen at the hotel. "You are not going to believe this!"

The investigator popped a tape into the recorder. Taken from across the street from the retired detective sheriff's house, Jack and Stephen watched Robert R. Coyote shuffle out of his house, walk over to his wife's Grooms to Grow dog-grooming truck, and fill up one of its tanks with water. An old motorcycle could be seen in the garage in the background. He stooped from the car injury and used a metal cane to help him walk. He was, however, limber enough to walk at a brisk pace a good quarter-mile down the block to his neighbor's house and also shuffle at that same pace back. Another segment showed Coyote climbing into what Stephen described as "their big humongous truck" to go to work. Coyote drove with his wife by his side and later filled up the truck by himself at a gas station. The doctors had painted a picture of Detective Coyote as completely bedridden, essentially unable to drive. This clearly was not the case.

Jack was elated. Coyote would have to testify, and Jack would make a motion to show this tape in court, which belied Coyote's medical note portraying him as an invalid.

Much of the trial played like the last one. Michelle Arrieta testified, as did Tony Martinelli, Michael Breece, John Aguero, and Judge Tobin. All made strong witnesses. As with the first trial, Michelle Arrieta explained how she was coerced into identifying people she knew to be innocent and how once she saw photos of the actual perpetrators, Carbonell and Phaedra, she immediately picked out Carbonell and then later when on the witness stand, ID'd Phaedra during his trial. Again, Judge Tobin, Stephen's former defense counsel, reprimanded the police for having blinders on. "These men," he said, "brought this case upon themselves because of their own machinations."

John Aguero, the independent prosecutor, supported this opinion. Aguero made it quite clear that he had looked over both cases and found great fault with the one assembled by BSO. Consequently, he freed three innocent men, arrested and successfully prosecuted the right suspects, and put them in jail.

"How did you know you had the right men this time?" Cicilline wanted to know.

Aguero explained the evidence, in particular the guns found in the lake, including the one that killed Joseph Viscido, Jr., which was registered to James Phaedra, one of the two thugs he successfully put away.

On the stand, Michael Breece explained once again how he located the real wheelman, Boyce Rickenbach, and how he tried to explain to Detective Coyote and Chuck Morton why their case was no good.

"I asked them to come by to interview my witnesses for themselves, but even though they came, they just ignored the testimony and belittled me," Breece said. Martinelli again confirmed that Phaedra and Carbonell returned to his house after the deed to throw the guns into the lake and clean the blood off Carbonell's shirt.

Where the first trial was cut short at four weeks, this trial would last ten. This time, the bookkeeper, Mrs. Salvadoro, testified, verifying that Stephen did indeed co-sign payroll checks every Friday throughout October 1986. Carlyn Benkhart, Stephen's sister, was also allowed on the stand. She confirmed that the day before the murder took place, Stephen picked her up at the airport. She knew he was in Rhode Island the following day as well. Neither Kara nor Elodie testified, but it didn't seem to matter. Key portions of their extradition hearing transcripts were read to the jury instead. There was no doubt that Stephen was innocent of this crime. That wasn't the point. It was the tactics of the police that were on trial.

A surprise witness for Rosati was Jeff Bloom, the man who—according to McNeil and Coyote's scenario—had the supposed safe house that Dallas returned to after Joe Viscido was killed. In riveting testimony, Bloom admitted he was petrified that he would die in the electric chair if he didn't play along and falsely ID the men he was told to ID: his friend Peter Dallas; Pete the Greek, whom he also knew; and Stephen Rosati, whom he had never met.

"I didn't have a choice," Bloom confessed. "I didn't want to die like my father, who was blasted in the back with a shotgun by the cops just a year earlier." Shocked, the jury sat transfixed as Bloom described the ordeal. "I didn't know nothing about how Joe got it, and I pleaded with the cops to give me a lie detector test, but they just wouldn't. I'll admit it, man. I was scared."

The judge sent the jury out of the room but allowed the reporters to stay. Bloom described how, like his father just a year before, his brother was murdered.

"Skip just wouldn't play along. And wouldn't you know it, just a couple a weeks after the grand jury meeting, we found his body by the side of the road. It was tossed out of a moving car in a blanket along with our dog. I was scared out of my wits, Your Honor, and I want it known that if they find me dead in the next few weeks it won't be a suicide."

On cross-examination, after the jury had returned, Jolly revealed that Bloom's father was killed in a drug raid that was unrelated to the Viscido homicide. He asked if Bloom had been convicted of any crimes. Bloom pleaded the Fifth Amendment. Jolly asked for Bloom's address, but he refused to give it.

"I'm afraid I'll be killed if the cops know where I live," he said.

The judge threatened to strike his testimony if he refused to answer questions and then called a break to cut this testimony short and to allow Bloom to speak to his attorney.

When the trial resumed, Jolly accused Rosati, Pete the Greek, and their attorneys of speaking improperly to Bloom.

"Your Honor," Jolly said "I am requesting," he paused a split second for full dramatic effect, "a mistrial, Your Honor, a mistrial."

"Request denied," Lynch said without missing a beat. "Mr. Bloom, you may continue."

Jolly feigned devastation by the denial. The jury smiled at his shenanigans.

"That will do, Mr. Jolly. Mr. Bloom, please continue."

Bloom admitted to two criminal convictions.

Chuck Morton followed. As with the first trial, he could not counter Cicilline's barrage. As an assistant attorney general, he had no excuse for not opening up the FDLE envelope, which contained information on Breece's competing investigation, so again he simply admitted mistakes were made.

Detective Coyote was up next. Contorted into a permanent hunch caused by his car accident, Detective Coyote limped into court with the help of his cane and a stomach pump that delivered a painkiller. Jack tore him apart in forty minutes.

"Your warrant stipulates that Rosati not only was accused of being involved in the Viscido homicide but also that he was living in Florida at that time. Isn't that right?"

"Yes, sir," Coyote replied, popping a pill.

"Well, if that was the case, why didn't you obtain your own handwriting expert to look at all the bank checks and gasoline credit card receipts he signed to see if it was really his handwriting?"

"I didn't think of it."

"Well, you saw the testimony of the Rhode Island expert whereby we established that these checks were signed by Rosati. Isn't that right?"

And so it went. Stephen described Coyote as "being crucified."

On cross, most of Coyote's strategy concerned his reading of the police logs. The testimony literally took hours as he went on and on in a monotone. Members of the jury were rolling their eyes. Coyote even played the audiotape of Peter Dallas's confession.

"It sounded exactly like he was leading Dallas on," Stephen said. "What a jerk."

Jack then called Detective Frank Puccini to the stand.

"I didn't have anything to do with it," Puccini protested, but a thorough shredding proved otherwise.

Cicilline and Bates culminated with the two plaintiffs followed by the grieving mother. As with the last trial, Stephen found himself bursting into tears when he described his ordeal, trying to survive in prison, dealing with the aftermath, the great loss of family business, his father's death, the endless delays of trying to have his day in court, his bouts with depression and alcohol, and finally the destruction of the life he thought he would have.

Pete the Greek was more staid. He did not deny that he had a criminal record. He just stated as clearly as he could that he was falsely accused of this crime and spent a year and a half in jail for something he didn't do.

Esther followed. In gut-wrenching terms, she recalled her family's own "personal holocaust." Poignantly, she described how Stephen changed from his time in jail in Rhode Island to his time in Florida.

"He was becoming bloated from the bad food and his skin had become sallow. He was a young man in his thirties, but now his hair was turning gray."

"That wasn't the worst of it," she said. "After a few months in the Broward jail, he seemed to give up. He didn't even want us to visit anymore. He got there in the summer of 1991, and by the winter he had become zombie-like, institutionalized. They just sucked the life out of him." Esther broke down and cried. The judge called a brief recess.

Sometimes the jurors went into the back room and came back with questions for various witnesses. In this instance, they wanted more information on the Rosatis' business losses. Esther recounted that the Rosati Group had a twenty-four-million-dollar quarry deal that fell through because of Stephen's arrest. The jurors wanted to know what their percentage of the deal was. Esther said 10 percent, which was standard. The prosecution rested.

The plaintiffs called back Detectives McNeil and Puccini. Stephen reported that on the stand, Puccini resurrected the idea that his father, Carl, was part of organized crime and that Jack was "a big-time mob lawyer. Jack objected and then really tore into him on cross."

Michelson then called Vic Giordano. Recalling an event that had happened eighteen years ago, Giordano stated that he still thought that Stephen was the culprit. Jack went through the height differences. At the time of the murder, Giordano described the "big guy" as considerably taller than him. Stephen and Giordano are about the same height. Giordano did concede, however, that if he had been shown a picture of Carbonell, it might have made a difference.

Over two months passed before the lawyers came to their closing statements. Stephen recalled that Cicilline "went through everything the cops had done, how they coerced witnesses, threatened us with the electric chair, hid evidence, the whole nine yards. And then he pointed to Puccini and said that he was right along with them acting as their enforcer. 'No! I did not, Mr. Cicilline,' Puccini shouted out. He called him 'Mr. Cicilline.' What a joke. He sounded like a frightened little kid. It was pathetic!

"Bates was very good," Stephen continued. "He showed how they tried to take our lives away and kill us in the electric chair. Michelson said that the only reason we didn't kill Viscido was that Phaedra and Carbonell got there first. Can you believe that, after all our evidence of my innocence? It's unbelievable."

"Defense attorneys for the officers fired back." Paula McMahon of the *Sun-Sentinel* reported on April 16 and 20, 2004, "calling Rosati and Roussonicolos 'drug dealers' and 'rip-off artists' and accusing them of trying to make money off the errors that were part of a difficult investigation. 'These guys are scam artists,' said attorney Stuart Michelson, who represented Detective McNeil. 'This case is another rip-off for Pete and Steve. . . .'

"In an unusual argument, Michelson speculated that Rosati and Roussonicolos had been planning to rip-off the victim, but the real killers 'beat these two guys to the punch.'"

In a follow-up article four days later, Jon Burstein, also of the *Sun-Sentinel*, covered Bruce Jolly, "the attorney for detectives Bobby Coyote and Frank Puccini, [who] argued the detectives thought they had the right men based on witness testimony. Jolly argued that Roussonicolos is a '22-time convicted felon' and a 'sociopath' who is looking to take advantage of the judicial system. The attorney portrayed Rosati as a man coddled by his parents whose life has taken a downward spiral since his jail stint because he is consumed by self-pity. 'Make no bones about it, [this case] is about money,' Jolly said."

The *Miami Herald* had less coverage for this final day, but their April 16 issue did report some of Jack Cicilline's closing.

"'These detectives had probable cause because they created probable cause!' Cicilline said. 'They threatened my client with capital punishment and then put him jail. He's been devastated ever since.' As Cicilline talked, it all came to a head for Stephen Rosati, and he burst out in tears once again. 'They destroyed a human life,' Cicilline said."

As I had done throughout both civil trials, I spoke to the Rosatis on a daily basis.

"How was the judge?" I asked Stephen while the jury was still out.

"He's been great. I've got no complaints. The jury loved Jack. When this is over, Marc, I'm going to buy you a house here in Naples. And you won't have to live in that pit in Rhode Island any longer."

"But I like my pit," I said protesting.

"So, you'll have two pits. It was just incredible. Ten weeks, ten fucking weeks and those assholes never won a single day. Do you get what I'm saying? Not one single day. We totally crushed them."

"So what do you think?"

"Well, Jack laid it all out in his closing. It came to about eight million. Almost a million in out-of-pocket losses and cost of litigation, the quarry deal, the hotel and industrial complex I was going to build, other land development deals blown because of this. And that doesn't count pain and suffering. There's got to be punitive damages as well. I mean, look what they did to me."

Stephen called the next day. "The jury is still out, Marc. They've requested from the judge pay instructions. They want to know how to calculate past and future earnings."

Stephen thought they might consider interest accrued and the time value of the money over a fourteen-year period and upped his guess to twenty-eight million.

"Jack says eight to ten. People are just not going to want to give out a big number, he tells me. Either way. What the heck, but they gotta figure not just business losses, which was easily eight mil. They've got to also punish these guys."

The Rosatis returned to Rhode Island emotionally drained. It was a hung jury. This trial had cost Esther another $80,000. Finally out of funds, an appeal was out of the question. She would be eighty years old in two years.

Four of the six jurors, including the builder, the teacher, and the architect, wanted to give Stephen nothing. This came as a total shock to the Rosatis and Jack, who completely misread them. The two holdouts were women who Stephen barely noticed during the trial. One, a nurse, felt that $3.9 million would have been a fair payout to Rosati and $500,000 to Pete the Greek. The other woman had a figure of $540,000 for Rosati and $80,000 for Pete the Greek.

Jeff Fuller, the private investigator, interviewed the nurse, the juror who was most sympathetic, and filed a report. She said that all six jurors believed that the plaintiff's civil rights had been violated. Four of them, however, did not accept the idea that Stephen's career was destroyed by his incarceration. The four who voted not to give anything to Stephen felt that he had been "coddled by his family and sought out Pete the Greek for excitement." One of the jurors said, "If you play with fire, you get burned."

Clearly, Stephen was hurt in this trial by trying this case with a man who had twenty-two convictions. The nurse said that had the jury known that Dallas had settled out of court, they may have been more likely to award some recompense because it showed that the police had admitted culpability. The four who ruled against paying out any money were concerned that the policemen might lose their homes. They also accepted the premise that although Stephen could account for the Friday and Saturday before the murder and the Tuesday after, he couldn't account for the day of the murder or the day after.

Jack had read Elodie's testimony from the 1990 extradition hearing into the record, and he had offered that along with the long-distance phone records showing calls to her house. But these jurors wanted to hear from Elodie in her own words that she definitely had been with Stephen that Sunday, October 12, 1986, the day Joe Viscido was killed. This clearly meant that Michelson and Jolly had been successful in planting a seed of doubt that maybe Stephen was part of the Mafia and maybe this really was a mob hit. It would have been easy for him to have flown down for two days to commit the crime.

The two ladies who held out were most swayed toward Stephen's position because of the actions of Detective McNeil, who held back the audiotape that ID'd the real killers. One juror saw Stephen as displaying several personalities. When he talked about his business dealings he was coherent, but when he discussed what had happened to him because of being arrested he appeared to be a broken man.

She said that Cicilline was strong but repetitive. "He kept beating a dead horse. We had a name for him, Mr. Redundant." On the other hand, concerning the detectives' attorney, she liked Mr. Jolly's theatrics and said that he was entertaining.

Concluding, the nurse theorized that the reason Stephen Rosati lost this trial was because he was sitting next to a career criminal. "If he goes to trial again," she said, "I suggest he go it alone."[4]

And so he did. Two years later, on November 9, 2006, the case was finally settled out of court between Stephen Rosati and the Broward Sheriff's Office. The Rosatis' compensation was one million dollars, a third of which went to Jack Cicilline, a percentage of which went to Michael Avery. Having achieved some measure of vindication, Stephen began a new life working with venture capitalists in analyzing and investing in small businesses. Pete the Greek settled for $80,000, which was less than half the amount that Dallas had received.

As for Esther Rosati, she was philosophical. After spending thirteen years of unrelenting work on the case, paying out hundreds of thousands of dollars, and spending her life's fortune to support ongoing lawsuits, she summed it all up.

"Stephen is a forty-six-year-old man now. I've taken him full circle My task is finally done."

NOTES

Prologue

1. *Miami Herald*. "Hanging Is Ruled a Suicide." August 23, 1992; *Sun-Sentinel*, "Prisoner Is Found Hanged in Jail." August 23, 1992, B1, 8.

Chapter 1: A Family United

1. *Providence Journal*. "R.I. Man Held as Fugitive in Florida Drug Slaying." September 23, 1990.
2. *New York Times*. "Father's Inquiry Leads to Arrests." January 7, 1991.
3. *USA Today*. "I Couldn't Let Them Get Away." January 2, 1991.

Chapter 4: The Tapes

1. Deposition of Peter Dallas, Monterey Shock Incarceration Center, Beaver Dams, NY, September 6, 1990, 8:25 a.m. by Detectives Bobby Coyote and Frank Puccini, Broward County Sheriff's Office, Fort Lauderdale, FL.

Chapter 7: The Criminal Attorney

1. Marc Seifer interview with Bobby Pazienza, August 26, 1991, high school football rival of Jack Cicilline, circa 1955–56.
2. Stanton, Mike. *Prince of Providence*. Random House, NY, 2003, 41.

Chapter 8: Federal Hill

1. During the week of December 18, 1994, *Providence Journal* ran

six full front-page stories on Suki (Soukky Luanglath), and Mooki (Khek Luanglath). Now out on bail and on appeal, they have been convicted of armed robbery. During the trial, their attorney, Gerard Donley, was so convinced that he had shattered the prosecution's poor case that he did not bother to put on the stand the fifteen people who saw these two men at a party. Due to language difficulties and Donley's inexplicable defense, the two men were convicted. A lawyer from the attorney general's office felt that they should have sued Donley for gross incompetence. Instead, he handled their first appeal. *Providence Journal* supports this as a case of mistaken identity. According to Aaron Weisman of the AG's office, as late as October 2003, the case was still pending. *Providence Journal* points out they could easily flee the country, but since they see themselves as innocent, they could not imagine ultimately losing their case. *Providence Journal.* "Guilty Verdicts Shatter Dreams for New Life." January 18, 1994, 1:2–4, 12, and follow-up page-one articles on January 19–23, 1994. Eleven years later, in January of 2005, it was announced that Suki and Mooki would get a new trial!

Chapter 10: Prayer Group
1. *Providence Journal.* "RI Murder Suspect Denies Being in State Where Crime Occurred." January 31, 1991, B3.

Chapter 12: An End Run
1. AFFIDAVIT IN AID OF EXTRADITION CARL STEPHEN RO-SATI had been previously established as a possible suspect. After interviewing [two] witnesses, I put together a photo lineup that included a picture of CARL STEPHEN ROSATI. Both witnesses positively identified him as being one of the suspects who forced their way into Mr. Viscido's apartment on October 12, 1986 and forced him into the bedroom where shots were fired that resulted in the death of Mr. Viscido. Danny Ek, who had purchased cocaine from the victim a few hours prior to his death, identified CARL STEPHEN ROSATI as one of the people he had seen at the residence of Skip Bloom on the evening of October 12, 1986. . . . CARL STEPHEN ROSATI and another person had arrived . . . with a bag of cocaine that matched the bag from which Joseph Viscido had gotten his purchase. He also said CARL STEPHEN ROSATI had an Uzi weapon he believed belonged to Viscido. Cory Franco, who

had been at the Bloom residence [the same] evening, also identified CARL STEPHEN ROSATI as one of the people who had been at Bloom's that night and talked about "ripping off" Joseph Viscido.

Another suspect has been identified as Peter Dallas. Mr. Dallas gave a sworn statement in which he admitted his involvement in this homicide and identified CARL STEPHEN ROSATI as the other person who was with him. Peter Dallas further named CARL STEPHEN ROSATI as the man who fired the shot that killed Joe Viscido. . . .

The Grand Jury returned an indictment. . . . CARL STEPHEN ROSATI is now to the best of my knowledge a fugitive from the State of Florida. I make this affidavit in support of the Indictment in Case No. 90-19433CFB and in aid of the extradition of said defendant.

ROBERT R. COYOTE, Broward Sheriff's Office
SWORN TO AND SUBSCRIBED before me this 8th day of October 1990.
STANTON S. KAPLAN, Circuit Judge

Chapter 14: Jack and John
1. Marc Seifer interview with Jack Cicilline, August 21, 2003.
2. *Providence Journal.* "Perjury Trial of Cicilline." June 20, 1984, A10.
3. *Providence Journal.* "Informant Admits Lying." June 22, 1984, A8.
4. *Providence Journal.* "Hung Jury Leads to Mistrial for Lawyer Cicilline." June 25, 1984, A1.
5. *Providence Journal.* "Von Bülow Lawyer, John Sheehan, Burns Midnight Oil." April 22, 1985, 1–2.
6. *Providence Journal.* "Jury Clears Cicilline." October 1985.

Chapter 15: The Trial
1. Marc Seifer interview with Jack Cicilline, August 21, 2003.
2. Marc Seifer interview with Francis Martin, October 26, 1994.

Chapter 16: Discovery
1. The entire police investigation, which follows throughout the text, derives directly from 1,500 pages of the signed daily Deerfield Beach Police Department Viscido homicide investigation report

and the Broward County Sheriff's Office Florida, released to Stephen Rosati's attorney during the course of Rosati's extradition hearing (heretofore referred to as BSO log). The dates of the log begin the day of the murder, October 12, 1986, and continue until Stephen's arrest on September 12, 1990. Detective Chevy McNeil's investigation covers October 1986–May 1989, and Detective Robert R. Coyote's investigation follows, covering May 1989–September 1990. All events, conversations, police interrogation techniques, and taped and transcribed sworn witness statements have been secured from these reports. The information provided on every witness questioned by Detective McNeil or Detective Coyote comes directly from this BSO log. Some specific depositions are highlighted below. Literary license such as addition of colorful language has occasionally been added throughout the text for the sake of readability. The bulk of the depositions appear verbatim and condensed with some name changes.

Chapter 18: Police Log

1. *Sun-Sentinel*. "Trial Opens in 1986 Murder Case." June 8, 1993, 3B.
2. BSO log by Detective McNeil of Michelle Arrieta, October 12–13, 1986.
3. Hayes, John. "Fathers and Sons. One Dad's Mission Puts Another Man's Son in Jail." *Palm Beach Post*. September 15, 1991, 1, 14.
4. BSO log by Detective McNeil of Vic Giordano, October 14, 1986.
5. BSO log/taped deposition by Detective Kenny of Chris Jones, June 5, 1987.

Chapter 19: The Grieving Father

1. Hughes, Sallie. "The Man Who Wouldn't Say Die; A Tale of Two Fathers." *Miami Herald* Sunday magazine cover story, September 29, 1991.
2. Hunter, George. "Devoted Dad Hunts Down Son's Slayers." *The Globe*. November 19, 1990.

Chapter 20: A Question of Identity

1. BSO log by Detective McNeil, October–December 1987.

Chapter 22: The Hearing

1. Extradition Hearing: Carl Stephen Rosati v. The State of Rhode

Island, Kent County Superior Court, December 10, 1990–June 10, 1991, KM 90-1287. The dialog that follows in all chapters that have the pretitle "The Hearing" are taken from the 1,400-page court transcripts. The dialog is almost verbatim but edited down for the sake of readability. Additional descriptions of what happened during this extended hearing are from personal knowledge (having testified myself at the hearing); from interviews with Carl, Esther, and Stephen Rosati and their lawyer, Jack Cicilline; from *Providence Journal* newspaper reporter Jim Hummel, who covered the trial; and from TV coverage, other interviews, and newspaper reports.

For the record, on this first day, the following precedent cases were cited:
   a. Mich v. Doran (U.S. Supreme Ct, 1978).
   b. Baker v. Laurie (375 A.2d 405)
   c. Puerto Rico v. Brandstedt (107 S. Ct. 2, 802, 1987).
   d. Calif. v. Superior Ct of CA, San Bernadino (107 S. Ct. 2433).

Chapter 34: Slickville
1. Detective McNeil's report dated April 28, 1988; Jay Prince's witness signature on photo lineup; Lantana Florida police transcript of Jay Prince and Terry Malone, April 28, 1988; Jay Prince interview, FDLE report, M. Breece, June 8, 1992.

Chapter 35: Back to Geebs
1. BSO log/taped deposition by Detective McNeil of Cory Franco, December 8, 1987.
2. Walsh, Barbara. "Bizarre Bond." *Sun-Sentinel.* July 1993, 1B, 5B; Carl and Stephen Rosati, face-to-face interview, with Rose Viscido, July 1993; Marc Seifer interview with Joseph Viscido, Sr., May 17, 1995.
3. BSO log/taped deposition by Detective's Burndt and McNeil of Cory Franco, June 2, 1988.

Chapter 39: The Hearing: The Right of Confrontation
1. State v. Limberg, Minnesota (1966).
2. White cited Morrissey v. Brewer; Gagnon v. Scarpelli (411 US 778); South Carolina v. Bailey; Muncey v. Cluff.
3. Cicilline cited Clark v. the Warden of the Baltimore City Jail, Maryland (358 A. Reporter, 2nd page 816); and State v. Limberg, (274

Minnesota 31, 142 N.W. 2nd 563); Smith v. Idaho, (373 Fed. 2nd 149th, a Ninth Circuit case); State v. Marrapese, (122 RI, pg. 501); Salvail v. Sharkey (108 R , pg. 63). Josey v. Galloway, (Supreme Court case 507 Southern Reporter, 2nd, 594). Cicilline relied on the Marrapese case.

4. The judge cited State v. DeRoche (120 RI, 523). See also State v. Babb.

Chapter 42: Tainted Witness

1. Description of Herbert Bloom's death provided to Marc Seifer by Pete "the Greek" Roussonicolos, November 24, 1993, Providence, RI; Also *Sun-Sentinel*. "Bloom Shot in Back by Officer Dustin." November 8, 1985. Coincidentally, Herbert Bloom had been a drug pusher for Robbie Newman.

2. Detective McNeil's police log, November 17, 1987.

3. BSO log/taped deposition before Detective McNeil, Detective Burndt, and Charles (Chuck) Morton, Assistant Attorney General, of Jeff Bloom, January 12, 1988.

4. BSO log by Detective McNeil, January 27, 1988.

5. BSO log by Detective McNeil of Kit Finch, August 29, 1988.

Chapter 43: Hidden Agenda

1. *Miami Herald*, Broward local edition. "Drug Pilot Named in Sheriff's Office Probe." June 30, 1991, 2–3 BR.

2. Higham, Scott. "Broward Sheriff's Office Probed." *Miami Herald*, Broward final edition, September 25, 1990, 1A, 10A.

3. Marc Seifer interview with Richard Rendina, December 8, 1993.

4. Marc Seifer interview with Peter Roussonicolos, Providence, RI, November 24, 1993.

5. BSO log/taped deposition by Detective McNeil of Vic Giordano, August 23, 1988.

6. BSO log/taped deposition by Detective McNeil and Assistant Attorney General Morton of Michelle Arrieta, October 14, 1988.

Chapter 45: The Hearing: Cicilline on Cross Continued

1. Marc Seifer interview with Jim Hummel, September 21, 2003.

2. Deposition of Peter Dallas, Monterey Shock Incarceration Center, Beaver Dams, NY, September 6, 1990, 8:25 a.m., by Detectives Bobby Coyote and Frank Puccini, Broward County Sheriff's Office, Fort Lauderdale, FL.

3. Page 12 of the December 8, 1987, Cory Franco transcript.

Chapter 47: Closing In

1. BSO log/taped deposition by Detective McNeil, Assistant Attorney General Morton, and defendant's attorney Hilliard Moldof of Jeffrey Bloom, November 10–11, 1987, January 27, 1988, December 12, 1988.

Chapter 48: Ambush

1. Walsh, Barbara. "Bizarre Bond." *Sun-Sentinel*, July, 1993, 1B, 5B; *Providence Journal*. "Florida Dad's Persistence Pays off in Murder Case with RI Angle." December 31, 1990, C6; *Miami Herald*, Broward edition. "Pompano Father Tracked Suspects Helps Indict 3 in Son's Murder." September 20, 1990.
2. Carl Rosati and Stephen Rosati. Interview with Rose Viscido, July 1993.
3. Walsh, Barbara. "Bizarre Bond." *Sun-Sentinel*, July 1993, 1B, 5B; Hayes, Ron. *Palm Beach Post*. "Fathers and Sons. One Dad's Mission Puts Another Man's Son in Jail." September 15, 1991, 1, 14.
4. From Joseph Viscido, Sr., audiotape of Viscido/Jeffrey Bloom meeting played before Michael Breece, April 1, 1993. Some literary license on peripherals, but Jeff Bloom suggested that Mr. Viscido was responsible for the death of his brother.

Chapter 52: Good Cop—Bad

1. Depositions before Detective S. Coyote, BSO, May–September 1990, of Michelle Arrieta, Vic Giordano, Victor Merriman, Danny Ek, Cory Franco, and Jeff Bloom.
2. Deposition before John Aguero, Governor-appointed Assistant State Attorney, and Cynthia (Cindy) Imperato, Assistant Statewide Prosecutor on behalf of the State, and Hilliard Moldof, attorney on behalf of the defendant James Phaedra, of Michelle Arrieta, Circuit Court, Broward County, FL.

Chapter 53: Final Arguments

1. The following two witnesses also testified: Carlyn Benkhart, Stephen's sister, was called back to the stand. She testified to a gasoline credit card receipt of hers that was written in Italian, verifying that she did, indeed, take the trip to Italy, and that she had her own credit card, not her father's. "That's all I have," Cicilline said.

Mr. Carl Rosati took the stand and provided a receipt of Stephen's showing that he stayed at the Quality Inn in Pompano Beach, Florida, in November of 1988. When Stephen Rosati took the stand, he verified receipts establishing that he stayed at the Quality Inn in Pompano from November 10, 1988, to January 13, 1989.

2. "As a point of reference, 'Habeas Corpus' is always referred to as the great writ. It is the legal avenue designed to test the legality of a detention." Jack Cicilline, November 4, 1994.
3. Randy White cited precedent cases South Carolina v. Bailey (1933) and Muncey v. Cluff (1905).
4. "That same evidence was applied, and I submit correctly, in the RI case of Baker v. Laurie," White said.
5. Jack Cicilline: "Now, Rhode Island followed basically the principles that were first established in this case but later on, habeas corpus came into following, actually, after the case of Joseph Smith in 1842." Rhode Island adopted Section 12-9-4 of the General Laws, and that statute specifically provides the foregoing quote.
6. Hogan v. Buerger (647, S.W., 2nd, 21, a 1983 MO case. 7); Nelson against the People (297 N.E. 2nd at 172, IL, 1973); Clark against the Warden of the Baltimore Jail (385 A. 2nd); Maine against Illinois (at 424 N.E. 2nd); State against Macreadie (123 Florida at pg. 9, 1936); Josey against Galloway; State against Scoratow (456 So. 2nd at 922, FL, 1984); Turino v. Butterworth (416 So. 2nd at 67 FL, 1953); People against Elrod (511. Sup. 559 Northern District, IL, 1981).
7. Motion to Modify Giordano's Sentence, April 17, 1991, Circuit Court of the 19th Judicial Circuit, St. Lucie County State of Florida, Case No: 90-843, signed by James Harpring, Public Defender. Order Modifying Giordano's Sentence, May 24, 1991, signed by Acting Circuit Judge James B. Balsiger, cc: Public Defender, State Attorney Probation and Parole, Indian River County Jail.

Chapter 55: The Hearing: I Accuse!

1. In Detective Coyote's deposition before Rosati Attorney Michael Avery, April 1996, Coyote said that he thought that Judge Sheehan or Randy White had ordered him (Coyote) to leave the courtroom when Giordano testified. Certainly the judge did not order him to leave, and it is highly unlikely that White would have, as Detective Coyote was present for the entire extradition

hearing.

Chapter 57: The Hearing: Copping Out
1. Marc Seifer interview with Jack Cicilline, August 21, 2003.

Chapter 59: Railroaded
1. Barry, Dan, and John Sullivan. "Porn Is Guarino Game: The Mob and Central Are Players on His Team." *Providence Journal*, June 26, 1991, 6, front page; *Providence Journal*. "Witness Puts Rosati at Scene of Slaying." June 26, 1991, 11, front page.

Chapter 60: By the Short Hairs
1. *Providence Journal*. "High Court Rules Rosati Must Stand Trial in Fla." July 30, 1991, front page, 10.

Chapter 61: Turning Tide
1. Dear Judge B. Goldstein, Please allow me a few minutes of your time. My name is Peter Dallas and this consists of the Joseph Viscido, Jr., murder case. I been sitting in jail in Florida for 15 months going onto 16 months terrified, not knowing what to do. Ever since those two Florida officer [sic] came up to [sic] the prison where I was at in New York, I did not know who or what to turn to. (I reached a decision and that's God) They threaten that they had physical evidence against me that could put me on the "electric chair["] if I did not tell them what they wanted to hear. That morning for over two (2) hours they kept me in a room threatening me about the electric chair, they made me listen to taped statements possibly threatened statement just like mine was. The word on my statements came out of fear, not knowing no better what the results were going to be, but "I can not live with this night-mare no longer ["]. I can not live with the thought of I put someone in jail or on the electric chair for something they had nothing to do with. But most of all I cannot see myself getting convicted for something I had nothing to do with. This problem would not of came this far if my family had a little money that I could of put a REAL lawyer on the case. I tried 2 or 3 times to take back my statements and Plea, but every time I tried they threatened to turn everything against me if I did. There is a lot more to this, but there is too many inmates around trying to read what I am writing. I'm ready to turn my case over to the hands of GOD and let Him judge me. I'm ready to tell

the TRUTH. Thank you very much for your time Your Honor. Sincerely, Peter Dallas, circa 1991.

2. This would not be the only time Randy White would err badly in a high profile case covered daily in the papers and on the six o'clock news. Six years later, White successfully prosecuted policeman Detective Scott Hornoff, accused of murdering his concubine, Vickie Cushman. Hornoff, who was married and had had an affair with Cushman, loudly proclaimed his innocence, but the prosecutor got what he wanted, a life sentence. With clairvoyant powers, White concocted a fictitious phone conversation between Scott and Vickie and then described how Scott put dishwashing gloves on his hands to open the window from the inside to make it look like a fake thief had entered from the outside. Likening the crime to the making of a spaghetti sauce, White said, just as you need tomatoes, oregano, and some secret ingredient like paprika to make that indefinable tasty sauce, Hornoff, since he was a detective, processed the crime scene to remove all evidence that he, Hornoff, had been there, and that is why he was guilty!

"When you put together the elements," White concluded with a culinary flourish, "the sum is greater than the parts." Hornoff looked on in shock as he witnessed what he described as "a fairy-tale scenario sadistic version of *This Is Your Life*. It's like the Salem witch trials," Hornoff continued. "He says he's not a witch, so he must be one." If Todd Barry had not had a conscience, Scott Hornoff would have spent his entire life in jail.

After six years of living with the lie, Barry turned himself in, as he was the real killer, and Hornoff was set free. The well-known Rhode Island news reporter Jim Hummel wondered how Randy White slept at night. When it came to big-time mistakes, such as sending the wrong men to death row, Randy White found himself with the wrong interpretation of the evidence in two major cases. The endnote is abstracted from "The Hornoff Conviction, Just a Fairy Tale Scenario," *Providence Journal*, by Gerald Carbone and Cathleen Crowley, January 6, 2003.

Epilogue

1. Entire epilogue based on Special Agent Michael Breece's interview, December 1994 and his official police files, FDLE, Broward

County, Florida. Also, Marc Seifer interviews with John Aguero, Governor-appointed Assistant State Attorney, December 28, 1994, and Assistant Statewide Prosecutor Cindy Imperato, December 29, 1994.

2. Assistant Attorney General Chuck Morton's deposition before Rosati Attorney Michael Avery, March 5, 1995.

3. Jensen, Trevor. "Trial Opens in 1986 Murder Case." *Sun-Sentinel*, April 8, 1993. "The Killing of Joseph Viscido Jr. was not unusual by South Florida standards, but the sequence of events from Viscido's murder to the trial . . . was anything but normal."

4. Davis, Kevin. "Victim's Father Still Seeks Truth in Slaying." *Sun-Sentinel*, 1992. "We never threatened him or coerced him. We never slammed him against any wall," Puccini said. "Me and my partner have been taken over the coals." Sgt. Richard Scheff, head of the Homicide Unit, said he supports the detectives.

5. On the TV program *Eye to Eye*, which was playing in the background on December 29, 1994, as I was typing out an early draft of this last chapter, Connie Chung covered a case of wrongful imprisonment. One of the focuses of the segment was to answer the question "Why would a person admit to a crime he did not commit?" In this case, an elderly lady was found tied up in her bed, burned to death. Robbers had come into the house, tied her up, robbed her, and then set the house on fire. A mildly retarded young man was arrested for the crime and admitted to it.

Connie Chung played a segment from the young man's interrogation. When asked by the arresting officer what color the lady's blouse was, he said, "White or maybe blue." "Let's say it was green," the officer corrected. Under questioning by Chung, the young man said that after hours of interrogation, he admitted to the crime to please the officers. They said that they could all go home if he would just admit to the crime, and he stupidly thought that they meant him as well. To avoid the death sentence, he pled to the crime and is still in jail facing a life term.

Chung located the actual killer, who is in prison on another charge. On camera, he admitted to the crime, saying, without any doubt, that he and a culprit tied the lady up, robbed her, and set the house on fire. He came forth because he was doing a life sentence anyway and because he wanted to help the retarded boy. When

Connie Chung brought this man's confession to the attention of the arresting officer and prosecutor, both said they didn't believe him. They were sticking to their case. The mother and grandmother of the young man, who has obviously been wrongly imprisoned, have no recourse but to appeal to the governor. It seemed clear that the prosecutor would not change his opinion because he did not want to look like a fool—that is to say, he did not want to face the possibility that he had simply made a mistake. "Right or wrong, I think we did an excellent job on this case," he said.

See also: *U.S. News & World Report.* "Innocent, but Behind Bars." September 19, 1994. This is the story about Johnny Wilson, a retarded individual who was "railroaded," tried, and convicted for a crime in Aurora, Illinois. After the frame-up was discovered, the prosecutor, Robert George, did not want to release Wilson because this would create "public distrust of the legal system"!

6. Walsh, Barbara. "Charges Against 3 Dropped." *Sun-Sentinel*, February 6, 1992. "Dallas said they were slamming him against the wall telling him if he didn't tell them what they wanted to hear, he'd get the chair," said Rosati's attorney, Victor Tobin.
7. Davis, Kevin. "Guitarist Offers Clue to 14-Year-Old Crime." *Sun-Sentinel*, local edition, October 16, 1994, 1, 2.
8. Brunais, Andrea. "1 body, 2 sets of guys? Puleeze!" *Tampa Tribune*, July 8, 1993. The Auer quote at the end taken from this article.
9. Hughes, Sallie. "The Man Who Wouldn't Say Die; A Tale of Two Fathers." *Miami Herald, The Tropic* magazine section, September 29, 1991, 1–3, 12, 15, 18.

Afterword

1. Marc Seifer's daily interviews with Stephen Rosati and Esther Rosati during the times of both trials, September 2003–April 2004, interview with Michael Breece, January 14, 2005. Much of the dialogue from the trials was taken from the newspaper articles covering the trial from both the *Miami Herald* and the *Sun-Sentinel*. See references for exact chronology of said articles, September 2003–April 2004.
2. Out of the Box Investigations, Hollywood, Florida, letter and report to Steve Rosati [sic] of the jury with an interview with one juror: M. H., re: Rosati v. Broward Sheriff's Office, June 28, 2004 by Jeff Fuller.

NOTE: This is a true story. Most of the dialogue is verbatim, derived from taped depositions, court transcripts, newspaper articles, and interviews. Some secondary characters were modified slightly, and a number of names and places were changed, including the following:

Jeffrey Bloom, Skip Bloom, Derek Bogard, Jeffrey Burndt, Bob and Jayne, Gary Crane, Crosby Caterers, Bobby Coyote, Steven DelBono, Kit Finch, Cory Franco, Calvin Fredrick, Vic Giordano, Red Gooseberger, Ruby Janeau, Susan LaPlante, Pastor Lottie, Kara Lynx, Joe McBridey, Blake McFadden, Chevy McNeil, Elton Magdeleine, Terry Malone, Tony Martinelli, Robbie Newman, Betts Olivetti, James Phaedra, Jay Prince, Frank Puccini, Boyce Rickenbach, Club Sirocco, Sweetie Sartucci, Tiffany, Billy Toronado, Elodie Vanderpyl, and Rick Whistler.

CHARACTER LIST

LEGAL

Jack Cicilline, Attorney
Randy White, Prosecutor
John F. Sheen, Judge

STEPHEN'S GIRLFRIENDS

Elodie Vanderpyl (nickname Ellie)
Kara Lynx

POLICE

Chevy McNeil (*BSO*)
Bobby Coyote (*BSO*)
Frank Puccini (*BSO*)
Michael Breece (*FDLE*)

HOMICIDE VICTIM

Joe Viscido, Jr.

SUSPECTS

Pete the Greek Roussonicolos
Peter Dallas (*Bug Eyes*)
Stephen Rosati

EYE WITNESSES

Michelle Arrieta (*Apartment*)
Vic Giordano (*Apartment*)
Chris Jones (*Apartment*)
Jeffrey Bloom *(Bloom complex)*
Skip Bloom *(Bloom complex)*
Danny Ek *(Bloom complex)*
Cory Franco (Geebs) *(Bloom complex)*
Kit Finch *(Viscido's friend)*

OTHER SUSPECTS

James Phaedra *(Poppa Jim)*
Kerry Carbonell
Boyce Richenbach

EPILOGUE WITNESSES

Tony Martinelli (Scally's Saloon owner)
Jay Prince (Slickville)
Terry Malone (Slickville)

REFERENCES

Interviews

Conducted by Marc J. Seifer
John Aguero
Michael Breece
Jack Cicilline
Cindy Imperato
Francis Martin
Richard Rendina
Carl Rosati
Esther Rosati
Stephen Rosati
Peter Roussonicolos
Joseph Viscido, Sr.
Jim Hummel

Conducted by Stephen, Carl, or Esther Rosati
John Aguero
Cindy Imperato
Michael Breece
Peter Dallas
Peter Roussonicolos
Victor Tobin
Joseph Viscido, Sr.
Rose Viscido
Kara Lynx
William Venturi
Jeffrey Geller

Depositions conducted by Michael Avery
Peter Dallas
Robert R. Coyote
Frank Puccini
Chevy McNeil
Chuck Morton

Depositions conducted by Detectives Chevy McNeil and Bobby Coyote
Michelle Arrieta

Marc. J. Seifer

Vic Giordano
Chris Jones Danny Ek
Cory Franco
Kit Finch
Victor Merriman
Peter Dallas
Jeffrey Bloom
Skip Bloom

Police Files

Broward County Sheriff's Office: (BSO)/Deerfield Beach:
Viscido Homicide Investigation, 1986–1990 (1,500 pages).

Michael Breece's, Florida Department of Law Enforcement
(FDLE): 25 pages.

Court Testimony

Rosati v. State of Rhode Island Extradition Hearing: December 1990–June 1991, 1,400 pages.

Depositions

Michael Avery depositions: 1994–1995, 300 pages.

Newspaper Articles

Two hundred articles: referenced mainly from the *Providence
Journal*, *Miami Herald*, and *Sun-Sentinel*. The list and sequence of
these articles follows:

1981
Ellsworth, Karen. "Patriarca, 5 Others Targets of Bugging at Lawyer's Office." *Providence Journal*, July 23, 1981, 1, 12.

1984
Providence Journal. "Lawyer Hires Crime Figure Bianco 'Para-Le-
gal' Aid to Cicilline." August 17, 1978, 1.
Providence Journal. "Perjury Trial of Cicilline." June 20, 1984, A10.
Providence Journal. "Informant Admits Lying." June 22, 1984, A8.
Breton, Tracy. "Hung Jury Leads to Mistrial for Lawyer Cicilline."

Providence Journal, June 25, 1984, front page.

Providence Journal. "Von Bülow Lawyer, John Sheehan, Burns Midnight Oil." April 22, 1985, 1–2.

Providence Journal. "Informant Admits Lying." June 22, 1984, A8.

1985

Duggan, Paul. "Von Bülow Lawyer, John Sheehan, Burns Midnight Oil." *Providence Journal*, April 11, 1985, front page.

Providence Journal. "Jury Clears Cicilline." October 1985.

Sun-Sentinel. "Herbert Bloom Shot in Back." November 8, 1985.

1989

Providence Journal. "Warwick Developers Plan Motel in Richmond." November 17, 1989, B1.

1990

Miami Herald. "Busting with Pride. Being a Bounty Hunter Means Never Having to Say You're Sorry," June 15, 1990, 1.

Providence Journal. "Rosati Group Brings Project to Richmond." July 20, 1990, 1.

Warwick Beacon. "Rosati Group Buys Land for Offices and Retail." n.d. (circa 1986).

Higham, Scott and Sallie Hughes. "Feds Issue Corruption Subpoenas. Broward Cops Targeted." *Miami Herald*, B1, 3–4.

Providence Journal. "R.I. Man Held as Fugitive in Florida Drug Slaying." September 13, 1990.

Hughes, Sallie. "Dad Helps Indict 3 in Son's Murder." *Miami Herald*, September 20, 1990, 3, front page.

Miami Herald. "Broward Sheriff's Office." September 25, 1990, 10, front page.

Hunter, George. "Devoted Dad Hunts Down Son's Slayers." *The Globe*, November 19, 1990.

Providence Journal. "Florida Dad's Persistence Pays Off in Murder Case with R.I. Angle." December 31, 1990, C6.

Walewski, Sandra. "Father Spends Four Years and $50,000 to Break Stalled Murder Investigation." *Westerly Sun*, December 31, 1990.

1991

USA Today. "I Couldn't Let Them Get Away." January 2, 1991.

Marc. J. Seifer

New York Times. "Father's Inquiry Leads to Arrests." January 7, 1991.

Hummel, Jim. "Rosati's Lawyer Seeks to Block Witness." *Providence Journal*, January 15, 1991, B1.

Hummel, Jim. "R.I. Man Fights Fla. Slaying Warrant." *Providence Journal*, January 25, 1991, B3.

Hughes, Sallie. "Suspect in Murder Fighting Extradition." *Miami Herald*, January 27, 1991, 1BR.

Hummel, Jim. "R.I. Murder Suspect Denies Being in State Where Crime Occurred." *Providence Journal*, January 31, 1991, B3.

Miami Herald. "Suspect Fighting Extradition, Says He Wasn't in Florida During Killing." January 31, 1991.

Hummel, Jim. "First Details of Killing Came from Police, Suspect Says." *Providence Journal*, February 1, 1991, B3.

Hummel, Jim. "Ex-girlfriend Testifies for Rosati." *Providence Journal*, February 14, 1991, B3.

Hummel, Jim. "Rosati Lawyer Seeks to Block Witness." *Providence Journal*, February 2, 15, 1991, B1.

Hummel, Jim. "Extradition Fight: Fierce Court Drama." *Providence Journal*, February 18, 1991, 10, front page.

Hummel, Jim. "Murder Witnesses Identify Cranston Man." *Providence Journal*, February 20, 1991, A3.

Hummel, Jim. "Witnesses Failed to Pick Rosati from Photo Lineup." *Providence Journal*, February 21, 1991, B3.

Hummel, Jim. "Rosati's Lawyer Clashes with Florida Detective at Extradition Hearing." *Providence Journal*, February 22, 1991, C4.

Miami Herald. "Broward Sheriff's Officer Acquitted of Drug Charges." February 22, 1991, front page.

Rowland, Christopher. "Detective Says Witness against Rosati Lied." *Providence Journal*, February 23, 1991, B10.

Hummel, Jim. "Investigator: Police Scared Witness." *Providence Journal*, March 19, 1991, B1.

Rowland, Christopher. "Rosati Extradition Case Has Final Arguments." *Providence Journal*, March 23, 1991, B1.

Hughes, Sallie. "Suspect Casts Doubt on Father's Sleuthing in Killing of His Son." *Miami Herald*, Dade County Edition, April 2, 1991, front page.

Hughes, Sallie. "Did Broward Dad Nail Wrong Guy?" *Miami Herald*, April 3, 1991, 1, 7, front page.

Hughes, Sallie. "New Delay Requested in Case." *Miami Herald*, May 9, 1991, G3.

Hummel, Jim. "Judge Delays Ruling on Sending Man to Fla. to Face Murder Charge." *Providence Journal*, May 13, 1991, C3.

Hummel. Jim. "Rosati Granted Bail in Fugitive Case, High Court to Review Judge's Decision." *Providence Journal*, June 5, 1991, A3.

Hughes, Sallie, "RI Judge Orders Bail for Murder Defendant." *Miami Herald*, June 5, 1991, BR1, 4.

Rau, Elizabeth. "Rosati Family Lashes Out at Fla. Police Officials." *Providence Journal*, June 6, 1991, A8.

Hummel, Jim. "Bail Ruling Due for Man Accused in Fla. Slaying." *Providence Journal*, June 10, 1991, A3.

Hummel, Jim. "High Court Bars Bail in Carl Rosati Extradition." *Providence Journal*, June November 1991, A3.

Miami Herald. "Suspect in Broward Murder Can't Leave RI Jail." June 11, 1991.

Providence Journal. "The Longest Fight against Extradition. Decision Near in Rosati Battle to Avoid Florida Murder Trial." June 23, 1991, 14, front page.

Westerly Sun. "Rosati Waging Battle against Extradition." June 24, 1991, 1, 10, front page.

Providence Journal. "Porn is Guarino Game: The Mob and Central Are Players on His Team." June 26, 1991, 6, front page.

Providence Journal. "Witness Puts Rosati at Scene of Slaying." June 26, 1991, 11, front page.

Miami Herald. "Rhode Island Man Is Killer, Witness Says at Extradition Hearing." June 26, 1991, BR1, 7.

Hummel, Jim. "Judge Vows to Make His Decision on Rosati Extradition This Week." *Providence Journal*, June 27, 1991, B3.

Hummel, Jim. "Judge Orders Rosati Returned to Florida for Murder Trial." *Providence Journal*, June 29, 1991, front page.

Higham, Scott and Sallie Hughes. "Drug Pilot Named in Sheriff's Office." *Miami Herald*, June 30, 1991, 1, 3BR.

Hummel, Jim. "Rosati Ordered to Fla. on Murder Charge: R.I. High Court: Let Guilt or Innocence Be Decided There." *Providence Journal*, July 31, 1991, A3.

Hummel, Jim. "Rosati's Lawyer Asks High Court to Hear Testimony." *Providence Journal*," July 3, 1991, D1.

Providence Journal. "Supreme Court to Consider Rosati Appeal on

Extradition." July 4, 1991, A3.

Providence Journal. "Rosati Parents Criticize Police." July 6, 1991, front page.

Rau, Elizabeth. "Rosati Family Lashes Out at Fla. Police Officials." *Providence Journal,* July 6, 1991.

Richards, Cheryl. "Rosati Family Asks FBI to Investigate Fl Sheriffs Actions." *Warwick Beacon,* July 9, 1991, 4.

Davis, Kevin. "Manhunt Ends. A Father's 5 Year Search Nets 3 Suspects in His Son's Murder." *Miami Herald,* July 31, 1991, 1, front page.

Hummel, Jim. "Rosati Lawyer: Key Witness Lied In Denying Deal with Fla." *Providence Journal,* July 20, 1991, A3.

Smith Maureen, Susann Ann Latz, William Castelluccio, Margot Walton, and Jeanne Tatton. Free Stephen Rosati. Four Letters to the Editor. *Providence Journal,* July 2, 1991, A11.

Hummel, Jim. "High Court Rules Rosati Must Stand Trial in Fla." *Providence Journal,* July 30, 1991, 10, front page.

Providence Journal. "Rosati Ordered to Fla. on Murder Charge." July 31, 1991, A3.

Hummel, Jim. "Rosati Drops Extradition Charges in Fla." *Providence Journal,* August 1, 1991, B1.

Richards, Cheryl. "Court OKs Rosati Return to Florida; Family to Continue Fighting Charge." *Warwick Beacon,* August 1, 1991, 2.

Providence Journal. "Rosati Quietly Taken to Fla." n.d.

Associated Press, Two Sons, Two Fathers: One Murder." August 7, 1991.

Providence Journal. "Cicilline Denies He's the 'Conduit' Between R.I., N.Y. Crime Families." 4, August 26, 1991, front page.

Algier, A.J. "Rosati Land Slated for Auction." *Westerly Sun,* August 27, 1991.

Hayes, Ron. "Fathers and Sons. One Dad's Mission Puts Another Man's Son in Jail." *Palm Beach Post,* September 15, 1991, 1, 14, front page.

Higham, Scott. "Broward Sheriff's Office Probed." *Miami Herald,* Broward final edition, September 25, 1990, 1A, 10A

Hughes, Sallie. "The Man Who Wouldn't Say Die; A Tale of Two Fathers." *Miami Herald,* September 29, 1991, 1–2, 11, 14–15, 18, magazine section.

Providence Journal. "Rosati Murder Trial in Florida Postponed; Lawyer Seeks Bail." October 8, 1991.

Hummel, Jim. "Judge Orders State to Give Rosati Team New Evidence." *Providence Journal*, November 8, 1991, B1.

Hummel, Jim. "Special Prosecutor May Be Appointed to Probe New Evidence in Rosati Case." *Providence Journal*, December 1991, A3.

Filkins, Dexter. "Murder Indictments Questioned." *Miami Herald*, December 3, 1991, 3B.

Filkins, Dexter. "New Investigation Casts Doubt on Murder Case." *Miami Herald*, December 3, 1991, BR1, 5.

Davis, Kevin. "Secret Evidence May Clear Pair in Murder." *Sun-Sentinel*, December 3, 1991, B1.

Hummel, Jim. "Questions Raised about Case against Rosati." *Providence Journal*, December 1991.

Walsh, Barbara. "Request for Bail Rejected. Attorney: Killers Remain on Street." *Sun-Sentinel*, December 10, 1991, B1.

Filkins, Dexter. "Accused Killers Denied Bail as State Case Falters." *Miami Herald*, Broward Final, December 10, 1991, 1, front page.

Filkins, Dexter. "Man Claims Police Coerced Him into Confessing to Role in Murder." *Miami Herald*, Broward Final, December 17, 1991, 1, front page.

Walsh, Barbara. "Murder Case Witness Claims He Lied to Police." *Sun-Sentinel*, metro edition, December 17, 1991, B1, 5.

Hummel, Jim. "Rosati Co-defendant Wants to Recant Story." *Providence Journal*, December 18, 1991, D8.

1992

Walsh, Barbara. "Murder Suspects Get Chance to Bail Out of Jail." *Sun-Sentinel*, 1, 1992, B1, 10.

Filkins, Dexter. "New Suspects Arrested in Murder Case. Others Held Earlier May Be Cleared." *Miami Herald*, Broward local edition, February 5, 1992, BR 1, 3.

Miami Herald. "Judge Delays Decision on Evidence That Could Clear Murder Suspects." January 15, 1992.

Providence Journal. "Cranston Man Freed on Bond in Murder Case," January 25, 1992.

Davis, Kevin. "Victim's Father Still Seeks Truth in Slaying." *Sun-Sentinel*, n.d.

Hummel, Jim. "Rosati Basks in Freedom but Still under Shadow of Murder Indictment." *Providence Journal*, January 27, 1992, 4, front page.

Richards, Cheryl. "Rosati Freed from Florida Jail, Faces March Murder Charge Hearing." *Warwick Beacon*, January 28, 1992, 2.

Davis, Kevin and Ardy Friedberg. "Arrests Gives Prosecutors 2 Sets of Suspects in Killing." *Miami Herald*, metro edition, February 1, 1992, B12.

Providence Journal "Arrest Made in Slaying in Which Rosati Was Held." February 4, 1992.

Sun-Sentinel metro edition. "2nd Man Arrested in Slaying. Charges against 2 Others Expected to Be Dropped." February 5, 1992, B 1, 4.

Hummel, Jim. "Rosati Charges Likely to Be Dropped. 2 others Arrested as Murder Suspects." *Providence Journal*, February 5, 1992, D1.

Filkins, Dexter. "Three Suspects Cleared in 1986 Drug Murder." *Miami Herald*, Broward local edition, February 6, 1992, BR1, 5.

Walsh, Barbara. "Charges against 3 Dropped. Mistake Admitted in Murder Case." *Sun-Sentinel*, February 6, 1992, B23.

Hummel, Jim. "Murder Charges against Rosati Officially Dropped." *Providence Journal*, February 6, 1992, A3.

Walsh, Barbara. "Wronged Men Get Reprieve." *Sun-Sentinel*, n.d.

Walsh, Barbara. "Man Falsely Accused of Murder Hoped for Miracle." *Sun-Sentinel*, n.d.

Miami Herald. "Lies Pervert Justice. Innocents Kept in Jail." February 8, 1992.

Brunais, Andrea. "The Legalized Rape of a Man Named Rosati." *Tampa Tribune*, March 16, 1992, FM4.

Greene, Ronnie. "'88 Tip Pointed to Man Now Charged in Murder." *Miami Herald*, April 2, 1992.

Sun-Sentinel. "Inmate Found Hanged in Jail." August 22, 1992.

Jensen, Trevor. "Hanging is Ruled a Suicide." *Sun-Sentinel*, August 23, 1992.

Miami Herald. "Prisoner is Found Hanged in Jail." August 23, 1992, B1, 8.

1993

Williams, Joseph. "Lawyer: State Hid Pembroke Evidence." *Miami Herald*, May 12, 1993, 1, front page.

Greene, Ronnie. "Cleared a Third Time." *Miami Herald*, May 13, 1993, 93.

Sun-Sentinel. "Jury Lifts Threat." May 13, 1993.

Keller, Larry. "Man Sues 2 County Officers." *Sun-Sentinel*, May 18, 1993, B1, 9.

Westerly Sun. "RI Man Sues Florida Detectives." May 19, 1993, 1, 14, front page.

Hummel, Jim. "Carl Stephen Rosati Files Suit Over Charge Brought against Him." *Providence Journal*, May 19, 1993, C7.

Williams, Joseph. "Cleared Murder Suspect Sues over Arrest." *Miami Herald*, May 19, 1993, LB1.

USA Today. "Fort Lauderdale. Stephen Rosati Files Suit against Two Broward County Detectives." May 19, 1993, 2.

Jensen, Trevor. "Trial Opens in 1986 Murder Case." *Sun-Sentinel.* June 8, 1993, B3.

Walsh, Barbara. "Bizarre Bond." *Sun-Sentinel*, July 1993, B1, 5.

Brunais, Andrea. "1 Body, 2 Sets of Guys? Puleeze!" *Tampa Tribune*, July 8, 1993.

1994

Providence Journal. "Skull ID Stuns Emery Theorists." September 10, 1994, A1, 6.

US News & World Report. "Innocent, but Behind Bars." September 19, 1994.

Sun-Sentinel. "Guitarist Offers Clue to 14-Year Old Crime," October 16, 1994, B1, 5.

Nickell, David. "State Persecutor, Michael Satz, The Most Powerful Elected Official in Broward County, Inspires Fear in Defendants and Employees Alike." *Miami Herald*, News Iron first section, October 19, 1994, 13–16.

Providence Journal. "Guilty Verdicts Shatter Dreams for New Life." December 18, 1994, A1, 12; December 19, 1994, A1; December 20, 1994, A1; December 21, 1994, A1; December 22, 1991, A1; December 23, 1994, A1.

1995

Breton, Tracy. "Supreme Court Upholds Gag Order on Rosati Ally." *Providence Journal*, June 25, 1995, B5.

1998

McCormick, John. "The Wrongly Condemned: How Many Capital Cases End in False Convictions?" *Newsweek*, November 9,

1998, 64.

1999

Brant, Martha. "Last Chance Class: David Protess's Students Have Freed Three Men from Death Row. They Have a Case Now That They Believe in—and Haven't Won." *Newsweek,* May 31, 1999, 32–33.

Gegax, Trent T., "Getting the Wrong Man: How a Seemingly Open-and-Shut Murder Case Fell Apart, Wrecking a Life and Leaving a Mystery." *Newsweek,* June 14, 1999, 38.

2000

Dwyer, Jim, Peter Neufeld, and Barry Scheck. "When Justice Lets Us Down." *Newsweek,* February 14, 2000, 59.

Fineman, Howard. "How Bush Made the Call: I Trust the Juries." *Newsweek,* June 12, 2000, 30.

Locy, Tony. "Lawyers, Life and Death: Inept Defenses Taint Many Capital Cases." *US News & World Report,* June 19, 2000, 26.

Newsweek. "Rethinking the Death Penalty." cover story, June 26, 2000.

Miller, Mark. "A War over Witnesses: A Texas Death-Penalty Case Raises Intriguing Questions." *Newsweek,* June 26, 2000, 55.

2001

DeMarzo, Wanda and Daniel deVise. "BSO's Role in False Confession Questioned." *Miami Herald,* April 2, 2001.

Providence Journal. "House OK's Ban on Exercise Equipment at ACI." April 17, 2001, A7.

2002

DeMarzo, Wanda, Daniel deVise, and Larry Lebowitz, "Handling of Behan Case Part of a Pattern, BSO Critics Say." *Miami Herald,* March 4, 2002.

DeMarzo, Wanda. "Broward Homicide Investigation at Center of DNA Controversy." *Miami Herald,* circa May 2002.

Jordan, Jennifer. "Criminal Justice under a Microscope: DNA Expert Barry Scheck." *Providence Journal,* September 18, 2002.

DeMarzo, Wanda and Daniel deVise, "Experts: Tape Police Interrogations." *Miami Herald*, December 12, 2002.

2003

deVise, Daniel. "Branded a Killer, One Man Seeks Justice." *Miami Herald*, August 3, 2003.

deVise, Daniel. "Wrongly Accused, Rosati Gets Day in Court." *Warwick Beacon*, August 5, 2003, 3:1–3.

McMahon, Paula. "Civil Trial to Start in Broward Wrongful Arrest." *Sun-Sentinel*, September 21, 2003.

Breton, Tracy, "Jury to Hear R.I Man's Wrongful Arrest Suit." *Providence Journal*, September 22, 2003, 1, 11, front page.

Seifer, Marc J. WABC-TV News, Providence, personal interview for feature story.

McMahon, Paula. "Wrongful Arrest Plaintiff Settles Lawsuit with Broward Sheriff's Office." *Sun-Sentinel*, September 23, 2003.

Wanda J. DeMarzo and Daniel deVise, "BSO Coercion Claimed in Civil Lawsuit." *Miami Herald*, September 23, 2003.

McMahon, Paula. "Sheriff Defends Arrest of 'Good Subjects'." *Sun-Sentinel*, September 25, 2003.

The Associated Press. "Woman Testifies against Broward Detectives in Wrongful Arrest Suit." The Emerald Coast.com, FL; Bradenton.com, Florida's Gold Coast, September 30, 2003.

DeMarzo, Wanda J., "Herald Watchdog: Troubled Cops." *Miami Herald*, September 30, 2003.

McMahon, Paula. "Broward Detectives Accused of Bullying Witness into Wrong ID." *Sun-Sentinel*, September 30, 2003.

McMahon, Paula. "Witness Says Police Pushed for Wrong ID." *Sun Sentinel*, September 30, 2003, B1–2.

Fantz, Ashley, "Two Jailed for Killing, Say Tape Cleared Them." *Miami Herald*, October 1, 2003.

"Florida Officer Forgets Evidence in Drawer." AP Wire, *Herald Sun*, October 1, 2003.

McMahon, Paula. "Broward Detective Says Key Evidence in Murder Was Forgotten in His Sock Drawer." *Sun-Sentinel*, October 1, 2003.

McMahon, Paula. "I Forgot Tape in Murder Case." *Sun-Sentinel*, October 1, 2003.

"Florida Officer Forgets Evidence in Draw." Associated Press; *St. Petersburg Times*; *Daytona Beach News*, *Naples Daily News*, *Newsday*, NY, October 1, 2003.

Marc. J. Seifer

"Florida Officer Had Evidence in Sock Drawer While Suspects Were in Jail." CBS National News, Fort Worth, TX; WOKV.com, Jacksonville, FL; NBC-6, South Florida; WKMG-TV, Central; FL; *Keith Olbermann Show*, CNBC; CBS-3, KYW-TV, Philadelphia, PA, October 1, 2003.

"Detective Stored Evidence in Sock Drawer While Men Sat in Jail." FreeRepublic.com, Newstrove.com, *TampaBay* Online, October 2, 2003.

Grimm, Fred. "Ghosts of Past Come Calling at Sheriff's Office." *Miami Herald*, October 2, 2003.

McMahon, Paula. "Ex-FDLE Agent Assailed." *Sun-Sentinel*, October 2, 2003.

Andron, Scott. "Coerced Confession Described." *Miami Herald,* October 3, 2003.

McMahon, Paula. "Fear Led to False Confession in 1986 Killing, Man Says." *Sun-Sentinel*, October 3, 2003.

McMahon, Paula. "Judge Testifies in Civil Lawsuit for Man Wrongly Accused; Held." *Sun-Sentinel*, October 4, 2003

Rosati, Esther, "Negative Spin on My Son's Life." Letter to the Editor, *Providence Journal*, October 6, 2003, A8.

deVise, Daniel. "Prosecutor Calls Rosati Case 'Weak'." *Miami Herald*, October 7, 2003.

DeMarzo, Wanda, Daniel deVise, and Larry Lebowitz, "Handling of Behan Case Part of a Pattern BSO Critics Say." *Miami Herald*, October 7, 2003.

McMahon, Paula. "Views Vary in Courtroom about Broward Murder Investigation That Went Wrong." *Sun-Sentinel*, October 8, 2003.

deVise, Daniel. "Witness: There Was No Smoking Gun." *Miami Herald*, October 8, 2003.

deVise, Daniel. "Two Once Jailed for Murder They Didn't Commit Tour Cell with Jurors." *Miami Herald*, October 8, 2003.

Associated Press. "Jurors Tour Jail in Wrongful Arrest." October 8, 2003.

deVise, Daniel. "Alleged Threat Could Jeopardize BSO Lawsuit." *Miami Herald*, October 9, 2003.

deVise, Daniel. "Suit against BSO, Judge, Jury Take Tour of Broward Jail." *Miami Herald*, October 9, 2003.

McMahon, Paula. "Views Vary in Courtroom about Broward Murder Investigation That Went Wrong." *Sun-Sentinel*, October 8, 2003.

McMahon, Paula. "Jurors Tour Broward Jail in Lawsuit over Erroneous Murder Arrests." *Sun-Sentinel*, October 9, 2003.

Miami Herald. "Mistrial Declared in Suit against BSO Officials."
October 9, 2003.

McMahon, Paula. "Mistrial in R.I. Man's Suit against Fla. Sheriffs."
Providence Journal, October 10, 2003, B6, B8.

McMahon, Paula. "Prosecutor's Improper Testimony Ends Trial on
Wrongful Arrests." *Sun-Sentinel*, October 10, 2003.

deVise, Daniel and Wanda DeMarzo. "Mistrial Declared in Suit
against BSO Officials." *Miami Herald*, October 10, 2003.

deVise, Daniel. "Mistrial: Lie Detectors Still Failing Legal Tests."
Miami Herald, October 11, 2003

Rosati, Esther. "Judge Thwarted Quest for Justice," Letter to Editor,
Miami Herald, November 2003.

2004

Sun-Sentinel. "Man Suing BSO for Wrongful Arrest Nabbed for Cocaine Possession." January 29, 2004.

McMahon, Paula. "Lawsuit Trial Restarts for Pair Falsely Jailed."
Sun-Sentinel, February, 27, 2004.

McMahon, Paula. "Former Detective Admits He Left Crucial Evidence in Murder Case in Drawer." *Sun-Sentinel*, March 3, 2004.

Bierman, Noah. "Wrongful-Arrest Case Hinges on Tale of Tape."
Miami Herald, March 5, 2004.

Bierman, Noah. "BSO Lawsuit: Witness: Plaintiff Made a Threat."
Miami Herald, March 10, 2004.

Burstein, Jon. "Wrongful Arrest Lawsuit Resumes in Broward over
Accusations in 1986 Slaying." *Sun-Sentinel*, March 17, 2004.

Burstein, Jon. "Broward Judge Rejects Mistrial after Outburst in
False Arrest Suit." *Sun-Sentinel*, March 19, 2004.

O'Boye, Shannon and Paula McMahon. "Sheriff Stiffens Rules on
Case Closings." *Sun-Sentinel*, March 20, 2004.

DeMarzo, Wanda. "Crime: BSO Changes How It Clears Cases."
Miami Herald, March 20, 2004.

Bierman Noah. "Wrongful Arrest Case: Plaintiff Threat of Death
Chilling." *Miami Herald*, March 23, 2004.

Burstein, Jon. "Deputies Threatened Death Unless He Falsely Implicated Suspects, Witness Says." *Sun-Sentinel*, March 26, 2004.

Bierman Noah. "Witness: Cops Threatened With Electric Chair."
Miami Herald, March 26, 2004.

McMahon, Paula. "Closing Arguments Get Under Way in BSO False

Imprisonment Case." *Sun-Sentinel*, April 16, 2004.

Sara Olkon. "Wrong Arrest Trial Ending. Lawyers in a Long-Running Wrongful Arrest Lawsuit Wrap up Their Case against the Broward Sheriff's Office Thursday." *Miami Herald*, April 16, 2004.

Olkon, Sara. "Wrongful Arrest Suit Goes to Jury." *Miami Herald*, April 19, 2004.

Burstein, Jon. "Jury Deliberates Case Involving 2 Men Falsely Arrested for Murder." *Sun-Sentinel*, April 20, 2004.

Olkon, Sara. "Broward Courts. Jury Gets Wrongful-arrest Suit." *Miami Herald*, April 20, 2004.

Olkon, Sara. "Mistrial Declared for Two Men Suing BSO for Wrongful Arrest." *Miami Herald*, April 21, 2004.

Ziner, Karen Lee. "Brothers Argue for New Trial." *Providence Journal*, October 10, 2004.

2006

Associated Press. "Settlement Reached in Broward Wrongful Arrest Suit." October 13, 2006.

DeMarzo, Wanda. "BSO May Pay $1 Million to Innocent Man." *Miami Herald*, October 25, 2006.

DeMarzo, Wanda. "Wrongful Arrest Case Settled." *Providence Journal*, November 9, 2006, B1, 3.

BIOGRAPHICAL SKETCHES

Marc J. Seifer, PhD: Internationally recognized handwriting expert has worked on over 10,000 forgery cases. Clients include the Attorney General's Office of Rhode Island, University of Rhode Island (URI) Crime Laboratory, Central Falls, Warwick and Narragansett, RI Police Departments, U.S. Defense Department, Naval Underseas Warfare, and the Public Defenders Office. Having testified in civil, criminal, and federal court, he is a past editor of the *Journal of the American Society of Professional Graphologists*. His articles have appeared in *RI Bar Journal, Lawyer's Weekly, Wired, Cerebrum, Civilization, Psychiatric Clinics of North America*, and the *Historian*. He is also recognized as an authority on the inventor Nikola Tesla.

Featured in the *Washington Post*, the *Wall Street Journal*, the *Economist, Cosmopolitan, MIT's Technology Review*, and in feature articles in *Rhode Island Monthly* and the *New York Times*, he has appeared on the *History Channel*, AP International TV, WJAR-NBC, the BBC and Coast to Coast Radio, and has lectured at the United Nations, Federal Reserve Bank in Boston, Cambridge University and Oxford University in England, Brandeis University, City College of New York, LucasFilms Industrial Light & Magic, and West Point Military Academy. His book *Wizard: The Life and Times of Nikola Tesla*, translated into eight languages, has been called "Revelatory" by *Publishers Weekly*, "Serious scholarship" by *Scientific American*, and "[A] Masterpiece" by Nelson DeMille. It is "Highly Recommended" by the American Association for the Advancement of Science. Fiction works include *Rasputin's Nephew, Doppelgänger*, and *Crystal Night*, and nonfiction works include *The Definitive Book of Handwriting Analysis, Where Does Mind End?* and *Transcending the Speed of Light: Consciousness and Quantum Physics*.

With a BS from the University of Rhode Island, five semesters of handwriting investigation at the New School For Social Research, an MA from the University of Chicago, and a PhD from Saybrook University, Dr. Seifer teaches psychology and forensic graphology as a visiting lecturer at Roger Williams University.

Carl Stephen Rosati (1960–2013): Mr. Rhode Island of 1983, Stephen returned to bodybuilding competition after nearly a fifteen-year layoff to win Mr. All New England in the Heavyweight Division in 1999. Stephen constructed seventeen luxury homes and ran a number of businesses, including real estate companies and East Coast Fitness Center. An avid skier who competed in jumping competitions, he also worked as a financial analyst and investor in promising companies.

22162538R10282

Made in the USA
Middletown, DE
22 July 2015